PRAISE FOR *Ci*

"Gorton explores the clash and interplay ~~~~~~~~~~~~ entity greater than the sum of its parts, absorbed in an endeavor as important now as it was then: molding coherent narratives that help readers—surrounded by a cacophony of daily stories—grasp the changes they are living through."
—*Atlantic*

"*Citizen Reporters* is a vibrant tale of courage and perseverance. With a thorough and steady hand, Stephanie Gorton guides the reader back in time, telling the origin story of America's long tradition of bold and incisive journalism. Ida Tarbell and S. S. McClure's inner lives are interwoven in a story of feminism and American journalism that will have a lasting impact on its readers."
—**Abby Phillip, anchor of** *CNN NewsNight with Abby Phillip*

"Reading Stephanie Gorton's smart and engaging *Citizen Reporters* summoned rhythms of a past whose cadence can be felt in the present. . . . Fascinating. . . . Gorton provides readers with a rich context for understanding the historical and cultural milieu."
—***Minneapolis Star Tribune***

"In an era newly conscious of journalism driven by exposing wrongdoing, *Citizen Reporters* stands as an essential read of America's long history with reporting on urgent matters of social justice."
—**Eliza Griswold, Pulitzer Prize–winning author of** ***Amity and Prosperity***

"Strong, well-written, and compelling. . . . Extensively researched, the book is written with flair. Readers will find themselves caught up in the story and rooting for the protagonists."
—***Christian Science Monitor***

"[As] Gorton reveals, *McClure's* magazine was instrumental in paving the way for reporters to battle corruption and drive change in society. . . . Readers interested in Gilded Age history and its parallels to contemporary society will enjoy learning about this trailblazing publication."
—*Library Journal*

"In this exciting portrait of giant-slaying journalist Ida Tarbell, visionary S. S. McClure, and his muckraking *McClure's* magazine as they blazed across the golden age of American periodicals and the founding battles of progressives and traditionalists, Stephanie Gorton has written more than a beautifully crafted and original narrative history. She reminds us of the courage and passion that fearless magazine journalists must find once again to reveal the true American landscape; her own elegant example shows that the printed word remains the radical technology for the deepest, clearest writing and thinking that changes the world."

—**Michael Capuzzo,** *New York Times* **bestselling author of**
***Close to Shore* and *The Murder Room***

"*Citizen Reporters* is beautifully written, deeply reported, and worthy of its very worthy subjects. Through the stories of S. S. McClure, his star reporter Ida Tarbell, and the writers associated with *McClure's* magazine, Stephanie Gorton gives us a fascinating glimpse of a formative time in American history—and reveals the urgent and necessary role played by investigative journalists."

—**Louisa Thomas, author of** *Louisa:*
***The Extraordinary Life of Mrs. Adams***

"Anyone who loves journalism will revel in this story of an unlikely partnership that shaped the media business, helped to define investigative reporting, and showed Americans the injustices and inequities in our midst. We wouldn't be the country we are today without *McClure's*."

—**Sasha Issenberg, author of** *The Lie Detectives*

"*Citizen Reporters* offers a fascinating exploration of the adventurous work produced at *McClure's*. In Stephanie Gorton's crisp, fast-moving narrative, we come to know, love, and fear visionary editor S. S. McClure. Even more memorably, we meet top journalist Ida Tarbell, whose stamp on the science and craft of in-depth reporting remains indelible more than a century later. This is a fun, absorbing story with surprises on just about every page."

—**Earl Swift, author of** *Hell Put to Shame*

"S. S. McClure altered the realm of magazines while educating the public. Then Ida Tarbell, while breaking gender barriers, altered American democracy for the better. Bravo to Stephanie Gorton for bringing the saga to a new generation of readers."

—**Steve Weinberg, former executive director of**
**Investigative Reporters and Editors**

"In an era echoing our own, two trailblazing journalists—one a fearless woman— confront the monied interests and political corruption that distort the fundamental fairness of American society. Stephanie Gorton's beautifully shaped and closely researched narrative shows how the same manic energy that propelled its founder to embrace such a high-risk and pioneering venture ultimately led to *McClure's* demise. We can be grateful that its legacy lives on."

—**Peter Stark, author of** *Young Washington: How Wilderness*
***and War Forged America's Founding Father***

# CITIZEN REPORTERS

# CITIZEN REPORTERS

S. S. McClure, Ida Tarbell, and the Magazine
That Rewrote America

## Stephanie Gorton

An Imprint of HarperCollinsPublishers

HarperCollins books may be purchased for educational, business, or sales promotional use. For information, please e-mail the Special Markets Department at SPsales@harpercollins.com.

A hardcover edition of this book was published in 2020 by Ecco, an imprint of HarperCollins Publishers.

FIRST ECCO PAPERBACK EDITION PUBLISHED 2024

*Designed by Michelle Crowe*

Library of Congress Cataloging-in-Publication Data

Names: Gorton, Stephanie, 1984– author.
Title: Citizen reporters / S. S. McClure, Ida Tarbell, and the magazine that rewrote America / Stephanie Gorton.
Description: New York : Ecco, 2020. | Includes bibliographical references and index.
Identifiers: LCCN 2019018623 (print) | LCCN 2019980437 (ebook) | ISBN 9780062796646 | ISBN 9780062796660 (ebook)
Subjects: LCSH: McClure's magazine. | McClure, S. S. (Samuel Sidney), 1857–1949. | Tarbell, Ida M. (Ida Minerva), 1857–1944. | Journalists—United States—Biography. | Editors—United States—Biography.
Classification: LCC PN4900.M28 G67 2020 (print) | LCC PN4900.M28 (ebook) | DDC 051—dc23
LC record available at https://lccn.loc.gov/2019018623
LC ebook record available at https://lccn.loc.gov/2019980437

ISBN 978-0-06-279665-3 (pbk.)

24 25 26 27 28 LBC 5 4 3 2 1

The quest of the truth had been born in me—the most tragic and incomplete, as well as the most essential, of man's quests.

—*Ida Tarbell,* All in the Day's Work

In America the President reigns for four years, and journalism governs forever and ever.

—*Oscar Wilde, "The Soul of Man Under Socialism"*

# CONTENTS

# *Preface*

In the Gilded Age, when the magazine was readying its ascent, cities sounded more like barnyards of the past than metropolises of the future. Hoofbeats punctuated the long avenues of New York, and the light step of a messenger boy was more frequently heard than the ringing of a telephone. But it was nevertheless a time shaped by the advent of the machine: the whirr of cable cars, the colonizing force of the railroad, the miracle of wireless telegraphy, even the boisterous new leisure activity made possible by the bicycle. Every facet of life was affected by a new reliance on mechanization and speedy communication that hadn't existed a generation before, opening new channels for the accumulation of money and social control. How could anyone hope to understand this as it was happening? Preachers and politicians did their best, but most people turned to the press.

A magazine seems to be a frivolous thing: a way to pass the time in a waiting room or on a commute, a way to take a break from the work of real thinking. But behind each pulp-and-ink issue lies a gargantuan effort to satisfy the curiosities of an anxious society. Each article represents a claim on the reader's attention, as well as a period of obsession, or at least dutiful fixation, for the writer behind it. In the years before radio, television, and the internet, this meant readers from all walks of life—from the president to the newly literate—turned to the written word to tell them what exactly they were living through, and what might come next.

The Gilded Age takes its name from an 1873 novel by Mark Twain and journalist Charles Dudley Warner. The two friends, provoked by a dare from their wives, collaborated on a story that satirized what they saw as a mindless, materialistic America around them. But it could have had a third allusion, to a sensational yet significant age of journalism—and of magazines, as a form. Out of a heated, competition-driven surge in print media, the now-vanished *McClure's* magazine rose up and leveled reportage and entertainment at a growing American readership, coming to embody the emerging art of investigative journalism.

With origins in immigrant-packed steerage quarters and the rapidly industrializing Midwest, the strivers who made *McClure's* brought long-held quests and biases to the task. They—the visionary Samuel Sidney McClure, dauntless Ida Tarbell, dedicated John Phillips, gentle Ray Stannard Baker, idealistic Lincoln Steffens, and dozens of other reporters and novelists in their circle—channeled their vision into print, creating a magazine whose roving interests paralleled the evolving concerns of the society around them. Their lives and loves, as well as their work, were consumed by the magazine's success and dissolution.

In the last years of the nineteenth century and the first decade of the twentieth, the frontier vanished, Victorian values were pushed aside, and entrenched political corruption sparked a grassroots reform movement. Railroads extended their reach across the continent, requiring American time zones to be standardized for the first time; town clocks no longer set their time by the sun or the local almanac, but by the railroad schedule. Electricity lit cities that had previously been dim and smoky with kerosene and whale oil, and telegraphy accelerated the end of the Pony Express. A dentist from Buffalo invented the electric chair, which dispatched its first murderer in early August of 1890. Life was brighter and more efficient, but also fraught with new ways to die.

Throughout the Gilded Age—and its hopeful successor, the Progressive Era—the United States was deeply divided between progressives and conservatives, stretched by recessions at home and wars abroad, and astonished by advances in speedy new communications technologies. Wealth inequality had never been higher. At the same time, gender roles were being renegotiated, and race relations seemed to have reached a postslavery crisis point. All this meant there was a demand for stories that could make sense of the brave new world and no shortage of material for socially conscious writers. A revelatory story or investigation could rock a political administration, bring together a reform campaign, and powerfully articulate tensions simmering in the surrounding culture. In 1892, in the words of reformer and lawyer Clarence Darrow, there was a declared shift in public taste from the romance of "fairies and angels" to instead "flesh and blood."

The written word never held as much power as during this period of transformations. Actors might have been known by name across the country, and traveling lecturers appeared in towns large and small, but many lacked the means or the time to attend plays and talks. Print was the only mass medium, and "the pulpit, the press, and the novel" influenced an increasingly literate population. In the post–Civil War years, the prevalence of magazines in America mushroomed. In 1860, there were about 575. That number practically doubled every decade until, by 1895, there were more than 5,000. Reporters' words did not only fill space on the page; they could make or break campaigns, careers, products, and fashions.

The rise of magazine journalism drew attention, attempts at shaping the narrative, and deepening dismay from those in elected office. "It is always a pleasure to a man in public life to meet the real governing classes," Roosevelt began a speech on April 7, 1904, in the ballroom of Washington's New Willard Hotel. He was speaking to the inaugural industry banquet of the Periodical Publishers' Association, including several members of the *McClure's* group. The rest of his speech focused on the theme of restraint. He urged his listeners to realize their own political influence and wield it with care. "The man who writes," the president told the crowd, "the man who month in and month out, week in and week out, day in and day out, furnishes the material which is to do its part in shaping the thoughts of our people is fundamentally the man who, more than any other, determines what kind of character, and therefore ultimately what kind of government, this people shall possess."

Out of all the loud-shouting newspapers and venerable magazines of the day, *McClure's* was unprecedented in its determination to entertain, to chase the allure of the new, and to expose injustice. *McClure's* stories agitated for change, though they also sought subscribers the way television producers now chase ratings. They exposed the dysfunction of mob-run cities like St. Louis and Pittsburgh and destabilized the monopoly on industry held by oligarchical tycoons, particularly John D. Rockefeller.

S. S. McClure's conviction that a magazine could be a cultural force kept *McClure's* sharply attuned to the demands of the reading public. The magazine embodied the muckraking genre; this term for investigative journalism was arguably invented for *McClure's*. By 1900, McClure was widely recognized as one of the most important men in America. In a later reflection in *Life,* the writer noted, "nobody's hand has been more perceptible than his on the crank that turns the world upside down." At its peak, *McClure's* had more than 400,000 subscribers, soundly beating its rivals *Harper's Monthly, Scribner's Magazine, The Century,* and *The Atlantic.*

S. S. McClure himself was "a queer bird, but a lovable man and a great one . . . stranger than any fiction," in the words of one reporter who knew him. He was a perceptive editor and larger-than-life man, described by his friend Rudyard Kipling as a "cyclone in a frock-coat" and likened to both Theodore Roosevelt and Napoleon. Today he might be seen as part Citizen Kane, part Wizard of Oz: a blazing talent with outsize self-belief and what might today be diagnosed as manic depression or bipolar disorder. He discovered and mentored obscure young journalists—including Ida Tarbell, Ray Stannard Baker, Lincoln Steffens, and Willa Cather—who became "the most brilliant staff ever gathered by a New York periodical," according to contemporaneous *Atlantic* editor Ellery Sedgwick.

The history of *McClure's,* as this book tells it, focuses tightly on a few characters and years—and then, only on certain aspects of their lives and legacies. The rise and fall of the magazine as narrated here runs from 1893 to the cataclysmic staff walkout of 1906 (though *McClure's* continued under various owners until it officially folded in 1931). The story is one of two major characters with an ensemble cast: manic "Chief" S. S. McClure, formidable Ida Tarbell, and their core group of colleagues and loved ones. The wider lens includes a small number of key people, including John Phillips, Ray Stannard Baker, and Lincoln Steffens, at the expense of trying to capture the full orbit of *McClure's,* which included many other fascinating figures. These were thinkers who believed their words could be aimed— "like a gun," in Steffens's words—and could leap off the page to become a movement. The magazine was, in Ida Tarbell's words, a "lively, friendly, aggressive, delightful" enterprise that demanded sacrifices of its makers that were worthwhile for a time—novels left unfinished, broken marriages, the impossibility of having a family at all. Then McClure flew too close to the sun. Buffeted by both internal strife and political pressure, *McClure's* moment of influence could not hold. In its slow-motion shattering, the end of *McClure's* as America knew it shows the effects of power, ambition, and human frailty—and love, both socially sanctioned and not—on a singularly original group.

\* \* \*

I CAME TO THIS STORY in a roundabout way. In my first assignment as a magazine office assistant, swamped under boxes of unsolicited submissions, I often wondered: What makes a writer write, knowing their work will likely be lost to the years? How precisely does a writer make a difference in the world? Later, as I moved through various publishing offices and editorial roles, I kept finding iterations of the McClure-Tarbell relationship, where important creative work emerged from a hothouse ecosystem of close, affectionate, yet often codependent or outright exploitative relationships. When I came across the story of the rise and fall of *McClure's,* these questions and experiences came echoing back, gave me a new lens for looking at the media landscape around me, and became the kernel of this project.

McClure, Tarbell, and their cross section of history came to possess my curiosity over the course of five unevenly disciplined years. In this retelling, their history is more personal than panoramic. My abiding interest in the characters' sense of identity, ambitions, and relationships guided the writing more powerfully than any model of scholarship, though my sources are restricted to the historical record.

In reading deeply on the relationships at the center of *McClure's,* my implicit focus has been on S. S. McClure and Ida Tarbell as their roles in the world evolved, how they were both driven and blinkered by their own time, what circumstances granted them tremendous influence, and what events took that influence away. While I am not a formally trained historian, this book allowed me to pursue my curiosity about the unique phenomenon of *McClure's* while learning about a story that is as timely and human today as it was in the Gilded Age. As Mark Twain so famously said, history doesn't repeat itself, but it does rhyme.

# Prologue

*I suppose there is no place where historians are so often wrong
as in dealing with men's motives.*

—*S. S. McClure*

da Minerva Tarbell, who lived alone, opened the door to her small, book-crowded apartment near Gramercy Park. Miss Tarbell, by then "a spirited seventy-six," was not particularly mellowed by age. An unusually tall, straight-backed figure, she did not soften her posture to make gentlemen more at ease.

New York had its coldest February on record in 1934. Outside, cars and trolleys rumbled in honking conjunction with each other, the hansom cabs of Miss Tarbell's youth now vanished. The visitor, a reporter, crossed the threshold, noting her "gray hair, gray eyes, sensitive, alert face, a body that is still straight and graceful," and her utter lack of vanity or frivolity. She welcomed him and her voice was pleasant to the ear, strong and resonant, though occasionally she seemed to trail off with a tremulous quiver, "as though it knew the meaning of years."

Miss Tarbell's rooms were cozy and stuffed with sturdy upholstery, enclosed by gray-green walls, littered with volumes thick and thin, newspapers, black boxes of pamphlets, a typewriter and Dictaphone. The living room had not become like this intentionally, the reporter thought, as his eyes scanned the Lincoln biographies, complete set of Emerson, and delicate tea set—the only visible domestic touch. It had, he decided, "grown around her," like ivy molding itself to a tree. Their interview took place in the middle of a weekday, and the reporter could see she was absorbed in work. Papers and files pressed in everywhere around them.

Miss Tarbell looked at the younger man with anticipation. His readers wanted to know how she—the original muckraker of *McClure's*, "terror" of tycoons, "notorious" unmarried woman—navigated the world. But the reporter hesitated. What should he ask first? Would she take offense? A colleague had warned him that this remarkable woman—"in many respects the most influential woman of her times—is no languishing, rose-cheeked girl." Instead, Miss Tarbell "has trained herself for her work as a soldier is trained for war." She was an old master, able to read him and his nerves like a grubby and familiar book.

At the moment she was regarding him with cold precision, but the reporter felt a current of interested sympathy running close below. Once he began his interview, Miss Tarbell answered his hesitant, prosaic questions frankly. She described a quiet, writerly life of waking at seven with a cup of coffee and the papers. Sometimes, while the water was boiling, she practiced her few dance steps to get her blood moving. She started work by eight, and by eleven had a secretary drop in to take dictation. Lunch was almost always taken with friends at the National Arts Club nearby. Then a wink of sleep if she had time, followed by a walk, often to the New York Public Library to catch up on some research. Evenings were usually quiet; after dark, she either kept company with a coddled egg and a detective story or a solitary trip to the movies. Among her favorites, she confessed, were Charlie Chaplin, Mary Pickford, and Rin Tin Tin.

In the cushioned, paper-strewn room, listening to Miss Tarbell's kind, grave voice, the reporter's nerves dissolved. She was more like his maiden aunt than a battle-ax. But at the end of their meeting, she left him with a single admonition, provoked by a question he'd thought perfectly innocent. She was *not* a muckraker, she told him, urging him to print that in the papers.

"I am a student of events and men," she said slowly, emphatically. Her hand shook a little, he noticed, but here her voice was firm.

* * *

**THE SAME YEAR,** Samuel Sidney McClure faced another reporter at a lunch table downtown. At seventy-seven he was garrulous and spry, a slight, small-boned man with "eyes as blue and as keen as a Norseman's" and a thick, tow-colored mustache. The reporter found himself opening and closing his mouth wordlessly as his companion, the so-called editor of genius and "Merchant of Men's Minds," didn't let him get a word in edgewise.

McClure, barely guided by his interviewer's questions, fidgeted as he spoke, modulating his tone but not the momentum of his speech. "Active does not begin to describe him," another reporter had marveled. He frequently raised a hand to tug at his tousled white hair when narrating a time of crisis or triumph, the many times he had run aground on financial ruin, the friendships and rivalries with artists and presidents. His reedy voice had a slight burr, a vestige of his rural Irish youth. Every digression led back to the same theme: regardless of what the reporter had originally thought to ask about, the subject "on the top of his mind and heart" was the singular triumph of *McClure's* magazine.

The interviewer contemplated the man across the table and began to understand how this faded figure of American magazines had so often been written up as an inimitable, volcanic force of nature. Once perpetually unkempt from sleeping in train cars and on transatlantic steamers, now McClure was neatly but inexpensively dressed. Still constantly in motion, he cut an old-fashioned figure, as though the Jazz Age had passed him by without notice. He had none of the ponderous solemnity of the more patrician magazine editors. The reporter considered how to portray this man who had led from behind the printing press. As though orchestrating from behind a curtain, McClure had defined the muckraking movement without actually authoring any investigative stories himself. Headlines often easily slid into calling him a "genius" or a "titan," but inventor, discoverer, or relentless pursuer of talent might have captured him better.

McClure—or "S. S.," or "the Chief," depending on who was telling the story—exhausted his writers while bringing out the best in them. An apprenticeship with McClure led faltering young people to glittering careers and positions in the American canon as journalists of authority and brilliance. McClure led by enthusiasm, rather than by example. He was impatient, extravagant, a veritable "concatenation of unusualness," and a one-track conversationalist.

The reporter listening to him now had heard the stories, all of which hit a similar refrain. "The thoughts and ideas that sparked out from McClure's mind, the impalpable emanations of his personality, became, by some process of nature undirected by him, material things," one former McClure protégé had tried to explain. "They became presses, offices, staffs, editors, paper, ink, hundreds of thousands of copies of printed magazines, hundreds of thousands of readers, millions of readers. It was not that McClure created these things, it was rather that they gravitated to him, came out of the air, to attach themselves to McClure's thoughts and make the immaterial material. They grew like coral, formed themselves into orderly structures like a cathedral of stalactites, except that they had life, which begat more life, multiplied itself, became an immense and complex living mechanism."

One riddle would befuddle interviewers and readers alike as they confronted the special case of S. S. McClure: it was hard to tell what had happened by design, and what had hit against circumstance like flint against steel. As McClure carried on his whirling torrent of talk, the reporter took notes as quickly as he could.

How had this little interloper come to shape America's very image of itself? And why, after his monomaniacal climb to fame, had he lost his grip on it?

# Part I

# ORIGINS

# A Country for Youth

S. McClure and Ida Tarbell were born in the same year, 1857. Until their lives converged nearly forty years later, they were a study in contrasts. Sam McClure was a boy out of the Old Country, accustomed to hunger and the scorn dealt to the Irish by his American peers. Ida Tarbell grew up well fed and well read in Pennsylvania's rapidly industrializing Oil Region, before making a life for herself as a writer in Paris. He was a restless, rumpled figure of a man, a bantamweight five foot six. She stood nearly six feet, a thick topknot of hair giving her extra height and a regal air, and was punctilious about keeping her modest suits brushed and mended. But both were ruled by a drive to prove something to the world—a drive born from coming of age among doubters.

For the first eight years of his life, Samuel McClure—he would add "Sidney" later, realizing important men had middle names—knew exactly where he belonged. It was not a magazine office, or a steamship, or the downtown apartment of a liberated female poet; not yet, anyway. It was a farm.

McClure was born on February 17, 1857, in his grandfather's sturdy stone house in County Antrim, Ireland, the first of four boys. He would later remember his childhood as a country idyll. The McClures' home sat on nine acres in Drumaglea, halfway between the port cities of Belfast and Derry, among pale fields hedged in with hawthorn that bloomed bright white and pink in the spring. His parents, Thomas and Elizabeth, had a low, stout cottage on a gentle slope, with flowers growing up to the windowsills and a thatched roof. Inside, the floors of the two modest rooms were of neatly packed earth.

The McClures, Protestants of Lowland Scotch and French Huguenot blood, belonged to the "well-to-do poor." They lived according to an unchanging annual rhythm, their lives governed by potato planting in March, peat cutting in July, and church. Sam grew up eating potatoes seasoned meagerly with bacon, oatcakes, and buttermilk, tea for company, and woke and slept to the soft sputter and reek of a peat fire. Thomas supplemented the farm's unpredictable earnings by working as a ship's carpenter. Elizabeth would take care of their nine acres alone—as well as Sam and the babies who followed—whenever her husband traveled for a job.

Sam's sense of himself began to take shape when he started school. "It was then that I first felt myself a human entity," he wrote. When he was four, he quickly grew tired and bewildered by long, numbing days on schoolroom benches, sandwiched between other reluctant students. But he quickly discovered that the faster he learned, the more opportunity he had to borrow books.

He had a need for stories. His parents' cottage held just three books: the Bible, *Pilgrim's Progress,* which he read over and over, and *Fox's Book of Martyrs,* a volume of grisly woodcuts showing the persecution of Protestants through the ages. Sam McClure knew well the scenes of martyrs burning at the stake, being flayed alive by Catholic tormentors, thrown to hungry pigs to be devoured, or hauled to the gallows, but while the scenes were striking, the narrative was always the same. Periodically, the schoolhouse received unwieldy boxes from Dublin that brought more excitement than Christmas, at least for boys who felt the way Sam did. "Opening those boxes and looking into the fresh books that still had the smell of the press," Sam wrote, "was about the most delightful thing that happened during the year."

Sam McClure was gregarious and often in the center of a knot of boys. He felt equally free and happy reading in the schoolhouse whenever there was a quiet moment or on evening tramps through the fields with classmates. Weekends were dull by comparison, full of obligations to farm and faith. Later in life he wrote, "I have always experienced a sense of dreariness on going into houses where one was supposed to leave [the interests and occupations of my life] outside. I have never been able to have one set of interests to work with and another set to play with. This is my misfortune, but it is true." Sam's mind raced furiously along its own singular track, groaning whenever it had to apply the brakes.

His father died young, shattering the McClures' modest, respectable life forever. On a carpentry contract in Scotland, while walking across the deck of a partially built ship, Thomas fell through a hatch and hit his head. He lay in a Glasgow infirmary for weeks before his death was recorded November 30, 1864. Sam would later think of his father as a kind, clever man with a brown beard, who every morning gave his oldest son the top morsel left over when he cracked into a boiled egg. The very ordinariness of this image—no portentous words of fatherly advice, in fact no words at all—shows what hollowness and deprivation his death meant to his children.

This was a devastating loss to a family that had narrowly avoided displacement or death from the Famine. They lived close to the land, thankfully not beholden to any landlord, but their sustenance depended on the constant labor of both parents. Elizabeth was twenty-seven and heavily pregnant when she got word of her husband's accident. Spirited and stocky, she had "unusual physical vigor and great energy" that awed her sons, for "[a]fter keeping up with the men in the fields all day, she would come in and get supper for them at night," Sam recalled. One of fourteen siblings, she had a formidable will of her own.

Back near Drumaglea, walking home from school on a mild November evening, Sam and his friends happened upon a patch of sweet turnips and fell to eating them "with great glee." As was later seared in his memory, Sam saw a man approaching on the road and heard him call, *Samuel, your da is deid*. His teeth crunching through a sweet turnip just pulled from the earth, seven-year-old Sam couldn't quite grasp what the words meant. When he got home, he found relatives crowded into the cottage, already debating what Elizabeth should do, speculating on how she might foster out the children and go back to work her father's land.

On the night she learned of her husband's death, Elizabeth firmly put her well-meaning family out of her house. In her grief, a mulish determination to prove them wrong possessed her. She and Thomas had made an independent life, they had been touched with good luck in their own health and their potato harvests, and if she could work hard enough, she believed she could keep her home. She took a ferry to Glasgow to recover her husband's body, which was given a simple burial in the nearby village of Clough. Now their cottage felt bereft, with Thomas's clothes and tools abandoned. Elizabeth likely returned to her father's house to give birth to her fifth child—named after a previous Robert who had died in infancy— two months later. She then continued working the land alone for nearly a year, falling further behind in her debts with each passing month. Without Thomas's income it was impossible to support herself and four surviving sons.

Still stubborn, Elizabeth refused to foster out her boys to separate homes. She knew her relatives and neighbors thought her fortunate to have the option, and unbalanced for rejecting it. Sam, Jack, Tom, and Robby were nine, eight, six, and one—none of them old enough to work much. Elizabeth could not stomach the notion of being a wage laborer for her parents while giving up her children, essentially signing on to live on familial charity.

Much later, keeping the brothers together would prove formative in more ways than one: when Sam founded *McClure's,* all three of his brothers (as well as a cousin, Harry McClure) came to be magazine men with him. Sam drew continual inspiration from his mother's defiant will, which he regarded as a great strength and the key to the family's survival. Elizabeth demonstrated how to reinvent oneself after a foundational blow, something Sam would practice more often and willfully than necessary or comfortable for those close to him.

America beckoned. Elizabeth had three siblings of her own in the Midwest and decided to try her luck where they were, around the southern tip of Lake Michigan near Valparaiso, Indiana. Elizabeth spent some of her vanishing savings and bought all four of her boys new suits, a size or two too big. They filed into steerage quarters on the steamship *Mongolia* and felt the deck rock beneath them as the port of Londonderry grew smaller against the horizon. The voyage was cheerful enough, once seasickness subsided. The steamer took the McClures to the port of Grosse Isle, Quebec, where they passed the health examination, boarded a slow, immigrant-packed train to Indiana, and disembarked at a rough, quiet little station on the prairie. Elizabeth's brother Joe Gaston met them there and took them, piled in the back of his wagon, to a sister's tiny farm, where they slept at last.

In the northern heartland of Indiana, in the midst of a vast frontier territory dotted with glacial kettle ponds, Valparaiso steadily drew fortune-seeking new arrivals through the nineteenth century. The territory had been purchased from the Potawatomi tribe barely thirty years earlier and was home to fewer than three thousand settlers, but the land was fertile, the forests full of game, and it was a promising place to stake a claim, trade furs, or elude an unsavory past in the Old Country. By the time the McClures arrived on July 3, 1866, Valparaiso was the county seat and had the advantage of a direct train line to Chicago.

After that first night crowded in with their unfamiliar American family, Sam's first memories of Valparaiso were of small-town Independence Day celebrations. He recalled sitting on a wooden chair looking at the land, a kind of bare terrain he had never seen before, taking in the speeches and firecrackers and looking at "a great stretch of unfenced prairie in place of the little hedge-fenced fields I had always known."

Someone thrust a cup of lemonade into his hand as he listened to a local politician's grand oratory about the land of freedom and unbounded opportunity. The world around him seemed very big and free. "Here was a young country for Youth," he later wrote of his impressions that night. It was a rare, idealistic, self-reflective moment for that particular youth. In the years that followed, both Sam and the young country around him struggled to build a future to live up to it.

* * *

**AS SAM McCLURE WAS CAUGHT UP** in his new home's July Fourth pageantry, America was adapting to its own changed landscape in the wake of the Civil War. The McClures were part of a demographic sea change. Immigrants flooded into the fractured country, while former slaves migrated to northern cities and towns, if they could. From 1860 to 1910, the rural population of the United States almost doubled while the urban population multiplied nearly seven times. But the McClures noticed little of that upheaval through their first year in America. They were preoccupied with survival.

Being poor was as much a liability in the New World as it had been in the Old, and Elizabeth's American family was unwilling to take in five more mouths to feed. After months scrambling to get by, moving her sons frequently between begrudging relatives and squatting in a vacant storeroom in town, Elizabeth finally found steady work as a laundress for a doctor's family. Sam took to spending long hours in the library of the doctor's house, where, he later wrote, "I lay on the carpet, face down, and read for hours at a time," books that fired his imagination like *Robinson Crusoe*. Like its hero, Sam had been pulled far from home by tides he could not swim against. When the doctor moved away, the McClures were cast out into a harsh midwestern winter. They crowded in with their aunt and uncle again, who had six children of their own, subsisting on "frozen potatoes boiled into a kind of gray mush." All were so malnourished by winter's end that the boys' hands shook.

Then came a pragmatic marriage. Elizabeth was noticed and courted by Thomas Simpson, a kindly Irish farmer who lived less than a mile away. It is unclear whether she returned the interest of this man who shared her dead husband's first name and profession; she certainly couldn't afford to turn it away. "Something had to be done," McClure later wrote, "and it seemed to mother that when she had this opportunity she ought to marry and give her children a home." The family moved to Simpson's unyielding patch of prairie, gaining a roof over their heads as Simpson gained four chore boys and a healthy, hardworking wife.

It was hard to get a sense of the wider world amid the demands of Simpson's farm. Sam liked his stepfather but hated the relentless grind of chores, which began with the cows needing to be milked and mucked out in the morning and progressed to planting and harvesting corn by hand. Everyone worked hard to eke a living from the land, soldiering grimly through bouts of fever, frostbite, and dysentery. They had a roof now, but lived as much hand-to-mouth as ever. "It seemed to me," McClure wrote in his memoirs, "that my mother worked hardest of all." She seemed to be in perpetual motion, though unable to dodge catastrophe. Elizabeth bore four more children, three of whom died in infancy. There was always a sick baby in the house, debts to worry about, and little time for school or stories.

Yet Sam refused to be penned in by his surroundings. Frustrated that his new country school only covered basic reading and math, he asked a neighbor to teach him algebra. When he had a break from the farm, he read and reread his stepfather's only literature, yellowing copies of *Agricultural Reports* and catalogs for farm equipment. Once, some hunters camped for the night on their land and left behind a scattering of old magazines and paperbacks. Sam seized them. "Here were good stories of adventure, stories of poor boys who had got on, stories of boys who had made collections of insects and butterflies and learned all about them," he wrote. They enthralled him and fed his daydreams for years. He wanted to be one of those worldly heroes.

Despite her astonishingly demanding days, Elizabeth was ambitious for her bright, dreamy eldest son. When he was fourteen, she took Sam aside: Valparaiso's first-ever high school had just opened, she told him. She offered him a chance to leave home, find a place as a chore boy in town, and try to get as much education as he could. Sam gratefully took this chance to escape. After screwing up his courage to knock on doors and ask for work, he was hired by the Scrooge-like Dr. Levi Cass, known to have "the most money and the fewest friends" in town. Each morning, Sam would emerge from his sleeping quarters in Dr. Cass's basement and rush to help with laundry and chores, then dash to school for the starting bell.

Sam McClure began to refashion himself on his first day of high school, creating a character who could pass within the slipstream of his mostly middle-class classmates. As he listened anxiously to roll call on the first day, he realized he was the only boy with no middle name. It suddenly seemed uncouth to have only two names, so he began to call himself Samuel Sherman McClure, borrowing a middle name from the Civil War general he had read about. Later he changed it to Sidney, possibly to sound more literary, and from his school days onward signed his name S. S. McClure. "[L]ike most things in my life," recalled McClure, this hurried self-invention was "entirely accidental." The extra initial gave a stateliness to his name, as though a word alone could add stature and a gliding elegance to a figure who would grow up slight and nervous.

But this superficial change did little to help him fit in. His poverty was obvious. A classmate recalled noticing him: "there sat a little tow headed, studious, energetic boy, whose almost homeless condition always appealed to my heart." Other boys mocked his Irish accent, and he was overworked and lonely in the great house nearby where he earned his keep. Much later, an up-and-coming writer would hear Sam McClure's stories of childhood and memorialize them in a novel, writing of her lonesome young hero, "under his weather-beaten old cap, perched sidewise on a tousled head, was a commotion of dreams and schemes, ambitions and plans, whose activities would have put to shame the busiest wharf in the world." At Christmas he went to his uncle Joe Gaston's farm and was so relieved to be with family that he overstayed his time off. When he returned to Dr. Cass's house late, he was turned away.

Sam wasn't sorry to find some other way to make a living, even if it meant dropping school temporarily. He rustled up work as an amateur butcher and a foundry boy, and worked the grade on the Baltimore & Ohio Railroad. For two months, he was a printer's devil for a local newspaper, arranging type and ink for the Valparaiso *Vidette,* his first brush with journalism. At fifteen he taught in a country school for a summer, where he resisted the convention of making children sit still all day and sent them to play outdoors instead.

Above all, he was restless. His need to move may have first stemmed from physical necessity: unable to afford an overcoat, Sam McClure ran from place to place in the wintertime to keep from freezing. Possibly he was spurred along by a need to get away from the humiliations of the classroom, the overbearing rule of Dr. Cass, or the sight of his mother bound to a home where she was buffeted by anxiety and loss. The compulsion never left him, and ideas always came more easily when he was in motion. At the first hint of warm weather, he liked to hop a freight train and ride out of town and then back again, just for the sake of moving. The train's momentum soothed him, and seeing familiar landscapes replaced by new ones made the cares of family, money, and school fall away. He wrote, "I escaped being a tramp so narrowly that I have always felt that I know exactly what kind of one I should have been. . . . This restlessness was something that I seemed to have no control over. I have had to reckon with it all my life, and whatever I have been able to do has been in spite of it."

His learning and roaming were cut short when Thomas Simpson died of typhoid. Doubly fatherless, Sam gave up his independent life and the elusive benefits of high school and went home to help Elizabeth. By now he and his brothers were old enough to run the farm, and together they resolved to do whatever it took to turn a profit. With Sam, Jack, Tom, and Robby McClure putting their full effort in, 1874 brought a bigger crop than had ever been produced on Simpson's land before. Eight years after the family's arrival in Indiana, they finally had a tenuous foothold. They had wrested self-sufficiency from the land, achieving a pioneer dream that much more frequently ended in bankruptcy or ruined health.

In late summer, just as they were harvesting and starting to prepare for another austere winter, Uncle Joe Gaston arrived for a visit. The McClures hadn't seen him in over a year, and he explained he had gone to study for the ministry at a place called Knox College in Galesburg, Illinois. He spoke of it as one of the greatest places in the world.

Sam was galvanized. By the time Joe stopped talking, Sam had resolved to go, too. In the small world of Valparaiso, Sam could make his way by working the land, or he could be a servant in town. He knew he hated both. The potential obstacles of a high school qualification and tuition money melted away as Galesburg gleamed like Athens in his mind's eye, and the decision became fixed: he was finished with the farm.

# 2

# *Oildorado*

da Minerva Tarbell was hardly more than three when she led her baby brother Will down to the footbridge, hoisted him up, and threw him into the creek that flowed by her family's rough little house. His pale, voluminous baby dresses floated up bright against the current, and as he bobbed there, held up by the clothes for a minute, he began to scream.

A neighbor quickly noticed what was happening and rescued the little boy. Examining Will's crumpled face as he was pulled from the creek, Ida was appeased. She had wondered whether the baby would float or sink. Classification, not fratricide, was her aim, and now she felt "the peace of satisfied curiosity in the certainty that my brother belonged to the category of things which floated." Though pursuing the question earned her a spanking, it was well worth the experiment.

This unsentimental child grew up surrounded by books, in a landscape glinting from hurried industrialization in Pennsylvania's Oil Region. Oil seeped through the bedrock of Ida Tarbell's childhood and returned to occupy her adult years, despite the great lengths she went to to leave it behind. The Oil Region was backdrop to countless dramas of hope, ingenuity, and violent death. Ida later wrote, "Of the pregnant, bizarre, and often tragic development going on about me I remember nothing; yet the uncertainties and dangers of it were part of our daily fare."

Her parents, Franklin and Esther Tarbell, were reluctant settlers in northwestern Pennsylvania's Erie County. They had talked of going west after their marriage and Franklin took an exploratory trip as far as Iowa, but a sudden recession evaporated their savings and kept them close to the comfortable log house—not a backwoods cabin, Ida Tarbell would later emphasize, but a real house—in the now-vanished settlement of Hatch Hollow. Their family grew, first in 1857 with Ida's birth and then with the arrival of William, Sarah, and finally Frankie, who died young of scarlet fever.

A boom in oil drilling transformed Erie County. Franklin Tarbell, though he had been a farmer and teacher, was a gifted designer and craftsman. Once he and Esther gave up their dream of a new life in the Midwest, he became an oil prospector and tank builder. The family moved to Rouseville, a prospectors' settlement at the mouth of a steep-banked stream called Cherry Run. A local observer reported, "Men think of oil, talk of oil, dream of oil; the smell and taste of oil predominate in all they eat and drink; they breathe an atmosphere of oil-gas, and the clamor of 'ile, ile—ile' rings in one's ears from daylight until midnight."

Oil hadn't always been worth much notice, except as a nuisance. "Rock oil" or "Seneca oil" had long troubled prospectors in Pennsylvania and the Midwest, contaminating salt wells and putting mines out of business. But it was valued as a tonic by Native Americans and pioneers, who rubbed it over injuries and sore muscles. To the rest of the world, it started to be important in the years just before the Civil War. Starting in the 1850s, along the Allegheny River, chemist Samuel Kier began to bottle and sell the thick, black oil that bubbled up in his father's brine wells. He and his neighbors were used to their oily terrain; since 1755, maps of the region helpfully pointed toward both "Oyl Creek" and "Petroleum"—itself the Latin word for "rock oil." Kier's salve sold at fifty cents per bottle, distributed by druggists as a cure for everything from sore eyes to piles. He heard rumors of other oils being refined into lamp oil, to compete with the expensive whale oil—a fuel that meant lamplight was generally a luxury reserved for the wealthy. With this in mind, Kier began tinkering with an old whiskey still on his property, chasing a vision of making his fortune.

Kier was edging into a market that needed innovators. City streetlamps and homes—those who could afford lamplight—were lit by coal gas, which was cheaper than the nearly odorless and smokeless fuel derived from whale blubber. Refining rock oil into kerosene was far cheaper and easier than extracting oil from coal or whales, and although it had only been done in small volumes, Kier knew there was money to be made—provided he didn't blow himself up in the process. When he upgraded his experiments to a five-barrel-capacity still, his neighbors asked him to move, for fear of fire. He persisted with his experiments, and soon Kier had a new kind of fuel and a new lamp for burning it. He neglected to file a patent for either.

Separately, in New Hampshire, lawyer and linguist George Bissell was visiting his alma mater, Dartmouth, when he got hold of a bottle of "rock oil" that happened to be in a professor's office. Bissell also intuited that it had potential as a new source of light. But one great obstacle stood in the way, the same thing that kept Kier from building a real business: no one had been able to harvest large enough amounts of the stuff to produce anything on an industrial scale. Soaking it up from waterways or salt wells was nowhere near as reliable as mines were for coal. Even whale hunting, dangerous as it was, seemed a more practical business. The traditional way to accumulate oil was to dam sections of oil-rich creeks to create a "seep," where oil then collected on the surface and could be skimmed off. But even the best seeps yielded just three or four gallons a day at most.

Kier's hunch connected with Bissell's ambition in New York City, as Bissell took a walk down Broadway. In the window of a drugstore, he caught sight of a bottle labeled "Kier's Petroleum, or Rock Oil. Celebrated for its wonderful curative powers. A Natural Remedy; Produced from a well in Allegheny Co., Pa., four hundred feet below the earth's surface." Among the words was a drawing of an artesian well; among the claims was that, applied internally or externally, the product could ease rheumatism, gout, asthma, "obstinate eruptions of the skin," diarrhea, cholera, and deafness. Bissell decided that he had to go to the place on the label, find the source of the oil that filled these bottles, and build a well that would pump the oil from the depths of the earth to the surface to fill barrels at a time. This method would do more than supply medicinal quantities: it had the potential to light cities.

Bissell paid a lab scientist at Yale, Benjamin Silliman Jr., to analyze and write about the potential of oil for illumination, lubrication, and any other use where he saw possibilities. Silliman told him what he needed to hear to get investors on board, writing a report that dryly foretells what we now take for granted: "Your company have in their possession a raw material from which they may manufacture very valuable products."

With this scientific backing, impartial or not, Bissell gathered funding and launched Seneca Oil in the spring of 1858. One of the stakeholders, an unemployed train conductor named E. L. Drake, became Bissell's head prospector. For Bissell, Drake's main qualification was most likely his free railway pass, a relic from his previous job that would save the new company a little money in prospecting costs. He had little notion that Drake would someday be seen as the founding father of the oil industry.

Drake began his experiments near the quiet town of Titusville, on the banks of the waterway that had been called Oil Creek for more than a century. His employers suggested he introduce himself as "Colonel Drake" to gain the respect of his new neighbors. Instead, their whispered name for him was "Crazy Drake." His efforts to design reliably productive seeps yielded almost ten gallons per day, double what anyone had produced before, but still an unprofitable harvest. Working with a blacksmith, he began drilling through the unyielding bedrock using steam-powered equipment. On good days they would get through about three feet. Drake had no practical, scholarly, or hobbyist's background that would qualify him for his job, and he was quickly running out of money. Finally, the company's investors decided the experiment was a bust and sent Drake a letter telling him to shut down the whole operation.

But the postal service between New Haven, Connecticut, and Erie County was slow. On August 27, 1859, the letter somewhere en route, with his well at 69.5 feet, Drake struck oil. He waited for the gush to subside and started reaping oil the next day, using a hand-operated pump borrowed from a neighbor's kitchen. He filled an unprecedented twenty-five barrels. Witnesses dashed off to spread the word, crying in disbelief, "The Yankee has struck oil." The source seemed inexhaustibly rich, and now men had a way of getting to it and a reason to sell it. As Ida Tarbell would later report in *McClure's* magazine, "In many places pumping was out of the question; the wells flowed, two, three, four thousand barrels a day; such quantities of it that at the close of 1861, oil which in January of 1860 was twenty dollars a barrel had fallen to ten cents." Drake himself had not secured equity in the company whose fortune he extracted from the earth. Though his grave monument in Titusville now hails him as "founder of the petroleum industry," he was broke when he died in 1880. A contemporary of Drake wrote in a posthumous profile, "He pumped the well serenely, told funny stories and secured not one foot of ground."

The strip of petroleum-rich land in the Allegheny river valley extended 160 miles, from western Pennsylvania up to New York, only forty miles wide at its broadest point. Once a quiet farming region with a few salt mines, the newly branded Oil Region now swarmed with fortune hunters tapping the earth for the light, sweet crude that promised to bring lamplight and wealth. In 1861 *Vanity Fair* commemorated the rapid change in a cartoon of whales drinking, dancing, and waving celebratory banners ("Oils Well that Ends Well") at the "Grand Ball given by the Whales in honor of discovery of the Oil Wells in Pennsylvania." Through the mid-1860s, popular music dwelled on the drama of the oil speculating life, with songs like "Pa Has Struck Ile," "Petroleum Galop," and the German-accented kitsch of "Ile, or Vay Down in Bennsylvany":

> *De ile it flow so shplendid,*
> *It make dem all to shmile,*
> *For "Greenbacks" dey is blenty too,*
> *Venever you "shtrike ile."*

The oil revolution transformed everyday life. Daily work schedules stretched to fill this new, longer, brighter day. Great Plains writer Hamlin Garland told of the night he came home from the fields in 1869 to find a kerosene lamp on the dining room table, brighter and steadier than any candle. Laura Ingalls Wilder, born a decade after Ida Tarbell, chronicled her family's reliance on a single kerosene lamp for light and cheer through dark winters in Dakota Territory. Uses for oil multiplied with the years, until, as French Prime Minister Clemenceau wrote to President Wilson after World War I, everything that rolled or sailed or flew required it, and suddenly oil was as necessary "as the blood of men."

By the start of 1872, northwestern Pennsylvania was responsible for kerosene-lit cities from New York to St. Petersburg. Oil was struck in Ohio and West Virginia, too. At the peak of the oil boom, Pennsylvania was supplying roughly one-third of the world's oil. The rise of "Oildorado" bred a landscape covered in derricks and engine-driven pumps, with speculators' settlements sprouting up in a matter of weeks after the discovery of each new source. The land became so densely settled that a local clergyman noted it was difficult to tell where one town ended and the next began. The oil boom made for a grimy and often desperate livelihood for most who relied on it. Rouseville was one of these newly sprouted oil towns: "a collection of pine shanties and oil derricks, built on a muddy flat—as forlorn and disreputable a town in appearance as the earth ever saw."

It was here that the Tarbells, contrary to their best-laid plans, made their life.

\* \* \*

IDA GREW UP STUDIOUS AND HEADSTRONG, a thin girl with deep-set eyes and slightly protruding ears, which she would learn to disguise under her plentiful dark hair. Rouseville's scenery, scorched, clanging, and cluttered from the paraphernalia of "Oildom," never felt like home, and she tried to run away as soon as she could confidently walk. "It aroused me to a revolt which is the first thing I am sure I remember about my life—the birth in me of conscious experience," she remembered decades later. The rise of oil defined the landscape Ida saw every day and governed her family's fortunes. Their home stood by a "creek rushing wildly at the side of the house, great oil pits sunken in the earth not far away, a derrick inviting to adventurous climbing at the door." Oil's expansion from niche market to big business coincided closely with Ida's coming of age, shaped her early encounters with both wealth and grief, and captured her emotions in a way that she didn't always like to admit. She later wrote, "No industry of man in its early days has ever been more destructive of beauty, order, decency, than the production of petroleum."

Most of their neighbors in Rouseville either drilled for crude oil or refined it. Drilling was expensive and risky. Refining oil to be turned into kerosene, on the other hand, required a simple apparatus: "a cast-iron still, usually surrounded by brickwork, a copper worm, and two tin or zinc-lined tanks." Crude oil was distilled at high heat, and then treated with chemicals and rinsed, before being left to settle. Ida Tarbell later wrote, "Anybody who could get the apparatus could 'make oil,' and many men did it—badly, of course, to begin with, and with an alarming proportion of waste and explosions and fires." As a child, Ida witnessed enough gruesome accidents to mark her for life. In her old age, when a gas station attendant spilled some fuel on her by accident, she began to scream.

Within, the Tarbells' home was dominated by Esther's outspoken, educated voice. Herself a product of a freethinking Scottish family with a supposed bloodline to Sir Walter Raleigh, she had been a women's rights advocate and teacher—inspired, as Ida later wrote, to "vindicate her sex" by securing higher education and possibly even a career. Despite her natural independence of mind, Esther's life was ultimately governed by the vagaries of her husband's career and the needs of their children. She and Franklin were staunch Methodists; travelers often knocked on their door hoping for a meal, as Esther and Franklin kept a sign of hospitality, a white cross, on the house, and had the coffee going all day. The Tarbells were liberal readers, both young and old, with a particular affinity for *Harper's Weekly, Harper's Monthly,* and the *New York Tribune.*

Ida had a botanist's inclination for dispassionate inquiry and the natural world. With the nature around her stamped out by the cogs and fumes of oil-drilling, she turned her eye to the social hodgepodge of Rouseville. Curiosity, not convention, possessed her, and her gaze did not shy from the things she was not supposed to see: "I saw from the corner of my eye as I walked sedately the length of the street saloons, dance halls, brothels; and I noted many curious things." She never forgot the sight of her father slowly walking up the hill, head bowed, in the spring of 1865, to announce to the family that Lincoln was dead.

Fifty years later, Ida Tarbell described her experience of a knowledge-thirsty child's inner life. She wrote in *The Ways of Woman* (1915), originally a series of *Woman's Home Companion* essays, "'Keeping a child busy' is no sure guarantee that her mind is not vagabonding in forbidden places." A sharp-eyed girl like herself knew to pretend to "sleep on the couch to listen to strange conversations she knows not to be for her ears. She reads every book 'kept out of the children's sight.'" Her family had built a bunkhouse on their land for rent-paying prospectors who left behind copies of the *Police Gazette,* a paper generally deemed improper for the ladies and children who were far outnumbered by fortune-hunting men in the oil-prospecting towns. Ida developed a habit of sneaking into the bunkhouse for the *Gazette* and its colorful reports on crime. It was a window onto a world no adult cared to explain to her directly. Through listening, reading, and blending into the background, she discovered and cataloged the dramas and hypocrisies of the adults' world. Ida held tight to her inner life, instinctively knowing it was "more enticing, far lovelier, than the life of work and play 'they' provide for her." She relished keeping secrets and always found a way to observe more than she was meant to.

Her imagination hungered for made-up stories, too. In her memoirs Ida recalled, "There are still family storeroom copies of *Harper's Monthly* stained with lemon pie dropped when I was too deep into a story to be careful. Here I read my first Dickens, my first Thackeray, my first Marian Evans, as George Eliot then signed herself. My first Wilkie Collins came to me in the *Weekly*." The British Victorian novelists had an indelible influence over her. Dickens's *The Mystery of Edwin Drood* was serialized through the summer of 1870, and Eliot's *Middlemarch* was also published in installments over the following two years. Ida Tarbell's career-defining Standard Oil series would be animated by a Dickensian portrait of a fearsome industrialist and richly descriptive prose worthy of Eliot, with the sweep and tone of a social novel.

By 1870, the oil boom in Pennsylvania had lasted for a decade. Cautiously flush, the Tarbells moved to Titusville, a proper town with a train station, schools, and churches, even an opera house. Franklin bought a grand, disused hotel from the nearby settlement of Pithole and used the materials to build his family a graceful house on Titusville's Main Street. Here Ida had a room of her own and a cupola nook with space for her desk, where she could watch everyone who came and went along one of the town's busiest arteries. The spacious, stylish home filled with a piano, solid furniture, and well-made clothes. That Christmas, Franklin gave his wife a fur coat. It was, in Ida's words, her first "notion of elegance." Like their neighbors on Main Street, the Tarbells tamped down most ostentatious signs of their new wealth: among this tight-knit Methodist community, college education and first-class travel were the preferred symbols of gentility. The Tarbells took a pleasure trip to Cleveland and stayed in the best hotel. In the summers, they drove the fifty or so miles out to Chautauqua Lake for all-day picnics and educational programs. Around that time, in the same city, the Rockefeller brothers formed a consortium that would have a profound effect on the nation and an uncommonly personal impact on Ida Tarbell's life: the Standard Oil Company.

As she entered adolescence, Ida resolved to live differently than her mother; total independence was the only sure way to avoid being trapped as Esther had. Ida later wrote of her vow, "I must be free; and to be free I must be a spinster. When I was fourteen I was praying God on my knees to keep me from marriage."

This equivalence of wedlock with bondage echoes Louisa May Alcott's vow never to marry, made in 1860 when the author was twenty-seven. On the occasion of her sister's marriage, Alcott remarked, "I'd rather be a free spinster and paddle my own canoe." If readers had not clamored for her most famous heroine to find a love match during the serialized publication of *Little Women,* when Ida Tarbell was just turning twelve, Jo March would have shunned the institution, too.

Working outside the home was a relatively daring goal for an educated white woman in small-town Pennsylvania. (It was far from revolutionary in the urban South, where nearly five times as many black women as white women did so.) In her resolve to be both educated and self-sufficient, Ida was pushing the bounds of a life of easy convention and social approval. She attached herself to ideals that were no longer radical, but nevertheless, not entirely safe. As she wrote, "Ours was a yeasty time, the ferment reaching into every relation of life, attacking and remodeling every tradition, every philosophy."

From the mid-1800s, the daughters of well-off, forward-thinking families saw their futures grow less circumscribed. The Seneca Falls Convention in July 1848, the first high-profile women's rights summit, stated in its Declaration of Sentiments that men had "denied [woman] the facilities of a thorough education, all colleges being closed against her." As the Civil War took many men away, universities tentatively opened their doors to women to fill empty seats. The same applied to professional positions that had been left empty, from clerical work to nursing to, in the South, managing vast plantations. Female wage workers became a large and confident enough population that in 1868, Susan B. Anthony and Elizabeth Cady Stanton formed the Working Women's Association, which encouraged working women to unionize. All-female colleges gained a foothold, especially in the Northeast, where the intellectual elite puzzled over what to do with accomplished, unmarried daughters. If college did not throw them in the path of an eligible man, it was hoped that these young women would hear an appropriately feminine and service-oriented "call" to teaching or missionary work, still the only career paths regarded by the middle and upper classes as truly respectable.

Beyond campus, new rights and roles for women came in fits and starts. A major force in the American women's rights movement of Ida Tarbell's youth came from Quakers and other abolitionists active during the Civil War, who saw the end of slavery as the primary pillar of their campaign. In 1868 the Fourteenth Amendment was passed, affirming the citizenship of freed slaves but explicitly excluding women from equal representation in government. In Ida's words, this milestone "for the first time introducing the word 'male' into the Constitution, aroused a sense of outrage, not only in the advocates of equal rights but in many women who had not approved of previous agitations." One new agitation, which Ida followed in the newspapers, came from the nascent Equal Rights Party, which in 1872 nominated Virginia Woodhull for president and Frederick Douglass for vice president of the United States. Woodhull won no electoral votes in that election—not that she was permitted to cast a ballot herself—and news coverage regarded her as the embodiment of a bad joke, frequently portraying her as a whip-wielding harpy or bewinged "Mrs. Satan."

As long as she didn't damn herself through a too-public, too-radical life, a woman could at least get an education and cultivate a life of the mind. In that same election year, Cornell became the first Ivy League school to open its doors to women, and fifteen-year-old Ida Tarbell decided she would go. Then one Sunday in Titusville she met Dr. Lucius Bugbee, charismatic president of Allegheny College, which had become coed even earlier, and her ambitions redirected themselves there instead. Here her plans diverged from those of other girls in her high school graduating class. Those who planned to work didn't need a college degree; a teaching certificate would fulfill the balance of their studies.

Ida's unusual vocation, as she prepared to leave home, was science. Her most treasured object was the microscope she had bought out of her allowance in her early teens. In her memoir, she saw the microscope as her "first intellectual passion, my first and greatest . . . With a microscope I could perhaps get an answer to my mystification about the beginning of life, where it started; and then, I believed, I should find God." She was compelled by the new theory of evolution—*On the Origin of Species* was published the year after her birth—which guided her sense of the world more powerfully than faith. She amassed her own collection of leaves, insects, rainwater samples, and saw that nothing—even her own skin and hair—had the smooth, cohesive surface visible to the naked eye alone.

Gazing into the microscope also offered a needed escape into a timeless and symmetrical world, impervious to society's ills. In that same tumultuous year of 1872, a crisis in the community overwhelmed the Tarbells and many of their neighbors. Even in adulthood, Ida remembered the experience as a bewildering physical trauma, a "blow between the eyes," which rocked her sense of stability and possibility even more than any election or thoughts of college.

The terror was set off by a scheme called the Southern Improvement Company: a sweetheart deal between John D. Rockefeller and three railroad companies that increased oil freight prices by 100 percent—with an exemption for oil from refineries controlled by Rockefeller's Standard Oil. Consequences came quickly; Oil Region families who had just arrived in the middle class were now terrifyingly destabilized. In Rouseville, oilmen cooked up "processions" and "raids," occupying the Titusville Opera House, defacing Standard Oil banners with the skull and crossbones, and, on one raw spring night, "[running] oil into the ground." This was an extraordinary and bitter eruption in a community where independent oil refiners and Standard Oil employees lived cheek by jowl.

Franklin Tarbell "came home with a grim look on his face and told how he with scores of other producers had signed a pledge not to sell to the Cleveland ogre"—Rockefeller—whose name was permanently tinged in Ida's mind with fear, repulsion, and contempt. The anger extended beyond the reaches of Oil Region territory; the Brooklyn refinery headed by Charles Pratt (of the Pratt Institute) quickly lost business to the Standard, and New York refineries sent a delegation to confront the railroads. Rumor had it that Rockefeller had started sleeping with a revolver within reach.

The rebels won the battle. In April 1872, the Pennsylvania state legislature repealed the Southern Improvement Company's charter and the scheme was dismantled, to the embarrassment of the railroad owners and Rockefeller associates.

Victory in the courts couldn't stave off a catastrophic shift for the Tarbells and many of their neighbors who made a living from oil. In the end, no oil was ever shipped by the Southern Improvement Company. But before the ruling came into effect, Franklin Tarbell and many other independent businessmen went bankrupt, leaving them permanently marked by shame and anxiety. Where Franklin had once cracked jokes, sang, and played the jaw harp of an evening, he now turned "silent and stern." For the rest of her life, when Ida Tarbell recalled the Oil War, she judged that "the sly, secret, greedy way won in the end, and bitterness and unhappiness and incalculable ethical deterioration for the country at large came out of that struggle."

At fifteen, Ida could see that Rockefeller and his ilk, despite the failure of their scheme, were insulated from anything like this fate. Three decades later, she heard of Rockefeller's son comparing Standard Oil to a prize rose in a speech at Brown University, saying that "in order to produce the perfect flower fifty or more small buds must be lopped off"; she used this phrase as one of the epigraphs for the book edition of *The History of Standard Oil*. The Tarbells had once been hopeful buds alongside Rockefeller's rose, stunted so that the stronger, showier specimen could flourish. "There was born in me a hatred of privilege—privilege of any sort," Ida later wrote. When, as an adult, she read of Rousseau's social contract and his defense of the right to revolt, she was "much elated" by how it resonated with her own instincts.

Her brother William would go on to become the in-house counsel for the Pure Oil Company of Pennsylvania, but he, too, never stopped seeing the oil business as a gamble, a will-o'-the-wisp of a trade. "Often I wish I was in some other business," he wrote to Ida in 1896, "and if I ever hit it rich, you bet I'll put most of it into something safe."

# 3

# *A Garibaldi Type of Mind*

S am McClure left Valparaiso in late summer 1874, wearing an old suit and cowhide boots burnished by heavy use. He was primed for transformation. In Galesburg, Illinois, he expected to become a man of the world, to emerge from the cocoon of subsistence work on the prairie into a realm of ideas. As he left his mother and brothers at the train platform, he carried a bulky suitcase covered in black oilcloth, eight dollars in his pocket, and little knowledge about his destination save that it would change him, and change his life, utterly.

On train and on foot, he was pointed two hundred miles to the west. Knox College was rooted in idealism that suited his vision of a great university. Both Galesburg and Knox (originally known as Prairie College) were founded in 1837 by antislavery social reformers and followers of Presbyterian minister George Washington Gale. The college drew dedicated abolitionists to Galesburg, which became a heavily used stop on the Underground Railroad. In 1858, Abraham Lincoln came to Knox and debated the morals of slavery with Stephen Douglas, who narrowly beat him to the Senate. (To reach the hastily built debate platform, the self-educated Lincoln had had to climb through a window; afterward he reportedly quipped, "At least I have gone through college.") Two years later, during Lincoln's presidential campaign, Knox awarded him an honorary doctorate—the first such degree Lincoln ever held.

A less-rigorous Female Seminary had been part of Knox almost since its founding, but women were at last allowed mainstream enrollment starting in 1870, four years before McClure arrived. One of those women, slightly ahead of him in years and scholarship, would become his adored Hattie, who reflected back his dreams of himself and chagrin at how the world saw him. But on the day he arrived, although he knew a revolution was about to happen in his life, its specifics were still a mystery.

Eagerly, he walked for the first time across the leafy, imposing, stone-and-brick campus. He was overwhelmed. "There are few feelings any deeper," he wrote, "than those with which a country boy gazes for the first time upon the college that he feels is going to supply all the deficiencies he feels in himself, and fit him for struggle in the world."

McClure never graduated from high school in Valparaiso, so before he could be admitted as a Knox freshman alongside the sons and daughters of established midwestern society, he had to sign on for preparatory work. In the end, he would stay in Galesburg seven years. He relished and drew from each one, testing his powers, forging a new identity, and throwing himself into relationships that changed his ideal of the future. "Everything of any importance in my life and career had its origin in Knox College, Galesburg, Illinois," he later wrote.

The seven years that McClure spent at Knox were a defining moment for literature, technology, and politics, though his awareness of that wider world was vague. This short, dizzying period saw the publication of *Leaves of Grass, The Adventures of Tom Sawyer,* and works by Henry James and Louisa May Alcott. Overseas, *Middlemarch, Around the World in 80 Days, Through the Looking-Glass,* and *The Brothers Karamazov* appeared. The first prototype telephone, light bulb, and phonograph were invented. In 1875 a Civil Rights Act was passed, only to be overturned as a failed experiment soon after. In the West, bitter Indian Wars ended in massacre, surrender, and broken treaties. McClure, meanwhile, was fully absorbed in that faulty microcosm of society, the college campus. "In seven years," he wrote later,

"I scarcely read a newspaper." Instead, he produced one: it was at Knox that journalism found McClure.

When he first arrived, McClure was alight with the joy of being free from his old life, and he resolved never to be a chore boy for anybody ever again. But he was quickly running out of money, and his physical existence became severely compromised. To keep body and soul together for the first month, he made do with bread, soda crackers, and Concord grapes. He moved his meager belongings into a series of cell-like rooms, including an ancient Knox dormitory called the Bricks. In the wintertime, merciless as only Illinois can deliver, one of McClure's neighbors joked the place "might cause some of our eastern friends to wonder as to which part of Northern Siberia we were brought up in." Water froze at night. McClure often ate his Spartan meals while pacing back and forth across his room to keep his blood moving and wearing a fur cap and mittens. Crawling between ultra-chilled sheets was a nightly exercise in brute willpower.

To afford food and tuition without resorting to servitude, he regularly had to disappear for weeks on end to sell small goods door-to-door, either on foot or by donkey, the most efficient means he found to settle his restlessness and make a little money. For several seasons he was a traveling peddler of coffeepots and gimcracks; one summer, he sold microscopes, possibly to customers with curious middle-class children like Ida Tarbell. He roamed all over the surrounding states, selling needles, pins, handkerchiefs, and stockings, tramping through Indiana, Illinois, Wisconsin, Minnesota, Michigan, and Ohio. He later claimed that he'd built a reputation in a large swath of Illinois as "the honest little peddler," and that no compliment ever suited him better.

Yet he easily looked past the harsh constraints on his presence at Knox, seeing instead a grand panorama of real and imagined opportunity. College was a new world; seen through the eyes of a striver fresh from the prairie, it was a place to reinvent himself. McClure quickly earned a reputation for his seemingly limitless, manic energy. "I have seldom seen so much enthusiasm and life in such a small carcass," a classmate remarked. Another presciently urged him to slow down: "Be *idle* once in a while!

You will be all worn out and old before you are thirty-five." For the first time, Sam had access to as many books as he could read. In time, peers at Knox sought McClure out, and many even admired him. He befriended two literary-minded boys from well-off families, John Sanburn Phillips and Albert Bird Brady, who would become his closest colleagues at *McClure's*.

Tall, gentle, and bookish, John Phillips made himself McClure's lieutenant and closest friend. He was four years younger than McClure, the son of a Galesburg doctor. Periodically, McClure felt the urge to brush off Phillips as a sheltered, wide-eyed boy who "hasn't an overplus of energy," but the two grew to be close confidants. Phillips's admiration cast a warm, instantly respectable glow on McClure, whose seriousness was doubted by Galesburg's establishment. In the Phillips family's comfortable living room, McClure first read *The Century* and *Scribner's Magazine*, magazines he would later consider inspirations and rivals to his own.

Albert Brady, an Iowan newspaper editor's son, saw Sam McClure as a way into a more dynamic, authentic life—and an opportunity to slum it now and then. He tagged along on McClure's peddling trips, amused by the novelty of sleeping in hayricks and seeing his friend charm housewives into buying the cheap odds and ends pulled from his traveling case. At Knox, Brady was generous to his constantly destitute friend: "I once ate a whole roast chicken in his room," McClure recalled.

Compared to John Phillips and Albert Brady, McClure was a rube, and worse, an Irishman at a time when the Irish were considered low society. Yet, with his original mind, perpetual air of excitement, lack of self-consciousness, and knack for spinning a good story, he already exerted a cultlike appeal. "He is a genius—or would be, if he could stick to one thing," said a perceptive friend.

For the first time, he thought seriously of love. He desired it less as a fulfillment of a romantic yearning and more as a means of affirming his reinvention of himself, a way of proving he was now less a tramp and more an eligible man, equal to his friends. At Knox, McClure encountered women different from the feminine roles he already knew: mother, servant, or lady of the house. Warm, elegant Louise Williston, wife of Galesburg's Congregational minister, recognized and defused his initial romantic admiration, but she was drawn to him in return. "Sam had a powerful effect on me," she later admitted. "Proud as I am, reared in the most rigid aristocracy New England maintains. . . . He could not pass my door but I felt the influence, nor sit in my room but, *if I chose,* I could draw from his vigor." She enjoyed adding his unpredictable, spirited talk, broadcast in a brogue that so contrasted with the bland tones of Galesburg, to her lunch gatherings.

He fell more deeply and fatefully in love with a remarkable woman who fit even better into his new intellectual imagining of himself. Harriet Hurd—Hattie, to her friends—was a brilliant Knox student nearly three years older than McClure. Confident, emancipated, and classically beautiful, she shrugged off suitors and declared herself destined for a teaching career. Her father was one of Knox's most respected professors, natural science lecturer Albert Hurd. McClure and Hattie were introduced at a lunch given by Louise Williston. McClure attended because he admired Louise, but over the course of the meal, his affections instantly redirected themselves toward the slim, almond-eyed Hattie, whose glossy dark hair and full lips struck him as the epitome of feminine perfection—as was immediately clear to everyone else at table.

Hattie was flattered and modest; Professor Hurd took a violent dislike to the situation. "Don't cry for the moon, Sam," was Louise Williston's advice, for Hattie Hurd was far above him, not only in looks and style but in class and fortune, too. Hattie was being educated for a teaching career, not for marriage, and certainly not for marriage to a penniless Irishman with no solid prospects.

Regardless, on May 30, 1876, McClure, with rare and painful shyness, presented himself with a bunch of wildflowers at the Hurd home to visit with Hattie. The parents frowned, but Hattie took to the stranger with the crackling blue eyes who provoked such a strong aversion from her family. Raised among books and deliberately trained for a life of the mind, she yearned for romance and had started to rebel against the scholarly spinster future her father had laid out for her.

The couple faced further opposition from McClure's mother, for reasons that are harder to discern. Seen through the eyes of a woman who raised her family thanks to her own redoubtable strength and ingenuity, it may have been that Hattie was too refined, built for the classroom or parlor rather than hard work. Elizabeth would not have wanted Sam, bright proof of her own aspirations, to be drawn into a too-early marriage and the burden of feeding a family.

Elizabeth was determined enough to dispel Sam's infatuation that she made him an irresistible offer: a trip to Ireland to visit his childhood home. Using cash from the recent sale of Simpson's farm, mother and son took trains from Chicago to Philadelphia and took in the Centennial Exposition of 1876, where McClure remarked that "the telephone exhibit, which was certainly the most important thing there, attracted little or no attention, while people crowded around the butter statue." Then they sailed for Ireland.

The trip was also a pretext for Elizabeth to attempt to redirect her nineteen-year-old son's life with astonishing boldness. If her words couldn't persuade him to forget Hattie, geography would. After a perfunctory visit, she surprised Sam with a blunt announcement that she intended him to stay in Ireland and find work near their family; his time at Knox was over. McClure was incredulous until Elizabeth boarded a steamer headed back to America without him. She had never even booked him a return ticket. It was bittersweet to see his grandfather Gaston's house again, his parents' stone cottage, and the hedged-in fields mostly unchanged. But there was no question in his mind that he needed to get back to Galesburg.

Sam finally worked his passage back across the Atlantic as a galley boy, baking fifty pies a day. In later years, when he was accustomed to traveling first-class, he delighted in recounting the experience, and on ocean crossings he enjoyed pulling the trick of descending to the galley for a pie-baking contest with the ship's cook.

The adventure didn't have the effect Elizabeth had in mind. McClure's feelings for Hattie were only invigorated by the effort required to get back to her. In Galesburg, meanwhile, Professor Hurd was as stern and possessive as ever. His attempts to banish McClure and his preordained plan for her to live as a model of intellectual womanhood sparked defiance in his otherwise affectionate daughter. "[He] just assumes that I have no capacity for affection, no love of home—that I am hardly a woman at all!" she wrote her suitor. McClure sensed the moment was right: he asked Hattie if, provided he could support her, she would marry him in seven years' time. Meeting rarely for a hushed conversation or walk, writing fevered letters relayed by sympathetic go-betweens, they became secretly engaged.

If this was happiness, it was on-again, off-again, characterized by distraught letters and ferocious parental opposition. McClure found that "outside powers can intervene very potently, and that such settlements [as engagements] can be to the last degree unsettling." When despair descended on him, as it did every few months, he daydreamed of vanishing from campus and heading to the frontier, of reinventing himself yet again. He couldn't quite believe Hattie would ever openly defy the Professor and needed frequent reassurance, which he extracted through dramatic threats. "Tomorrow I start for the West," he wrote in one letter, though he was not to leave Galesburg for several more years. "I leave forever. Hattie if you love me as you say you do & as you wish to I won't go. We won't break the engagement." His uneasiness was founded on reality: Professor Hurd had no intention of letting McClure win. He arranged for Hattie to begin graduate school and orchestrated her sudden disappearance from campus, then forbade anyone from telling Sam where she was going. For more than two years, they had no contact at all. Being jilted didn't lessen his fixation, and he took up the habit of reading the local newspaper to see if Hattie's engagement to someone else had been announced.

The experience ignited a lasting defiance toward others' narrow expectations of who he was and who he might become. In an essay titled "Intolerance," dated March 1880, McClure angrily dismissed the obstacle that had broken up his first deep love. "Social intolerance is a less formidable phase of this evil," he wrote. "It scarcely deserves mention as it often falls upon those who regard with indifference + sorrow the self-conceived assurance, falseness + superficiality of the so-called social world."

Deprived of his own father and rejected by Hattie's, McClure created his own model of manhood—and he shaped it out of stories, some received through the books at Knox, others dreamed up by his fervid imagination and instincts. At Knox, McClure embodied the self-made man as few of his classmates did, lending him a kind of mythic status he recognized and embraced. While the myth was based in the reality of his hardscrabble origins, he amplified it as best he could, mastering the art of self-promotion early on. McClure held tight to a central story; a later biographer noted that throughout his career, McClure "buttonholed almost everybody to tell of his rise from rags to riches."

Occasionally, though, he had to contend with skeptics. The Hurds were outright disbelievers, as they saw Hattie dangerously in love with an irretrievably inappropriate upstart. Others simply discovered that McClure, charismatic as he was, could not always live up to the character he'd constructed. When a friend decided to accompany McClure on a jaunt from Knox to make some money, he was dismayed to find he "tried to get him to work and he could not; that McClure would lie awake half the night making plans for the next day and then do nothing . . . he does no work to amount to anything, and then he crowds all into a few days and nights." One of Hattie's friends spread the word that he borrowed money frequently and had publicly dropped suggestive hints about his and Hattie's engagement.

The cracks in McClure's legend of himself lined up with contemporaneous slurs about the Irish, stereotyped as impulsive fabulists who enjoyed the charity of others without qualms or pride. Even Hattie sometimes indicated her uncertainty about his moral character in her letters: was he a hero, or a winsome con man?

\* \* \*

FIRST WITH AMBIVALENCE, then almost alarming energy, McClure began to ruffle feathers well beyond the Hurd household. Phillips and Brady were both interested in journalism and they launched a coup on their campus newspaper, the Knox *Student,* nominating McClure as editor-in-chief. He commissioned long pieces and then cut them enthusiastically; he bluntly told established humor writers they weren't funny. He worked at the paper seriously but with little idea of journalism as a career, though Phillips assured him he was "the readiest and easiest writer on the staff." In manic phases, he joyfully pulled all-nighters—on at least one occasion "killing off," or exhausting past the point of consciousness, three assistants who were inspired to try to keep up. His peskiest obstacle was that his hand eventually got tired of scribbling notes and editorials, but his spirit was flying. "Everything *hums*," he wrote. It was a glorious, treacherous feeling.

Soon after, Hattie visited Galesburg from the ladies' college in Canada where Professor Hurd had sent her, and the two soon crossed paths on the college quad. As though no time had passed, once reunited, they resumed a secret correspondence.

The frank, impassioned letters between Sam McClure and Hattie Hurd show how Hattie already saw herself as the better angel of McClure's nature. As she kept her involvement with McClure a secret from all but a couple of close friends, she occasionally heard the casual gossip about him. She wrote him, "[I]t is agony to me to hear people . . . say what an impractical visionary you are. . . . I pray to God to make you *wise* and *careful,* and bless you with His love and grace. You are very different from other people. . . . You are so full of force and intensity of life and feeling that if God takes the helm of your life you will certainly sail on to a beautiful success; but a little willfulness or fanaticism would bring an overwhelming shipwreck." She knew he had a deep dread of failure.

These private exchanges contain the first written evidence of McClure's periodic depressive moods, attacks of darkness when he could do nothing. He was already aware that these came and passed like the tides. He wrote her, "To tell you the real *real* truth, I am deeply depressed this morning. . . . I'm blue about the debts, about the future, about uncertainties. . . . Next time I'll write you from some Mount of joy and life that will surprise you." In his phases of despair, McClure saw only the worst in himself, "nothing but weakness and unrest." He knew he was clever and adaptable, perhaps even brilliant, but was terrified that outside of Knox, in a world where men of fortune could not also be indecisive dilettantes, his "cursed mediocre versatility" would be his ruin.

Most often, the lovers' letters expressed powerful yearning, to the point of spiritual possession. To McClure, Hattie was an object of chivalrous worship: he often called her pure, ethereal, lovely, womanly, exquisite, delicate, tender, one who lit "the insatiable desire of my soul." To Hattie, he had awakened her. "Nobody dreams how I can love. I am just as quiet and moderate as anybody else, and one cannot know how my heart is full of fire and feeling. I dare not show it," she wrote. Sam McClure was different from other men; something about him made her unafraid to confess her longing for him. In October 1881, she wrote him, "There are very few men who have any idea of a woman's sensitive devotion, who will notice her care to please. But you are just different as if you were a woman yourself. . . . I feel as if I should leave the body and fly to your side." McClure replied the same day, "I can't tell you at all how much I love you. I have cast my soul + my life + my entire future on this thing. *I must have you I will have you* at any cost."

Graduation from Knox came as an exile. McClure had anticipated this, but it still stung. He had expected to be transformed by university, yet after seven years felt like "just the same boy." He considered himself and his achievements and was exasperated by them. Academically, he was third in his class of thirty. He had no definite plans for building a life, only large nebulous visions that floated roughly along the same terrain as the philosophy of Ralph Waldo Emerson, whose death had come barely a month before commencement. McClure and Hattie both identified with the poet's version of American romanticism, and one of McClure's handwritten notes from this period carefully transcribes a line of Emerson that had particular meaning for him: "Live not to apologize but to live!" Like another Emerson quote much repeated today—"Consistency is the hobgoblin of little minds"—this reflects McClure's determination to live boldly, though thus far the specifics eluded him.

At five feet six inches tall, with thin cheeks and an antsy, barely contained presence, he was not even distinguished looking. The only notice-able physical difference to the farm boy of seven years earlier was the thick blond mustache that had come in. Crucially, he had none of the pro-fessional contacts that most of his classmates counted on to make a start of a career. His ideas for the future shifted from one day to the next. He shuffled through a grab bag of ambitious but hazy prospects, speaking of taking up a timber claim in the Dakota Territory, or becoming a diplomat; he didn't consider there could be any money or greatness in newspapers. As a finale to his tenure editing the *Student,* he compiled and printed a *History of Western College Journalism* that made him a little cash from ad-vertisement sales. "Many of my friends advise me to become an editor," he wrote Hattie, and his professors "intimated that with my powers of mind I could easily take the first place in almost any field if I would only concen-trate," but he had no possibilities lined up as commencement drew close. Privately, he thought his future would look far smaller and less remark-able than his college years had felt. Most probably, he would wind up a teacher.

McClure was still on uncertain ground with Hattie, as the Hurds and doubtful friends continued to chip away at her faith in him. She was once again outside the immediate radius of his personal charm, teaching in An-dover, Massachusetts. Guileless and interested in his reaction, she relayed her doubts directly back to him, and in reply he sent impassioned defenses against her family's charges that he was egotistical and unrealistic. "I can't imagine why your people should think that I would remain poor," he wrote. "The reason why so many think me egotistic is this: I talk of my plans in a straightforward way & more, I *do* things with an assurance of success that they imagine to be conceit. . . . I don't care what anyone says or thinks. Be-cause I happen to be poor, people deem it allowable to criticize me & my ac-tions." McClure's self-reliance and capacity for hard work had already been tested beyond that of the Hurds or anyone in their circle, and he forcefully urged her to disregard their objections. "Don't fear. . . ." he wrote. "*I'll get what I want* & you may depend on it."

* * *

**ON JUNE 30, 1882,** McClure made his way to a small town near Utica, New York. His mission was to find Hattie, who was visiting an old classmate. He expected to steal some time with her, out of the Professor's thunderous gaze, and then return to his family to figure out the rest of his life. Just in case he ran out of cash on the way, he threw a few peddling supplies in his valise. He didn't yet know he had left the West for good.

His encounter with Hattie that day dramatically derailed his plan. She first refused to answer his knock, then dismissed him face-to-face with a coldness he had never seen before. McClure was bewildered and racked his brain to figure out what he might have done wrong. Just as disconcerting was the presence of Hattie's friend and chaperone, Miss Potter, sitting critically in the room with them as Hattie stonily told him, "I do not love you and I never can." She had already sent him a letter severing their engagement and expressing a wish never to meet again, but it hadn't reached Galesburg before he graduated and took off in pursuit of her.

As McClure began to understand that Hattie meant what she said, no resolution came to mind, and neither did any persuasive words that might mollify her. Uncharacteristically quiet, he obeyed her request to leave and agreed to return her letters. Walking along the railroad tracks back to Utica, he heard an engine behind him, and "for a moment . . . thought that it was not worth while to get out of the way."

His very idea of himself had become tangled up with marrying Hattie Hurd. McClure waited at the station lost in grief, and his suitcase was promptly stolen. The first train that opened its doors to him was going to Boston. McClure had never thought of going to Boston before, but he boarded it anyway. He had heard that a former Knox elocution teacher, Malvina Bennet, lived in nearby Somerville, and he made his way haltingly "in a terrible storm of thunder and lightning" to her house, where he was welcomed, dried, and fed. McClure awoke the next morning with the realization that, with his peddling supplies gone, he was once again in the position of muffling his feelings and going from door to door asking for work.

He had one other connection in Boston: bicycle magnate Colonel Albert Augustus Pope. After the Civil War, Pope had started as a sewing machine manufacturer but switched to bicycles in 1878, just as a craze for them began to take off. Penny-farthings, the precipitous high-wheelers, were the most popular model at first, but the positioning of the seat over the high front wheel meant riders were frequently thrown over the handlebars. Pope's classic Columbia Roadster had a seat that was nearly five feet off the ground. During the 1880s, the "safety" model, with a design much closer to today's bike, began to be seen on the roads, and Pope's ingeniously designed models followed suit. Ads for the Pope Manufacturing Company and the Columbia bicycle were plastered everywhere, from the national papers, magazines, and catalogs to college newspapers like the Knox *Student*— where Sam McClure had first seen them.

On his first Monday morning in Boston, McClure went to the address listed on Pope's billboards. McClure quickly charmed the Colonel, and Pope offered him a trial run as an instructor at a cycling rink where he expected to be a man short the next day.

The following morning—the Fourth of July, 1882—McClure walked into a cycling rink for the first time. The place bustled with families and courting couples learning to ride, echoing with the cries and clatter of collisions, falls, and enthusiasm. He had never been on a bicycle in his life. "I was," he thought, "in the predicament of the dog that had to climb a tree." Before the morning was over, McClure taught himself to ride the high-wheeler convincingly enough to teach others. He was paid one dollar for the day's work, and, sore but hopeful, returned the next day. After a week Pope promoted him to manage another rink. Shortly thereafter, he took McClure aside and asked if he would be interested in editing a magazine. Pope wanted to put a highbrow sheen on his business interest, and intended to launch a magazine that would "weave the bicycle into the best in literature and art."

Journalism, along with a new and idiosyncratic mission, had found McClure again. Still dazed from Hattie's reversal, he tried to fire up some enthusiasm for work. Together, Pope and McClure launched *The Wheelman* from an office at 608 Washington Street, Boston. With eighty pages of text, woodcut illustrations, and as many ads as it could carry, it sold for twenty cents an issue, on par with other serious journals. Soon McClure had persuaded Pope to let him hire his brother Jack and his Knox friend John Phillips. Jack was simply glad to have a job, but Phillips leapt in with both feet, meaning to make McClure somehow part of his life's vocation. "You always alight on your feet. . . . Great Heavens I wish I were with you," he had written McClure shortly after graduation.

The three men shared a garret apartment for four dollars a week, but McClure was seldom there. Trusting the others to run the office, he gave in to his restlessness and hopped trains to cycling events as far south as Washington, D.C., and as far north as Maine, reporting and commissioning pieces from far-flung wheelmen, traveling as much as Pope's expense account would allow. In the words of a later colleague, "He was not a swivel-chair editor."

It was both exhilarating and sobering to have a start in a career. "Up to this time I had always lived in the future and felt that I was simply getting ready for something," wrote McClure. "Now I began to live in the present." He recognized that the stakes were higher now, as both Valparaiso and Galesburg were far behind him. Now he lived in the epicenter of patrician New England, a port to Europe, and a hub for trains whose tracks snaked all the way to the other coast. McClure felt his bare-subsistence midwestern youth turning into a stable, citified adulthood. On the threshold of Pope's office, "I said good-by to my youth," McClure wrote. "When I have passed that place in later years, I have fairly seen him standing there—a thin boy, with a face somewhat worn from loneliness and wanting things he couldn't get, a little hurt at being left so unceremoniously. . . . I went into business and he went back into the woods."

*The Wheelman* was an unabashedly literary magazine. McClure was inspired by the then-venerable magazine *The Century,* perhaps the most respected serious monthly publication coming out of New York, with its wide-ranging contents, glittering list of contributors, and lush illustrations. *The Century,* in the eyes of a contemporaneous *New York Times* critic, "made

New-York, instead of London, the centre of the illustrated periodicals published in the English language." McClure copied every aspect of font and
page design wholesale from *The Century*. Most articles were written by the
three-man staff, with a smattering sent in from hobbyists who were often
paid in kind with one of the Colonel's velocipedes. McClure sought out
high-profile contributors and knocked on Oliver Wendell Holmes's door to
suggest a poem about cycling (Holmes obliged, though he amused himself
by answering McClure's subsequent inquiries, "I will neither be lured nor
Mc-lured into anything of the kind!"). They turned out lively, high-quality
work, and it began to attract attention.

Though the Colonel was an amiable employer, McClure did not feel
his vocation lay in the bicycle. He began toying with the idea of launching
his own magazine. In his imagining, it would be for readers as omnivorous
as himself, and would translate and reprint articles from leading French,
German, and Italian journals, covering interest areas from literature to
social science to technology. He gave it the long-winded title *The Eclectic
Magazine of Continental and Periodical Literature* and began ending meetings
and interviews for *The Wheelman* with a pitch for the new magazine. But
this editorial effort was quickly nipped in the bud, stymied by the discovery that G. P. Putnam's Sons were already publishing a monthly magazine
based on the same concept, *Topics of the Time*.

His free hours were still given over to thoughts of Hattie Hurd. Every
Sunday, he took a walk from his garret to Boston's Devonshire Street post
office to ask if any letters awaited him there. For weeks, there was nothing;
then, in mid-September, a letter arrived. Hattie wrote that she was returning
the books he had lent her, a terse message, but her civil tone immediately
revived his hope. He replied eagerly, and in turn she sent the letter he had
dreamed of since their separation. Hattie's love for him had never truly
died, she wrote, but she had felt compelled not to betray her father. Now,
having tried to live without his love, she wanted to explain herself.

That was all McClure needed to hear. He began visiting her at the
school where she taught. He befriended her colleagues, brought her books,
and wrote her frequently, even when an attack of typhus put him in the

hospital. Once again, she must have been struck by the contrast between her present life and the one McClure offered, and she warmed to him. "It seems so strange to be happy," McClure wrote in return. His revived campaign to win her hand took less than a year to succeed.

At last, almost coinciding with the seven-year engagement they had secretly plotted at Knox, Harriet Hurd resolved to marry Sam McClure. When she broke the news to her family in Galesburg, her father responded with a letter warning her that "[McClure's] personal appearance, his bearing, & his address are not pleasing to me; I think him conceited, impertinent, meddlesome, &c., &c., and, of course, would not choose him for your husband. I regard it as a misfortune that you ever made his acquaintance. . . . You are going into a family which we can never enter. We fear you are making a sad mistake." This time, however, Hattie was not swayed.

She was forced to choose between two men who were oddly alike in character and yet intractably opposed. Professor Hurd never admitted how much he had in common with his unwelcome son-in-law, though it must have been evident to those who knew both men. Like McClure, Hurd was magnetic and had an instinctive command over listeners, a man of probable genius and changeable temper. A dean at Knox wrote, "Professor Hurd's was a volcanic temperament, and ever boiling in its depths were feelings, emotions, that waited only a worthy occasion to pour forth in an enthusiasm that kindled even the most susceptible." Hattie felt she belonged to both of these fiery and volatile men, but this time her decision held firm. On McClure's side, he brushed aside Elizabeth's vocal reluctance. Once his marriage was imminent, Pope raised his pay from $12 to $15 per week. McClure thrilled aloud to his colleagues, "I shall be married next month and able to keep my wife nicely in Cambridge in a beautiful home."

They were married on September 4, 1883, in Galesburg. The romance and its hard-won culmination was on nearly everyone's tongue at Knox that summer, driving the Hurds to further teeth-gnashing and despair. Rather than enact their wedding in a church, with pews full of well-wishers, the couple exchanged vows in a simple ceremony in the house where Hattie had grown up. During the ceremony, McClure was jumpy and said "yes" too soon, and then had to say it again. Few people were invited. John Phillips was the best man, and McClure's family nervously crowded in, but his uncle Joe Gaston was turned away by the Hurds. Hattie, cringing at her parents' hostility, had decided not to invite any classmates and confessed to feeling "indignant and wicked" throughout the day.

Afterward, the couple moved into a frame house with a vine-covered verandah at 22 Wendell Street in Cambridge, just near Boston. Though Hattie didn't instinctively take to keeping house and got Sam into the habit of serving her breakfast, she enjoyed contributing short pieces and sketches to *The Wheelman* when he needed to fill space. When McClure came home in the evening, they sometimes went to the theater or to lectures. They were very happy.

It was a steady, modest life—one McClure soon itched to escape.

# 4

---

# *Among the Furies*

A s the summer waned in 1876, Ida Tarbell beheld for the first time the sober, graceful outlines of Allegheny College. It seemed a world apart from Titusville, though she was less than thirty miles from home. There was no sign of oil-dom here in Meadville, among the stone halls and green slopes of the school. Forty other newcomers streamed around her, carrying suitcases into dormitories and looking askance at her. Without meaning to, she already stood out; she was one of the only women among them.

The exhilaration of plunging into such a place compensated for the unexpected pitfalls. In Ida's case, her family paid her board and tuition, but there was no residence hall yet for women, so she moved between rented rooms in various houses in town. Like Sam McClure, she was filled with an earnest reverence for the institution and the enlightenment it promised, though she could not maintain this awe and seriousness constantly. The "rebelling, experimenting child," as Ida saw herself, absorbed diverse influences from her college years. Another Allegheny girl, her close friend Iris Barr, described Ida as a perfectionist who escaped being labeled a "grind" because she was "too interested in people."

The early weeks of her new life were punctuated by a trip to the future.

Ida's father swept in and took her on a quick visit to Philadelphia to see the Centennial Exposition. (Just a month or two earlier, Sam and Elizabeth Mc-Clure had walked the same halls, past the Statue of Liberty's torch-bearing arm and through the throngs surrounding the butter sculpture.) It was the farthest from home Ida had ever traveled, and there was so much to see that she was overwhelmed. On her return to Allegheny, science professor Jeremiah Tingley excitedly asked if she'd seen the telephone. In between the marvels of Heinz ketchup and the Corliss steam engine, she had missed it. Tingley then gathered the student body to give a lecture on the change that was about to happen in the world: "New York will talk to Boston," he proclaimed to a skeptical crowd. Perhaps few of the young people listening that day expected to see New York or Boston, or cared whether the two were on speaking terms.

Ida was captivated—not by the telephone, precisely, but the way Tingley talked about it. "This revelation of enthusiasm, its power to warm and illuminate was one of the finest and most lasting of my college experiences," she wrote. Through her adult life, Ida would be drawn to people who lent her their grandness of vision and who had genuine, unforced passion for new ideas in spite of conventional thinking. Tingley's enthusiasm was so different from the "sullen" demeanor of most of Ida's professors. The way he perceived this new invention, seeing the miraculous in this odd machine that bent unseen forces and cleanly did away with geographical barriers to communication, moved her. She resolved to make him her mentor.

Tingley had spent a summer with renowned natural scientist Louis Agassiz and often quoted him to his impressionable student: "Nature always brings us back to absolute truth whenever we wander" and "It is not the outside, it is the inside of things that matters." Taking Agassiz at his word, in Tingley's lab she set out to dissect and write the definitive study of a repulsive local river creature known as a "mud puppy," a rust-colored salamander with both gills and a lung. Her peers were bemused; what glory lay in the mud puppy? It was a "slimy, loathsome" project, Ida admitted, but she was fired up by Tingley's reverence for nature, and she worked over it with devotion. She was drawn to the unexamined intricacies of nature and the chance to be the first to fully understand one lowly creature.

When she lifted her gaze from the mud puppy, Ida confronted a world of boys. She scolded herself for reaching eighteen "without ever having dared to look fully in the face of any boy my age," which was at odds with her otherwise omnivorous curiosity about nature and society. Once she looked, she quickly realized that she was regularly examined in return, and with great interest, especially as women were a small minority of the student body. Ida had never been seen as beautiful, but she had an appealingly straight and serene bearing, perceptive gray eyes, strong features, an intelligent low voice, and plentiful dark hair drawn back from a broad, clear forehead. "You see such countenances among the unaffected Celtic women of Ireland and Brittany," a later admirer said of her. If she had any vanity, it was in keeping her modest wardrobe up-to-date with new styles, replacing sleeves, underskirts, and buttons rather than investing wholesale in new dresses. She was not shy, and she approached the rituals of courtship and romance with more irony than blushing excitement. Determined to make up for lost time, she accumulated pins from all four of Allegheny's fraternities—tantamount to a pre-engagement commitment—though she could not bring herself to take this seriously. When she wore all four of her pins to chapel it caused a minor scandal. By the end of her senior year, in 1880, she begrudgingly thought that "possibly some day" she might marry, and a yearbook caption under a photo of a young man named Warren Shilling notes that he was engaged to Ida Tarbell. But the relationship, if there was one, ended before any further announcements were made.

Besides her handful of suitors, the men of Allegheny struck Ida as a discouraging and dismissive lot, a foretaste of what her professional life would bring. Her male classmates were "hostile or indifferent," and Ida herself was "dimly conscious that I was an invader, that there was abroad a spirit of masculinity challenging my right to be there, and there were taboos not to be disregarded." More than fifty years later, when she read Virginia Woolf's *A Room of One's Own,* Ida recognized her experience immediately in Woolf's description of women excluded from certain spaces at university. Even an institution like Allegheny, whose Methodist roots encompassed fervent support of equal rights for women and rallying behind the campaigns of Elizabeth Cady Stanton and Susan B. Anthony, belonged primarily to men. Ida wrote later that the sense of alienation reinforced her vow to keep a distance around herself. "I was learning, learning fast, but the learning carried with it pains. I still had a stiff-necked determination to be free. To avoid entangling alliances of all kinds had become an obsession with me." She found instead a sense of belonging as part of a coterie that gathered at the home of Professor Tingley and his wife. Near fifty and childless, they hosted informal salons that gave Ida an early inkling of how good society can feed the life of the mind. "It was my first look into the intimate social life possible to people interested above all in ideas, beauty, music, and glad to work hard and live simply to devote themselves to their cultivation," she wrote.

As she studied lab specimens and men, Ida also began to test her voice. She edited a college publication and was an active member of Ossoli, the ladies' literary society named for author and women's rights advocate Margaret Fuller Ossoli. This predecessor's life and work loomed large in Ida's imagination. In the early nineteenth century, Fuller had progressed from teacher, to journalist, to major Transcendentalist thinker, and finally moved to Italy, where she married and had a child before all three died tragically in a shipwreck. Her *Woman in the Nineteenth Century* (1843), widely recognized as America's first feminist manifesto, inspired Ida's peak moment of fame on campus, a much-discussed speech in which she argued that every woman "must be educated not for man, but for her Creator."

The question of what to do after graduation troubled her. If she ever seriously contemplated moving home to her parents after graduation, their straitened circumstances jolted her into seeking other options. Forced into selling his business to Standard Oil, Franklin Tarbell had taken a train headed to the Dakota Territories, hoping to find some business there. The train was full of other fortune hunters, and Franklin soon came back to Titusville, tired and discouraged. He grieved that Rockefeller was turning independent Oil Region men into wage workers, in his mind the ultimate failure for an American. Ida drew on this philosophy when she later wrote of oilmen like her father, "They believed in independent effort—every man for himself and fair play for all. They wanted competition, loved open fight."

Ida puzzled that her friends and teachers "were constantly urging me to follow a 'call' which somehow I myself couldn't hear." Family, professors, trusted mentors—all expected that if she was seriously determined neither to marry nor to move back home, she should follow one of the two professional paths open to women: teaching children or serving God as a missionary. She hadn't yet found a way to channel her passion for scientific exploration into a practical future. Missionary work was impossible: she didn't have the necessary dogmatic belief, and during her Allegheny years, she had even begun calling herself a "pantheistic evolutionist." She was to be a teacher, then.

When Ida received an offer to teach in rural Ohio, she accepted it with alacrity. "If I had been going on my honeymoon, I should scarcely have been more expectant or more curious," she wrote. It would allow her to support herself, at least, and see a new part of the country. She abandoned both the mud puppy and fraternity society and boarded a train to an unknown place, "to begin," as she later wrote, "what women were then talking of in more or less awed tones as a Career."

* * *

POLAND, OHIO, NOW A SUBURB OF YOUNGSTOWN, was in 1880 a small mining town clustered around the slow-flowing Yellow Creek, lodged between coal pits and farms. Ida arrived for her first day of work and encountered a strange, unwelcoming atmosphere among students and neighbors alike; she soon discovered that she had been hurriedly recruited to replace a beloved teacher who had resigned out of the blue.

Ida's high hopes for a stimulating professional life were quashed. Her role as preceptress of Poland Seminary was, despite the imposing title, constant and badly paid work. She served under a scowling, lackadaisical president, whose sole duty as far as Ida could tell was leading chapel service "with more or less grandiloquent remarks." With the help of an assistant, she taught Greek, Latin, French, German, geology, botany, geometry, and trigonometry, as well as two survey courses in grammar and arithmetic. It was a "killing" workload that left her no time for her microscope, which she had brought with her, but now lay "dusty on the table," she wrote, a relic from a past life that she contemplated in the seconds before dropping off to sleep. Any refreshing perspectives that struck her as she moved alone to a new place faded quickly, as each day she soldiered on alongside fellow teachers who saw her as a bumbling neophyte. She nearly left after two weeks, burned out by the grind of teaching teenagers.

What eventually made her exile in Poland bearable was a new friendship, with the enterprising Clara "Dot" Walker, daughter of the town banker. Both women had a fully fledged investigatory zeal. Together, both clad in the crisp shirtwaist, tailored coat and skirt, and sensible shoes of independent-minded women of the 1880s, Ida and Dot took drives to the slums on the edge of Poland, just to see. One evening, coming home from a play, their way was blocked by a procession of corpse-laden carts—a furnace had exploded and killed several men. They witnessed protests spearheaded by women whose husbands had lost their jobs and livelihoods during mill closings.

As they had been during the Oil War, the inhuman demands of the new industrial economy seared themselves into Ida's consciousness. For now, all she could do was observe: her career, though she despaired to think it, was restricted to the schoolroom. Her rambles with Dot piqued an interest in the exploration and categorization of social forces that had affected her own upbringing. She began to realize her own privilege compared to women who had no bargaining power except the violence they could deploy when they joined together. Ida wrote, "I learned the meaning of Maenads, Furies, as we came upon a maddened, threatening crowd rushing towards the offices of the mills which had been shut down without warning. It was led by big robust shrieking women, their hair flying, their clothes disheveled. It was a look into a world of which I knew nothing."

After two years, Ida left Poland. Considering her teaching career a bust, she found a job back in Meadville organizing the office of *The Chautauquan,* a monthly pamphlet that grew from the Chautauqua Assembly Institute's popular adult education programs. Having failed at her proper feminine vocation, this was, at least, a secure place from which she could regroup and form a larger strategy for the future. "To me it was only a temporary thing," she wrote. "I had no inclination toward writing or editing work. This was a stop-gap—nothing more."

At *The Chautauquan,* Ida began to write and edit for the public. She was able to flex her curiosity for a magazine that openly advocated for the moral and intellectual betterment of its readers. It was no match for *The Dial* in Margaret Fuller's day, a nexus of important Transcendentalist writing and thought, but in this context, finally, Ida felt comfortable, useful, and liked. In 1886, the editor-in-chief, Dr. Theodore Flood, named her assistant editor. Toward the end of her career, she gave it substantial credit as the place "where I learned my trade."

The agenda of the Chautauqua Institute—progressive, bent on self-improvement, and offering a multitude of correspondence courses for those with no time or access to school—gave Ida a broad canvas for ideas of stories she might write herself. Originally a religious training ground for Methodist Sunday school instructors, the institute had grown to include a robust general education program designed to bring a "college outlook" to middle- and working-class people nationwide. Ida learned to adapt to the voice of the magazine, which served a thriving, earnest, sometimes stiflingly wholesome community. William James wrote of the Chautauqua world, "Sobriety and industry, intelligence and goodness, orderliness and ideality, prosperity and cheerfulness, pervade the air. . . . And yet what was my own astonishment, on emerging into the dark and wicked world again, to catch myself quite unexpectedly and involuntarily saying: 'Ouf, what a relief!'" James concluded that Chautauqua represented a kind of utopia, one that was enlightening for many, but intolerable for the truly questing mind; as he wrote, "This order is too tame, this culture is too second-rate, this goodness too uninspiring.'"

Within this tamely edifying world for the next five years, Ida made a content and controlled life for herself. The strictures that kept it predictable also allowed her to push boundaries and toy with ideas for the future. After a period boarding with Dr. Flood and his wife, she set up "co-operative living," a very modern arrangement by the standards of the time, with three colleagues. The women shared living expenses, cooking duties, and evening conversation. And though Ida dismissed the relationship as being "as informal . . . as non-committal," she allowed herself to be sedately courted by Judge John Henderson, fifteen years her elder and one of the most eligible bachelors in Meadville.

Gradually, she developed a philosophy for editorial work—specifically, how to successfully work on a magazine while female—that underpinned her later work, too. Her career was less adventurous and more servile than she wanted, but she was learning to make herself indispensable to the man in charge. By earning his trust, she might be given more authority. "A woman is a natural executive," she reflected. "Intuitively she picks up, sets to rights, establishes order. I began at once to exercise my inheritance." She quickly became invaluable to Dr. Flood, though she had to mute her stronger opinions to peaceably keep the job. She advised other women interested in journalism, "The editor-in-chief knows what he wants and does not want, and all work must be done in accordance with his views; often in direct opposition to personal tastes." Of the delicate matter of women trying to forge a path in journalism alongside the men who controlled it, she later wrote, "She must not put forward her femininity to such an extent as to demand that the habits of an office be changed on her account; nor can she presume on her womanhood."

She began to admit to those she trusted that she wanted to be a writer. With Dr. Flood's cautious encouragement, she started writing for *The Chautauquan*. Her favorite project was a series on exceptional women, a relatively daring topic for the magazine. One of her subjects in particular caught her deeper interest—a feminist who was guillotined in the French Revolution, known as the "Queen of the Gironde," Madame Manon Phlipon de Roland.

Like so many Americans before and after her, Ida dreamed of Paris. She studied French with émigrés until she could read and translate from it fluently. As the novelty of *The Chautauquan* and Dr. Flood faded, she wondered how difficult it would be to move to Paris. She saw herself at the Sorbonne, writing a book on Madame Roland. That distant vision silently followed her on her pleasant, underwhelming days. "I had never wanted things," Ida wrote, ". . . but I wanted something cheerful and warm and enduring. There I could work over that which interested me, day in and day out, with no alarm for my keep." Her family's sudden loss of fortune in the Oil War still weighed on her memory and tempered her dreams. *The Chautauquan* was not a place where Ida could fulfill her yearning for "fresh attempts, fresh adventuring," but the steady work ensured she could support herself. It was daunting to break away from a safe, wage-earning job with no idea how to make ends meet in a city she'd never been.

She was not alone in her economic anxiety. The whole country's fortunes were in flux: Ida wrote that the tumultuous 1880s in America "dripped with blood," between the enduring post–Civil War economic devastation of the South, the overexpansion of railroads, and the fearmongering as communists and anarchists fanned the most heated labor disputes and called for direct and revolutionary action. Ida felt herself swept up in the country's oscillation between booms and busts. At one point, she stood with crowds of panicked townspeople to withdraw her entire deposit from a Meadville bank that was rumored to be going under. Despite her determination to be sensible above all else, she was unable to stay calm when faced with the reality of losing her meager fortune—and it shamed her.

These strands of experience—monotonous days at *The Chautauquan* contrasting with the existential threat of another recession—knotted together within her and emerged as a kind of epiphany about the future. One Sunday she was taken aback by the exhortations of an elderly Scottish minister who "leaned over his pulpit and, shaking his fist at us, shouted, 'You're dyin' of respectability.' Was that what was happening to me?" She reflected that she had avoided the trap of marriage, only to trap herself in another limited role. Ida began to rebel—both inwardly and in conversation with friends—against the limits of her *Chautauquan* life and also the bounds of her future possibilities, as history indicated what she could expect them to be. Women, Ida thought, seemed to be permitted three roles in society: "doormat, toy, and tool." None appealed to her.

Despite this deep conviction, Ida recused herself from supporting the larger cause of women's suffrage. Raised by her parents to be a staunch supporter, Ida hesitated to wholeheartedly agree, and her inability to claim a strong, instinctive position frustrated her as much as anyone. "Why must I persist in the slow, tiresome practice of knowing more about things before I had an opinion?" she wrote. "What chance for intuition, vision, emotion, action?" This line of questioning brought her to another persuasive reason to devote herself to writing about Madame Roland and the French Revolution. If she could trace the rise and success of one political woman, perhaps she would gain clarity on what was right for all women.

Those quiet years did allow Ida Tarbell to begin to live her ideals. Where there was security and a little boredom, there was also room to experiment. "I at last knew what I wanted to do," she wrote. "It was no longer to seek truth with a microscope. My early absorption in rocks and plants had veered to as intense an interest in human beings. I was feeling the same passion to understand men and women, the same eagerness to collect and classify information about them." Research and writing had become her main bridge to understanding, and she began to hope they would bring her a livelihood, too. She began keeping a notebook, writing down scenes she had witnessed or thought up, assembling the elements of a novel. As chapters of a novel, it did not pass muster with its most critical reader: "Poor stuff," Ida judged her own effort at fiction, and abandoned it. Instead she resolved to report on life and history as they really were, to get as close to the truth as possible as a journalist.

Meadville continued in its comfortable rhythm, a new crop of Allegheny freshmen every fall, a sudden calm when the campus emptied every summer. Ida turned thirty-three there, where nothing extraordinary was asked of her and days slipped past. Her talk of Paris and writing a book grew louder, raising eyebrows around town. She had disavowed the traditional feminine calls to service; now she rejected other conventions. "There were friends who said none too politely: 'Remember you are past thirty. Women don't make new places for themselves after thirty.'" It was as though they expected physical laws of inertia to constrain her. Their doubts strengthened her resolve to unmoor herself from her cozy harbor.

Her ambition to go abroad struck others as a judgment on their own, self-circumscribed lives. Dr. Flood anxiously suggested that she was simply not a writer and would not be able to support herself. When he realized Ida was stuck on the idea, he curtly predicted, "You'll starve." Their previously genial collaboration went sour. Her parents, though "puzzled and fearful," supported her plan, and two other single friends expressed interest in joining for a year. She determined to leave and to discover something new in herself, within the unknown rhythms of another city. She wrote, "It was not to be 'See Paris and die,' as more than one friend had jeered. I knew with certainty it was to be 'See Paris and live.'"

In the early spring of 1891, her idea turned into an urgently needed escape when something highly disturbing occurred in *The Chautauquan*'s offices. The precise details aren't clear from the existing historical record, but the trouble left Ida demoralized and convinced Dr. Flood was a humbug. From the remaining personal letters, it seems that Dr. Flood decided to install one or both of his sons at *The Chautauquan,* giving them seniority over the team of women who had long made the magazine function and thrive. His son Harry possibly even made some drunken overtures that proved too insulting to bear for the fiercely self-respecting Ida, who denounced "Harry's escapades" to her family and resigned alongside her close colleague Mary Henry. Harry was quickly shunted to another local paper where Dr. Flood had influence, but he had trouble holding down a job: he drifted around the Midwest, sought treatment for alcoholism, and died in Cuba at thirty-five.

Ida, meanwhile, discouraged her family from letting the Floods "worry you into any kind of retaliation." She referred vaguely to the "Meadville matter" as a traumatic rupture, but one that hadn't tarnished her own reputation a whit. In her letters, she made Dr. Flood into a recurrent character nicknamed the "Gyascutus," an imaginary, bigfoot-like creature that bumbled through rural folklore and traditional tall tales. For his part, in his letter accepting her resignation, Dr. Flood offered Ida the barest respect: "I esteem you as a high minded, honorable Christian woman, whose strength and force of character I have learned to admire."

This final commendation may have been issued through gritted teeth, but it was fair. As she moved from the small town that fostered her voice to a city more strange and old than she could fathom, Ida would need every ounce she could muster of that force of character.

# 5

## New York

In December 1883, Sam and Hattie McClure boarded a steamship in Boston Harbor, making their way to New York on the Fall River Line. They arrived in the metropolis after dark, in a fine rain. Hattie wrote of catching sight of the city for the first time, "Just before dawn, I sprang up and saw a beautiful sight. We were approaching the Brooklyn Bridge, which is lighted with seventy electric lights, and the river was full of great steamers all lighted in the windows."

The McClures were spellbound by New York and its cacophony of different tongues, faiths, and flavors. The streets thumped with horses' hooves pulling every shape and size of vehicle, while sidewalks fairly seethed with people, with occasional influxes of crowds from the docks, from which a briny breeze also filtered in. The McClures had great hopes for the freedom that the city would bring: New York was, after all, the engine of the future, with brand-new electrical illumination blazing from streetlights, hotels, and theater billboards, sharpening silhouettes and casting long shadows past the skyscrapers-in-progress. And it was the center of the media universe.

For McClure, this new upheaval launched his ascent into literary society. For Hattie, it led to the logical consequence of her rebellion against the Professor: the exchange of an intellectual career for an affectionate domestic life, with its varying degrees of honesty and harmony. As she wrote to a friend two months after their inauspicious wedding, "I think you told me the truth when you said my liberty was gone, the night I was married, but captivity is sweet to me."

Their accelerated departure from Boston came after a blunder by Colonel Pope. He had merged *The Wheelman* with another adventuring magazine, *Outing,* and had assigned McClure to lead the new and expanded magazine alongside a co-editor. McClure, already friendly with New York magazine editors who sent him freelance assignments, reacted quickly. He was allergic to the idea of losing his autonomy, began to seek an escape, and set his sights on the busiest hive of American literary magazines. Phillips also took the restructuring as a chance to leave, but he drifted amicably away from both Pope and McClure and enrolled at Harvard.

McClure had one particular destination in mind—or rather, a person. Roswell Smith, publisher of *The Century,* embodied McClure's ideal of a literary tastemaker and inspired the younger man to emulate him as closely as he could. *The Century,* McClure considered, was "the uttermost limit of my ambition"—it set the bar for the perfect magazine, "devoted to matters of timely, though not temporary, interest." In the past year, McClure had absorbed a staggering range of stories from the magazine, delighting in tales about pirates in Louisiana, a chronicle of a visit to Venice by Henry James, poetry by Robert Browning and Emma Lazarus, descriptions of the photographic process, and florid illustrations of war heroes, cityscapes, and New York tenements. McClure resolved to work his way into it somehow. He and Hattie had visited Smith just weeks before their steamboat journey and secured a bittersweet offer. Smith generously arranged a job for him, but it was at a printing house downtown; unexpectedly, he hired Hattie to help him with his latest project, the *Century Dictionary*. It was far from the offer he had hoped for, but McClure's mind had been set in motion, he was determined to leave Boston, and he accepted.

Their new life refused to settle comfortably into place. They lived first in a Manhattan boardinghouse, wanting to be in the thick of the towering city around them. McClure's work itself quickly dulled the sparkle of their fresh start. As a compositor in *The Century*'s print shop, he was on his feet from seven in the morning until six at night, measuring and proofreading. For him, it was unbearably dull, claustrophobic work. "Everything about the work was distasteful to me," he wrote. In his half-hour lunch break, he would walk to City Hall Park "and look up in desperation at the sky and buildings, like a man in prison trying to find a way of escape."

Four months later, their situation shifted again. Hattie was pregnant, and she felt bound by propriety to leave her work on the dictionary project as soon as her condition became apparent. McClure, meanwhile, never directly expressed how he felt to his superiors at the printing house, but his unhappiness must have been palpable. His kind boss, Theodore De Vinne, seeking a diplomatic way to let him go, suggested he try again for a job at *The Century*. As it happened, the company secretary was on leave, so McClure was given some of his work for six months.

Just when his family's needs were starting to press on him, McClure's restlessness made office life impossible. He freely admitted the friction at work was his own fault, or as he put it, "I was not satisfactory because I forgot important things." He would absentmindedly put proof pages into his pocket and forget about them for days, vexing everyone and jamming up schedules. A friend noted that, hemmed in by an endless routine of clerk-level tasks, McClure "was a round peg in a square hole or a square peg in a round hole, whichever is the most uncomfortable."

The McClures moved to East Orange, New Jersey, ahead of the birth of their daughter Eleanor in July 1884. New fatherhood brought McClure two weeks away from the office and a burst of entrepreneurial spirit. With the Hudson River between him and the drudgery of the office, he felt his old energy return. One Sunday evening he sat down at his desk and wrote up a proposal for a new business, an idea that seemingly coalesced in his mind fully formed. It was a literary syndicate, with McClure as chief discoverer and purveyor of new fiction, editorials, and cartoons that would be published by newspapers in every state in America. The plan appeared to him as "huge transparent globes like soap bubbles," he wrote. "I saw it, in all its ramifications," he recalled, "as completely as I ever did."

It was not exactly an idea pulled out of the void. The French had established a similar system of feuilletons, or printed galleys of stories sold to multiple newspapers to be published simultaneously. An article or short story could be printed in multiple cities on the same day, with each newspaper owning exclusive rights within a defined circulation area. Charles Anderson Dana, editor of the New York *Sun,* had started the first American syndicate and added to the fortunes of his paper by acquiring stories by Henry James, Bret Harte, William Dean Howells, and other renowned authors of the day, to be sold to newspapers across the country. McClure became infected with the idea of doing this himself. It solved the problem of how to ascend to the position of literary tastemaker, as Roswell Smith had, without toiling along the traditional apprenticeship path of a larger magazine office, which he found unbearable. He was half-convinced he was originating a new business model, and half-conscious that he was imitating Dana. "To be sure, the thing was in the air at that time: somebody had to invent it," he wrote.

McClure was, it was now clear to all his employers so far, temperamentally incapable of being subordinate to anybody. Roswell Smith advised him directly that he didn't seem to be "fitted to work to advantage in the offices of a big concern," and should probably "go out and try to found a little business" of his own. Everyone liked McClure, but it had been exasperating trying to manage him; there was no place for his grand disruptive visions in the machinery of a magazine. His salary would be paid for two months, and if nothing had turned up by then, Smith agreed to find some sort of position to last him through the winter.

McClure had the advantage of not hearing criticism when he really believed in an idea. His family and friends were skeptical of the syndicate plan. "Everyone with whom I discussed the idea," he recalled, "manifested a great indifference." Hattie must have been anxious that the gamble would fail, and that they would be thrown on the Hurds' baleful charity. John Phillips wrote and advised against the idea. "I surmise that many would object to the manner of publication—which will be quite indiscriminate," he wrote McClure, to no effect.

There was reason for concern. Syndicating fiction, though a fledgling business, already had a dubious reputation; the prevailing assumption was that even the finest literature, when marketed via a syndicate, would be repackaged into sensational literature by newspaper editors. Publishing was a bespoke business, and syndication turned it into ready-to-wear. One of the most valuable writers in Dana's own stable (and one whose byline seemed ubiquitous in the literary magazines of the early 1880s) was Henry James, whose story "Georgina's Reasons" was sold through the syndicate; a western newspaper published it under a bold subtitle that read, "A Woman Who Commits Bigamy and Enforces Silence on Her Husband! Two Other Lives Made Miserable by Her Heartless Action!" The novelist Ouida described the way syndicates treated authors "precisely as the Chicago killing and salting establishments treat the pig; the author, like the pig, is purchased, shot through a tube, and delivered in the shape of a wet sheet (as the pig is in the shape of a ham), north, south, east, and west, wherever there is a demand for him."

Yet as one who came of age reading agricultural catalogs for want of good books, McClure considered that the publication of fiction in newspapers had not been indiscriminate *enough*. How he would have devoured tales of adventure if they had ever reached Simpson's blasted farm! He was an admitted monomaniac when it came to his venture, "as I had been when I was determined to get an education, as I had been when I was determined to get my wife." Pursuing his own idea at last, he was possessed by a feeling of unconquerable joy. "My blood [is] like champagne," he wrote, in a vivid evocation of a manic phase. He believed in his scheme to such an extent that he secured a respectable Manhattan address for it, moved his family and career to 114 East Fifty-Third Street, behind the Steinway piano factory, and opened a bank account, the first he'd ever held. Then he ordered a bulk supply of purple ink—the color that *The Century* used for its business correspondence—and began to scribble.

\* \* \*

**THE McCLURE NEWSPAPER SYNDICATE** sent out its first pitch on October 4, 1884. McClure and Hattie copied out nearly a thousand letters, bound for every city and town where they knew there was a newspaper, announcing their new business and the rationale behind it. "Dear Sir," they addressed editors, "This method of publication has been employed very successfully in England and France for a very long time; leading novelists publishing their works in a London or Parisian newspaper, and at the same time in several provincial journals"—lending their letter a worldly air—"there is no reason why American newspapers should not reap great advantages from a similar arrangement."

Its first deal fell short. McClure bought a story by H. H. Boyesen, a then-popular Norwegian American scholar and writer, for $250, and was $50 in the red after exhausting his sales opportunities. Generally, the syndicate's model was to acquire a story for about $150, and then sell it at five dollars to at least a hundred newspapers. Once the syndicate's quality had proved itself, McClure hoped newspapers would subscribe at a steady five to ten dollars per week.

Money didn't flow the way he'd projected it would. Despite McClure's years of door-to-door peddling, he was an untested salesman in the literary marketplace. Writers were eager to sell him work, but newspaper editors were far less consistent in wanting to buy it. McClure glossed over his early, messy handling of business finances, writing, "[T]he men who wrote for me were usually willing to wait for their money, as they realized that my syndicate was a new source of revenue which might eventually become very profitable to them. And it did." In practice, no one was at peace with McClure falling short month after month. An early supporter, Sarah Orne Jewett, finally snapped after months of delay, "if I do any more work for you I must have my regular price and be paid at once."

Each morning's mail and dearth of profitable responses sent McClure on long, anxious walks around Manhattan. He got into the habit of going out with the baby carriage to meet the letter carrier. When he was in the office, he had a tic of "trotting his foot and pulling his front lock . . . fiercely" when worry descended on him, aggravating the unruliness of his light hair and his general manner of anxious impatience. He took a temporary job at the

Columbia College library filing newspaper clippings for three and a half dollars a week, trying to stem his descent into bankruptcy.

Near despair, he abruptly left the filing job and persuaded Hattie that if he went on the road and sold his stories in person, the numbers would improve. Since their savings had already been eaten up, he borrowed money from a former *Century* colleague, borrowed more from his family, and traveled to Philadelphia, Baltimore, Washington, Boston, and finally Albany, selling his wares directly to newspaper editors. When he returned to New York, several inquiry letters awaited him: more editors had heard of his new service and wanted to subscribe. At last, the new machine was on the verge of taking flight.

McClure's fledgling syndicate only avoided failure through luck and force of personality. Through its first quarter, the syndicate sank deeper into debt every week. McClure was twenty-seven, responsible for a wife and child, and close to friendless in New York. Grocery stores started to refuse them credit. Relatives were either reluctant or unable to help. "It was a business of a most awful sort," he wrote. "You had to please different editors in different parts of the country with the same thing." By the end of 1884, about thirty newspapers had signed on, which McClure rounded up to fifty in his pitches. He made a smart purchase of a series of articles on Mormonism— combining a serious subject with the tantalizing topic of polygamy—and gained back a little ground. Because his determination and charisma were second only to his profound belief in himself, the business limped onward.

The McClures' domestic life thrived under pressure. Hattie cared for their baby daughter, wrote her husband's letters, prepared copy, translated stories from French and German, and rearranged household finances so the syndicate could afford stamps. The couple worked together Monday through Saturday, from eight in the morning to ten at night. Early in their marriage, the McClures had realized that neither of them could cook; Hattie's father had educated her to be a teacher, not a housewife. So McClure took a few lessons in the kitchens of Astor House, then New York's preeminent luxury hotel. This gave him enough know-how to write a series of cookery articles that he sold via the syndicate, claiming they were by an "expert" cook named Patience Lathrop. Responses from newspapers began to be warmer. Early on, McClure had opened poison-pen notes from the likes of the *St. Paul Pioneer Press,* where an editor clearly enjoyed telling him, "Some of the daily stories you send out are fossil chestnuts from the antediluvian strata of literature." Others, like the *Newark Evening News,* began to treat McClure more as a peer: "Please send me a good short story by some unknown writer. I want one that people who are not 'literary' will appreciate."

Newspaper publishing was on the brink of a great expansion. In 1884 there were fewer than twelve hundred dailies in the United States, but in the next decade that number grew by almost a hundred per year. One British visitor in the 1880s noted the liveliness of the American press; there was roughly one newspaper for every 10,000 Americans, compared with one for every 120,000 in Great Britain. Newsprint was cheap: the technique of making it from wood pulp, rather than rags, had begun in the 1840s and slowly spread across the United States and Europe.

For the McClure Syndicate, this meant more buyers: from the *Boston Globe,* to the *Hartford Times,* to the *New York Commercial Appeal,* to the *Hoosac Valley News,* and the San Francisco *Argonaut.* After a year, the better-known authors H. Rider Haggard and Joel Chandler Harris, known for the Uncle Remus tales, were writing for McClure. Between March and June 1885, the McClures began to shakily trust that they could cover their monthly expenses. McClure wrote to his in-laws, who still refused to allow him in their home for more than twenty-four hours at a stretch, "[E]veryone thinks that I have established a business that will give me an independent income and make me rich besides." Riches were elusive, but breaking even was already a kind of victory.

John Phillips moved to New York and joined the syndicate the following year. The business was growing, Hattie was preoccupied by motherhood, and McClure was befuddled by the rote copying, correspondence, and bookkeeping required of him. Phillips slipped back into the role he had had alongside McClure since their term editing the Knox *Student.* He had a gift

for imposing order while adapting swiftly to many of McClure's extravagant, past-deadline ideas.

For the next twenty years, he would be McClure's professional foil—his
"seismograph, measuring the tremors and apparently controlling them," in
the words of one observer. Another wrote, "His job as partner to McClure
was to rope him, sit on his head, take the idea away, consign the fantastic
seedling to the compost heap, and cultivate the practical." Journalist William Allen White recalled, "We used to say that Sam had three hundred
ideas a minute, but JSP was the only man around who knew which one was
not crazy."

Phillips's formidable talents belied the gentle impression he gave to
friends and rivals alike. A tall, dome-headed, mustachioed figure who was
modest to the point of enigma, he developed a reputation among fellow editors as "the kindest man alive." There was "nothing flamboyant about him,"
wrote Ray Stannard Baker, who worked for him for nearly a decade. Ida
Tarbell's memoir notes, "He was no easy editor. He never wheedled, never
flattered, but rigidly tried to get out of you what he conceived to be your
best." As beheld by his closest friends and colleagues, Phillips was a kind
of Atticus Finch of editors, a barometer of correct judgment and exquisitely
controlled action. Though one humorous letter of introduction warned the
recipient, "Be not deceived by his ministerial air. He has a blackjack in his
pocket. . . . If you want to avert a deep indentation in your forehead, hand
him the stuff he wants without an argument, otherwise, the hot breath of
the wolf is on your cheek and the fangs of the magazine hyena are in your
throat." Phillips left all the hobnobbing and travel to McClure. He kept his
personal life strictly separate from his work, and most nights he went home
to his wife and young family rather than frequenting Manhattan's literary
clubs. He had known tragedy—his first wife, a girl from Galesburg, had
hanged herself—and absorbed himself in the syndicate, spurred on by a
sincere belief in McClure and dedication to their unconventional trade.

At thirty, McClure had all the trappings of an established media man,
another New York hustler experimenting with a business model plucked
from the future. By July 1887, the syndicate was publishing Jules Verne in

thirteen American papers. McClure renamed his business the Associated Literary Press, moved into a downtown office in the high-rise Morse Building near Newspaper Row, and hired a stenographer. McClure himself did not formally draw a salary, but usually took between $3,000 and $5,000 per year, as needed. And in the syndicate's early years, his needs grew quickly: he and Hattie had three more children, two daughters and a son, between 1886 and 1891. McClure was starting to accumulate renown of his own, a notoriety that would yield him mixed returns.

\* \* \*

WHILE DANA DESIGNED the first extensive literary syndication in America, McClure made it a mainstream business. He built relationships with editors across the country and inspired serious competition, turning syndication into an industry. But his real talent was his literary sensibility. "To find the best authors," McClure said, "is like being able to tell good wine without the labels." Still, he signed extravagant contracts to woo anyone whose stories caught his eye. He had to contend with other entrepreneurs who had noticed his formula and were edging into the same territory—syndicates launched by Irving Bacheller in New York, and agent-publisher William Tillotson in England—and, dealing with this rising competition, his days took on a new urgency.

Robert Louis Stevenson wound up on the receiving end of McClure's quest for the next literary coup. Through their often-tense relationship, the two men alternately boosted and deflated each other. McClure first approached Stevenson three years into his experiment in running his own business. Stevenson, already famous from *Treasure Island* and *Dr. Jekyll and Mr. Hyde,* had an adventure story, *Kidnapped,* that had been published in England but not yet in the United States.

After months of unanswered letters, McClure had all but given up on *Kidnapped* when he heard that the author was in New York. McClure didn't wait for an invitation. Whisking Hattie along, he called at the Hotel St. Stephen, where Stevenson received them in his pajamas and nightcap, surprising them with his untidy, tobacco-stained presence and his kindliness. McClure quickly proved himself as a man of action: the same afternoon, he negotiated to sell Joseph Pulitzer's New York *World* a year's worth of short weekly essays by Stevenson for $10,000.

Stevenson couldn't quite believe the money was real, but he enthusiastically welcomed the talkative, hustling upstart into his life. He invited McClure to his rented cottage in the Adirondacks, on Saranac Lake, where, when they weren't talking of what profits they might share someday, they went ice skating and chatted constantly. Stevenson and his wife had brought from Montreal an extraordinary assortment of indigenous-made goods, including fur caps, buffalo skins, and snowshoes, and in the sparsely heated house, family and guests wore them as they plotted, turning negotiations into a pageant of rugged frontier trading. "If Mr. McClure's generosity and push were a revelation to Stevenson, accustomed to old world methods," one biographer remarked, "Stevenson's conscientiousness and diffidence may have been a revelation to Mr. McClure, experienced in many types of men." McClure gambled heavily on the author to be sure of keeping him. He offered steep advances that had to be paid from sums originally marked for other writers or for staff salaries, instructing Phillips, "John, I want the syndicate to be run exactly as if it were being conducted for the benefit of Robert Louis Stevenson." When they weren't bundled up together and sharing confidences in Saranac, McClure sent regular, affectionate letters.

The first story that Stevenson gave McClure to sell, "The Black Arrow," had never been published in America—perhaps because it was about the English Wars of the Roses. Stevenson allowed McClure to edit it heavily; he cut the first five chapters and had it illustrated with line drawings. He also, in the absence of copyright enforcement, advertised it under the title "The Outlaws of Tunstall Forest" to pull the wool over the eyes of impatient American editors who might be tempted to pirate the story directly from Stevenson's British files. It was the syndicate's first illustrated story, and it brought in more money than any single piece they had sold before. Thanks to the conjunction of this first deal with Stevenson and Phillips's eagle-eyed office management, McClure began to make a steady profit. When the

McClures' son was born in November 1888, he was given the name Robert Louis Stevenson McClure.

Stevenson's career was likewise transformed by his connection to Mc-Clure. While he considered himself "an obscure 'literary gent' at home," he realized "American appreciation" showed itself quite differently—with more money and adulation than he was used to—and that "a little of that would go a long way to spoil a man." Stevenson suddenly made enough money to fulfill his dream of sailing to the South Pacific.

Stevenson was astonished enough by this windfall to accept it despite other commitments. Momentarily forgetting that he had a contract with Scribner's for his next novel, the sequel to *Kidnapped,* Stevenson accepted 1,600 pounds—worth nearly $200,000 today—from McClure for the same book. Stevenson was caught out when Scribner's reminded him of his original contract, and immediately backpedaled with both his word and pocketbook. Habitually forgetful when it came to managing his publishing affairs, Stevenson described himself as "a kind of unintentional swindler," but he found a convenient scapegoat in McClure, who had tempted him into the deal in the first place.

The mutual dependence began to chafe Stevenson in other ways, too. The two men had widely different sensibilities when it came to Stevenson's writerly reputation. McClure advertised the author in proud, purple prose, which embarrassed Stevenson—who had never branded himself "the foremost romancer of today" or "the Knight Errant of the Nineteenth Century." Stevenson referred privately to McClure as "my benignant monster." He took further vengeance, as novelists do: in his novel *The Wrecker* (1891), he put an undisguised McClure into his character of Jim Pinkerton, an "irrepressible," "bright-eyed" figure whose "questionable" ways nevertheless "fattened" any author who signed a contract with him. To save face when asked about *The Wrecker,* McClure rehearsed a smooth dismissal: "Louis knew I was not like that," he would say; "he just described how somebody like me might have behaved under certain circumstances."

Their alliance held. Both men knew there was enough to be gained that their collaboration was worth the aggravation. Together they worked out a plan whereby Stevenson would buy a yacht and embark on a South Pacific voyage, and McClure would receive reports about his inevitably exotic and colorful travels, to be published through the syndicate. The advance was enough to get Stevenson to San Francisco, where he equipped the *Casco* to take him far away from his benignant monster and the rest of America.

McClure never saw Stevenson again. The author stayed out of his reach, mainly on his estate in Samoa, until his death in December 1894. The relatively lackluster "South Sea Letters" took their time to arrive, throwing McClure into a brief panic. When they came, they seemed written by somebody else, or as McClure regretfully wrote, they drew from the wrong aspect of Stevenson's two-sided psyche: "it was the moralist and not the romancer which his observations in the South Seas awoke in him."

But there were tabloid pages to fill, and despite disgruntled editors questioning McClure as to the lack of "song, flowers and hula stuff," the "Letters" appeared in papers across the country through the early 1890s.

\* \* \*

**AS HE HAD AS A BOY,** and then at *The Wheelman,* McClure kept moving. "I never got ideas sitting still," he admitted. "I usually lost interest in a scheme as soon as it was started, and had no power of developing a plan and carrying it out to its least detail." Drumming up business for the syndicate, he "sometimes spent as many as seventeen successive nights in sleeping-cars," he wrote. "Whatever work I have done has been incidental to this foremost necessity to keep moving." An author in South Carolina opened the door of her cottage one day and quickly sketched a description of the man in front of her, "the indefatigable editor of a New York literary syndicate, to whom distance is a myth, and topography a plaything."

McClure justified his wandering easily, saying he wanted to find out what audiences were reading and what interesting writers were writing about, but he knew he was fitting his life around an intractable and imperative idiosyncrasy. "The restlessness which had mastered me as a boy always had the upper hand of me," he wrote, "and it was my good fortune that I could make it serve my ends." Travel brought out the brash energy that had sustained him when he was a sleepless student and a broke peddler. It inspired and extended his wildly productive manic phases. When he was feeling this way, the limits of ordinary men did not apply to him. On the night of March 12, 1887, McClure went out to London's Savage Club with Harold Frederic, a *New York Times* correspondent. They attended a late variety show and returned to the Hotel Metropole for a brief sleep. The next morning the two men reunited for breakfast, where, according to Frederic, they "talked a few minutes apparently & it was two o'clock! I then lunched with him & we talked a few minutes & then it was . . . evening." McClure wrote Hattie, "I am getting very strong & young & fresh & feel the old boundless vigor in my veins & feel the conscious thrills of perfect life & health, I feel as if difficulties would melt before me."

Each year now, he went to London. His friendships there were fruitful, though his letters of introduction from Stevenson sometimes fell flat. "I found," McClure noted, "that most of Stevenson's set was very much annoyed by the attention he was receiving in America." McClure was surprised by the hostility he encountered, but it did not present an obstacle for long. He wrote Hattie in early March 1887, "My main success was this: I find that Bret Harte, H. Rider Haggard, Wilkie Collins & a great number of the most famous authors in England do all their business through a gentleman named Mr. [A. P.] Watt. I called on him, found him a most agreeable man." Watt, a wily literary agent, was pleased to bring his authors word of fresh money coming their way, even if the news arrived via a jumped-up American with odd manners and a faint Irish brogue.

McClure initially landed squarely within the English perception of Americans as "a very uneducated, pushing, money-grabbing race." He acutely sensed their distaste. "I was the limit—an American editor," he recalled of his trips for the syndicate. Despite his déclassé enthusiasm for Jaeger clothing and a vegetarian diet, he charmed them. His volubility and genuine excitement for his work were hard to resist, especially combined with his philosophy of doing business. "There was never any haggling," McClure was quick to say. "I just paid better than anybody else." For struggling writers who were fortunate enough to pocket a check signed by McClure, this made the difference between continuing to write and not. Robert Louis Stevenson complained that by the age of thirty-one, "I had written little books and little essays and short stories, and had got patted on the back and paid for them—though not enough to live upon. I had quite a reputation. I was the successful man . . . yet could not earn a livelihood." With his fast-won reputation as an editor who paid, McClure was an almost mystically wonderful outlier in the literary marketplace.

Socially, he was received with less grace. Henry James wrote in a letter to Stevenson that "the natural McClure" unabashedly pursued close friendships with his new English acquaintances, who reacted with bemusement. Most were used to a more formal, old boys' publishing culture. One American writer noted the contrast between McClure's guileless "high spirits" and the London office of Messrs. Hodder and Stoughton, who, "noted for their Victorian appearance and manner, sat at opposite ends of a long desk, and on the side next to the wall carried on a sign language that could not be seen by the contracting author." His money, rather than his New World presumption of familiarity, kept doors open to McClure.

At lunch with a curator at the British Museum, McClure heard a name "so unusual that I had to write it down to remember it," that of twenty-five-year-old Rudyard Kipling. Soon after, McClure visited novelist and poet George Meredith and asked Meredith if he'd heard the name Kipling mentioned as a "coming man," a writer worth betting on. "The coming man," Meredith intoned, "is James Matthew Barrie." Barrie had four novels behind him then; it would be another fifteen years before *Peter Pan* appeared on-stage. His first byline in *McClure's* was a poem in Scottish dialect. When he returned to New York, McClure's notebook was full of recommendations like these, his scrawled lists the first link connecting a golden age in British fiction with American readers. In June 1890, McClure would introduce Kipling to America as the English "literary sensation of the hour," with the short story "At the End of the Passage" and the serialization of *The Light That Failed*. Soon after, he started touting Barrie as "great, almost equal to [Robert Louis] Stevenson."

Five years after its launch, McClure's venture had managed to secure and sell work by Thomas Hardy, whose *Tess of the D'Urbervilles* had to be amended for immorality before any magazine would accept to serialize it. Already-burnished names also came to McClure, including Alfred, Lord Tennyson; Henry James; Joseph Conrad; H. G. Wells; Anthony Hope of *The Prisoner of Zenda;* and Emile Zola. To manage the volume of European literature piping through the syndicate, McClure set up a London office and installed his brother Robby to run it. He also hired *Secret Garden* author Frances Hodgson Burnett to head his new Youth's Department—mainly as a figurehead, but a potent one—in 1889. He sold "Esther" by H. Rider Haggard, Winston Churchill's Boer War letters, and a defense of celibacy by Tolstoy, and rode the coattails of a successful *Century* series on Lincoln with a supporting piece, "The Real Lincoln," by one of Lincoln's former law partners. And he grasped after ever-more-illustrious authors, who, in the case of Charles Darwin and William Morris, graced him with curt letters of dismissal. On the home front, he had Mark Twain's letters from Europe, articles by Mrs. Henry Ward Beecher and Susan B. Anthony, and a young Theodore Roosevelt had promised three pieces on wild-game hunting.

In spring 1889, McClure took a train to Scotland to visit an acquaintance who told him about a forthcoming novel by a doctor named Arthur Conan Doyle. As he waited to take the train back down to London, McClure noticed a "shilling-shocker" on the newsstand, Conan Doyle's only publication to date. He read "A Study in Scarlet" on the way south and immediately asked Watt for the American rights to the stories. The first twelve Sherlock Holmes tales were brought to the United States for sixty dollars each. They weren't at first popular with American readers, because the stories tended to run long—eight or nine thousand words, instead of the standard five thousand. McClure contended with newspaper editors who complained "the Doyle stuff was a nuisance." But public interest picked up, and editors' eagerness chased after. After a handful of slow years, while England went "wild over Sherlock Holmes," McClure reported, the fever for Holmes made its way across the Atlantic.

Once his business had found its footing, McClure looked to the future and swung between ambivalence and grandiosity. "I suppose I am completely wedded to journalism. People at our age cannot profitably change their occupation," he wrote to an old Knox classmate.

McClure considered journalism a risky career but admitted it had set a hook within him: "By studying the present you see the animal growing, you see it developing . . . you have the fun and excitement of watching the gradual growth and the tendencies of the times." Publishing was then a young man's game. In many offices, a generational shift had taken place; the average age at *Scribner's* was twenty-four, and the new editor-in-chief of *Ladies' Home Journal,* Edward Bok, was barely thirty-three.

Being an outsider, even a late-to-books Midwesterner, turned out to be an advantage for someone whose trade was in timely entertainment. McClure wrote, "I could never believe in that distinction made by some editors that "this or that was very good, but it wouldn't interest the people of the Middle West, or the people in the little towns. My experience had taught me that the people in the little towns were interested in whatever was interesting—that they were just like the people in New York or Boston." They were potentially even more demanding of a wide-ranging magazine they could savor, for books were sparser and newspapers often provincial. McClure trusted himself—in fact, trusted his own ignorance—though he knew an ebullient mood might persuade him to buy a story that, in a more sober light, he would have declined. He set a rule of reading a story three times before buying it, writing, "I always felt that I judged a story with my solar plexus rather than my brain. . . . I have often been carried past my station on the elevated, going home at night, reading a story."

On very good days, he reveled in the upward swing of his career. He wrote to Hattie in October 1891, "I propose to down *all* competition, and in short time I can dominate the *world* in my line." The combination of instinct and luck that drove him was working, and magazines from *The Cosmopolitan* to *Harper's* began to court him for stories. McClure's roving eye scanned a wide range of genres, from poetry to self-help, as he cannily sold Walt Whitman's "The Dying Veteran" and Jay Gould's "How to Succeed in Business" in the space of a few months.

Talcott Williams, managing editor of the *Philadelphia Press,* was in the front ranks of the changing world of journalism. He got to know McClure and, years later, wrote with the benefit of hindsight: "This revolution, this discovery of a new audience, has multiplied by millions those who read and know the first authors of the day in certain classes of literary work; as the short story, it has doubled and trebled the price before paid, in all it has widened the market of the pen. . . .

"These are great fruits to come from a life of thirty-four years. They have made a spare figure, the gray-blue eyes, the thin, light hair, and the keen, mobile face of the author and inventor of this revolution, known in more newspaper offices and to more authors than any other man in the two centuries in which our letters have known newspaper."

McClure had the instinct—and the luck—to find talent and strike deals. He had learned the business of editing, and had built relationships with major writers and newspapers on both sides of the Atlantic. However, his livelihood depended on selling to fickle newspaper and magazine editors. He began to feel it was time for him to start a magazine of his own: to seize the role of editor-in-chief who ruled on what reached the eyes of the world, and what did not. "I would rather edit a magazine," he told Hattie, "than be President of the United States a hundred times over." As the last decade of the nineteenth century began to unwind, McClure began to put his new scheme into action.

# 6

# "I Fall in Love"

n August 1891, Ida Tarbell closed the door of *The Chautauquan* behind
her for the last time. Accompanied by two friends from Meadville and
a third girl who joined them at the dock, she took a train to New York
and boarded a steamship for France, leaving her family and the disgruntled
Dr. Flood far behind. She had never traveled so far from home. All too soon
after she had left Titusville, with a "dewy parting" from her family, she finished the sandwiches and peanuts she had packed. As the train chugged
up to each successive station, halted, and lurched onward again, she fought
the urge to disembark and scuttle home.

The steamer was another world, one where the young ladies passed
the days in unaccustomed idleness. They walked the deck and accepted
gifts of candy from amiable gentlemen who had heard that the clutch of lady
travelers preferred sweets to wine. Among their foursome, Ida, as usual, fell
into the role of chaperone. Soon they all had established nicknames among
the first-class passengers: Ida was "Mammy," Jo "Sport," Mary "Midget,"
and Anne, because she was often ill, was "Patient." One night after dinner,
her group gathered at the rail and pitched coins at the steerage passengers.

It wasn't all bonbons and hijinks. The success of her Parisian experiment depended on whether she could turn her curiosity into copy. Mustering

her fledgling reporter's spirit, Ida visited the lower decks and was shocked by the crowd and the smell. Keenly aware that she was living by her pen alone, she asked her family to save her letters in case she needed to draw from them for a future article. At first, those letters reflected a consciousness that still clung to the Oil Region; the red-tiled roofs of Antwerp, she wrote, "look exactly like Standard Oil tanks and I grew pale to think of that combination swallowing Belgium too."

In Ida's memoir, the title of the Paris chapter is "I Fall in Love." She loved it with a simplicity and gusto that was impossible for a decent unmarried woman to freely express in human relationships. The city exerted a powerful pull on her, a delight unabated by the "obvious fleas" of her new living quarters. The group found shabby but well-located rooms in the Latin Quarter, close to the Sorbonne at 5 rue du Sommerard, run by a kindly landlady, Madame Bonnet. Most mornings, Ida woke around six, went out to buy rolls and coffee, and then walked to the Bibliothèque Nationale, where she worked.

Here she breathed the same air, saw the same streetscapes as Madame Roland. She passed the house where her heroine was born, her family's church, the prison where she had spent her last hours, and the path she had walked to the guillotine. "The roofs of Paris are silvered by moonlight," she wrote. "The streets under the softening influence of the night and weariness are quiet. It is a vastly different Paris from that of today—this Paris of 1763. Tall, stiff houses arise on all sides. The narrow streets are unpaved, unclean, unlighted, deserted save here and there by noisy revelers from whom the few belated foot passengers shrink." It was awe-inspiring, chilling.

Far from their starchy Methodist families and the coddled morality of *The Chautauquan,* the women went to the Moulin Rouge to see what the fuss was all about. Ida took in political protests and the Annual Ball of the Beaux Arts, witnessing the French tradition of street demonstrations—including one that erupted into a hail of bullets while Ida was among the crowd, trying to take notes—and long, decadent evenings. She even flirted with a wealthy Frenchwoman who wore specially tailored men's suits. All in the name of journalism, naturally: "You mustn't think I am getting Frenchy in my morals because I do things here on Sunday which I don't at home," she assured her family in a letter. "I only do these things to see what the French life really is."

In Paris, she experienced what it was to live at a global crossroads. Next door at Madame Bonnet's lived a group of aristocratic Egyptian men with whom the Americans started having weekly parties. For the first time, she had friends with different-colored skin than she, men of wealth and sophistication who teased and cajoled their earnest American neighbors. "They were quite the most elegant-looking male specimens so far as manners and clothes went than any of us had ever seen," Ida wrote. "Here was more in the way of flavor than we had bargained for." Drinking sugar water—being Muslim, the men abstained from alcohol—and engaging in lively debates about the most civilized configuration of marriage and mistresses, Ida compared their typical Wednesday evenings to "children's parties at home, for the Egyptians loved games, tricks, charades, play of any sort."

Her plan was to report on how Paris maintained her charms. How did the city keep clean? Where did its food come from? How was it that even the poor seemed to have an attractive quality of life? How come hired workers seemed to have an intrinsic dignity that the same group in America didn't seem to have in the least? Or could it all be an illusion? The French simply seemed better at living. After several months in Paris, she wrote her family, "It is remarkable how a plain, steady, digging creature like me gets into so many wildly exciting places. I seem so *out of place*." Yet despite her mousy image of herself, she was powerfully inquisitive and a ready, hungry observer.

By mid-November, Ida received her first check, from the *Cincinnati Times-Star*. Its $6 gave her courage. Being paid, albeit sporadically, to dream up and write her own stories seemed like unbelievable good fortune, even if her rooms were so cold that she slept in all of her clothes. In time her clients grew to include *Harper's* and *Scribner's*. The latter also bought a short story she had written for a munificent one hundred dollars and expressed interest in her biography of Madame Roland, which gave her the validation she had quietly craved. Dr. Flood's dire predictions would not come true before the year was out, at least.

As she reported on the French, Ida felt herself moving closer to a kind of self-realization. She sensed she was noticed by her new neighbors, not for her "charm, beauty, chic, or *l'esprit*" but for her "seriousness, capacity to work, intelligence, *bonté* [goodness]." Ida knew she was not a scientist, teacher, managing editor, nor a girl who lit up the room at parties. She wore the same comfortable green suit for much of her first year in Paris and fended off the advances of persistent Frenchmen who tried to pick her up in the library. A "*femme travailleuse*," her French neighbors said of her: a working woman. It was a term of respect, and she kept busy enough to justify it, often making her workday last until midnight.

She and her friends were merry and poor. Every once in a while, they splurged on forty-cent meals, but usually they frequented bohemian bars with sawdust on the floor where the food was half that price. Ida didn't think much of French food and begged her family to spare her descriptions of luscious home-cooked chicken dinners. She dreamed of buckwheat cakes, beefsteaks, and even American toast. "Things aren't so good," she wrote. "You expect to get mule for beef and leather for cake." Despite their nonexistent travel budget, the group resolved to go somewhere every weekend— even if it was only a short boat trip on the *bateaux mouches* through Paris or a tram ride to Versailles. Their apartment became a base for American women who had come to tour Europe, and they developed a stock itinerary of entertainments that didn't cost much. On occasion, Ida dressed in a man's suit so that she and her friends could wander the boulevards without feeling vulnerable or unchaperoned.

Having to count every franc brought an as-yet-abstract reality into sharp focus. Ida wrote that for the first time, she classed herself for practical purposes with "those whom we call the poor. . . . I had belonged all my conscious life to the well-to-do, those who spent a dollar without seriously weighing it. Society had seemed to me to be chiefly made up of such people." Though her family had grappled with grave financial insecurity, when times were tight they always had the fallback of selling portions of the land that Esther had inherited. Their pantry was always full. Now, in Paris, Ida saw, felt, and lived what it was to be hungry.

After a bracing year, Ida's friends returned to Pennsylvania. They were ready to be dutiful daughters again. Ida was not, even if she had started feeling isolated and pinched for cash. Her sister, Sarah, an artist who lived at home and painted when her frail constitution allowed, was in bad health, dabbling in the new fad for spiritualism, but still sent Ida money when she could. Ida's guilt at deserting her family intensified in June 1892 when news of a deadly flood and fire in Titusville made her walk the streets in a panic until the arrival of a telegram from her brother Will. She backed into a corner to lean against a wall for support while she opened the message, which simply read, "Safe."

By August 1892, Ida was living alone, eating most of her meals alone, and had no intimate friends nearby. She moved to a smaller, fourth-floor flat on the quiet, cobbled rue Malebranche, and there her homesickness surged into a depression. When she could, she forced herself into the grand department store of the Bon Marché to look at the latest fashions, or boarded the top of an omnibus so that she could ride loftily across Paris, a favorite cheap diversion.

Slowly she found friends and reemerged into fitful good spirits. She was the only American invited to a lively Wednesday night salon where she was warmly entertained as "Mademoiselle Mees"—"Miss Miss." Though her French was not fluent enough yet to make her an easy conversationalist, Ida reveled in the talk that swirled around her: "There was nothing on earth that was foreign or forbidden. Opinions were free as the air, but they had to fight for their lives." She didn't have to contribute much to exist as a figure of great interest; the basic facts of her being were enough to intrigue those around her. "They can't get used to the idea of a woman really working," she wrote, and she was amused to be continually thrown together with eligible Frenchmen. She was regarded as an exceptional American, one who exhibited a sophisticated discretion and refreshing independence of spirit and who understood the innate superiority of France. America was, Ida learned from her French circle, a nation of scammers, criminals, and fanatics. She attracted the attentions of a Sorbonne history professor, who impressed upon her an Old World way of looking at America: it was a nation of "lesser men," he told her, a product of money and organization, but not capable of producing a true intellectual elite. "Five hundred years from now Chicago may be fit for scholars," he argued, "but not now."

At the salon, Ida was introduced to a descendant of Madame Roland's who offered to take Ida to the ancestral house in Beaujolais where Roland had actually lived. It was only once they were en route that Ida realized her companion wanted to keep the trip quiet because she was traveling with a "heretic"—a non-Catholic. The secrecy only intensified Ida's wonder at the dreamlike pocket of France that she found herself in, "a high broad country, striped by many colored ribbonlike farms, dotted by stout buildings of dull yellow, the stone of the country, sprinkled with splendid trees, vineyards and orchards." It was a place that belonged to a mythic past, a world away from Pennsylvania's Oil Region.

Even as Ida dispelled the preconceptions of others, her own illusions were being dismantled. After exhaustive research of Madame Roland's writings in the chateau's library, Ida found herself mistrusting her heroine, who was more flawed than the principled woman she had imagined. Madame Roland was not, Ida decided, a case study for the role of women in public life. Ida had intended to tell the story of a character who was "a steady, intuitive, dependable force," but instead found "a politician with a Providence complex." Before the revolution, Roland had tried to secure a title for herself; once the upheaval was under way, she pursued a husband with more fervor than her supposed ideals. Roland was also disturbingly—to Ida's mind, grotesquely—frank, writing in plain language about being molested by her father's apprentice and thus being driven to move to a convent and avoid marriage for a time. Ida was put off by her subject turning out to be so human. Perhaps what she needed was a dose of time at home and then a fresh start in Paris, as she hoped, to "[clear] up my mind on women and revolution."

* * *

**ONE DRAB DAY NOT LONG AFTER** in that late summer of 1892, she opened her door to a jittery man in his mid-thirties who introduced himself as S. S. McClure. He had noticed Ida's article on the streets of Paris, "The Paving of Paris by Monsieur Alphand," in the syndicate's submissions pile back in New York. It was an unexpectedly engrossing article that cast new light on an everyday necessity; the piece revealed the man who held himself responsible for the streets trod by Parisians rich and poor. As he finished it, McClure held it up and said to Phillips, "This girl can write." He asked Phillips who she was. "No idea," answered Phillips, "but from her hand-writing I should guess she's a middle-aged New England schoolmarm." McClure was eager to snap up young, interesting reporters whose talent might feed his literary syndicate, and he later wrote that this first story "possessed exactly the qualities I wanted for *McClure's*." He wrote to Ida M. Tarbell, as she signed herself, and offered to buy syndication rights for ten dollars. Then he sailed for Europe.

Ida wrote that he arrived "in the meteoric fashion I found was usual with him." She opened her door to see "a slender figure . . . a shock of tumbled sandy hair, blue eyes which glowed and sparkled . . . a vibrant, eager, indomitable personality that electrified even the experienced and the cynical. . . . His utter simplicity, outrightness, his enthusiasm and con-fidence captivated me." In later years, making notes for the story of her life, Ida reenvisioned how "[h]e stood at my door, the most vivid, vital creature that I had ever seen." He stood shorter than her, holding a watch in one hand. McClure insisted he had only ten minutes before his train left for Switzerland, but in the end he stayed for three hours.

It was the start of a transformative relationship for both, but those few hours hardly promised what was to come. She was soon listening to his full Horatio Alger story, from peddling around the midwestern prairies to try-ing to learn every word in the dictionary at Knox, winning Hattie, building the syndicate with John Phillips, and a new plan that was sure to take the world by storm. He spoke to her as though she were familiar with Galesburg and New York, and as if she had already met the other people in his life, and knew already that he was at heart a magazine editor; as Ida recalled, it was "always John this, John that, and last a magazine to be—soon."

She allowed herself to be swept up in his talk. When McClure left her apartment to catch the Geneva train, it was with the understanding that Ida would write for him regularly. He also asked to borrow forty dollars. Ida happened to have enough in a drawer, in preparation for a final vacation to Mont St. Michel with her friends. She readily gave it away to this outsize character who had blown into her apartment and brightened her hopes for the future; she assumed she would never be repaid. The day after his visit, she received a wire from McClure's London office reimbursing her the full amount.

One of McClure's utterances in particular made her stop and think. During his torrent of speech, he had offered her a full-time job at the syndicate, promising that she would have time to write for the soon-to-be magazine as well. She had cheerfully declined. Despite the bare sufficiency of her freelance income, Paris was too compelling to abandon. Her instinctive refusal made her realize just how much another office job represented compromise to her, and she wrote her family as much: "It would be a good joke on the Mogul [Dr. Flood], wouldn't it? . . . But I shall not do it if I'm going to make this literary business a go—if there's anything in me." Like her father, Ida resisted the loss of frontier spirit that came with a wage earner's life—but increasingly, that seemed the only viable way to make a living.

Nevertheless, when McClure sent assignments her way, Ida ran with them. She found that his magpie-like interest in the science and society around him corresponded to her own, and in a sense woke her up to the kind of writing she liked best. She wrote of his effect on her, "my natural enthusiasm for the physical world and its meanings . . . was not dead, only sleeping." Ida interviewed Louis Pasteur—uncovering his "inconsolable" regret that he had been distracted by fermentation from his original subject, crystals—and Emile Zola: "a rather small man, slight and nervous with exceedingly penetrating eyes." She covered rising social science theories, like the Bertillon system of criminal identification, which started the

American police procedures of keeping fingerprints, mug shots, and physical measurements of offenders.

McClure's keenness for stories that helped readers imagine the future and understand the present was infectious. His editorial direction could be frustratingly vague, as when he shot her a request for "something startling." Working for him, even with the expanse of the Atlantic between them, forced her to stretch.

By February 1893, Ida was "in deep with McClure." The sense of connection was mutual. McClure wrote her with an assignment and added a concluding line to tell her that her early articles pleased him "extremely. In fact, all your work does, as well as the fine spirit you show us which makes us admire you greatly." She began spending time with another dazzling new acquaintance who had entered her orbit thanks to McClure, the brand-new art director for his future magazine, August Jaccaci. Jaccaci (pronounced "Yakatchy") was a "marvelous fellow," Ida thought, nearly as charismatic as McClure himself, though in a very different tenor. Gossip had it that Jaccaci was Italian, had killed a man in a duel in Mexico, and had painted the murals in the Havana Opera House. He spoke French and Polish fluently and dodged polite inquiries about his past. A bon vivant regardless of his shoestring budget, he treated Ida to Parisian dinners at restaurants she had previously felt too poor to enter. Ida had a new sense of being a peer to this gypsy-like artist; no longer was she merely one of Dr. Flood's office girls, but a worldly journalist, sent around Paris to be McClure's eyes and ears and suck the marrow from all that was interesting. She wrote of this significant change in circumstances, "It raised my interest in the venture to a high pitch. . . . It meant something more than I had dreamed possible in magazine journalism."

When *McClure's* first came off press in May 1893, Jaccaci asked her to meet him at the Gare St.-Lazare train station at five thirty in the morning, as he was passing through, and there he showed her the first copy. Together they turned its pliable pages, smiling that S. S. McClure had really done it. Ida had a story in the second issue.

But the dozens of articles she filed from Paris that year, so painstakingly accumulated, did not translate to financial stability. The catastrophic financial panic of 1893 meant that all magazines were short on cash. In March 1894, she wrote from London: "As usual, I'm on the ragged edge of bankruptcy and gay as a cricket about it. The McClures are very taken with my work, so they write me. I suppose they can't find anybody else poor enough to tackle these wretched subjects." She poked fun at her situation as though it were just another bohemian lark, but in fact she was in a bind. Worried that she would not always be able to survive alone by her pen, she was also starting to see her future allied to McClure's. As she wrote to her family, "I've just received a letter saying the magazine is growing. . . . They ask me what I'm going to do the next five or six years and hope I'm not going to get married and thus 'cut short my career' (I wish to goodness I was and then I'd have a notion that I had a career)."

The world still seemed to be waiting for her to come to her senses and marry—and at the same time, it was falling apart. Ida found herself facing the awful necessity of having to ask her family for money. First, she pawned her richest possession, her sealskin coat. In this period of being utterly broke, praise for the integrity of her writing fell flat. "It seems my articles have had some compliments from high sources for their *accuracy*"—she practically rolled her eyes while writing this letter home—"which is some like complimenting me for being able to add up well." Kind words were easy currency, and exasperating, when no one was sending full or punctual payment for her work. Scribner's was still interested in her book on Madame Roland, but they, like her other sources of income, had stopped sending checks.

She often wondered when she would reach her limit of anxiety about the future. The protagonist of one of Ida's few short stories, Helen Walters, sheds some light on her thoughts and on the effort it took to wake up each morning and face the gaze of her more conventional peers: "She could endure overwork, grumbling editors, loss of position, she could make her way out of tight places with cat-like agility. What she could not support was the critical stare of women of assured position." In the end, Helen marries, but only because she is too tired to do otherwise. She tells her betrothed, "I have no judgment left. . . . I don't think that it is you in particular. It is simply that you offer to look after me and I should love anybody who should do that." Clearly, Ida was acquainted with the temptation to give up, blend in, and be looked after by a sympathetic suitor. She must have been grievously worn down by the itinerant writer's life, which put her firmly on the margins of respectable society, but she had a strong hunch (and ample evidence in the couples she saw around her) that marriage and children would mean suppressing a vital part of herself.

She decided to master the loneliness that she had found to be the shadow of marginality. It was a challenge memorably articulated by a later, equally daring journalist, Martha Gellhorn: "I tell you loneliness is the thing to master. Courage and fear, love, death are only parts of it and can easily be ruled afterwards. If I make myself master of my own loneliness there will be peace or safety: and perhaps these are the same."

After three years in Paris, Ida boarded a steamship headed back across the Atlantic. She could not afford not to. McClure, still wooing her, had sent enough money for a second-class ticket. At first she saw the return as a chance to inject new energy and opportunity into her writing life. She would drum up writing assignments with New York editors, spend time with her family, and then, her purse replenished, return to her true home in Paris's Latin Quarter. Perhaps she would convene her own salon. McClure seemed on the verge of bankruptcy himself, and she wasn't certain the job would last. "I know I was never meant for journalistic work, but here I am," she wrote home in late April, shortly before her return voyage. And so, uncertain of her commitment to McClure, Madame Roland, or anything else, Ida exchanged her ticket for a third-class passage and used the extra cash to buy her nieces a porcelain doll. She assured herself this trip was only a visit.

*Part II*

---

# RISE

# 7

# The Moving Spirit of the Time

S. McClure stepped off the train and into the frigid New England air. It was early spring in 1893, and the days were short. His friend Rudyard Kipling awaited him, if not on the platform then at his little house near Brattleboro, Vermont, called Bliss Cottage. The two men—one a thirty-four-year-old Irish American, shock-haired, and bursting with energy, the other twenty-seven, Anglo-Indian, bespectacled, and restrained—stayed up far into the night, sitting close in a room flickering with firelight.

The visitor did most of the talking; he had a particular idea to test. "[McClure] entered, alight with the notion for a new magazine," wrote Kipling later. "I think the talk lasted some twelve—or it may have been seventeen—hours, before the notion was fully hatched out." McClure's syndicate was thriving, and he was finally—for the most part—out of debt. His dream of launching his own magazine seemed within reach. Unfortunately, Hattie and Phillips were hesitant. They were on the brink of a comfortable life; why must he jeopardize it? So, impulsively, McClure had bought a train ticket to Vermont and sought out his new friend to see if his plan had any merit.

Kipling barely said a word as McClure, a "cyclone in a frock-coat,"

"whirled round [the] little shanty explaining, exhorting . . . and prophesying."
He spun one idea into another, each one enlarging on the last. He had come
to put into words the storm of ambitions that possessed him. "[McClure] is
a great man," Kipling wrote, "but he'd kill me in a week with mere surplus
of energy."

Their friendship had started with contracts. McClure pursued Kipling
to get stories for his syndicate, though Kipling, who had already left India for good, had lost his savings in a bank failure and was struggling to
catch on in America. He had submitted all of his existing work to Harper &
Brothers and was decisively rejected. Bliss Cottage, where he lived with
his American wife and baby daughter, was sparsely furnished and lacked
running water. That winter, Kipling started writing the stories that would become *The Jungle Book*. He rarely sought outside company, but he "liked and
admired McClure more than a little, for he was one of the few with whom
three and a half words serve for a sentence, and as clear and straight as
spring water." The two shared an understanding born of early hardship;
both were uprooted from an idyllic home at a young age, in Kipling's case
from Bombay to England. In the author's depiction of the boy Mowgli, an
odd species among the creatures who raised him but also among "civilized"
men, McClure might have recognized himself.

It was a visit that Kipling would remember and retell the rest of his life,
and one that sketched the blueprint for McClure's unlikely fame. McClure
offered to buy Kipling's entire output of the next few years, to help guarantee a steady source of fiction for his magazine. The author couldn't promise as much, but he was flattered that McClure considered him worth the
gamble. In time, even before he became a Nobel laureate in 1907, volumes
of Kipling's work, ranging from schoolboy tales (*Stalky & Co.*) to serialized
novels (*Kim*) to science fiction ("With the Night Mail") to grandstanding
verse ("The White Man's Burden"), would make their debut in *McClure's*.

The next morning McClure's torrent of talk finally came to an end,
and he bid the Kiplings thanks and farewell. After McClure returned to
New York, he sent an extravagant gift up to Bliss Cottage: a tandem bicycle,
which, Kipling wrote, "made good dependence for continuous domestic

quarrel. On this devil's toast-rack we took exercise, each believing that the other liked it." McClure, too, faced discord at home as he insisted on his risky new venture. But not for long; Hattie was soon swept up in her husband's enthusiasm and—for better or worse—put her faith in his scheme.

* * *

**OUTSIDE BLISS COTTAGE,** the rest of America was preoccupied with money. McClure would need that, in addition to ingenuity and a cache of winning material, to bring his magazine to life. In the weeks after his visit with Kipling, McClure took to the road to raise cash. Selling his syndication services to whoever would listen, he visited literary agents and newspaper editors from London to Chicago. He threw himself into the hustle, seeking the next Conan Doyle, adventure tales in the vein of Robert Louis Stevenson, and rising voices like J. M. Barrie. But now, on a tour that encompassed two passages over the Atlantic and sleeper trains through the Midwest, McClure came face-to-face with economic catastrophe.

The Panic of 1893, the most severe financial crisis to hit America before the Crash of 1929, had just struck. Its effects were visible and terrifying. The longest leg of McClure's trip took him to London and then to the western states, and from there he returned to New York via every major newspaper office that would meet with him. No city was untouched. In Chicago, McClure visited the editor of the *Inter-Ocean,* hoping to chase up a handful of syndicate payments and put aside the money for his magazine.

"Money?" the editor protested. "Oh, no! We can't give you any money. Look out there!"

From the upper floors of the newspaper office, McClure looked out the window at the street below and saw "masses of people seething from curb to curb before a building." They were trying to enter a bank and withdraw their savings, which, according to headlines, were on the brink of dissolving into nothing. McClure rushed to wire Hattie and Phillips, only to find a message from Phillips advising him to get to the bank and withdraw any cash he could.

On the train between Chicago and New York, McClure couldn't help but see the dire reports in every paper. "The doors of the Union Square bank, New York, were forced open and the watchman found dead, having killed himself because of the burden of supporting a large family," reported one local sheet. As the Panic rippled across America, the run on the banks that McClure witnessed was reenacted again and again. In six months in 1893, eight thousand businesses and more than three hundred banks were shuttered. About 20 percent of the labor force was out of work.

McClure realized that "[t]here never was a more inopportune time to launch a new business." But the gears of his mind were already in motion. Boldness, he hoped, was all. He would pursue his vision, and hope America could recover in time to welcome it.

* * *

JUST AHEAD OF THE PANIC, 1892 and early 1893 brought a new sense of pride in American ingenuity. The World's Columbian Exposition opened in Chicago, and Thomas Edison built the first working movie studio in West Orange, New Jersey. Untrammeled immigration and steady westward migration turned prairie into farmland, and cities shot upward and outward. From 1880 to 1900 alone, the population rose 50 percent—from about 50 million to about 75 million—as seven new states were admitted to the Union.

Increasingly, these recently arrived American city dwellers were readers, too. Before and through the Civil War, less than 6 percent of American teenagers attended high school; by the turn of the century, it was just over half. As a form, the magazine was ripe for growth, serving the needs of this increasingly literate citizenry. By 1899, the public, noted Chicago reporter Ray Stannard Baker, "would swallow dissertations of ten or twelve thousand words without even blinking—and ask for more." Newspapers tended to have an established allegiance to one political party, but the magazine was meant mainly to explain and entertain. As a whole, the press was integral to the American colonies' shift to nationhood. "Were it left to me to decide whether we should have a government without newspapers, or newspapers without a government," Thomas Jefferson remarked, "I should not hesitate a moment to prefer the latter." (Twenty years later, Jefferson's feelings swung in the opposite direction; once in his second term as president, he wrote in a letter, "Nothing can now be believed which is seen in a newspaper. Truth itself becomes suspicious by being put into that polluted vehicle.")

The word "magazine" is derived from the Arabic *makazin,* or storehouse, whose other descendants include the French *magasin,* or shop. The word was first used to refer to a collection of printed material by England's *The Gentleman's Magazine,* founded in 1731, which brought together news, editorials, and fiction. The concept took a decade to cross the Atlantic; Benjamin Franklin launched a monthly magazine for the colonies—whose purpose would be to aggregate noteworthy material from books and newspapers—and launched his *General Magazine and Historical Chronicle for all the British Plantations in America* in Philadelphia in 1741. (Bostonian Andrew Bradford preempted this by three days with his *American Magazine, or Monthly View of the Political State of the British Colonies,* poaching Franklin's chief contributor and engaging in a price war before a single copy had been printed.) Though neither Franklin's nor Bradford's magazine lasted longer than six months, the titles of both indicated there was a growing market for in-depth reporting on what the colonies were becoming, and on the independent identity they were starting to claim.

From the start, women's magazines had a substantial share of the market. From 1830 through the late nineteenth century, the "queen of the monthlies" was *Godey's Lady's Book.* This was required reading for genteel women, guiding their behavior, appearance, and which social issues they ought to care about. Its editor, far from being a woman of leisure herself, was the formidable, black-clad Sarah Josepha Hale, a widow with five children who had long supported herself. Under Hale's watch, *Godey's* advocated for women's education—though the magazine was at heart conservative, and did not support women's suffrage. (Hale is also credited with campaigning for Thanksgiving Day to be recognized as a national holiday, finally proclaimed by Lincoln on October 20, 1864.)

By 1890, the bestselling general-interest magazines—*Harper's Monthly, Scribner's Magazine,* and *The Century*—reached between 150,000 and

200,000 every month. They had gained a hold over readers in slightly varying ways: *Harper's* ran serialized novels by Dickens, Thackeray, and Trol-
lope, while *The Century* published Civil War articles written by generals
who had served on both sides. Their only rival for quality, *The Atlantic
Monthly*, voice of the Boston intelligentsia rather than New York, trailed
them at about 12,000. Magazines traditionally made money from subscriptions, which were priced to cover the cost of production, but increasingly they were growing flush on advertising, an industry that rode the
gathering swell of American consumerism—a swell interrupted by the de-
stabilizing Panic of 1893.

Magazines established themselves as an essential platform for American writers who could quickly introduce a sense of drama and timeliness.
These writers tended to be of two schools, old and new. For the first three
quarters of the nineteenth century, most journalists rose up from appren-
ticeships, typically starting out in the composing room and needing no
qualification but a willingness to do the inky, repetitive work. A college
education was not looked for among these reporters, nor was any degree
of intellectualism or literary sophistication. This generation had reported
from the frontier, and had seen the advent of the telegraph snaking across
the country, which had the effect of shaping news stories into brief, tight
dispatches without a single extraneous word. Once the telegraph network
was established and timely news could be circulated to many newspapers at
once via syndicated wire services, magazines added value through analysis
and illustrations. This demand, combined with a gradual professionaliza-
tion of the field, brought in a new cohort with more writerly aspirations.

Magazines also started to shape fiction. The bestselling novel of the
nineteenth century, Harriet Beecher Stowe's *Uncle Tom's Cabin*, was serialized in weekly installments for *The National Era* magazine during 1851–52,
before its publication in book form. Edgar Allan Poe coined the word
"magazinist" for writers whose living depended on such contracts, and the
magazine was instrumental for his own career: nearly everything he wrote
was for the magazines. With his efforts occupying the magazines alongside those of his contemporary Nathaniel Hawthorne and others, the con-

cise, plot-driven American short story came into focus as a mainstream and recognizable form.

The character of *McClure's* announced itself through fiction as well as its reporting. McClure told a reporter a decade later, "What I have always felt is that a magazine, to be successful, must have a distinctly ethical background. Every article and every story must be definitely uplifting, and have a moral influence on the reader, though this may be expressed in any of the thousand different ways which are the province of art and literature." He sought to set himself apart from more liberal editors of the dangerous French realist tradition; none of these, it was said, "is able to feel himself fully sincere in fiction unless he is indelicate." Magazines were expected to have morals as well as artistic sensibilities; editors of the old-guard magazines resisted even allowing fictional treatment of slums in their pages.

As early as the syndicate heyday of 1886, McClure had seen himself having "a powerful agency in destroying the market for vile literature." His guidelines for syndicate authors required that stories have high moral tone, and that no story should agitate for class conflict or hostility between North and South. In 1888, he enclosed a circular with a story by Emile Zola called "The Dream" to justify his promotion of a chaste story by a daring writer: "[H]is exposures of the depravities of the worst side of Parisian life, and his seeming preference for immorality and vice as a theme for fiction, have hitherto prevented American readers from appreciating his marvelous talent as a novelist, and his vigor and brilliancy of style as a writer."

When Ernest Poole submitted a draft of a report on the lives of newspaper boys to McClure, the Chief initially cut his coverage of sexually transmitted disease among them, then revised his feedback: "Now I'll tell you what to do. Imagine yourself in a room with six grown-ups and six little girls. Tell this part of your story so that the grown-ups will get it but the six little girls will not—and then I'll print it." He may have received letters like that of a New York banker who wrote to *Scribner's* to say that "a young female member of his household," reading an article on French art, found that illustrations of nudes accompanied the story. The girl "uttered a low cry and fled from the room."

Magazines began to position themselves in a theoretical position of power, addressing the question of what larger social forces united disparate events and upheavals. In a nation too sprawling to be adequately covered by any daily paper, the monthly magazine was able to step in and give a larger-scope perspective on "what it was all about." As journalist and future *McClure's* staffer Will Irwin wrote, "The reader who skimmed day by day the [newspaper] stories . . . missed often the connective passages or overlooked the significance of small details."

From points east and west, workers were testing their power via collective action, threatening the complacency of the industrialists who had become America's aristocracy. Between 1870 and 1903, government troops, militias, or the National Guard were deployed in more than five hundred labor or labor-related disputes. A French observer noted, "The police in the United States have become another of the armed bands of the Middle Ages which were found in the service of the barons." This was exemplified most starkly in July 1892, when workers at the Carnegie Steel Company in Homestead, Pennsylvania, went on strike. The protest ended in the murder of eleven strikers, with sixty more wounded by the army of Pinkerton enforcers who were mustered to restore order. On the same day as that slaughter, an anarchist in Pittsburgh confronted Carnegie ally Henry Clay Frick and shot him twice before being subdued.

McClure knew he could make a magazine that would capture the zeitgeist more cannily than *The Century,* with bolder reporting than *Munsey's,* and with more heartland appeal than *The Atlantic.* After his trip to see Kipling, he overwhelmed the opposition at home and at work. The concept was soon set up and funded—or, at least, pulled together convincingly enough to publish the first issue. Phillips and Robby agreed to buy shares in the new magazine, and the division of ownership was soon settled: out of the initial 1,000 shares, valued at $100 apiece, Robby held 50, Phillips held 45, and McClure had the rest. His entire capital for the enterprise was $7,300, more than half of which had come from Phillips. They rented their first offices at 743–45 Broadway, the Charles Scribner's Sons building.

Practical matters settled, McClure turned to weighty creative decisions, beginning with what to name the new magazine. They thought about naming it *The New Magazine, Galaxy,* or *Elysium,* avoiding any hint of being regional or citified. *McClure's,* suggested by English critic Edmund Gosse, was the name that stuck.

The magazine's voice was harder to nail down. The new editor-in-chief bought advertising space in other magazines to announce his broad-stroke ambitions: "*McClure's Magazine* is designed to reflect the moving spirit of the time," he promised. Readers would encounter "the character and achievements of the great men of the day . . . the new discoveries, tendencies or principles in science." The scope of the writing would range from "the human struggle for existence and development" to "the best imaginative literature." It sounded like a close sibling to a newspaper's Sunday supplement, or to a variety show.

McClure's first source of material was his own syndicate, and this proved to be a great advantage. In years past, there had been times when he hadn't been able to sell a story he loved, written by an author he had made promises to, because editors weren't as receptive as he'd assumed they would be. Having his own magazine meant liberation; the magazine, he said, "was my syndicate work grown up."

He had a model in the London magazine *Strand,* launched in 1891 by another working-class entrepreneur, George Newnes. No one was particularly proud to read it, but everybody did. From the start, "[i]t seemed to be in everybody's hands," wrote a London critic after the first issue appeared in January 1891. "It entered every omnibus, and took itself off in every departing train. In the evening it dined out—so to speak—at innumerable literary dinner parties." Another critic called *Strand* "a six penny edition of *Scribner* or *Harper* [*sic*]," as it included celebrity profiles and plenty of pictures.

Savvy, seasoned magazinist Frank Munsey was perhaps McClure's nearest competitor among the editors of monthlies. In 1882 he had launched the popular "boys' literature" magazine *The Golden Argosy,* one of the first periodicals printed on ultracheap pulpwood paper. Munsey then started the general interest *Munsey's Magazine* as upbeat entertainment for working-class readers, and went on to newspapers; the *Washington Times,* New York *Daily News,* New York *Sun,* the *Globe,* and other papers were at some point acquired by Munsey, who was known to ruthlessly merge publications and lay off entire offices if profits did not satisfy expectations. Both he and McClure embraced the idea of literature as a commodity that everyone could consume. But they also had contrasting notions of their ideal reader. Munsey liked to rib McClure for making a "magazine to suit his own taste," rather than "human nature as I [Munsey] understand it."

It took more than the right stories or a firm grasp on an ideal readership to make a magazine survive, though. Munsey liked to claim that, because it took a month to get the advertising and illustrations right and then another month to print and distribute, the magazine was the most difficult literary product to get right. "The magazine, then," Munsey wrote in an article about the business, "must depend for its hold on the people upon its superior excellence throughout, both mechanical and literary; its superior illustrations, its more perfect letterpress, its more carefully selected and carefully written contents, and upon its convenient and preservable shape." All McClure's competitors' magazines were illustrated, and traditionally those illustrations were reproduced using wood engravings of drawings—at a steep cost. "The *Century Magazine* used, when I was working at it, to spend something like five thousand dollars a month on its engraving alone," McClure recalled. The process required a team of artist-engravers working with expensive boxwood, imported from the Middle East. Even before paying staff or contributors, McClure was concerned about being run into debt by illustration expenses.

Circumstances worked in his favor. The invention of photoengraving, or "halftone reproduction," by Cornell photography professor Frederic Ives gradually came into general use through the 1870s and 1880s, and it revolutionized the process. Then the linotype or "hot-type" machine, invented by German American Ottmar Mergenthaler in 1894, made typesetting faster and cheaper. The price of paper, too, went down. Immediately after the Civil War, manufacturers had started using wood rather than cloth as the basic ingredient. By 1900, the per-pound price of paper had diminished from eight cents to two. Every component of magazine making was faster, cheaper, and more vivid than it had ever been.

McClure and Phillips arranged their first issue with the best ammunition they had. It had a handsome cover designed by Art Nouveau–inspired American artist Will Low, with the table of contents framed on a rich, leather-colored background. Its pages featured Alfred, Lord Tennyson, a piece on evolution titled "Where Man Got His Ears," and the debut of a series called "Real Conversations," where well-known writers interviewed even more renowned figures (later, these included Alexander Graham Bell and Jules Verne).

In May 1893, the first issue of *McClure's* came off press and landed in newsstands (as well as making its way to Paris, via Jaccaci's valise, and to Ida Tarbell). Within weeks, all manner of readers and critics responded. Theodore Roosevelt, then at the Civil Service Commission, sent McClure a letter praising the first issue of his "excellent magazine" that "rendered a real service to the cause of good government." The *Review of Reviews* hailed the new magazine's fresh, living qualities, saying of the first issue, "It throbs with actuality from beginning to end." The Albany *Argus* put it, "He is a rash man who attempts to start a new magazine, unless he is so favored by circumstances that he is certain of an audience from the beginning. A man so blest, we are sure, is S. S. McClure." In *The Outlook* magazine, the reviewer claimed to have read "every line" of the first issue with interest, and asked its audience, "How often does this happen, one wonders, with the average magazine reader?" A verse by English poet J. K. Stephen poked fun at the newcomer who had seemingly set off a new era of wide-eyed tale-telling:

Will there never come a season
Which shall rid us from the curse
Of a prose which knows no reason
And an unmelodious verse:
When the world shall cease to wonder
At the genius of an ass,
And a boy's eccentric blunder
Shall not bring success to pass:

When mankind shall be delivered
From the clash of magazines,
And the inkstand shall be shivered
Into countless smithereens:
When there stands a muzzled stripling,
Mute, beside a muzzled bore:
When the Rudyards cease from kipling
And the Haggards ride no more.

Rival editors zeroed in on another, more startling feature of the new magazine: the price. McClure had decided on an old-fashioned way of attracting attention: he made himself the cheapest option. *Scribner's, Harper's,* and *The Century* were all priced at thirty-five cents—for that sum, a hungry New Yorker could obtain three boiled eggs, an order of pancakes, and a cup of coffee at a breakfast counter. *McClure's* cost fifteen, equivalent to toast and coffee.

The competition, who referred to McClure behind his back as a "bog Irish" interloper, were aghast. McClure's model disrupted the traditional notion of what a magazine was worth; it assumed that advertising sales would make up for the losses incurred by selling the magazine below the cost of production. Within four months, *The Cosmopolitan* was at twelve and a half cents and *Munsey's* cost only a dime. McClure had gotten his edge—or so he believed.

* * *

**DESPITE THE LOW PRICE**, the Panic of 1893 hit the fledgling magazine hard. Of the 20,000 copies of the first issue that came off the press and onto the streets, 12,000 were returned unsold. For more than a year, the magazine lost close to $5,000 a month. Instinct and generosity frequently took hold of its editor-in-chief, regardless of his slim pocketbook. Another newspaperman made a crack repeated more than once by those who worked under McClure: "If he had been a woman, he would have been pregnant all the time." This generally did not serve the magazine all that badly. But now, in its infancy, it seemed to predict certain downfall.

The new magazinist took on the mission of recruiting a staff using a giddy combination of referral and whimsy. During a syndicate sales tour, in Davenport, Iowa, he met with Albert Brady, his Knox friend, who was publisher of a local newspaper. By the end of their meeting, McClure had hired Brady to be the advertising manager for his new magazine at the handsome salary of $5,000, angering Robby and Phillips, who admired Brady but despaired of being able to pay what the Chief had promised. Over the following years, Brady's brothers Oscar and Curtis would join the staff, too.

The Panic was personally formative for the newly formed *McClure's* group. They were part of the first American generation to have no living memory of the Civil War; McClure had landed in the United States a year after the war's end. The Panic was the first national-scale trauma witnessed by the *McClure's* generation since they had reached adulthood and embarked on careers. In June 1893, writing from Chicago, where he planned to visit the World's Fair, McClure wrote Hattie, "We are nearly on the verge of failure. . . . Have you the strength to go through a squeeze?" The Panic gave them a baseline familiarity with economic catastrophe that proved both the might of Wall Street and the fragility of their livelihoods.

The magazine survived McClure's impulsiveness because he managed to win over enough publicity and favors to continue sending issues to press. Colonel Pope bought advertising worth one thousand dollars. The printer agreed to extend a month of credit. McClure avoided paying the syndicate's English authors—his most valuable clients—and traveled to London in the spring to find new voices. During one meeting on that trip, he found himself weeping with one author who was about to be evicted from his flat because he hadn't received his counted-upon check from McClure. For several months in 1894, during which Robert Louis Stevenson, Henry Rider Haggard, and Bret Harte appeared in *McClure's* regularly, the magazine shrank from 96 to 88 pages and used smaller illustrations, which helped, but not enough; *McClure's* continued to bleed money. Phillips persuaded his father to mortgage his home in Galesburg, and McClure extended his borrowing power with Pope. To save money, McClure and Hattie moved with their children and a nursemaid to Bay Shore, Long Island. He wrote of these careworn days, "I felt, day after day, as if I were trying to walk into a granite wall."

Luck turned at last in the autumn of that year, at a chance meeting with Arthur Conan Doyle. Since McClure had orchestrated the American discovery of Sherlock Holmes via his syndicate, the author came to regard him as a kind of wizard. Conan Doyle was just then on an American lecture tour and invited McClure to lunch with him at the Aldine Club in New York. McClure apologized for not having attended any of his friend's lectures, and, unable to maintain a suave façade for long, confessed his business worries. In response, Conan Doyle left him with a check for five thousand dollars, allowing McClure to pay off all of his English authors and regain equilibrium. Then Ida Tarbell, who had until now resisted accepting a full-time job, answered McClure's summons and boarded a steamer for New York.

Science and technology had a special focus in *McClure's*. Electricity, wireless communication, vaccination—the triumphs of experimental science fascinated and spooked McClure and his readers. Technology was not wholly separated from spiritualism, in many readers' minds; Rudyard Kipling's story "Wireless" (1902) illustrates this in its portrayal of a man attempting to use a wireless device to connect with another experimenter, who instead channels the long-dead poet John Keats.

The series "The Edge of the Future" featured interviews with great men of science, starting with Thomas Edison. The January 1894 issue speculated about communications in the future: "The telegraph ties together continents, and puts a girdle around the earth. . . . Who shall say that the telephone may not, in a few years, give us the power to speak with friends in the Orient, or on the continent of the antipodes?" The race to the North Pole, herculean efforts to build railroads across the continent, and breakthroughs in medicine ran alongside "Stories from the Archives of the Pinkerton Detective Agency," "The Destruction of the Reno Gang," and stories that played into American readers' fascination with old-world society ("Stranger than Fiction: Stories of the Brontë Family in Ireland").

There were violent, anarchical stories to make sense of, too, for the century seemed determined that it would not go quietly. In June 1894 the magazine printed Hamlin Garland's "Homestead and its Perilous Trades," a report on conditions in Carnegie's steel town since the violent strike of 1892. McClure himself had assigned thirty-four-year-old Garland, better known for his short stories set on the northwestern prairie and his carefully groomed hair, to write the piece, which turned into a revealing portrait of "labor pass[ing] into the brutalizing stage of severity." The "squalid and un-lovely" town was more like an army camp than a civic center, while the iron mill itself initially gave the impression of glowing peacefully from within; the illusion was interrupted by the screams of saws, thunder of engines, deafening hiss of steam, the "wild vague shouts" of the ragged men feeding the machines for twelve hours at a stretch in a mill building pounding with heat and nicknamed the "death-trap." "I'd as soon go to hell at once," Gar-land told his guide. His article concluded that, in the midst of Pennsylvania lush with green hills and the wide Monongahela River, Carnegie's "town and its industries lay like a cancer on the breast of a human body."

McClure surrounded himself with young people, hoping they would expand his own energies. He was propelled by an anxious certainty that, without a steady influx of fresh voices, he might miss out on what was most current, brilliant, and saleable. His generosity and inveterate absent-mindedness combined toward this end; McClure hired young people for jobs that didn't exist and ordered unplanned articles from writers without telling anyone in the office, himself forgetting his promises shortly after he had made them.

Besides the permanent staff, writers whom McClure had spontane-ously hired for a few months to help them out regularly drifted through the office. There was a thin, shy young man who pitched in with proofreading: Frank Norris, from San Francisco. He was working on a trilogy of novels about the West, though only one, *The Octopus*, would be published before his death. (When Norris resigned from *McClure's,* he contritely wrote to Phillips, "It is not that I distrust Mr. McClure in the slightest degree—you know that. But I am afraid that he would forget all about me in one week's time.").

Presently there was also a stocky, lethargic kid from Terre Haute, Indiana, who sometimes wrote short articles for the syndicate, nothing too literary: he signed his work Theodore Dreisser (later he would drop an *s*). And there were countless aspiring journalists fresh out of college in the Midwest: by the turn of the century, one editor remarked, it was routine for "every man who had graduated from Knox in the last few years to write to *McClure's* asking for some position." The magnetism of the *McClure's* office was not just due to the Chief's default welcome; the magazine symbolized the future. One observer remarked, "The very name *McClure's Magazine* had an irresistible attraction for any young man who believed the American world susceptible of improvement," and who wanted to be on the vanguard of the action. Willa Cather later wrote of McClure's success with young people: "You often thought them a little more able than they really were, but those who had any stuff in them at all tried to be as good as you thought them, to come up to your expectations. You had such a spirit of youth yourself that you knew how to strike a spark in young writers." The magazine publisher who initially encouraged McClure to strike out on his own, Roswell Smith of *The Century,* did not live long enough to witness his protégé's rise as an editor. But McClure was doubtless watched with chagrin by the likes of Frank Munsey, as *McClure's* began to build a reputation for incisive, wide-ranging journalism.

As young writers began seeking him out as a kind of rite-of-passage pilgrimage destination, McClure outgrew the upper floors of the Scribner's building. He found a new home on the upper floors of a soaring, arch-bedecked building on Twenty-Fifth Street, between Lexington and Third Avenues, the gilded environs of Madison Square. By its third birthday in June 1896, *McClure's* had the largest publishing offices in Manhattan, at thirty-three thousand square feet. The immense space was a constant work in progress, split between glass-paned cubicles—the latest in interior design—and a printing plant. McClure, in an editorial for the third-anniversary issue, gave the reader a virtual tour of the place. "These offices, taking into consideration the perfection of their mechanical equipment, the amplitude of room and light, and convenience of location, are not surpassed—are scarcely approached—by any of their kind in the country," he wrote. The magazine occupied much of a city block, with windows and skylights frequently thrown open to liberate any hint of the stuffy, inky atmosphere McClure had encountered at De Vinne's printing house.

Crossing the short couple of blocks across Fifth Avenue and up Twenty-Third Street, between the *Century* office and *McClure's,* was, in the words of one visitor, like stepping "out of some 'ancient volume of forgotten lore' into an unexpurgated dictionary of tomorrow." At *McClure's,* transparent partitions glinted; bright yellow tables and hard chairs populated the floor; presses clattered; ink flew; McClure himself dashed about. A "bristling and busy atmosphere" was the visitor's first impression.

The tools of their trade—typewriters, desk telephones, fountain pens, the toothy, clanking presses—were recent, all invented since the Civil War. Two typesetting machines cast hot metal ingots into plates of text, which were then molded in wax, and finally coated in copper and burnished to be readied for the presses. The fleet of whirring, state-of-the-art presses was serviced by a freight elevator that could hold a wagon full of paper as well as the team of four horses. Mark Twain and Kipling both requested to see the technological wonder of the new press, and were amazed. "My God!" cried Twain. "Can that thing vote, too?"

McClure was proud that his enterprise ran on the clean, invisible fuel of the future: "The power throughout is electricity," he explained to subscribers, "and both in the press-room and the bindery each machine has its individual motor. The lines of shafting and web of belts that scatter dust and grease, and worry and even endanger life, in the old-time factory, have no place here. All is clean and remarkably quiet, and the comfort of the workman is complete." Fourteen of the latest Cottrell rotary presses devoured enormous spools of paper, folding, stitching, covering, and trimming, while flat presses turned out covers and illustrated layouts. Then to the bindery, and then the mailroom, where a team in shirtsleeves wrapped and addressed each subscriber issue, packing them into tall, unwieldy post office bags for shipment.

Manuscript reader Viola Roseboro, who had started at the syndicate, joined the *McClure's* editorial staff in 1896 and became the guiding hand of the magazine's fiction department. An auburn-haired, blue-eyed actress from Nashville, "Rosey" kept up the unusual habits (for a woman in public) of going uncorseted, cursing, and smoking cigarettes—thin, sharp-looking ones she rolled herself. She presided regally over two barrels filled with unsolicited manuscripts. She was "fidgity" by nature and preferred to do her reading on a park bench. Most evenings, she would lug home more manuscripts in a suitcase for her nighttime reading. In November 1897, Rosey opened a batch of stories from one W. S. Porter of Austin, Texas; the syndicate bought "The Miracle of Lava Canyon," the first time Porter had sold his fiction. Shortly afterward, he was imprisoned for embezzlement and took on the pen name O. Henry, conveying his work to Miss Roseboro from the Ohio State Penitentiary. She picked out his "Whistling Dick's Christmas Stocking" and the magazine published it the following year. Booth Tarkington, now best known for *The Magnificent Ambersons,* was similarly noticed and plucked from the barrel by Miss Roseboro. When McClure tried to reject a story loved by Rosey, she sometimes drew on her theatrical training and wept until he changed his mind.

Shortly after Rosey's arrival, McClure read an editorial titled "What's the Matter with Kansas?" reprinted in the New York *Sun.* Its author, William Allen White, was the twenty-eight-year-old owner of the *Emporia Gazette.* In his vitriolic editorial, he issued a withering takedown of the populist cause, which he saw as discouraging to businesses who might have otherwise invested in Kansas. The piece seemed to be on the lips of every politically conscious editor and reader, and so McClure wrote to White at once, wooing him to join *McClure's* as a regular contributor. White duly came to New York to see if the offers were bona fide. "The McClure group," he wrote in his autobiography, "became for ten or fifteen years my New York fortress, spiritual, literary, and, because they paid me well, financial." He was especially struck by McClure, "a Swedish blond with a yellow moustache, big, sensitive but challenging eyes, and a sharp, hard but still ingratiating high voice snapping orders like a top sergeant," with Phillips speaking softly and authoritatively in response.

The night of White's first visit, the motley crew of *McClure's* took him uptown, their streetcar scattering hordes of bicycles, to Grant's Tomb, where they spent hours dining and talking. "They were at heart Midwestern," White decided. "They talked the Mississippi Valley vernacular. . . . They were making a magazine for our kind—the literate middle class."

On the heels of the Panic, recovery took a heady, hopeful turn, and *McClure's* found its way to increasing numbers of firesides and club tables. The Klondike Gold Rush sent tens of thousands of prospectors, including a young Jack London, swarming west. Brands still sold today began to shout from market shelves—including Cream of Wheat, Aunt Jemima, Kellogg's Shredded Wheat, Juicy Fruit gum, Coca-Cola, and Quaker Oats. Patent filings multiplied sixfold between 1871 (12,688) and 1896 (72,470). *McClure's* remarked that it was an age of "applied intelligence": "Not only is there extraordinary fertility of invention, but also, what is perhaps more striking still, there is apparently an instant readiness on everybody's part to make use of the things invented."

It would be ten years before that surge of prosperity—and *McClure's* grip on America's attention—was abruptly cut short.

# 8

## *The Uneasy Woman*

I n the steamy July of 1894, through the prospectors' hamlets along the malodorous banks of Oil Creek, Ida Tarbell and her brother Will explored the landscapes of their childhood. She was now, in the eyes of her family, confirmed in her life as literary spinster aunt (as opposed to the painterly one, her sister, Sarah). Will was a careworn father of three, living close by his aging parents in Titusville.

In the town of Pithole, they saw "stripped fields where no outline of a town remained." They searched for the location of their father's former shop, and of their pre-Titusville home, finding only that "[t]he day left us with a melancholy sense of the impermanence of human undertakings." Returning to the Oil Region made Ida want to make a fresh attempt at novel writing, but, as she'd realized during her Panic year in Europe, securing a regular income would have to come first. McClure had paid her steamer ticket home and allowed her two months in the grown-over, reconfigured landscape of her childhood, and in return she had agreed to sign on with the magazine and mold herself to his very definite ideas for her.

Her first assignment required a disorienting relocation to Washington, D.C. Hearing that *The Century* was planning an illustrated life of Napoleon Bonaparte, McClure decided he wanted his new reporter to write essentially the same story—but faster. Ida Tarbell later wrote, "The success of a feature spurred him to effort to get more of it, things which would sharpen and perpetuate the interest. He was ready to look into any suggestion, however unlikely it might seem to the cautious-minded. He was never afraid of being fooled, only of missing something." He had already secured the exclusive cooperation of a private collector with a deep specialty in Napoleon.

Ida hardly had time to get her bearings as a *McClure's* staffer when she alighted in Washington to begin her research. John Phillips happened to be passing through and called on her to introduce himself, curious about the woman with looping handwriting who had brought Paris to life for *McClure's*. She offered him a beer—a gesture so awkward it was amusing, for it wasn't yet noon—and she was surprised and glad to find McClure had such a courtly, thoughtful counterpart. Most of her mind was already on the daunting assignment ahead.

Miss Tarbell, as her colleagues now addressed her, spent her days in the private Chevy Chase library of the remarkable Gardiner Greene Hubbard. A graceful country estate called Twin Oaks—a name Ida would one day give her own refuge—the house was to Miss Tarbell "the most beautiful home into which I had ever been admitted." Hubbard was founder and first president of the National Geographic Society, as well as father to Mabel Hubbard, who had been deaf since a childhood illness. One of the innovative teachers the family recruited for her—and her eventual husband—was Alexander Graham Bell, in Miss Tarbell's opinion "the handsomest and certainly the most striking figure in Washington."

From the vantage point of this exceptional household, Ida Tarbell encountered a new and regrettable facet of McClure's character. He arrived in Washington to go over the project with her and threw the entire residence into disarray. The Hubbards professed to be "accustomed to geniuses," as they reassured Miss Tarbell after a particularly chaotic visit from her employer, but Miss Tarbell admitted she was "horrified" by his manners. As she wrote, "He would burst unexpectedly into the house at any moment which suited his convenience . . . and almost before he had made his greet-

ing the bag was open and the proofs spread helter-skelter over the carpet."
Miss Tarbell saw for the first time that McClure's impetuosity might not be
charming to everyone, or in all contexts. He disturbed the refined atmosphere of Twin Oaks and seemed unconscious of doing so. It was an uncomfortable study in contrasts that made her realize how powerfully she wanted
others to like McClure as she did.

That summer, Miss Tarbell spent her hours immersed in Napoleon
and exploring the swampy, bucolic capital. The Napoleon series, though
pulled together in a hurry, increased the fortunes of *McClure's* beyond expectations. At the start of the series in late 1894, monthly circulation was
about 24,500, and by the end, it was close to 80,000. Ida Tarbell had quickly
become the lifeblood of *McClure's*.

In December, on a chill Thursday evening, McClure went out on the
town as a magazine editor to be reckoned with. Miss Tarbell's name was
not yet on the guest list for glittering events such as this one, but because
of her contributions, McClure was. He joined a select crowd at Delmonico's
for the American Commerce Banquet, rubbing shoulders with John Jacob
Astor and William Rockefeller (brother to John), politicians Mark Hanna—
the biggest fixer in the Republican Party—and William McAdoo, and fellow
publishers William Randolph Hearst and Frank Munsey. Even in evening
dress, McClure was "the whippy little Irishman, with the rumpled hair and
rumpled suit," but he was the only man on the guest list frowning at the
French menu who had landed there after starting life in a dirt-floor house
in Ireland.

Miss Tarbell's next venture, her twenty-part profile of Abraham Lincoln, once again doubled the circulation of the magazine. This was an unqualified feat; even in the 1890s, Lincoln's life had already been exhaustively
covered. Again, McClure had assigned her a subject that in theory belonged
to *The Century,* which had published excerpts from Nicolay and Hay's four-
thousand-plus-page biography. What set her work apart was the thorough-
ness of her research with living people. As Miss Tarbell began to dig into
the facts behind the drama, she turned up fresh material where there was
thought to be none left. Given license—and an expense account—to cast a

wide net, she deployed the skills she had learned in Paris and approached the historical material critically and with deep contextual and archival background. She also befriended librarians and curators. The Scranton *Tribune* noted, "We know of no other biography which so clearly brings home to present day readers the human qualities of Lincoln and puts into such interesting relief the comedy and pathos of his boyhood days."

From research through publication, the Lincoln series took four years. No one had expected great things of Ida Tarbell; *Century* editor Richard Watson Gilder scornfully announced to his colleagues that "McClure's got a girl trying to write a life of Lincoln." Her method was workmanlike, with the advantage of unusual stamina. Like her contemporary Nellie Bly, who in 1889 traveled around the world in seventy-two days as a stunt for the New York *World,* Miss Tarbell was unfazed by cold-water hotels in unfamiliar landscapes. When she sent word to McClure that Knob Creek, Kentucky, was colder than she expected, he worried enough to write, "Have you warm *bed socks*? We'll send you some if not." A fellow reporter marveled, "she could mobilize just as swiftly as any lad in the place—could accept a decision at noon to start for Chicago that night without turning a hair. I suppose there have been other females like that—I glimpse them in books [on] great travelers but she is the only one I ever saw keep it up right along; thereby in her case wiping out one good ground for paying women less than men."

Fellow journalists openly expected her to falter. Long after their *McClure's* years together, Lincoln Steffens would wonder that she "never seemed to get tired." Women writers typically wrote columns from the comfort of their homes, rather than taking to the road or newsroom. Instead, Miss Tarbell systematically identified potential leads, pursued them regardless of distance or difficulty, and kept bringing new material to light. The Lincoln series put obscurity behind her, for better or for worse.

With each subject, she allowed a surprising capacity for obsession to take over and became immersed in as many archives, interviews, and follow-up fact checks as resources allowed. A woman writer traveling on her own for work—a modern, somewhat bohemian concept—she quickly earned her interviewees' trust and sympathy, and knew how to shape her discoveries into clear, lively articles.

Her gifts of questioning and tact became profitable advantages when she met the president's son. Robert Lincoln took to her, and shared a daguerreotype that had never previously been published. The effect of this image alone shows the power of portraiture in the nascent days of mass-published photography. Taken when he was about thirty-nine, the daguerreotype featured an attractive, darkly poetic face, coinciding more with popular images of Emerson than the greasy backwoodsman young Lincoln was thought to have been. From that article in November 1895 to the next month's issue of *McClure's,* circulation rose from 175,000 to 250,000, surpassing even *The Century.*

The method of an editor-in-chief hiring a salaried magazine writer permanently, rather than story to story, was not common. McClure later claimed that, as a key part of "the peculiar character of *McClure's Magazine*," Miss Tarbell "inaugurated in America the idea of regular staff writers," who internalized the voice of their magazine and were in turn "given sufficient time to get the work just right."

Their partnership set the model for the now-established norm of matching a particular voice with an idea plucked from the editor's consciousness. The staff writer, in McClure's vision, was more than a "mere contributor"; her voice was an asset, she worked "in close sympathy" with himself, and she was, in McClure's description, "intrusted [sic] with the espression [sic] of the conviction and principles of the magazine." If he invented the role of staff writer for Miss Tarbell, it conveniently made sure that she was accessible to him year-round. From the moment he got used to her company in the office, he craved her approval, esteem, and calming influence; the persistent theme in McClure's letters is that he never felt he had enough time with her. After their meetings, he always felt there was much left unsaid; he was "lonesome" for her, the same word he used in a courting letter to Hattie, and hankered after her letters when he was away.

In the course of the Napoleon and Lincoln series, McClure felt increasingly bound to Miss Tarbell. "I lean on you as no other," he would write to her. "[I]n all great & noble qualities you are peerless to me." Hattie, too, admired her from the start as a "noble woman," and when Miss Tarbell finally arrived at her desk and into a working routine in New York, their acquaintance deepened into friendship. McClure was fascinated by her fixedness and patience, capabilities he had never known in himself. For Miss Tarbell, meanwhile, the work was weighted with personal meaning. McClure was compelling because he not only supplied ideas and a steady wage, but also offered a sense of convivial shared purpose. "Chiefly, it was the sense of vitality, of adventure, of excitement, that I was getting from being admitted on terms of equality and good comradeship," she wrote.

Most irresistibly, she felt needed, and in a way that transcended the requirements of the magazine alone.

*  *  *

IDA TARBELL LIVED ALONE IN MANHATTAN, first on Eighteenth Street and then in a handsome high-rise at 40 West Ninth Street, where she took on two cats and an Irish maid. Home life was exactly according to her desires: solitary and free.

Her ambition from a young age had been to achieve independence and a thriving intellectual life, and nothing she experienced since taking her vow of spinsterhood at fourteen prompted her to seriously rethink that choice. As she wrote in one article on an inner-city Domestic Relations Court, "There are in the city of Chicago, let us say, five hundred thousand pairs of men and women who have undertaken to spend their lives in the appalling intimacy of marriage—to create homes where they may rear children." Her single-mindedness to avoid that "appalling intimacy" was concentrated by a dose of fear that she would end up like her mother: idealistic but silenced and stilled by family life. Her determination was also bolstered by her reluctance to become a figurehead for the cause of women's suffrage.

She was living a life of ambition and stories, conventional enough for most journalists. Doing so while female, however, was like wearing a garish, cumbersome accessory she couldn't take off. As she sought her next investigative project after Lincoln, she was often reminded that her life was conspicuously different from the majority of her peers'. To the men of *McClure's* she was a maternal or sisterly figure to whom they could bring their frustrations, an authoritative peacemaker of editorial scuffles and bruised egos. The terminology of family relationships helped put everyone's mind at ease; motherhood and sisterhood were, after all, safe and socially approved ways for men to relate to women. Miss Tarbell regarded herself as "a species of big sister to the group." All except McClure were younger than her. They had the habit of greeting her with a kiss when they met in public, sometimes startling observers. But beyond the comfortable bounds of *McClure's,* her life and work raised questions about where she stood on that long-running anxiety, the Woman Question.

At the office, Miss Tarbell was instrumental in governing the Chief, because "[s]he could change him. No one else could." Her methods were those of the diplomat, not the seducer, and she kept a distance around her always. When McClure was in the office, he was generally in an upholstered easy chair within earshot of Phillips, while Miss Tarbell sought a quieter spot for her orderly desk. Poetry editor Witter Bynner wrote that she was essential in leading from below: "Whereas S. S. was the motor, the galvanizer of the staff . . . Phillips and Ida were in control, especially Ida. I can see her still, sitting there and gravely weighing prospects, possibilities, checking errors, smoothing differences." He continued: "The rest of us tided around her. And this was not only in matters of magazine policy or contents. It was in personal matters too. She was pacifier and arbiter, guide, philosopher and friend."

It was unusual that Bynner used her first name, for she managed to inspire awe as well as affection in her colleagues. Years later, when they no longer worked together as closely, John Phillips noted, "The main staff of our magazine was composed of men; someone probably S. S. McClure himself said 'Miss Tarbell is the best man among us.' . . . Our deep respect never allowed us to address her familiarly; she was always Miss Tarbell to us." A newspaper sketch by humorist Finley Peter Dunne proclaimed, "Idarem [Ida M.] is a Lady, but she has the punch," and Phillips admitted "that amusing name [Idarem] hung about the office, but did not change our habitual form of addressing our comrade-in-arms." Her byline remained Ida M. Tarbell, but in person, no matter how intimate the colleague—even to S. S.—she was Miss Tarbell.

Around her, other women were getting hired to write for the ever-increasing number of general-interest magazines. The widespread adoption of the typewriter and telephone also meant a steady rise in secretarial jobs, which were increasingly held by women. The media called this suddenly visible population of educated, outgoing young ladies New Women: they rode bicycles, played tennis, and wore skirts that showed some ankle, as in Charles Dana Gibson's pen-and-ink drawings. The "experiment" of women in higher education was, after plenty of hand-wringing anxiety that it could only result in vice, deemed harmless. As one of Miss Tarbell's fellow newspaperwomen, Rheta Childe Dorr, wrote, women increasingly sought "to belong to the human race, not the ladies' aid society to the human race." Equality in the workplace was another question.

The New Woman—as Ida Tarbell was inevitably labeled—was a target for heavy-handed commentary from all sides. "I hate the phrase 'new woman,'" wrote Emma Wolf in her 1896 novel *The Joy of Life*. "Of all the tawdry, run-to-heel phrases that strike me the most disagreeably. When you mean, by the term, the women who believe in and ask for the right to advance in education, the arts, and professions with their fellow-men, you are speaking of a phase in civilization, which has come gradually and naturally, and is here to stay. There is nothing new or abnormal in such a woman."

There were few examples in popular culture that normalized the young woman as a person capable of a full intellectual life. The middle-class feminine ideal of English critic John Ruskin's essay "Of Queen's Gardens" persisted on both sides of the Atlantic. In Ruskin's quintessentially Victorian words, "The man's power is active, progressive, defensive. He is eminently the doer, the creator, the discoverer, the defender." The "woman's power," on the other hand, is "for sweet ordering, arrangement and decision. She sees the qualities of things, their claims, and their places. Her great function is Praise."

By the time Ida Tarbell's byline rose to prominence, the disruption of Ruskin's ideal was a recognized and much-mourned phenomenon. In the *Gentleman's Magazine* of 1894, the anonymous author of a piece titled "The Wail of the Male: By One of Them" declares that "I am not a fanatic. I am only a husband. I am not against woman's rights. I don't think all women ought to be married. I am glad that women should be newspaper reporters. . . . Still . . . the serpent's tooth is hid in the new movement . . . the angel in the house is gone."

The latest scientific studies made a clear and damning case. As articulated in a *Popular Science* article on "Mental Differences of Men and Women" by evolutionary biologist George Romanes, it was commonly thought that women simply had less brainpower than men. "Seeing that the average brain-weight of women is about five ounces less than that of men," wrote Romanes, referring plentifully to Darwin, "on merely anatomical grounds we should be prepared to expect a marked inferiority of intellectual power in the former." He admitted there were "extraordinary" women, and that women had sharp yet superficial powers of observation—for noticing their neighbors' new bonnets and shoes, for example. Women also tended to be more sensitive to art and religion. But his conclusion was unambiguous: "Lastly, with regard to judgment, I think there can be no real question that the female mind stands considerably below the male." These claims, especially when parroted in the media, also bolstered arguments against equal pay for equal work. "[A] female," remarked a *New York Herald* reporter, "eats ordinarily one-third less than a man."

For women writers in particular, this "scientific" conclusion validated a near-universal scorn for their efforts and ideas. Women's psyches were considered easily corruptible—famously, Edith Wharton was forbidden by her mother to read novels until after her marriage—and incapable of producing important art. "Women can't write. And they ought not to try," says a respected literary man in an 1892 short story by Constance Fenimore Woolson, "In Sloane Street." He continues: "[T]hey can write for children, and for young girls, extremely well. And they can write little sketches and episodes if they will confine themselves rigidly to the things they thoroughly know, such as love stories, and so forth. But the great questions of life, the important matters, they cannot render in the least."

The literature of the 1890s mocked, admired, and wrung its hands over women who wrote. As Ida Tarbell was making her name at *McClure's,* the woman reporter was appearing frequently in major and minor literature, an ambivalent, rarely successful, and sometimes tragic or villainous figure. Charlotte Perkins Gilman's "The Yellow Wall-Paper," published in *The New England Magazine* in 1892, startled readers with its interior landscape of a woman kept in comfort but forbidden to engage in creative work. "John laughs at me, of course, but one expects that in a marriage," the narrator remarks when she tells him there's something eerie about the mansion where they live. Her husband and brother, both physicians, believe she is mentally incapacitated by a "temporary nervous depression—a slight hysterical tendency" and prescribe a strict regime of pills, fresh air, rest, and absolutely no work of her own. She silently disagrees, but obeys. "Personally, I believe that congenial work, with excitement and change, would do me good," she tells the reader. "But what is one to do? I did write for a while in spite of them; but it DOES exhaust me a good deal—having to be so sly about it, or else meet with heavy opposition." Gilman's portrayal was plausible; melancholia, neurasthenia, and hysteria were easy labels to assign to restless wives and daughters.

Frank Norris, a novelist closely allied with the *McClure's* group, noted the absence of positive portrayals of young women in fiction when he credited Louisa May Alcott as the only one who had ever "written intelligently for girls." He pointed out the literary territory still unexplored, and concluded that "the great majority of twentieth-century opinion is virtually Oriental in its conception of the young girl. The world to-day is a world for boys, men and women. Of all humans, the young girl, the sixteen-year-old, is the least important—or, at least, is so deemed. Wanted: a Champion. Wanted: the Discoverer and Poet of the Very Young Girl." Miss Tarbell would not be that Champion. She asked readers to consider her as a "bachelor soul," defined by her solitary freedom but by no means an example of typical womanhood. On this question, she asked to be left alone.

Ida Tarbell was raised to believe in equality of the sexes. "I grew up among people who believed in women's suffrage as much as they did in the abolition of slavery [or] the observance of the Sabbath," she wrote. "It was part of the creed I learned as a child—a part of the liberal program of the day." She had been hungry enough for education to insist to the doubters of Titusville that it was perfectly respectable. "To go to a man's college and to fit myself for a man's work—that was to be my contribution to the cause!" she wrote; it was to be "My little revolution!" Her education opened the way to a career and brought personal fulfillment, but she saw this success as separate from the campaign for equality. However, her forward-thinking peers were hard to deflect. A voice like Miss Tarbell's would have been a welcome addition alongside Jane Addams's or Carrie Chapman Catt's in the grinding effort for women's suffrage, but she steadfastly refused to contribute.

Once she moved to New York and made her name at *McClure's*, Miss Tarbell found the Woman Question, as many called it, inescapable and exhausting. Everyone wanted to know where she stood in the fight. "The most conspicuous occupation of the American woman of to-day, dressing herself aside," she chided, "is self-discussion."

Privately, she struggled in letters and conversations with the men of *McClure's* to clarify her thoughts. In two late-career series, *The Business of Being a Woman* and *The Ways of Woman,* she outlined their progression. Miss Tarbell saw the possibilities faced by the comfortably-off woman with access to education—Miss Tarbell dubbed her the "Uneasy Woman"—and mused on the compromises she had made in navigating them.

She took a grudging stance against women's suffrage, arguing that it was a mistake for women to confuse equality with sameness. The ballot, she said, "seems to me like an alien tool" in a woman's hands, "as alien as a gun." Even as she had studied revolutionary women for *The Chautauquan,* the subject disturbed her: "Radical and conservative, Royalist and democrat, aristocrat and proletariat. I had the same revulsion against them all," she wrote; "I think it possible that I was not quite fair to any of them." She felt sure and clear on this, and declared she didn't mind when younger feminists, among them Helen Keller, dismissed her in the press as "old."

Alternately starry-eyed and detached toward her female readers, she considered herself a fluke among women and excused herself from advocacy outside her journalism, or from being the symbol of any political movement. "The central fact of the woman's life—Nature's reason for her—is the child," she wrote. The capacity to birth and raise children struck her as powerful, enviable—and, ultimately, enough. "I confess I've always pitied men a little," she wrote, "that they could not know the death struggle for a new life and I always had a feeling of superiority over them." This sentiment is repeated in her memoir, where she claimed to be following in the spirit of Marie Curie: "Madame Curie so saw it," she wrote. "[T]he important thing was the beginning, and that beginning, Madame Curie insisted, was in the home, the center of small things."

The status quo struck her as natural, if ripe for improvement—especially when it came to family planning. Withdrawal and abortion were the most commonly used forms of birth control in the nineteenth century. Faced with what she saw as a stark choice between family life and self-sufficiency, she opted for the latter, and there is no evidence she ever had a romantic relationship. Miss Tarbell liked to quote the French revolutionaries: "'Celibacy is the aristocracy of the future.'" She must have felt herself visibly different from mothers and mothers-to-be, and compelled to prove herself fruitful in another sense.

When needled by friends who disagreed with her stance on suffrage—among whom John Phillips was the most direct—she confessed she didn't think much of other women, as a rule. She mistrusted their "intensity and implacability" and natural tendency to "go with her man" when it came to political views. "That is the way she is made," she told Phillips, allowing for a few exceptional "sexless" women who managed to maintain their own individual views—and these, she was certain, were not to be fully trusted, either. The assumption of many readers—that she was a mannish bluestocking—bothered her less than the prospect of being drawn into the quicksand of the Woman Question, forced to publicly argue a point on behalf of an entire gender, and associated forevermore with a movement that left her cold. Interrogating herself on the Woman Question, Miss Tarbell found a malleable and uncertain core, a swirl of emotion within. She confided in John Phillips, "I have always found it difficult to explain myself, even to myself, and I do not often try."

* * *

AS MISS TARBELL SETTLED INTO HER ROLE AT McCLURE'S, she began to believe, as its founder did, that the magazine gave her some sway over the "moving spirit of the time." Ida considered that her early years with McClure's "aroused my flagging sense that I had a country, that its problems were my problems." It is debatable how much of the crusading newspaper work of the Gilded Age was driven by moral scruples, and how much by the need to sell papers. The limit of readers' appetites for outrage-provoking stories had not yet been reached, and so manufactured drama inevitably became a cornerstone of news. Yet real change came from reporters' stunts, too; Julius Chambers and Nellie Bly, writing for the New York Tribune and World respectively, went undercover in mental hospitals, resulting in new laws, upgrades, and the closure of the most inhumane asylums.

McClure was attuned to the new style and pursued it. Bosses, politicians, tycoons, cops, meatpackers, quacks, gamblers, robber barons, reformers—and their native settings of oil refineries, slums, saloons, and city halls—fueled narratives that aimed to make government and big business publicly accountable. Journalism was no longer a commodity for the privileged; it featured a cast of characters and crises that reflected readers' everyday lives and struggles. He recruited his own ex-tramp, Josiah Flynt, who supplied the magazine's series "True Stories from the Underworld." "The stories are intended to point a moral as well as adorn a tale," an editorial specified, anticipating the accusation that McClure's was trying to join the ranks of sensational newspapers.

Technology increasingly preoccupied readers' imaginations—one angle where McClure's early hunch and personal curiosity paid off for McClure's. Science was, in the beginning, the major focus of McClure's nonfiction, closely followed by war, and then more distantly by railroads, business and labor, crime, animals, and polar expeditions. A common theme was that technology was making the world grow smaller and move faster; increasingly, this was a topic of prophetic and bewildered, rather than wholly positive, media attention. Jack London wrote in "The Shrinkage of the Planet," "What a play-ball has this planet of ours become! . . . The telegraph annihilates space and time. Each morning every part knows what every other part is thinking, contemplating, or doing."

It had been more than twenty years since the first light bulb, but the desire to slow the pace of change persisted. Guglielmo Marconi attempted the unprecedented feat of sending a wireless signal across the English Channel in early 1899. One of the witnesses in Dover who stood amazed at Marconi's success on March 27 of that year was Robby McClure. This was a revelation. "How could any sensible man," marveled a contemporary reporter—"the kind who prides himself upon 'keeping both feet on the ground'—accept the crazy idea of sending messages through space, with no wires to carry them?" When *McClure's* published their report in the June 1899 issue, it was a clean scoop.

When the battleship *Maine* blew up in Havana harbor on February 16, 1898, heralding the start of the Spanish-American War, Miss Tarbell was working on the profile of the head of the army, General Nelson Miles. Reporting from the army headquarters in Washington, Ida was appalled by the indecorous excitement of the man she saw abandoning his post to form his own unit in Cuba: Assistant Secretary of the Navy Theodore Roosevelt. Roosevelt in the late 1890s fit his caricature too well, with his button-bursting energy. Ida inwardly agreed with a humor writer who said of him, "Don't he make you think of a boy on a roller skate hobby horse tearing up and down these halls, brandishing a wooden sword[?]" He was frequently laughable, a constant show—and astoundingly effective. "Theodore had a clear idea in his mind to what that boyish performance ought to get for him," Miss Tarbell later admitted, "and he got it." To Viola Roseboro, she confided that she "thought him a delight and a wonderful person and of great value as well as of some disadvantage to his country."

She felt increasingly implicated in the society she observed and wrote up for the readers of *McClure's*. When she reached her eighties, Ida Tarbell would look back on a long and storied career and determine how that moment in 1898 had set the course for her writing life: the start of the Spanish-American War. "I could not run away to a foreign land where I should be a mere spectator," she wrote. "I must give up Paris."

America was newly fascinating to her as she reexamined her nation's contradictions and potential through well-traveled, inquiring eyes. In March 1898, *McClure's* editor-in-chief celebrated her by featuring her photograph in the magazine and noting in the caption that "no name is more familiar to readers of *McClure's Magazine* than that of Ida M. Tarbell."

She put down roots in New York, moving to her own apartment on West Ninth Street in May 1899. Apartment living, which she'd been used to in Paris, was a relatively recent circumstance for middle- and upper-class New Yorkers. Those who couldn't afford otherwise were in tenements; many occupied a range of boardinghouses, from shabby to refined; and the well-to-do had single-family homes. To live in an apartment by choice was, up until the mid-1870s, a novelty. (In *The Age of Innocence,* Edith Wharton's character Newland Archer remarks on the jarringly intimate experience of being able to see a bedroom from the entryway, calling it an "architectural incentive to immorality.") But "French flats" had taken fashionable hold in the city, brought in excellent rents, and suited citizens who worked but didn't keep servants, as was the case for a growing population. The city itself was newly expanded, heightened, and connected; the Brooklyn Bridge opened in 1883, the Statue of Liberty was dedicated in 1886, and the five boroughs were incorporated in 1898. Each morning, as Miss Tarbell walked from her stately brick Greenwich Village building uptown and across Madison Square to take up yesterday's work, she was surrounded by a city in a state of high-speed evolution.

\* \* \*

THE MAGAZINE NOW MOVED FROM survival mode to taking on a larger, more global, and more urgent role. "The war had done something to

*McClure's* as well as to me," Miss Tarbell put it. Its character had been wholesomely entertaining, as she wrote, "an ambition which it must be admitted opened the pages occasionally to the cheap, though it rarely excluded the fine." Its agenda shifted, with crucial consequences, following 1898 and the Spanish-American War, when war reports jostled alongside articles about scientific marvels and illustrated, futuristic fiction; in the same year, H. G. Wells's *The War of the Worlds* was serialized in *The Cosmopolitan*.

In *McClure's,* the popular and the political converged. Through 1899, *McClure's* dwelled on the feats of Admiral Dewey in the Philippines and Mediterranean, ranged from the mines of Cornwall to the Nile, included illustrations of the Dreyfus Trial in Paris, featured a short piece on "The Origin of the Sun and Planets," and purveyed short stories of adventure and romance. *McClure's* itself "was a citizen and wanted to do a citizen's part," she wrote. "Having tasted blood, it could no longer be content with being merely attractive."

McClure's omnivorous editorial eye, with the quiet dedication of Phillips and Miss Tarbell and an ever-enlarging circle of writers who blew through the office, meant circulation rose quickly through 1899, when it was at about 360,000 readers per month, or well over the entire population of Washington, D.C., neck and neck with *Munsey's*. As the nineteenth century drew to a close, *McClure's* was determined not only to report on the world they inhabited, but to change it, too.

# 9

# Facts Properly Told

When he joined the staff of *McClure's* in 1897, Ray Stannard Baker brought a new kind of presence: that of a cheerful, prolific midwestern newspaperman. He started out as the *Chicago News-Record's* least discriminating reporter, covering murders and fires, galas and the opera, churning out three to four thousand words per day. Baker would always yearn to publish a novel, but instead he turned to journalism, pasting above his desk lines from one of his favorite books, *Leaves of Grass*:

And I say that genius need never more be turned to romances,
(For facts properly told, how mean appear all romances)

Ray Baker grew up, like Theodore Roosevelt, believing in the value of a strenuous life. His father, Joseph Stannard Baker (known as Stannard), had been recruited as a spy during the Civil War and wound up commanding a Union battalion. After the war he settled in Lansing, Michigan, and married the social, churchgoing Alice Potter. Ray was the first of their six sons, born April 17, 1870. Five years later, the family moved to rural Wisconsin, where Stannard oversaw the interests of a logging speculator.

St. Croix Falls was a tiny settlement on a tributary of the Mississippi, home to about two hundred people, where French was as commonly spoken as English and many of their neighbors were, in Baker's words, "half Indian and half river-driver." Young Ray grew up fascinated by untamed landscapes and compelled to seek them out. Later, in the crises that arose in his life, he would seek out a rugged, uninhabited place as an escape.

The Bakers believed in a stern and vengeful God. Stannard framed his hikes with the boys as an opportunity to "walk the devil out of the children," but he also had a secret love of a good tale. Stannard and Alice filled the house with books that strayed from what might be expected for a Calvinist household into the romantic and fantastic: Norse legends, Shakespeare, *Uncle Tom's Cabin, 20,000 Leagues Under the Sea,* and subscriptions to *Harper's* and *The Atlantic.* When Stannard read from the Bible, he made the fearful Old Testament stories so vivid his sons clamored for more. Even the walls of their privy were plastered with high-minded insulation: pages from *Scribner's Monthly* and the *Pioneer Press.*

Early on, Ray had a sense that he was an observer and interpreter of larger-than-life men. His father was his first specimen of this breed, a man too original for what Ray later called "this age of machinery in social organization as well as in industry." His children attended the St. Croix Falls schoolhouse, but Stannard set a second curriculum for them: butter making, hog butchering, fishing, fossil and mineral collecting, typesetting and printing, and dominoes. Stannard was also hard of hearing, and on his business trips upcountry, he took Ray along to be his ears. They grew used to Chippewa camps where winter moccasins could be bought, and the cabins of Scandinavian settlers who had little English. "I know you pioneers!" Ray later wrote; "I have eaten your bacon and beans. I have sloshed at daylight down your wet trails, and returned at dusk through your uncut forests. . . . I was never one of you, but I knew you and I shall never forget you." Acting as his father's interpreter, he had started assembling a journalist's skill set without knowing it.

Ray Baker left St. Croix Falls for Michigan Agricultural College in Lansing, where he was an indifferent student and lived uncomfortably. Stannard could well afford to send regular checks, but he wanted Ray to build character by earning his tuition and keep. For the first time, Ray resented the patriarch. One professor gave real meaning to the place, botanist Dr. William Beal, whose subtle, critical mind became Baker's touchstone for how to study the shape of things. In Dr. Beal's laboratory, under the rather sententious rule of a scientist intent on turning out trained investigators, Baker absorbed the maxims that governed his work henceforth. "An eye trained to see is valuable in any kind of business," Dr. Beal once wrote on his blackboard.

Like Ida Tarbell, Baker tumbled into a fascination with the compound microscope; the first article he submitted to a national publication—the children's magazine *St. Nicholas*—was about single-celled organisms. It was rejected, but the botanist's way of seeing stuck.

In January 1892, after graduation and a temporary return home, he started studying law at the University of Michigan at Ann Arbor. More captivating than his law classes was a newly created journalism workshop, "Rapid Writing." Though he dreaded Stannard's disapproval of such an unstable trade, he decided that "it was writing or nothing for me." In June, Baker had had enough, and he took the train for Chicago. To his family and anyone else who asked, he claimed to be seeking a summer job in a law firm, but he hoped to break into newspapers.

At twenty-two, Ray Baker was handsome but not fully aware of it, just under six feet tall, with blue eyes shielded by spectacles, brown hair, a thick mustache, and a cleft chin. Because of a slight spinal asymmetry, one shoulder hung slightly lower than the other. On his rumbling journey on the sleeper train into Chicago, the novelty of his deception kept him awake. Upon arrival he bought a newspaper, then found a rooming house for three dollars a week.

In the afternoon he went directly to the offices of the most widely distributed morning paper in town, the *Chicago News-Record,* to ask for a job. "My ignorance of the newspaper world," he remembered later, "was equalled only by my interest in it." The formidable *News-Record* was independent in politics and sympathetic to labor, and seemed apart from the sensational journalism that had begun to characterize New York's papers.

When he cheerfully presented his Michigan Agricultural College diploma, the expression on the editor's face made Baker realize he had marked himself more as an object of amusement than a fellow soldier in the trenches of great reporting. The paper was already overrun by hungry graduates seeking work, assuming that there would be plenty to go around because of the World's Fair season. But the city editor, perhaps sensing that Baker was at least sober and earnest, gave him a chance. He told Baker there were no positions open but that he was welcome to wait around the city room in case an assignment came up.

For weeks Baker worked as a stringer, sporadically writing up weddings for the society pages. He was paid meagerly—he took his "string" of newsprint to the payroll desk each week, to be paid by the inch. He lived off heaps of ten-cent potato salad from the city's hash houses and pawned his silver watch to stave off eviction. When he wrote to his father confessing his new situation and describing the work, Stannard replied with surprising equanimity: he exhorted Ray to hang on, comparing him to a boy tasked with riding a reluctant colt.

On free afternoons, he returned to the *Record*'s city room to pitch lighter stories—"glimpses, street scenes, common little incidents of the daily life of a great city, which could be treated more or less humorously." When he managed to catch stray assignments, they were sometimes the most gruesome to be reported that day, and he composed each article with as much hard detail as he could gather at the scene: "After she had fallen dead with three gaping wounds in her body, the infuriated man still [not] satisfied with his bloody work, stooped and crushed the woman's skull with heavy blows from the butt of his revolver. A baby lying on the mother's breast fell from her relaxing arms when the first shot was fired and fell into the gutter, which contained several inches of water, and narrowly escaped drowning," read a bulletin in late August. Baker was trained to produce an unflinching, on-the-ground perspective for the city pages. He had a stroke of luck when he covered a restaurant workers' strike for four consecutive days, when the regular who "did" labor happened to be out. By early autumn he was hired as a staff reporter.

At the *News-Record,* Baker was daily immersed in the surfeit of crime, homelessness, and labor conflict in the city around him. If there was another city in America that was grand and sinister enough to rival New York City, it was here. The Chicago that Baker navigated had been transformed in the two preceding decades. The great fire of October 8, 1871, had destroyed its center and led to expansive redevelopment. Its population had grown to over 1.2 million, second only to New York, which had about 1.8 million. Baker wrote about soup kitchens, hungry lines of men, and flophouses where many spent nights marginally warmer than on the street. He took notes at meetings of unions, congregations, and the new settlement houses.

Chicago, for Baker, held "all the evils that plagued the body politic." Many working Chicagoans had scrimped before the Panic of 1893; now desperation crept through the streets. Even those with a reliable trade confronted privations and despair. A cigar maker who earned five dollars a week was asked how he supported his wife and three children; "I don't live," he said. "I am literally starving. We get meat once a week, and the rest of the week we have dry bread and black coffee." In New York, Rahel Golub, eleven-year-old daughter of a Russian Jewish tailor, asked her father, "[D]oes everybody in America live like this? Go to work early, come home late, eat and go to sleep? And then the next day again work, eat, and sleep?"

With its clean white stucco, imposing domes, spires, and promenades illuminated by blazing electric lamps, the White City on the shores of Lake Michigan—the grounds for the World's Fair, or Columbian Exposition—announced the renaissance of a place that had recently lain buried under a cloud of ash. Chicagoans hoped the fair would bring the city a reputation for culture and modernity rather than the more uncouth image it had at the end of the Gilded Age: for industrial reek, corruption, and violent crime. The inventions unveiled at the fair worked toward that end, with the dishwasher, fluorescent light bulbs, Pabst Blue Ribbon beer, and Ferris wheel on display for the first time.

Despite the potential for debauchery along Chicago's late-night beat, Baker led a wholesome life. He never completely shook off his regimented, rural childhood, or sought to. He hoped to marry Jessie Beal, daughter of his old professor, but needed at least one substantial promotion before he could support a wife. He still counted his father as his closest friend and correspondent, and was stung by a suggestion from Stannard that many newspapermen went no further in their careers than "the plateau of mediocrity." Hoping to make a quick fortune and prove him wrong, Baker and a colleague schemed to write a commercial novel together, a Horatio Alger–esque tale they submitted to just one publisher, Harper & Brothers. It was quickly, impersonally rejected. Still he was a relentlessly upbeat presence in the noisy, smoky city room, where a colleague once told him, "I wish I could feel as much interest in anything in this world as you apparently do in everything."

* * *

WHEN *McCLURE'S* LAUNCHED IN JUNE 1893, Baker was one of its early and enthusiastic readers. The magazine, he wrote, was "fresh and strong and living in a stodgy literary world," with articles "not merely about people . . . but the people seemed to be there in person, alive and talking." *McClure's* filled a void for readers like Baker—twenty-something, educated, raised on an older generation of magazines and eager to find a bold and contemporary equivalent. Even before the magazine gave him work to do, *McClure's* granted Baker a sense of belonging and intellectual companionship.

Then, in the spring of 1894, an unpromising newspaper assignment changed the young reporter's life and work when he was sent to cover an outlandish mass demonstration. A prosperous businessman, Jacob Coxey, planned to march a crowd of twenty thousand unemployed men from northeastern Ohio to Washington, D.C., aiming to arrive on May Day and present a petition to Congress demanding a federal jobs program. It was a stunt on a grand scale, and newspaper editors throughout the Midwest felt compelled to send their junior men to see if Coxey was a crank or a man of action.

At first, there was a circuslike atmosphere to Coxey's Army, as it was soon nicknamed. This was largely conjured by Coxey's buckskin-sheathed, fur-caped, sombrero-wearing partner, Carl Browne. An enigmatic Califor-nian, Browne was, in the words of another journalist covering the move-ment, "a great, big strong fellow with a hearty bass voice, part fakir, part religionist, part Wild West cowboy, and withal a natural leader of men." Despite Browne's showmanship, Baker assumed Coxey, a mild-mannered, round-shouldered churchgoer, was doomed to fail. Surely the marchers would begin to disagree among themselves, or they would be attacked by some state militia or Pinkerton men pursuing a bounty. Or maybe they would starve. From Baker's frugal Presbyterian perspective, there was some-thing repulsive about the jobless hordes. "Bums, tramps! Why didn't they get out and hustle?" he wondered privately. But, intending to keep his job, he joined the ragtag gathering and dutifully telegraphed notes back to the *News-Record*.

He was not immune to the picaresque, and he took pleasure in every eccentric detail of Coxey's campaign. When Coxey's Army began its march, Browne rode ahead in a procession that included a standard-bearer and trumpeter. Coxey's teenaged son wore a blue-and-gray uniform represent-ing unity; in a coach, Coxey, his wife, and their youngest son—christened Legal Tender Coxey—rode alongside the men all the way to Washington. Three or four hundred men formed the kernel of the crowd. They came from all over the Midwest and were welcomed into the march with hot cof-fee, bread, and roast ham. They sang and flew banners, and were escorted by commissary wagons bearing the sign SELL WHAT YOU HAVE AND GIVE TO THE POOR. At night, they slept "spoon fashion" in their tents to keep warm. At each stop, the army seemed to grow in numbers. Farmers and workingmen joined, protesting the fact that they could not afford to buy or rent land, or find a job that would support their families.

Baker was confounded at the absence of "tramps" and "vagabonds" among the growing horde. The marchers wanted jobs rather than a radical redistribution of wealth: they were not revolutionaries. Even more surpris-ing was that towns tended to embrace the cheery crowd. On May Day, Coxey and his men reached the Capitol steps, as planned. Amid the crowds lining the streets and cheering for the ragged army, police officers came forward and arrested Coxey before he could address the people or present his petition. Along with many of the marchers, who panicked as they tried to dissipate in the unfamiliar streets of Washington, Baker wound up in jail that night, exhausted and transformed.

The two-month assignment remade Baker's sense of America. He returned to Chicago deeply stirred, his notebook full. He wrote, "I had seen groups of people, ancient citizens, like the Amish and the Mennonites of Pennsylvania, whom I had never heard of before. I had had glimpses of the large population of foreigners in the mines and factories of Ohio and western Pennsylvania, where a great strike was in progress. I had also seen, for the first time, something of the Old South with its distressful Negro population. . . . I had even caught sight of President Cleveland driving down Pennsylvania Avenue behind a spanking pair of horses."

The demonstration of a common cause across far-flung communities had fired his imagination. Other writers observed its importance, too; among them was L. Frank Baum, who was rumored to be inspired by Coxey's march as he drafted Dorothy's hopeful trek to the Emerald City in *The Wonderful Wizard of Oz* (1900). Whether Baker would make a great novel out of it, or put that aside and once again embed himself in the heart of American unrest for the newspapers, was yet to be seen.

\* \* \*

**WHILE THE MARCH TO WASHINGTON** gave Baker closer knowledge of America's discontents, the desperation of the Pullman Strike marked him even more deeply. George Pullman's company town, designed by World's Fair architect S. S. Beman and built in the 1880s on the South Side of Chicago, billed itself as a "town from which all that is ugly, discordant, and demoralizing is eliminated." The houses were roomy, and they had indoor plumbing.

The town's morals were designed as carefully as its buildings. Liquor was restricted to one location, the bar of the Pullman-run hotel, but served only to visitors. Pullman's theater had twice-monthly shows, which were vetted for propriety and carefully selected by a company representative. Rents were not especially cheap, but Pullman and Beman were proud that their town not only met their workers' needs but brought them into a cleaner, more modern mode of living.

When the Panic of 1893 threw increasing numbers of businesses into bankruptcy, demand for Pullman cars crashed. Consequently, Pullman workers were increasingly transferred from salaried pay to piecework: they were paid less, but their rents remained the same. The company deducted workers' rent from their pay, and as the Panic settled in, they started to receive ludicrously small pay slips, forcing Pullman families to choose between food and fuel, or go without enough of either.

When Baker got to Pullman in May 1894, he learned that a strike was imminent. Its leader was Eugene Victor Debs, the young head of the American Railway Union. Debs seemed an unlikely revolutionary. He was gentle, almost awkward in his sensitivity, but Baker also noted his "gift of explosive profanity" and utter devotion to the cause. When he was offered a more lucrative job outside the union, Debs responded, "If I rise, it will be *with* the ranks, not *from* them"—a fitting pronouncement from the man who would become the five-time presidential candidate for the Socialist Party and cofounder of the Industrial Workers of the World. In Pullman he had mustered three thousand men to walk off the job in protest through the streets of the model town. On the scale of strikes at that time, this action was notable more for its impact than its size. American unions had grown stronger over the preceding generation; in the year 1880, there were as many strikes and lockouts as in the previous 140 years combined. Still, striking was dangerous—it was close to an invitation to violence, and many were desperate enough to accept any wage, even if it meant siding against fellow workers. Another railroad speculator, Jay Gould, claimed, "I can hire one half of the work class to kill the other half."

To the rest of the country, the strike was more than inconvenient—it meant terror. In the spring of 1894, Americans were riveted by the news of anarchist attacks in London, Rome, Barcelona, and especially Paris. Tourists avoided Paris that year, and the wealthy grew cagey about frequenting restaurants or shops that were too ostentatious. Everyone was on edge, especially in a crowd: one night at the theater, after being surprised by a loud thump from backstage, the audience fled in a panic, crying *"Les anarchistes! Une bombe!"* It turned out to be a piece of scenery that had fallen over. And then, on June 24, 1894, while riding in an open-topped carriage, President Marie François Carnot of France was stabbed to death by an anarchist. American readers were electrified and saw parallels with the discontent making news on their own shores.

The media drew a straight line between the Pullman workers' mutiny and a total tearing down of the established power structure. On July 2, 1894, United States attorney general Richard Olney obtained an injunction ordering the strikers back to work for blocking the mail service—an offense the strikers had scrupulously avoided. The following day, President Cleveland ordered U.S. troops into Chicago; they arrived on July 4, giving an ominous cast to the holiday, which soon erupted into open fighting. Suddenly, "[all] southern Chicago seemed afire," Baker wrote. Freight trains were set alight by strikers and unemployed men from all over the city who had joined the protest. Battles erupted between union members and the U.S. Army, between strikers and the police, and between sympathizers and the state militia.

Baker, writing from the front lines, was deeply conflicted about where his sympathies should lie. On the one hand, he saw a rich employer starving workers and their families. On the other hand, mob justice didn't have a place in his vision of a civilized society. On July 8, his sense of distance from the issue vanished at a railroad junction besieged by strikers in Hammond, Indiana. Baker's first bulletin described the tracks "strewn with overturned freight cars, battered and burned coaches, twisted rails and broken switches." He saw men heaving a Pullman car to tip it over. A moment later a shot rang out, and a man next to Baker was hit: he "slumped to the ground, and I saw blood spurt from his breast." Soldiers were approaching, rifles at the ready. The mob scattered, howling. The dead man, Baker learned, had been an onlooker who didn't belong to the union or work for Pullman at all. The battle broke the strike, but thirty-four people were killed.

Baker decided to spotlight the human stories of the strike, especially the innocent strivers who had been betrayed by the system. He returned to Pullman and began to interview the workmen and their families. There was a Swedish family of six who hardly spoke any English and relied completely on the relief committee to live day to day. Then a Greek family who weren't able to heat their apartment because Pullman company watchmen had been posted around the town dump, forbidding strikers or their wives from gathering anything that might be used as fuel.

His project had a startling result. Readers, moved by the plight of Baker's subjects, sent checks and bills for the Pullman families to the *Record*'s office. "I can recall, to this day," Baker remarked in his memoirs, "the wave of intense pleasure, complete satisfaction, that swept over me." His words had made a tangible difference. Deciding to deliver some relief, Baker spent the money himself: on bulk quantities of coffee, tea, sugar, salt pork, and beans. He rented a truck and drove everything to the Swedish family's doorstep, then to the Greeks' and beyond. The grim Dickensian scene turned merry: "What crowds gathered, and followed, and cheered! What thanks were showered upon us!"

After a summer in court, the American Railway Union was beaten and Debs spent a month in prison. But the ferocity of the strike had, for a brief time, shaken industrialists and inspired workers across the nation. For Baker, it drove home his deepest dilemma as a newspaper writer: "[E]vents would not stand still and wait to be thoroughly examined and written about: they rolled majestically onward, absorbing and terrifying, confused and complicated. What was a man to do?"

\* \* \*

**AFTER MARCHING WITH COXEY'S ARMY** and witnessing the bloodshed of the Pullman Strike, Baker grasped his vocation tighter than ever. He found his youthful interest in journalism confirmed by intense experience. It was, he decided, a worthwhile life's work. He began toying with the idea of taking over a newspaper of his own, perhaps in some small town, but this was in reality a far-fetched scheme: "My soaring fancies . . . crashed upon the rock of my poverty," he wrote.

His job gave him a platform of sorts, but increasingly it began to feel like a narrow one. Kept to a telegram-like brevity in his newspaper articles, Baker itched for expansiveness, to maximize his chronicling of society rather than be trimmed back by judicious editors. He began to fill a journal with vignettes and impressions and kept the habit for the rest of his life. Those sketchbooks became his diary and storehouse of literary material, some copied scraps from other books and papers, and also memories from long before that suddenly occurred to him and demanded to be set down. He hoped to clarify his role in the world. "I am trying, since I am the only person I have to deal with when I write, to *realize* myself."

He still saw himself on the same wavelength as that daring newcomer on the newsstand, *McClure's*. Ida Tarbell's series on Lincoln had fascinated Baker, and he dared himself to write to her suggesting a piece about his uncle, Lieutenant L. B. Baker, who had commanded the party that captured John Wilkes Booth. Miss Tarbell herself replied, encouraging Baker to work up a draft. The article was accepted for publication in the May 1897 issue of *McClure's*, sandwiched between stories by Arthur Conan Doyle and Robert Louis Stevenson.

The first notice that his life might change came just before the article's publication, when Baker received a letter from S. S. McClure. "Would it be possible for you to come on to New York to see us?" It was a surreally wonderful question—elevated even higher when Phillips sent along a rail pass to cover the trip. McClure's invitation didn't specifically mention a job, but Baker was delirious with joy anyway. It was his first time in New York. His anticipation mounted as the train passed through the Mohawk Valley and along the Hudson River, and as he checked in to the Continental Hotel on Twentieth Street and Broadway. Baker arrived at the *McClure's* offices to find that "Mr. McClure had suddenly dashed off to Europe, as was his custom." Nevertheless, the visit introduced him to a "marvelous new world." Miss Tarbell, Phillips, and art director Jaccaci took him out to lunch at their usual haunt, the private dining room at the old Ashland

House, a stately hotel-restaurant near Madison Square. Baker felt within their company "a quality of enthusiasm and intellectual interest I had never before encountered. . . . I was in the most stimulating, yes intoxicating, editorial atmosphere then existent in America—or anywhere else." He kept quiet, but Miss Tarbell noticed and was glad when he burst into unguarded laughter. They had a proposition for him: Baker should move to New York and write features for them.

It was the culmination of a strange season for Baker. It had been more than two years since Pullman, and his newspaper work felt increasingly mundane. Sweeping questions about life and writing came into focus for him after he finally married Jessie Beal in 1896. They had known each other since the age of fifteen; both were now twenty-six. Their first child came quickly, and the growing needs of his family made Baker see the world through a mercenary lens. After his daughter's birth, he noted, "Our baby herself, who was blue-eyed and fat and happy—altogether quite satisfactory—had cost me, at the lowest calculation, about seventy thousand words, a small volume like Emerson's essays." The offer to join *McClure's* left him ecstatic, and torn. He decided to persevere where he was, though his salary stagnated and he yearned for more of the sparkling camaraderie he had tasted at *McClure's*.

Battling the twin specters of debt and Stannard's "plateau of mediocrity," Baker peppered his editors at the *Record* with ideas. Once in a while they allowed him to publish a pseudonymous letter or editorial, but his frustration mounted. By early 1898, Baker was persuaded that the benefits of trying a new life in the New York magazine world outweighed the risks of leaving Chicago, and he accepted a position at McClure's syndicate with the understanding that he would be writing for the magazine, too. He moved to New York ahead of his family, and in late May he wrote Jessie that his actual job was still somewhat mysterious: "Mr. Phillips says that he is unmethodical and that he can't get anything done as it is because he has so many interruptions," wrote Baker. "In short he wants me, your humble servant to go into the office as a kind of supervising editor and gradually get control of things there so as to let him out and permit him to take a closer interest in the business. . . . I don't altogether understand just what the work is but they assure me that there is a great opportunity for advancement both in position and in salary." He was in the office from nine to six, with a "good long hour for lunch, however, going out with the 'crowd.'"

He first met his editor-in-chief in July of that year, and wrote to his wife, "I've rubbed up against Mr. McClure at last. It would take 10 of these sheets to give any sort of conception of him. He is a perfect cyclone, an electric shock." Over the next several weeks he would amend his description again and again: McClure was "active as a cat," a "hypnotist," and a spider who had Baker tangled in his big gray web.

Despite uneven first impressions, *McClure's* was in many ways an idyllic place to work. Staff writers received generous salaries and Phillips's acute, gentlemanly editing on multiple drafts of their work. Many articles in *McClure's* took weeks, if not months, to be researched and written, and cost between $1,500 to $2,500 in expenses—more than the typical annual salary for writers just starting at the magazine. Compared to how its rivals worked, it was shockingly extravagant, and yet it resulted in a creative and investigative hive, animated by writers who recognized their unique good luck. "[W]hat a boon for a writer!" Baker marveled.

Most pieces were edited three times before they went to press. "We maintained no society of mutual admiration in those good days," said Baker of Ida and their editors. They were blunt with one another, though they also had to be close allies in attempting to subdue McClure's restless enthusiasm. Anyone who joined the staff soon learned that friction was the norm, not the exception, and lulls were not to be trusted. One assistant reported to Miss Tarbell, "Personal gossip in the office seems to be reduced to a minimum. . . . I have actually heard nobody sassed all day long. Of course you know nothing is interesting when everything goes right."

McClure was the central energy—and threat—to the whole endeavor. The magazine office operated in a permanent state of tension between his passionate, unschedulable instincts and the need to turn out a respectable magazine once a month. Ida Tarbell, Phillips, Miss Roseboro, and a rotating staff of assistants had the challenge of balancing McClure's demanding leadership, which was "all intuition and impulse, bursting with nervous energy," pouring forth from "one of the most unorganizable, impatient, and disorderly men I ever knew," wrote Baker. Baker's origin myth of the magazine was that it started when McClure "literally erupted, like a live volcano, with ideas." The editor's frequent travels and spontaneous schemes for new projects—manifested by the dozens of clippings and notes he would eagerly bring out of his pockets by the fistful—dazzled and exhausted his staff. McClure demanded articles on color photography, on Tiffany glass, on Nikola Tesla, and on the horseless carriage. "Everything with him in those days was 'stupendous,'" Baker sighed. And yet, undeniably, often his plans contained "flashes of extraordinary penetration." "A week in the McClure office," editor (and future owner of *The Atlantic Monthly*) Ellery Sedgwick wrote after his brief tenure at *McClure's,* "was the precise reversal of the six busy days described in the first chapter of Genesis . . . From Order came forth Chaos."

Despite the chaos, McClure seemed to see his writers' potential more sharply than they could themselves, and he applied that vision—and his open pocketbook—to those he believed in. "[W]ith all his pokings and proddings the fires he kindled were brighter than any flames his staff could produce without him," Sedgwick admitted. He funded Stephen Crane's tour of Civil War battlefields with the idea that Crane would produce journalism; instead, Crane wrote short stories drawing from the experience and McClure published them. When he read a story by the unknown Jack London in the magazine *The Black Cat,* McClure was immediately excited by London's tales of adventure and sent him a letter: "We are greatly interested in you and want you to feel that you have the warmest kind of friends right here in New York," he began. Disregarding London's youth, inexperience, rage-prone disposition, and struggles with alcoholism, McClure sent London $125 a month—a living wage—for at least five months, on the understanding that London would be writing a novel. "Did I tell you that McClure has bought me?" London wrote in a letter, continuing that the sale had left him "filled with dismay in anticipation." The product, *A Daughter of the Snows,* was "a failure," as London admitted. Despite McClure having to turn it down, and going on to decline future stories that the author similarly admitted were "preposterous, untrue and impossible," London consistently praised *McClure's* as "the best publishers, or magazine editors, in their personal dealings, that I have run across."

\* \* \*

**BAKER MOVED TO NEW YORK** to find that the Spanish-American War had mesmerized the nation and its newspapers. Phillips had summoned him with a peremptory telegram: "Making war number. Good subjects for you. Come Quickly." The June 1898 issue had been about to go to press when McClure decided it should be devoted to the war. Baker reassured his wife that "there is not the slightest chance of my going to Cuba or to any other place where there is any especial danger, so you needn't feel the least worried." In the end, Baker was sent to Cuba for one of his early pieces for the magazine.

The war's effect on Americans and their magazines, according to Baker, was a sudden awakening "to a sense of a swiftly expanding world in which, whether we liked it or not, we should have to play our part." Intervention in Cuba was justified at home through hearty media excitement about America's role as a noble, civilizing force in barbarian lands, as the British Empire was widely seen to be. *McClure's* ran a much-talked-about article, "How the War Began," by war correspondent Stephen Bonsal, that compared Cuba's Spanish rulers to "vultures" hovering over the remains of the *Maine,* and justified the declaration of war as "the only argument which a savage race will heed."

The Philippine-American conflict quickly followed the events in Cuba, again an outright conquest boosted by media attention. Kipling's "The White Man's Burden," subtitled "The United States and the Philippine Islands," was first published in *McClure's* in February 1899 and became a kind of anthem for the nation's new colonial enthusiasm. It urged America to join in the effort to take responsibility for the races who couldn't govern themselves ("Your new-caught sullen peoples, / —Half devil and half child").

English scholar Beatrice Webb, who attended an Independence Day celebration shortly after the start of the war, satirically noted the "unique character" that governed such proceedings in America—"the Americans being the chosen people who had, by their own greatness of soul, *discovered freedom,* and who were now to carry it to other races (notably to the Cubans)."

The attack on the *Maine* rippled through an American society that, despite its strikes and privations, was already engaged in a fervid romance with itself. In 1893, Wellesley professor Katharine Lee Bates had written the lyrics to "America the Beautiful," inspired by the sight of Pikes Peak in Colorado. Three years later, John Philip Sousa penned "The Stars and Stripes Forever."

Magazines leapt to the sales and merchandising opportunities brought by this wave of patriotism. *Youth's Companion* coordinated a nationwide flag day for schoolchildren, and a publicist there, Francis Bellamy—a thirty-five-year-old ex–Baptist minister—spent two hours after dinner one night writing a salute that the students could recite. The Pledge of Allegiance first appeared in print in the September 1892 issue of *Youth's Companion.*

The frontier had long been an essential component of the young nation's idea of itself, and when it ceased to exist, according to the census in 1890, American Manifest Destiny needed to expand its definition. Theodore Roosevelt, who had thrived as a sheriff in the Dakota Badlands, theorized that the Winning of the West had forged a new people—and he now blamed the loss of the frontier on increasing urbanism, materialism, and what he called an "intellectual flabbiness." Roosevelt's was the first generation of American leaders that looked out at other nations for a strange wilderness and empire-building, rather than the western edge of home.

For the first time, *McClure's* pursuit of timely, entertaining material intersected with a weighty political event. In 1898 the magazine—along with every other paper in New York's feverishly competitive press—sent its reporters to shadow the war's most charismatic fighters. Baker went to Oyster Bay, Long Island, to greet Roosevelt on his return from Cuba. The circulation of *McClure's* rose to over 100,000 copies more than the same months of the previous year, and by 1900 it had risen to 370,000 total—beaten only by *Munsey's* among the general-interest monthlies. Demand for war stories surged, and *McClure's* eagerly joined in the simple patriotic fervor for a new and potentially bloody frontier. "Flags were flying everywhere, crowds were clustered around the bulletin boards and the boys were crying the extra 'All about the war' in the sheets," Baker wrote Jessie from a reporting trip in the Midwest. "It was enough to stir even my blood." In New York, the furor was intensified. "Everyone here is war crazy," Baker remarked. "Crowds have been standing all day . . . reading the wildest kind of nonsense." He was swept up in the swell himself: "Spanish rule has always meant cruelty, oppression and corruption and I hope a good thrashing will bring the haughty dons to their sense," he declaimed to his wife. "[The] American eagle screams."

*McClure's* faithfully covered the war, but its reporting faced the challenge of competing with more sensational reading: the newspapers. News and manufactured drama often seemed to blur into each other. Joseph Pulitzer's two-penny Democratic paper the New York *World* was at the peak of its popularity, while William Randolph Hearst, according to Baker, "was rising on the journalistic horizon like an ominous cloud." Pulitzer, a Hungarian immigrant and Civil War veteran, bought the *World* in 1887, and among the innovations that turned the paper into the country's largest-circulation daily were banner headlines, reenactment drawings, pseudoscience, and voyeuristic reports of crime and scandal.

There seemed to be no boundary to what a journalist could allege. The scare quotes and gratuitous melodrama were hallmarks of yellow journalism, named for the *World*'s comic strip "Hogan's Alley," whose main character always wore an oversize yellow nightshirt. Hearst, a Californian mining heir who came to New York by way of Harvard, admired Pulitzer but quickly set his ambitions even higher. After the sinking of the *Maine,* the Hearst papers—without any hard evidence—boldly blamed the Spanish, and American opinions soon demanded action in response. The two publishers' rivalry inflated the war into a circulation battle and a contest for eye-grabbing human interest stories.

Another channel between press and audience opened with the new popularity of the camera. From the wars to the early years of the new century, the camera turned from professional tool to popular diversion, and then to personal image-builder. This in turn provoked withering editorials about the potentially disastrous self-absorption of a new generation, as "The Cynic" wrote in *Town Topics*:

> Click! Click! Click!
> Look at the crowds and the cameras!
> Everybody posing, smirking, attitudinizing!
> Trying to look their best while being photographed,
> Trying to look intellectual unconscious, beautiful!
> Good Lord, what are we coming to?
> Is the world going to be one vast Rogues' Gallery?

Baker saw McClure's ambition as a publisher in a similar light: the urge to be eye-catching and captivating trumped all else, though the detailed, lengthy feature stories possible in a monthly magazine set *McClure's* apart from the outright sensationalism of the dailies. "[I]t was not the evils of politics and business . . . that impressed him most," remarked Baker, "but the excitement and interest and sensation of uncovering a world of unrecognized evils—shocking people!" At times, he thought, McClure's keenest ideas seemed almost cynical: they were the "banal stand-bys of editors who sought large circulations. . . . He told people more about things of which they were already hearing a good deal," Baker wrote.

After his initial few months at *McClure's,* Baker remained baffled by his new Chief. McClure never positively articulated what qualities he sought in a story; "interesting" and "best" were his watchwords, and they seemed to mean whatever would sell without veering into pulp. He freely owned up to the fact that he rarely seized on completely original ideas for his writers. "The proper policy of doing business is never originate if you can imitate. It is my policy. . . . I am so conservative I am rarely willing to perform experiments myself," he would say. Rather than covering brand-new territory, he valued accuracy and timeliness above all else. After all, he wrote, "A marksman who fired before there was any possibility of hitting the objective, or who used up his ammunition for an impossible object, or who fired too late, would accomplish nothing." The unifying element for his disparate collection of ideas and writers was his own opinion of what would sell.

After work, once his family had followed him to New York, Baker took the train home each evening to Bronxville, a small village about fifteen miles north of the office. The suburbs were a welcome balm after each day's fevered work. He covered the military campaigns and domestic unrest at the end of the nineteenth century, and on the train or at his desk at home, after playing with his children, he continued to fill notebooks with personal reflections. Writing purely for himself gave him more patience for journalism, but it also made him reflect on the mistakes and confessions he set down in ink. "I am appalled when I think of the sheer bulk of this self-disclosure," wrote Baker in later life when considering the number of books he had filled—all seventy of them. "Everything I am I have here set down. *So much I wish were different!*"

McClure, by contrast, did not dwell in self-reflection. Propelled by a renewed zeal for empire building, he vaulted into the twentieth century with the secret conviction that one magazine was no longer enough.

# 10

# The Brilliant Mind

I n the summer of 1901, Ida Tarbell stood on the breezy steamer deck and watched the Atlantic swell. She was forty-two. Part of her was surprised to be going to Europe, an extravagant trip just to pitch a magazine story. But McClure was there, shut in a Swiss clinic, and this story could not wait.

By the turn of the century, she wasn't quite famous enough to be stopped on the street, but she was the most senior writer at a heavyweight magazine that had risen from obscurity largely on her shoulders. *McClure's* now had close to 400,000 subscribers, making it one of the most-read magazines in the country. Journalists looked to her technique and persistence as a model; as she told a colleague, "I proceed on the theory that there is nothing about which everything has been done and said." It helped that she had become McClure's confidante, worthy of inventing the position of staff writer—the realizer of his visions. He did not have the sustained focus to research any subject in such depth himself, but they had evolved into a neatly effective symbiotic unit.

Behind Miss Tarbell was New York Harbor and her office at *McClure's;* ahead lay a bumpy train connection to Lausanne, where S. S. and Hattie had promised to meet her. Her present mission was to pitch a series on John D. Rockefeller and Standard Oil. It seemed uncertain that this could be the germ of her next great undertaking: Miss Tarbell was used to writing about conquerors and heroes, not the misdeeds of businessmen. She liked writing about the dead, conjuring bold lines of character from archives and interviews. But *McClure's* needed a big investigative story on corporate trusts, and fast. The trusts were already a subject of outrage in the press, yet *McClure's* was behind the curve.

They needed a subject that already had a direct and personal impact on households across America. At first Phillips proposed a series on steel or sugar. Then Baker wrote from California that oil had been discovered there, and there ought to be a story in it. In January 1901, news filtered in that an unprecedented "gusher" well had been tapped in Spindletop, Texas. The more the *McClure's* staff discussed an oil story, the more it made sense: Standard Oil was the largest and oldest trust of them all, run by an enigmatic tycoon, John D. Rockefeller. By the turn of the century, he controlled more than 80 percent of oil production and sales in America.

For Miss Tarbell, the topic evoked unwelcome emotions. Her memory of her father's bankruptcy when she was fifteen was still fresh. Franklin Tarbell regularly talked of Rockefeller and his company as the "Cleveland ogre" and "the great Anaconda." Newspaper cartoons commonly used snakes or octopi to represent the big trusts, sometimes wearing top hats and always extending tentacles farther than any man could reach. Miss Tarbell tried to write what bankruptcy had truly felt like, before the newspaper cartoons had come about: "a big hand reached out from nobody knew where, to steal their conquest and throttle their future," she began. "[A] blow between the eyes," she called it.

She had been fifteen when it happened, and the shame still rankled. It had even inspired her only attempt at writing a novel—she wanted to parse the crisis, to "catch it, fix it," and portray the human catastrophe in a way outsiders could understand. She'd been too critical of her own fiction to show it to anyone, but *McClure's* offered another channel to tell the story. At Phillips's request, in spring 1901 Miss Tarbell wrote an outline for a series of articles, though the process made her balk. What if, after all, the history of the petroleum industry was uninteresting to readers who hadn't grown up within it? The other risk was that her research would reveal John D. Rockefeller as a natural and highly organized entrepreneur who had earned every bit of his immense harvest of wealth and power. In late April she wrote to Baker, "I shy a little at the subject. I do not see how it could be made a McClure article." The staff awaited McClure's judgment. Months passed; they hadn't reckoned on the "McClure method." He wanted to mull it over, and he boarded a steamship bound for a European rest cure without giving an answer.

Around *McClure's,* journalism and art were grappling with the question of how to live in an age of dehumanizing industry. Booth Tarkington, who was to become a Pulitzer-winning novelist, was discovered by Viola Roseboro in the *McClure's* slush barrel. In his fiction, he described a "deteriorating social order caused by urbanization and industrialization" and contrasted it critically with the Indiana of his youth. In his version of events, "Not quite so long ago as a generation, there was no panting giant here, no heaving, grimy city; there was but a pleasant big town of neighborly people. . . . No one was very rich; few were very poor; the air was clean, and there was time to live." Powerful corporations had risen up thanks to the untrammeled free play of market forces, but there was widespread discontent and puzzlement about the consequences. Corporate stakeholders profited wildly, while small-scale oil refiners, ice manufacturers, beef packagers, and others were shut out of the competition. Social Darwinism did not seem to be working for the common good.

In Frank Norris's novel *The Octopus,* published in 1901, a frontiersman confronts this issue when his land is about to be seized by the railroad company: "Forces, conditions, laws of supply and demand—were these then the enemies, after all?" By the end of the novel, Norris's narrator concluded that "*Nature* was, then, a gigantic engine, a vast Cyclopean power, huge, terrible, a leviathan with a heart of steel." Miss Tarbell knew Frank Norris from the office; *McClure's* had published his stories since 1898. She kept his conclusion in mind as she contemplated writing about another vast Cyclopean power.

Miss Tarbell had made a certain kind of *McClure's* story famous: the deeply researched, "documented narrative" that told a story "so people would read it." Her colleagues knew that if anyone could turn a big-business profile into a page-turner, it was she. And also, though it went unspoken, they may have liked the idea of seeing the unflappable Ida Tarbell confront her childhood demons.

The reason she had to seek out her editor-in-chief a continent away, however, was that he was wrestling demons of his own.

\* \* \*

**THE POPULARITY OF THE MAGAZINE** after its launch in 1893 shocked the competition, and McClure reveled in it. Those early days were some of his best. The farsighted, high-quality science coverage he commissioned had even forged an unexpected truce with Professor Hurd, who in early 1896 sent a sincere note of appreciation for a recent *McClure's* profile of prodigious natural scientist Louis Agassiz. But even that feat seemed diminished as McClure confronted a worrisome development: the readily rebounding energy of his college days was turning traitorous and unreliable.

As the nineteenth century ebbed, McClure seemed to lose something with it. Doctors prescribed rest, which went against his nature. He traced the beginnings of his frailty to the days of building the syndicate, even before the magazine. "From 1890 on," he wrote, "I was overcome more and more often by periods of complete nervous exhaustion, when I had to get out of my office and out of New York City, when I felt for my business the repulsion that a seasick man feels toward the food he most enjoys in health." Hattie, whose own health was delicate, was nevertheless poised to respond to his needs; she was loving, good-humored, and took comfort in her Christian faith, but it must have been arduous work.

Just as the June 1896 issue of *McClure's* marked the magazine's third anniversary, its editor-in-chief found himself inexplicably depressed. Travel was the most reliable panacea. In railcars he could envision the future; on steamer decks he could see his past in perspective; and in hotel bathtubs his rising spirits burst out of his frame and into loud, atonal song. As Phillips and Miss Tarbell ensured steady magazine production, he took a whirl-wind trip on horseback through the Middle East and briefly moved his fam-ily to the French resort town of Beuzeval. It was an extravagant year, but McClure was seeking resurrection rather than luxury. He was on a quest to banish the funks that overtook him at least once a year, for weeks at a time.

Miss Tarbell and her colleagues grew used to long spells without their Chief. When he returned, McClure was simultaneously unbearable and gal-vanizing. First, flush with energy, he would impose new ideas on the office, assigning new stories, swiping edits from Phillips's desk and scribbling his own sweeping changes, hotly debating new fiction with Miss Roseboro, and booking steamer tickets to London to scout new talent. "Everyone about him caught fire," noted a later staffer, "and he would inflame the intelligence of his staff into molten excitement. The mood would be too hot to last but would bring results." Arranging his exit was one of the few tasks every staff member was glad to take on. A rising journalist who spent time at *McClure's*, Mark Sullivan, remarked, "it is no wonder McClure's associates and editors took on toward him a protective manner of coldness, and were only warm to him on the occasions—they were, happily for his staff, frequent—when he came to the office at nine in the morning to announce that he was sail-ing for Europe at twelve. Facilitation of the hurried getting of tickets and other preparations for departure was about the only function in which Mc-Clure's associates served him with unqualified cheerfulness." One of Mc-Clure's quixotic requirements for his voyages was a cache of fresh milk that would last as his only sustenance while aboard, a necessity that sent staffers scrambling—in the age of glass bottles and no mechanical refrigeration, it meant McClure never traveled light.

His agitation was not driven by any particular pressing threat, as the magazine now dominated former titans of the media world. It was mainly fueled by his desperation to reinvigorate himself. In the process, he further revealed his knack for discovering men whose names and legacies would eventually outshine his own; he also rushed into contracts that could have foundered his already precarious financial stability.

In the spring of 1897, McClure poached a *Scribner's* business manager,

Frank Nelson Doubleday, to help direct a new books department, Doubleday & McClure. Walter Hines Page, an editor at *The Atlantic Monthly,* also joined the venture, which was embarking on an encyclopedia project that would never come to fruition. Doubleday had a dangerous personality type, at least when drawn into proximity with McClure's. He was, Curtis Brady noted, "attractive and agreeable . . . whenever he wanted to turn it on." His close friend Kipling gave him the nickname "Effendi" (Ottoman "Lord" or "Master"), a play on his initials, but the kingly honorific suited him.

McClure's faith in the much-trumpeted new man vanished from the office as quickly as it had appeared. And Doubleday himself was never entirely comfortable in partnership with McClure, as he said of the Chief, "He was erratic to the last degree, and to be his partner was something like sitting on the top of a volcano with a very hot interior." Privately, Doubleday wondered about the wisdom of McClure's "very warm heart," which hustled him into supporting writers who were of little to no benefit to the magazine.

Doubleday's natural grasp at authority chafed McClure, who decided to separate from him and Page by September 1899. Effendi agreed to leave when McClure asked, cleverly negotiating to keep the rights to the Doubleday & McClure Co. catalog, which laid the foundation of his considerable success and the publishing house that still bears his name.

Miss Tarbell, meanwhile, was aggrieved; she had welcomed Doubleday's rationality. The news that McClure had separated from him reached her when she was away, recuperating from Lincoln-induced exhaustion at a sanitarium outside the city. Her note after receiving the news let the Chief know she was daunted by the newly slimmed-down staff and what the pressures might do to him. She wrote him, "I do not like to see Mr Doubleday and Mr. Page go. They are strong men in their way and would relieve you and Mr Phillips of much heavy care."

That same year, McClure made a bid to expand the magazine into a media company with a roster of venerable properties. In 1899, Harper & Brothers was the largest publisher in America, encompassing a books department as well as four magazines—*Harper's Monthly, Harper's Weekly,*

*Harper's Bazaar,* and *Harper's Round Table.* When the company teetered toward bankruptcy, major shareholder J. P. Morgan offered to sell the whole company to McClure. McClure agreed enthusiastically, as one witness described him, "like the intoxicated rabbit went for the bull-dog." The staff at *McClure's* was decidedly against the merger, as a Harper takeover would decisively change the scope and character of the company. Bringing out a single monthly magazine was complex and chaotic enough. McClure dismissed any objections, but the merger fell through in any case. The staff allowed themselves to feel relief: perhaps now, McClure momentarily sobered, they could get on with their work.

Then, invariably, the cycle began again: after a couple of months of radical scheming McClure was overtaken by anxiety and exhaustion. His symptoms matched up with a prominent medical theory of the time, which cast the human body as an electrical machine; when people expended too much of their nervous energy, the machine collapsed into a state called neurasthenia. Neurologist George Beard coined the term in 1869, seeing it as a direct consequence of a modern life spent in teeming cities. During neurasthenic crises, victims were beset by chronic aches, weight loss, irritability, impotence, insomnia, lethargy, and the blues. Like its elder cousin melancholia, it was a bit of a catch-all, but linked to contemporary life and its demands: "steam power, the periodical press, the telegraph, the sciences, and the mental activity of women," wrote Beard, were prime culprits. Because it was a disease of mental energy, it was a diagnosis generally reserved for the privileged. In these phases, McClure resorted to any remedy that promised to stabilize his disposition. He did rest cures by the sea, in the mountains, at sanitariums. He traveled with increasing desperation, bringing a large entourage on quests to improve his mental state.

It was on these journeys that nefarious new whims and longings began to play on him. As the weather grew warm in June 1899, he took the children, a handful of in-laws, a cook, maid, French governess, and bicycle handler to Europe; this meant twenty-one trunks, a dozen bicycles, and much hand luggage, telescope, and steamer rugs. Just before they left, Hattie needed urgent surgery at Johns Hopkins, where, to address her mysterious chronic pains, she underwent a hysterectomy. McClure left her in the surgeons' capable hands and tasked Miss Tarbell with checking in on his wife from time to time.

For the duration of the steamer trip, he regaled company with stories and, when he could find copies of his magazine or when urgent thoughts crossed his mind, fired critical cables back to Phillips. That would prompt extensive, hair-tearing repentance: "My dear, dear John," the Chief wrote his partner on one such occasion, ". . . I do not understand my Paris letter. I feel utterly different in all respects. . . . I seem to have lost something. I am a mere animal. . . . My poor friend, how I have hurt you. *I do not understand it.*" He explained how he planned to get well again: "Destroy the Paris letter, it was the expression of jangled nerves & a crazy brain. . . . [The cure] is like taking off a leaky roof before putting on a new one, for a while the condition is worse than ever."

Hattie and Miss Tarbell began corresponding, trading notes on McClure's state of mind after he suddenly dashed back to New York without his family. "You must not be over-anxious," urged Miss Tarbell. "I am sure he will be quite himself by Thursday." She cast herself as the family's rock, implacable despite the Chief's instability, hoping this was a temporary crisis.

On this particular trip just before the turn of the century, McClure landed in the stately spa village of Divonne-les-Bains, nestled by the imposing mountain ridges of French-speaking Switzerland. He and Hattie would return to Divonne every year as long as they could afford it, subjecting themselves to intensive regimes of thermal baths, massages, and weight management diets (S. S. always needed to gain, Hattie wanted badly to lose). Their frequent and affectionate letters began to dwell on their neuralgia, digestive trouble, and other symptoms rather than love or work.

The wandering Chief knew it was an unorthodox life for a family man without ready money, but he justified it as the secret ingredient ensuring the special power of *McClure's*. He knew that "if I am too much in the machinery of the office and too close . . . I lose the ability to judge." He couldn't sink his focus too deeply into matters of editing or management, but had to turn his face "towards the world, the activities of the present time." This itinerant life allowed him to "freshen" himself, to fill his mind with a kaleidoscope of sights, sounds, and characters. And indeed, he returned with riches for the magazine. On his 1899 travels, his discoveries included Bram Stoker, author of *Dracula,* and Joseph Conrad, whose *Lord Jim* was published that year (despite Robby McClure deeming *Heart of Darkness* "not very saleable").

In November 1900, McClure took his family to Egypt and hired a king-sized boat to float them ponderously up the Nile. His Knox friend and *McClure's* business manager Albert Brady, en route to join, suddenly took ill and died in Rome, aged thirty-eight. McClure was seized by grief and anxiety. He left his children in the care of a capable nurse, Mary Cloud Bean, and took Hattie with him back to New York. Miss Bean's letters return again and again to her dismay regarding McClure's agitation. "He has at last concluded that the children are better off without his constant presence. . . . I feel sorry for Mrs. McClure every day that I live, and of course I feel intensely sorry for Mr. McClure himself. Whether he will ever permit himself any calm of existence is very much to be doubted." McClure's anxious spells were miserable, not only for himself, but for his entourage—and he always had one, hoping to distract himself from the sinking within. His exuberance sometimes returned without warning. On a later trip, McClure was once seized with such uncontrollable glee that he grasped the arm of a young poet next to him and insisted they run up a nearby hill and roll down it together.

The first really dangerous impulse surfaced a few months after this burdensome Egyptian trip, when McClure was again on a steamer to London. He'd had a cable from his brother Robby, saying Kipling had a new novel and how much should he offer? The novel was *Kim;* McClure intended to buy it in person if he could. After securing the rights, he found himself courting an old acquaintance, Mark Twain. McClure spontaneously pitched a scheme to launch a new magazine edited by Twain—though, McClure assured, "There will, under no circumstances, be anything in the relationship that will cause you the least anxiety or loss of freedom." Just as Twain was about to sign on, the Chief changed his tune. He began peppering Twain with reminders about what a grave responsibility it was to edit a magazine.

The loss of freedom would, after all, be substantial: Twain would need to be in "intimate physical contact with the magazine" for a "considerable part of the year," and to manage everything from paper quality to illustration contracts to advertising. Twain was wily enough to decline, and the plan disintegrated.

In 1901, McClure got the itch again. He wrote Kansas newspaperman and author William Allen White to urge him to come east and run a new magazine under the *McClure's* umbrella. White explained his refusal to a friend: "I would rather live in a country town and be absolutely free to make my own particular damn fool," rather than move to the epicenter of "the wicked"—McClure's New York—as a "court jester." Eventually McClure's underlings began to joke that they should throw a grand dinner for all the prospects he had enticed with an editorship that never came to be. Reporter Samuel Hopkins Adams suggested they hire out Madison Square Garden— then a Beaux Arts–style indoor arena—to hold them all.

Restless once again, McClure fled with Hattie to the mountains of Europe, hoping this time he could finally find peace. But instead work would find him, in the form of Miss Tarbell.

* * *

AT THE END OF THE OCEAN CROSSING and train journey, Ida Tarbell sought McClure at his Lausanne clinic. When he and Hattie emerged it was only to sweep her up and move immediately onward—Vevey, Lucerne, the Italian lakes—with McClure deflecting any conversation about oil in an enervated search for rest. Miss Tarbell finally presented her outline to McClure in the hills of northern Italy. The town of Terme Salsomaggiore is built over wells of briny mineral water, and, as she wrote, among the "mud baths and steam soaks" McClure listened at last. Seizing the day, editor and journalist quickly dried and dressed, and an improved plan was sketched out on the yellow stationery of the Hôtel des Thermes. She took heart from his confidence in her, and in the story. For his part, there was something healing about sitting across a table from Miss Tarbell and envisioning a bold new investigation. He felt ready to work again, and they booked passage home on the same boat.

It was a temporary calm. That summer, the days at *McClure's* felt fractious and discontented. In June 1901, Baker wrote his wife that the office was "a fearful place . . . surrounded by 'temperaments,' with the matter of editorial control up in the air."

McClure's tempestuous visits and emotional tirades, both in person and via telegram, about revitalizing the magazine put the office on edge. Junior editor Bert Boyden was on the front lines of one of these fits of despair. Boyden wrote an exasperated report to Miss Tarbell, who replied: "*He* is a very extraordinary creature. . . . Able methodical people grow on every bush but genius comes once in a generation. . . . You probably will be laid up now and then in a sanatorium recovering from the effort to follow him but that's a small matter if you really get in touch finally with that wonderful brain." She assured him, "The big things which the magazine has done have always come about through these upheavals. Try not to mind." She found herself soothing her colleagues' nerves, trying to make them see that proximity to McClure was uniquely dazzling as well as maddening, and encouraging them to buck up. He had given her more confidence and support than she had expected as she pursued a career, and had assigned stories that were harmonious with her own interests. She was deeply invested in keeping *McClure's* healthy and whole.

Before Miss Tarbell could completely smooth things over, McClure had boarded another steamship for Europe, intending to rest at Divonne once again. More and more, the magazine relied on her faith and diplomacy. Miss Tarbell often doubted her own originality and brilliance, but she had no suspicions about McClure's.

This kind of labor was depleting in a way that writing and reporting had never been. Confronting the uncertainty that the Chief would ever improve, she began to admit to herself that a career at *McClure's* could be as much a Sisyphean boulder as it was a golden egg, that it was in fact both at the same time. Her unending, unrewarded task was calming the storms of the office. She wrote to Hattie, thanking her for a letter on the occasion of her forty-fifth birthday, "How kind it was of you. . . . I am so busy most of the time that I fear I am unfit to be anybody's friend. But you take me as I am and I feel that I can count on your understanding even if I do not have the pleasure of seeing you often or long."

She focused as much as she could on McClure the editor, the brilliant mind, trying to quiet her mind when it drifted to his latest eruption. She began a story that would transform their fortunes and bring her a most unwelcome and unshakable fame.

# 11

## The Gentleman Reporter

B y 1901, McClure should have been coasting into paunchy, laurel-cushioned midlife. Instead, he was troubled, his anxiety feeding on the constant elevation of his vision for *McClure's*. He itched to grasp the present, to report on events in real time, as newspapers did—an impossible task when a magazine took a month to come off press. The people closest to him stood in his way, insisting there was little greatness or money in the newspaper business after Hearst and Pulitzer had had their share. And so McClure decided to bring the best of the newspaper reporting clique under his wing, and sought out a new man. Fresh blood would reinvigorate *McClure's* and consolidate its position as a center of gravity, the best of its class, the essential among all periodicals—at least for the time being.

McClure's search led him to Lincoln Steffens, a newspaperman who had got into the trade late and reluctantly, and had then risen up with startling speed. Thirty-five and widely traveled, Steffens was already a New York media insider. He also had a brash forcefulness to his opinions that may have reminded McClure of himself.

* * *

**JOSEPH LINCOLN STEFFENS WAS BORN** in 1866 to a well-heeled family in Sacramento, California. He grew up a source of worry to his parents, preferring to ramble on his pony than work, and once at the University of California, Berkeley, he drifted away from his studies to experiment with novel writing, fraternity hijinks, romance, and paranormal phenomena.

Spiritualism and thought transference were discussed in serious intellectual circles; in 1884, William James had helped found the American Society for Psychical Research, which included committees on Thought Transference, Hypnotism, Apparitions, and Haunted Houses. Arthur Conan Doyle openly believed in communication with the dead (as well as being acquainted with the fairies who lived in his garden). The main recipient of Steffens's own psychic efforts was an impressionable young woman, Gussie Burgess, who had fallen in love with him and agreed to a secret engagement. Once Steffens finished at Berkeley, he tried a few times to keep in touch with Gussie via thought transference, but new surroundings soon distracted him from old games. He was headed to Berlin, with nebulous plans to read philosophy.

Europe granted him a freedom to explore that hadn't existed in California, where his family was close enough to try to hold him accountable. He duly studied philosophy and ethics at the University of Berlin, then art history at Heidelberg, psychology at Leipzig, and finally half-finished courses at the Sorbonne and the British Museum. He lived by a bordello, lost himself in the Black Forest, spent time at an American artists' colony in Munich, and met a woman with whom he hoped to build a life.

Josephine Bontecou was thirty-five to Steffens's twenty-five—old enough for her remarkable intelligence to have developed shades of cynicism. She had landed in Berlin with her mother, a wealthy American rebuilding her life after a divorce. Josephine was a freethinker and aspiring novelist, and she and Steffens talked openly about everything, including whether marriage was really a good idea. Yes, they were deeply in love, but could she really have a writing career if she were also a wife? After much deliberation, they decided that they couldn't *not* be together. In October 1891, without fanfare, they married.

Happiness was elusive, puzzling them both. Despite long analytic con-versations to try to pinpoint and banish the awkwardness between them, a distance gradually grew. One source of clues is, potentially, Josephine's novel-in-progress, *Letitia Berkeley, A.M.,* which depicted a heroine who struggled to retain a sense of her own identity after falling in love. Letitia, raised by a straitlaced father in a small town, abandons all that she knows and moves to New York to grow acquainted with "real life." There she falls into a sudden passion for a society playboy, allows herself to be seduced, and then moves abroad to a life of guarded independence. The *New York Times* would eventually say of the book, "Perhaps 'Letitia Berkeley' is rather risky at times, and written in a rather pessimistic vein." In her own married life, Josephine toed the line: she attempted to contain her rage against the prevailing cult of virginity and domesticity but gave it free rein in her writing.

Soon, with Steffens finding his father's checks arriving less and less frequently, they decided to move to New York, hoping that stability, money, and literary renown might come to them both. It was October 1892 when Steffens landed at New York Harbor, his wife and mother-in-law in tow. By stepping off the ocean liner and confronting the swarm of Manhattan in the crisp fall air, Steffens was facing up to a reality he dreaded. He needed to make a living. It was a distasteful idea to him, but he resolved to grit his teeth, throw himself into the most lucrative business he could find, and retire as young as possible. He also hoped for his family's support while he found his feet, anxious that his parents' sympathy might be jolted by the news that he had married in secret during his years away. It was perhaps a relief that his imposing father, Joseph, was home in Sacramento, and sent a note rather than coming in person to greet his son in New York.

But when Steffens opened the envelope handed to him after the ship had moored, he found one hundred dollars and the following message:

*My dear son: When you finished school you wanted to go to college.*
*I sent you to Berkeley. When you got through there, you did not care*
*to go into my business; so I sold out. You preferred to continue your*

*studies in Berlin. I let you. After Berlin it was Heidelberg; after that
Leipzig. And after the German universities you wanted to study at the
French universities in Paris. I consented, and after a year with the
French, you had to have half a year of the British Museum in London.
All right. You had that too.*

*By now you must know about all there is to know of the theory of
life, but there's a practical side as well. It's worth knowing. I suggest
that you learn it, and the way to study it, I think, is to stay in New
York and hustle.*

Steffens was furious, then weary. The ground had been pulled out from
beneath his feet. His first thought was to make his father sorry—he would
become a true bête noire, get himself hired as a dock laborer, vanish into a
social class he knew mainly from books.

In lieu of financial support, Joseph Steffens sent letters of introduction to New Yorkers who might be able to help his son find a job. Josephine
had to implore Steffens to forget his pride and use them. It was only after
he'd tried to get hired as a laborer and been roundly rejected that he dedicated himself to the unaccustomed task of looking for white-collar work.
One of his father's letters was addressed to Henry Wright, city editor of
the *New York Evening Post,* who hired Steffens as a reporter.

As he learned the trade, Steffens began to develop a promising interview style. His manner was congenial but not obsequious. Responding to a
timber baron who declined to meet with him with the line, "I don't care for
write-ups," Steffens countered, "I don't propose to write you up . . . I want
to write you down." He had nerve, and a puckish quality that suggested
anyone in his company need not worry about being bored.

Steffens became known on Wall Street as "the gentleman reporter." He
readily agreed to hold long, off-the-record conversations with his subjects,
which sometimes lost him the story but more often charmed them into
sharing more than they had intended. By mid-January 1893, when he had
been at the *Post* only a few weeks, Steffens had already met three former
mayors of New York and J. Pierpont Morgan. He was transferred from the

city desk to the Wall Street beat, and finally to the police beat, which was to him the most exhilarating of all.

In 1845, New York had been the first American city to organize a police force, which was modeled after London's. For most of those years, however, it was recognized as a source of criminal activity itself. Starting in the 1870s, Captain (and later Inspector) Alexander "Clubber" Williams, who amassed a fortune through bribes and protection rackets, was known to tell his underlings, "There is more law in a policeman's nightstick than the Supreme Court."

Who knew that working for a living could be so stimulating? "My present contentment," Steffens wrote to his father while at the *Post*, "is . . . in finding myself an active sharer, a busy part, of the noisy, hurried, over serious life about me in New York. I enjoy this American living, working and running. . . . I revel in the new life of America."

This "new life" was specific to the rapidly developing American metropolis, barely harnessed by the law and looked upon with moral aversion by many. The growth and problems of the city were aptly demonized in *Everybody's Magazine* in 1901, in a screed by the Reverend Percy Stickney Grant of New York: "More horrible than a disease, they [cities] appear like diabolical personalities which subsist on the strength, health, virtue, and noble aspiration produced in the country. A city is a Moloch: the fagots of its fires are human bodies and souls."

Aesthetically, the city's "multitudinous skyscrapers" irritated observers including Henry James, who disliked the way they resembled "extravagant pins in a cushion already overplanted, and stuck in as in the dark, anywhere and anyhow." Steffens embraced it. In New York City, regarded by much of the rest of America as a cesspool of sin seething with unwelcome foreigners, radicals, Jews, and Catholics, a city of grime and new steel, he found a far richer canvas than Berkeley or Berlin. "What I want," Steffens wrote in one of his letters, "is to gain a deeper insight into the heart of my day."

The *Post* where Steffens cut his teeth was run by Edwin Lawrence Godkin, the Irish American journalist who founded *The Nation* in 1865. The

*Post* was socially conservative, disdainful of party politics, and pro-reform, particularly of the city government corruption that was the legacy of William Marcy "Boss" Tweed's Democratic Party machine, the legendary Tammany Hall. At a time when the *Sun*'s editor Charles Anderson Dana, the *World's* Joseph Pulitzer, and William Randolph Hearst of the *Journal* expected daily numbers in the hundreds of thousands, Godkin's *Post* rarely sold more than 20,000 copies. Yet the paper spoke to and for the powerful. "To my generation," wrote William James, "Godkin's was certainly the towering influence in all thought concerning public affairs."

In early 1894, Steffens moved offices to the Lower East Side, directly across from the police headquarters at Mulberry Street—a world away from the home he'd made with Josephine and her mother in quiet Riverdale-on-Hudson. Though the rule of the Irish Five Points gangs was on the wane, the neighborhood was a maze of dissipated sights and whispers. The Anti-Saloon League and Woman's Christian Temperance Union had little impact here, in restaurants and beer halls tucked near the elevated tracks where cops, pickpockets, and Tammany stooges partook side by side.

Steffens's new environs were also experiencing a cultural transformation. While the Irish and Germans had long streamed from the wharves to settle lower Manhattan, waves of newer immigrants created Little Italy on Mulberry Bend, a Russian Jewish quarter (simply labeled "Ghetto" on city maps) around Hester Street, and Chinatown clustered around Pell Street. The expansion of Chinatown itself had slowed since the Chinese Exclusion Act of 1882, but roast pig could still be bought cheaply there, while a Hungarian enclave created "Goulash Row" off East Houston Street, and "Little Syria" dotted with fruit sellers and cafes sprang up on the Lower West Side. The established Kleindeutschland ("Little Germany") radiated from Tompkins Square Park, and the Irish were simply everywhere.

While covering the neighborhood's living and working conditions, Steffens became friendly with the longtime police reporter for the New York *Sun,* the Danish American Jacob Riis, who himself had landed on an immigrant-packed boat in 1870 and was newly famous after the 1890 publication of his photojournalistic book about the Lower East Side, *How the Other Half Lives*. That book had demonstrated the camera's power to open channels to other worlds, in this case enabled by the recent innovation of the flash, which brought to life the darkest corners of overcrowded tenements and alleyways bereft of daylight.

When Theodore Roosevelt was sworn in as police commissioner in May 1895, Steffens gained as much access to the "charging . . . dashing" Roosevelt as he could keep up with. The commissioner, reporter, and photographer developed a mutual affinity through their shared determination to expose the city's lawless actors and wrest a functional justice system into being. Roosevelt began to enforce the Excise Law, forbidding saloons from opening on Sundays and every day between 1 A.M. and sunrise, a rule hitherto ignored by most. He took up a habit of walking the city at night, finding police officers asleep at their posts or engaged in even worse forms of vice. A year after they met, Roosevelt recommended Steffens to the editor of *The Atlantic Monthly* as "a personal friend. . . . He and Mr. Jacob Riis have been the two members of the Press who have most intimately seen almost all that went on here at the Police Department." In the dynamic of their clique, Steffens was a man of quick words and ideas, Roosevelt all energetic action, and Riis the sharp-eyed emissary from the ranks of bootstrapping immigrants.

Riis, whose camera philosophy was to "tell the facts," and Roosevelt, who was so earnest about reform that he did his own rounds in the dead of night to catch policemen slacking, inspired Steffens to report on police corruption. As he combed the city for stories, his forays brought him in touch with a high-profile reformer, the Reverend Charles Henry Parkhurst. Parkhurst had made it his mission to gather evidence of bribery in the police force, and he was engaged on a mission of public denunciation, often from the pulpit, to try to embarrass city leaders into investigating the issue with some muscle. He found police officers in on every sort of game: saloons, opium dens, gambling halls, and brothels. (One of his undercover missions in Manhattan's Tenderloin district inspired a street chant: "Dr. Parkhurst on the floor / playing leapfrog with a whore.")

Together, over the course of 1894, Parkhurst and Steffens uncovered the hard economics of police work. The department received about $5 million from taxpayers every year, but that was supplemented by $8 million from brothels alone, $2 million from saloons, and the unofficial fees charged for promotions within the force. When Roosevelt was appointed police commissioner, Tammany lost its brazen hold on the force. Parkhurst continued to fight organized crime until his death at the age of ninety-one, when he sleepwalked off the roof porch of his seaside home in New Jersey.

Throughout Steffens's career, Roosevelt would be a correspondent and a critic, as well as a wily manipulator who strung the reporter along with the occasional scoop and flattering note. Already, Steffens and Riis regularly debated the chances of Roosevelt running for president. Riis seemed sure that it would happen soon, while Steffens thought it would be a long game. When they asked the commissioner, he recoiled. "Don't you dare ask me that," he hissed. "No friend of mine would ever say a thing like that, you—you—" He finally concluded, "I won't let myself think of it . . . if I do, I will begin to work for it, I'll be careful, calculating, cautious in word and act, and so—I'll beat myself. See?" To Roosevelt, the soldier's or frontiersman's gut instinct was superior to more contrived political maneuvering. Steffens was impressed at his friend's aversion to consciously crafting an image. He would later discover that this in itself was a kind of mask.

As he watched Roosevelt maneuver toward Washington, Steffens realized he wanted a wider arena, too. He took time in the evenings to write feature stories for magazines, enjoying his forays into satire, long profiles, and travel chronicles. He wrote a humorous monologue for *Scribner's,* a business story for a trade magazine, and was offered a commission to travel out to the Klondike. In September 1897, his account from the gold fields, complete with maps and photographs, spread over twelve pages of *McClure's*. It was a classic of the type of story that excited McClure, portraying not only a landscape of snowy, staggering wilderness, but also a reluctant community of prospectors, spiritual seekers, and cynical long-timers. After reading Steffens's evocation of the Klondike, McClure's radar sounded, and he began tracking Steffens as a talent fit for *McClure's*.

Career success did not buoy Steffens's home life. He and Josephine had grown into a very livable companionship, but when her novel was rejected by several publishers, she broke down and left Steffens and Riverdale for a sanatorium in South Carolina with her mother. Steffens further separated himself from them, taking an apartment in Greenwich Village— the shorter commute was an easy justification—and distracted himself in the evenings, either with work or an informal dining club of journalists who called themselves the Cloister.

He was lured away from the police beat and his burgeoning magazine work by a prestigious offer. Henry Wright, the editor who had originally hired Steffens for the *Post*'s city desk, had taken the helm at the *Commercial Advertiser,* New York's oldest newspaper. He took Steffens on as city editor in 1897, but the new man pushed the limits of his post almost immediately. He frustrated the management by treating his department more as a salon than an office, encouraging long afternoon discussions when reporters should have been out getting stories. When hiring his subordinates, Steffens snapped up recent Ivy League graduates whose lack of experience invited chaos and missed deadlines; he ran his department as an incubator for social theorists rather than a market-conscious workplace. Steffens urged his fellow newspapermen to find a sense of deep-seated purpose in their work. "Care like hell!" he used to tell them. "Sit around the bars and drink, and pose, and pretend, all you want to, but in reality, deep down underneath, care like hell."

He believed he was thriving. His editors, meanwhile, murmured their concern behind his back.

\* \* \*

**WHILE STEFFENS WAS STILL AT THE *ADVERTISER*,** McClure became more and more convinced that the younger journalist belonged on the *McClure's* staff. He had built his magazine's circulation on Miss Tarbell's biographies of Napoleon and Lincoln, and now McClure looked to other obvious targets. Jesus Christ topped the list, but McClure also wanted to profile a rising leader of his own time. He had his eye on the man who had just entered the race to become governor of New York; Steffens's closeness to Roosevelt was a valuable asset. McClure commissioned Steffens to write the piece, on a freelance basis, and Steffens eagerly accepted. Boosted by his independence at work, growing reputation as a writer, and the news that Josephine was well enough to come home, Steffens bought a handsome new home for them in midtown Manhattan.

Steffens began the project willingly, but his interviews were cut short when Roosevelt left the country to lead the Rough Riders in Cuba in 1898; the abbreviated text was published as a *McClure's* article in May 1899. Still, McClure was thrilled with Steffens's work. "A jim-dandy," he called it; "a rattling good article. I could read a whole magazine of this kind of material."

McClure deployed his staff to begin the process of making Steffens part of *McClure's*. First, art director Jaccaci invited Steffens to meet, and the two talked long into the night. From that evening on, they were close confidants; Steffens later wrote of the gregarious "Jac," "He could not be a friend; he had to be lover." Steffens quickly grew devoted to Jac, who in turn lobbied for Steffens to get a good salary.

Then Phillips took Steffens out for lunch and "gradually, cautiously—characteristically—he revealed his purpose: to find a managing editor for the magazine." Their interview was a study in contrasts both superficial and temperamental, between the tall, solemn Phillips and small, witty Steffens. "What will be your policy on the magazine?" Phillips asked. Steffens did not hesitate in his reply: "Put news into it." He was beginning to be intrigued. There were some news stories, he realized, "which ran so long and meant so much that the newspaper readers lost track of them. A weekly might comment upon such stories, but a monthly could come along, tell the whole, completed story all over again, and bring out the meaning of it all." Unlike Miss Tarbell, Steffens was positively excited by living, breathing subjects. He was an original new breed, half philosopher, half shoe-leather reporter, averse to his colleague's belief in burying herself in stacks of dry court documents and archives and skilled at cozying up to villains and reformers alike.

The managing editor's desk would be a convenient place for Steffens to learn the ropes. But despite the possible opening for telling new stories in more depth—and although he was enjoying being courted by *McClure's*—Steffens "was not eager." As he recalled, he "disliked the idea of leaving my staff and all the fun we were having." In May 1901, Phillips put the offer on the table: $5,000 a year and a strong preference for Steffens to start soon, "in one week rather than two." Ida Tarbell had taken on the temporary job of managing editor, sharing the work with associate editor Bert Boyden, but Miss Tarbell badly needed to be freed from the office to write.

At this point Steffens had been at the *Advertiser* for more than three years. The paper was starting to lean more conservative, and Steffens's vivid essays and experimental leadership style were increasingly pitched against the editors' preference for plainer, less colorful reporting from the city desk. While Steffens recognized and resisted the encroaching staidness of the *Advertiser*'s editorial voice, he was surprised to hear that his fellow editors considered him to be past his prime. Overhearing a passing conversation by chance, his ears caught his own name and the words, "We've got out of that man just about all there ever was in him." Others agreed, saying he was clearly "used up." Steffens was thirty-five and incredulous. He told his editor-in-chief about the offer from *McClure's,* and the *Advertiser* "rather encouraged [him] to go."

Steffens first negotiated a stretch of time off. Packing his bags, he included plenty of paper and writing implements. If he could produce a great novel over the next four months, he figured, perhaps he wouldn't need to learn the eccentricities of another office.

The summer of 1901 found Steffens and Josephine wandering the country, letting their minds go gloriously fallow. Her novel had been published, and again she and Steffens were coexisting peaceably. They visited family in California, and then rented a cabin in the Adirondacks. Steffens fell into a rhythm of sleeping into the day, plunging into the mountain lake by the cabin, and passing long summer days observing nature. He wrote his father that he was at a crossroads: he wanted to write a novel, this was his chance to do it, and the end of the summer would bring a final decision about whether he was "an author or a journalist." Despite these intentions, he wrote little.

In the end, the choice was made for him, by an anarchist with a gun. On September 6, 1901, President William McKinley was shot by Leon Czolgosz; he died of gangrene eight days later. Vice President Theodore Roosevelt assumed the presidency. Steffens instantly cast off his novelistic ambitions and telegraphed *McClure's* that he was ready to start. He was back in New York and at his new desk within days. "It was just like springing up from a bed and diving into a lake—and life," Steffens remembered. "The water was cold."

\* \* \*

**FROM THE BEGINNING,** Steffens was adrift in the rhythm of publishing a monthly magazine. He could see why Phillips had been so keen to hire someone—"the editorial department needed organization," he noted—but was quick to disqualify himself from the task, admitting, "I was not an organizer." At the *Advertiser* he'd had a staff of junior reporters and the rapid-fire pace of a daily newspaper, but at the magazine he had no staff, and his new colleagues Miss Tarbell and Baker were frequently out of the office, researching Standard Oil and preparing a series about Germany, respectively. Where he was used to being in a huddle of deadline-pressed reporters who looked to him for authority, Steffens now faced a void. He began to lose confidence. "I simply was not an editor," he wrote in his memoirs. "As I wandered around that magazine office looking for work, I realized that I was a false alarm." Bert Boyden ended up doing much of the managing-editorial work.

Sitting at his desk, helping Phillips and Viola Roseboro evaluate manuscripts, hoping his great opportunity at the magazine would reveal itself soon, Steffens studied the individuals around him. McClure was "wild . . . Blond, smiling, enthusiastic, unreliable." He was "rarely in the office," and when he was, he was never afraid to "raise a rumpus." "I can't sit still," McClure would shout. "That's your job. I don't see how you can do it." It was clear from the start that McClure's staff had one tacit duty. Steffens wrote, "my job, the job of all of us, to hold down S.S. . . . . There was always some act of his enthusiasm for us to counteract."

The editor-in-chief was a riot of ideas and when the staff needed to vote them down, it often involved a large amount of vigorous, noisome arguing. "We had to unite and fight against, say, five out of seven of his new, world-thrilling, history-making schemes," wrote Steffens. "If a new author rose on the horizon, or an explorer started for it, or a statesman blew in over it, S.S. went forth to meet him and 'get him into *McClure's*.' To Africa he traveled, to Europe often. . . . He would come straight from the ship to the office, call us together, and tell us what he had seen and heard, said and done. With his valise full of clippings, papers, books, and letters, to prove it, he showed us that he had the greatest features any publisher had ever had, the most marvelous, really world-stunning ideas or stories." Dryly, Steffens ended the scene: "Sometimes he had good things."

In his quiet early days at the magazine, Steffens assessed each of his colleagues in turn and thought about his own niche among them. He was jealous when he saw them purposefully move about the office and the country, driven by exciting and urgent work. Phillips, thought Steffens, was "hard, patient, but immovable," a business-conscious and meticulous editor. His ally Jaccaci was "like S.S. himself, temperamental and explosive"; as Miss Tarbell warned, his rages were "like terrible summer thundershowers." Baker was not yet a confidant, but he was becoming a friend.

And then there was Ida Tarbell, the coolly accomplished veteran and "devoted friend of S.S." Miss Tarbell seemed exempt from the "idiosyncrasies and troubles" that McClure found fault with in the rest of the staff. Despite being favored by the editor, she was well liked by everyone. Steffens regarded her not only as the star journalist of their group, but as McClure's lieutenant and the magazine's most effective broker of compromises: "When we were deadlocked we might each of us send for her, and down she would come to the office, smiling, like a tall, good-looking young mother, to say, 'Hush, children,'" Steffens wrote. "She would pick out the sense in each of our contentions . . . and take away from all of us only the privilege of gloating.

The interest of the magazine was pointed out, and we and she went back to work." The arrival of staff writers who bristled against the Chief repositioned Miss Tarbell from a regular reporter to a parental surrogate. She was the better part of a decade older than Baker and Steffens, with a way of tacitly questioning whether their argument was germane or a strategy to delay finishing the day's work.

As editorial confrontations mounted in number and intensity, Miss Tarbell observed that Steffens was "incredibly outspoken, taking rascality for granted . . . never doubtful of himself." That rascality was deliberate; he would later comment, "Nobody will remain long a friend of mine who doesn't perceive that I say lots of whimsical things that are to be rejected and forgotten as meaningless or the opposite of what I mean." He was blunt, sarcastic, and, most anathema to her way of working, he disregarded deadlines. Still, each found much to admire in the other, and she ultimately agreed with McClure that Steffens was "the most brilliant addition" to the staff. She even took secret pleasure in their dustups: "I knew our excited discussions were really fertile," she wrote. "They also were highly entertaining." McClure had been farsighted in recruiting Steffens, she realized.

But their satisfaction was not shared by the recent arrival. Less than a year after moving to *McClure's*, Steffens was suffocating beneath the mundane tasks that piled up on his desk. On weekends, when he and Baker would sometimes go sailing together, Steffens began talking about buying the weekly paper in Greenwich, Connecticut, to fulfill his yearning to publish something of his own. But as much as Steffens was unready to fit himself to the duties of a managing editor, he was equally attached to life in New York and the tantalizing prospect of somehow proving himself as a *McClure's* reporter.

Part of his frustration may have been that there was a place and a need at *McClure's* for the investigative work he knew how to do—only it was being handled by others. Josiah Flynt, the pen name of Berlin-educated sociologist Josiah Flynt Willard, had spent years as a professional vagrant and petty criminal, and his series "In the World of Graft" appeared in *McClure's* through the spring of 1901. Able to nimbly move between social strata, Flynt would submerge briefly into his old vagrants' milieu and surface with highly readable studies of bribable policemen and the shadowy side of life on the streets. He wrote anonymously and swiftly and—a crucial difference to Steffens's craft—called his stories fiction, though they were drawn from life.

McClure and Steffens, who stood eye to eye at exactly the same height, had widely divergent editorial priorities. Steffens's intellectual leanings, shaped in European laboratories and lecture halls, stood in contrast to McClure's preference for more accessible, even sensational material. But they admired each other from the start. Even during Steffens's aimless early days at the magazine, McClure was certain he had the instinct to discover and secure promising stories for the magazine. He told the other editors that Steffens was "the only great editor of them all—all but [himself]." Despite their deeper-grained differences, the two men "became pals."

As the weeks wore on, Steffens's unfitness as a desk editor became increasingly irksome for all—especially McClure. Robby McClure, the brother who ran the London office but also helped manage things in New York, thought Steffens was a waste of the magazine's money, and one of his brother's temporary, ungrounded enthusiasms. Then, in October 1901, Steffens published a freelance piece titled "Great Types of Modern Business—Politics" in *Ainslee's* magazine. It had all the crackling energy that had beguiled McClure. In many ways, that piece foreshadowed the themes of the next five years of Steffens's writing career: "[P]olitics is a business. That's what's the matter with it," he wrote. "That's what's the matter with everything—art, literature, religion, journalism, law, medicine. . . . Make politics a sport, as they do in England, or a profession, as they do in Germany, and we'll have—well, something else than we have now,—if we want it, which is another question."

McClure, after weeks of fraternal squabbling, came to a resolution. Steffens needed to show his chief's belief in him had a real foundation by finding a great story and bringing it to the magazine. McClure decided to reorganize his staff: he hired junior editor William Morrow, who later went on to found a publishing business of his own, and gave Steffens his marching orders.

"Get out of the office," McClure finally told the reporter in a private meeting in late December 1901. He laid his hand on the younger man's knee and told him, "You can't learn to edit a magazine in this office." Then he sprang to his feet and gestured vaguely with his arms. "Go to Washington, Newfoundland, California, and Europe. Meet people, find out what's on, and write yourself."

Steffens dreamed that he would be free from desk work thereafter—and that if he could uncover an urgent story for the magazine, he would still have a job.

The two-room house in County Antrim where S. S. McClure lived until he was eight. McClure stands in the doorway.

S. S. McClure in 1882, the year he graduated from Knox College. His professors, he wrote, "intimated that with my powers of mind I could easily take the first place in almost any field if I would only concentrate."

Harriet Hurd at age twenty-four. She wrote to S. S. McClure, "Nobody dreams how I can love. I am just as quiet and moderate as anybody else, and one cannot know how my heart is full of fire and feeling. I dare not show it."

After The Battle          December 1895

S. S. McClure and John Phillips in the *McClure's* office, December 1895. The original caption, "After the Battle," may refer to the magazine's survival of the steep recession following the Panic of 1893.

In this illustration from S. S. McClure's memoir, S. S. and Hattie McClure visit Robert Louis Stevenson in bed. This meeting signaled the start of a fraught but lucrative relationship.

Rouseville as Ida Tarbell knew it at age ten. She recalled of her childhood there, "I saw from the corner of my eye as I walked sedately the length of the street saloons, dance halls, brothels; and I noted many curious things."

Ida Tarbell and her father, Franklin, ca. 1867.

E. L. Drake (*right foreground*) stands with a friend at the drilling site of America's first commercial oil well.

Ida Tarbell in 1880, the year she graduated from Allegheny College.

Ida Tarbell in 1894, after returning from Paris and joining the staff of *McClure's*.

The monstrous snake of Monopoly threatening Lady Liberty in a cartoon titled "In Danger: What Are You Going to Do About It?" by Joseph Ferdinand Keppler, published in the humor magazine *Puck* in 1881.

Ray Stannard Baker

Lincoln Steffens

Issues of *McClure's* from 1893 and 1902. As technology and competition evolved, monochrome, type-heavy cover designs gave way to eye-catching artwork.

Theodore Roosevelt and reporters at his Long Island home, Sagamore Hill. Though this photograph was taken after the crisis at *McClure's*, it shows the kind of scene that Ray Stannard Baker knew well from his encounters with the president.

"The Crusaders: Marching Embattled 'Gainst the Saracens of Graft" by C. Hassman, published in *Puck* in February 1906, featuring McClure (*foreground, with crossbow*), Tarbell, Baker, Steffens (*on horse, at right*), and fellow magazinists.

S. S. McClure. "Able methodical people grow on every bush but genius comes once in a generation," Ida Tarbell insisted in the magazine's later years, as she struggled to rally the staff around the Chief.

Ida Tarbell in 1904.

John D. Rockefeller in 1909, the year the Department of Justice filed a federal antitrust lawsuit against Standard Oil.

Ida Tarbell with her sister, Sarah, and mother, Esther, in 1905, near the time of Franklin Tarbell's death, on the steps of their Titusville home.

S. S. McClure in 1903 in one of his favorite places—a steamship bound for Europe—with his son Robert, Florence Wilkinson (*center*), Cale Rice, and Alice Hegan Rice.

S. S. and Hattie McClure with (*clockwise from top right*) Robert, Elizabeth, Enrico, Mary, and Eleanor, ca. 1907.

S. S. McClure attempting to rest.

S. S. McClure, Willa Cather, Ida Tarbell, and Will Irwin in 1924.

Ida Tarbell at Twin Oaks, the farm in rural Connecticut where she took refuge and offered it.

# 12

## *Big Game*

The first article of Ida Tarbell's "History of the Standard Oil Company" appeared in the November 1902 issue of *McClure's*. It was a tense season in America, but now more because of domestic discontent than war overseas; civil unrest aimed against trusts had built to a five-month strike by coal miners. Writing about architecture, Walt Whitman criticized the era as having a blind "pull-down-and-build-over-again spirit," a tendency to believe too fervently in the new at the expense of the old. The old ways seemed corrupted and past saving, but what did that mean for the future?

Even in this climate of existential angst, Ida Tarbell's story of Rockefeller's rise to power hit the newsstands at a particularly sensitive time. After McKinley's assassination, Roosevelt hardly took the oath of office before proceeding to channel his energies toward reform. McClure, Steffens, and Baker already knew Roosevelt, and Baker had even written to his father that he'd hoped for his ascent: "I think we have nothing to fear concerning his reputed rashness and impetuosity," he wrote. "He seems to possess a very keen sense of his tremendous responsibilities, and he is highly amenable to advice and wise counsel so that he will make no foolish departures."

Standard Oil was already in Roosevelt's sights. In a speech early in his presidency, he pointedly declared that the nation had to grapple with the problem of fortunes in big businesses, with the portentous words, "no amount of charities in spending such fortunes can compensate for the misconduct in acquiring them." As one Rockefeller biographer wrote, Roosevelt "had a glint in his eye for Standard Oil. He was a big-game hunter, and Standard Oil was big game."

Others had put the Standard in the crosshairs long before Miss Tarbell or Roosevelt did. It had been targeted by the media and the courts for years, even before the passage of the Sherman Anti-Trust Act in 1890 and an exposé in *The Atlantic* of Standard Oil's monopolistic practices. That series, *Wealth Against Commonwealth,* by Henry Demarest Lloyd, was published as a book in 1894, just as Miss Tarbell was leaving Paris. She determined to dig deeper than Lloyd and reach a much larger readership.

To begin, Miss Tarbell started with what she knew: western Pennsylvania's boom and bust. She excavated some notes from her old room in her parents' house in Titusville, first written back when she was at *The Chautauquan.* She recalled, just after her return from Paris, when she spent a day driving through the ruined sites of the Oil Region with her brother Will, finding many of the landmarks they knew obliterated. Now she began looking beyond the landscape, at the legal charters and government records that would let her trace the ascent of Rockefeller and his empire.

Before approaching Standard Oil itself, she amassed documentary evidence that told most of the story she had set herself to write. She delved into dense stacks of documents from Standard Oil's past legal battles. Since the 1870s, oilmen who had been disadvantaged by the ever-expanding Standard had periodically sued the company, and there was a wealth of sworn testimony on the relentless expansionist methods of Rockefeller's organization. The Standard had been under federal investigation almost continuously since its founding in 1870, under the allegation that it was "practicing methods in restraint of free trade." Miss Tarbell went directly to the courts, requested the records, and painstakingly dissected them, hoping to dig up something new in the transcripts. The typed covering letters she received back from records departments and businesses often bore the same correction in pen: they were so accustomed to starting letters with "Dear Sir" that the "Sir" needed to be struck and replaced with "Madam."

The material she found—though some files had mysteriously vanished—spurred her onward. She wrote, "These experiences had exactly the quality of the personal reminiscences of actors in great events, with the additional value that they were given on the witness stand." In other words, it was juicier than she expected. Congressional committees and state legislatures had investigated Standard Oil several times already, but it was these private lawsuits that yielded the stories never previously reported by journalists.

She mapped out the sources that would allow her to paint as detailed a picture of Rockefeller as possible, pending an interview with the man himself. Writing about a subject that was alive presented problems that were by turns irritating and sinister. Many seeming well-wishers sternly warned her against taking on the Standard. Even her father, still scraping together a living from oil in Titusville, cautioned her, anxious that Rockefeller would somehow ruin *McClure's* before Ida could make any real headway. "Don't do it, Ida," he said. "They will ruin the magazine." Some fellow journalists took the trouble to send Miss Tarbell murky warnings that Standard Oil would "get" her in the end.

Determined to keep her trepidation concealed, she proceeded stubbornly through the fog of suspicion and fear that surrounded her investigation. She was used to resurrecting stories from dry records and accounts, in a foreign language if necessary. Even Lincoln's death had been distant enough to approach more as a historian than a contemporary. But in the case of Standard Oil, her subject was not only living but thriving, at the height of its powers. Miss Tarbell, her *McClure's* colleagues, and other journalists who knew of the series waited uneasily to see how the Standard would retaliate.

* * *

HER FIRST INTRODUCTION INTO THE ranks of the Standard itself came from an unexpected source. As she wrote, rumors about her work had started to alarm Rockefeller's men: "Mr. McClure dashed into the office one day to tell me he had just been talking with Mark Twain, who said his friend Henry Rogers, at that time the most conspicuous man in the Standard Oil group, had asked him to find out what kind of history of the concern *McClure's* proposed to publish."

Nicknamed "Hell Hound Rogers" for his ruthlessness at the negotiating table, Henry Huttleston Rogers was Rockefeller's corporate PR man, in Miss Tarbell's eyes "as fine a pirate as ever flew his flag in Wall Street." He was curious about the forthcoming *McClure's* story, but he also saw another advantage to talking with Miss Tarbell. It was a chance to repaint the damning picture that Henry Demarest Lloyd had drawn in *Wealth Against Commonwealth,* the prior *Atlantic* series and book.

If anyone had the guile to sway Miss Tarbell, it was Hell Hound Rogers, then in his early sixties. Miss Tarbell frankly thought him very appealing indeed; "the handsomest and most distinguished figure . . . tall, muscular, lithe as an Indian." She liked his fluid, masculine way of moving, the "hint of the mechanic & laborer" in his bearing, "despite excellent grooming." She liked looking into the sharp dark eyes under his gray mane, "narrowed a little by caution & capable of blazing." Rogers, she thought, had "[the] devil in him all right." Both Twain and Rogers assumed the latter would charm the spinster reporter, and they were right. In this, however, they underestimated her ability to remain focused on the mission at hand.

Rarely had a man engaged her so completely. Armed with her instinct and experience in gaining the confidence of volatile men, she had cultivated a self-effacing manner that quickly made interviewees trusting and voluble. "She got in the habit of protecting herself from people that way," Viola Roseboro perceived, "and the other side is that when she gets with the people who have what she wants she is masterly in keeping them talking." Men, especially. When a younger writer once mentioned the impressive number of men that Miss Tarbell associated with, she was taken aback; beyond the *McClure's* group, those meetings and lunches were all incidental to a specific goal: the story. "Men were as impersonal as the pitcher on the table," she thought to herself, "but they always had a good time." Rogers, however, affected her personally, and soon both discovered they shared more than a mercenary interest in each other's work.

In an odd coincidence, Miss Tarbell and Hell Hound Rogers realized early in their acquaintance that they had once been neighbors in the derrick-covered settlement of Rouseville. She had been a child then, while he was first starting out in business. "Probably I've seen you hunting flowers on your side of the ravine . . . I was never happier," confessed Rogers, as he faced the sharp-eyed reporter seated on the other side of his desk. She warmed to the nostalgia for his obscure pioneer background, which reflected her own.

She went to the Standard Oil offices at 26 Broadway regularly for two years. Each time, she entered the imposing colonnaded building and was immediately whisked by an assistant from the lobby via a circuitous and private route to Rogers's office, kept out of sight from Standard Oil employees who might recognize her, and spoken to by no one but Rogers and his secretary. Once they were in his office with the door closed, even sensitive subjects were fair game for Miss Tarbell's spirited questioning. When reminiscences of Rouseville led naturally to a conversation about the Oil War, Rogers's reaction was quick. He forestalled her, saying it was "an outrageous business. That is where the Rockefellers made their big mistake." She made a deal with Rogers that she would bring all of her discoveries to him in the interest of hearing his clarification and context—although the final narrative would ultimately be shaped by herself and her editors alone.

Privately, she found his poise in the heat of her interrogations remarkable. "He's a liar and a hypocrite, and you know it," she "exploded" at Rogers in one of their long interviews, speaking of a man who remains unnamed in her papers. Rogers refused to be moved by her outburst and replied, with ostentatious calm, "I think it's going to rain." She was leery of relaxing too much in his presence, and of any situation that might compromise her in his eyes. In her sessions with Rogers, she would even refuse the glass of milk he habitually offered her unless he let her pay for it.

The exchanges with Rogers solidified her approach with a living subject who was seemingly determined to outmaneuver her. She asked Rogers to confirm the factuality of her findings and neatly batted away his attempts to steer her toward his own narrative. "Mr. Rogers," she would say good-humoredly, "if you will look at my letter you will see that I did not suggest that you make the article correspond with your opinion of this case. I feel convinced I could never do that. I asked you to examine the article and see if I had made any errors in statement or had omitted any essential testimony on either side." Her efforts at verification—including checking sources' affidavits and only using stories that could be confirmed—were unique to the Tarbell method decades before they became common practice for journalists.

Both enjoyed their sparring matches and were enlightened by their interviews, but those meetings could also be strangely obfuscating. How could she believe him on every count, seductive as he was, when he was a key part of Rockefeller's machine? Once, after he had given her some documents to review and she was bent over them in concentration, she glanced up suddenly and "caught him looking at me with narrowed eyes and an expression of great cunning. He straightened his face out at once." She kept her own expression neutral, but never forgot that ruthless, predatory gaze behind Rogers's suave façade.

Rogers was her only key to the tycoon himself, who had essentially retired around 1897. When she wasn't using her meetings with Rogers to fact-check documents and allegations she had turned up, Miss Tarbell gently prodded him about arranging that meeting. In one of their first interviews, Rogers agreed, "a little doubtfully," to try to set something up with Rockefeller. Gradually the possibility faded. "If I hinted at it," she wrote, regretfully, "he parried." Rockefeller remained tantalizingly out of reach—for now—and she was at a loss for how to close the gap.

Rogers had his own agenda for Miss Tarbell. He framed the company's accelerating growth as a patriotic necessity. What would happen to the Oil Region's lucrative product if it were outstripped by an upstart competitor, perhaps Texas, or California—or Russia? Rogers suggested Miss Tarbell and her story should see that threat, and not Rockefeller's familiar reign, as the "anaconda" squeezing the Oil Region workers. "It looks as if something had the Standard Oil Company by the neck, something bigger than we are," Rogers pushed. Miss Tarbell took notes, unmoved. Her judgment of the company's desire for total dominance echoed like a drumbeat through her articles.

Rogers's anxiety was, in fact, backed up by the headlines. The recent Spindletop, Texas, oil well had yielded close to 100,000 barrels of oil per day for nine days before it was capped to control the flow. Meanwhile, in St. Petersburg, American kerosene had been the main light source until drills hit massive oil reserves near Russia-controlled Baku. The streets and homes of Shanghai had burned the Standard's product since the early 1880s, creating valuable consumers abroad just as electric light was starting to shrink the American oil market. But what if Shanghai could strike a better deal with Russia? Miss Tarbell resisted being drawn in; her story was about oil in America, but Rogers had a way of complicating her thoughts.

The Rogers connection also aroused suspicion among valuable sources, even those she assumed would be the most sympathetic. Henry Demarest Lloyd, whose *Wealth Against Commonwealth* had presciently attacked the Standard, at first offered to help with her research; but when he heard that she was meeting with Rogers he did his considerable best to keep independent producers from talking to her, for fear she was feeding information to the wily PR man. Later, when her articles began to appear, Lloyd had another change of heart. "I want to congratulate you on the extraordinarily interesting and effective work that you are doing in *McClure's,*" he wrote her in April 1903. "When you get through with 'Johnnie [Rockefeller],' I don't think there will be very much left of him except something resembling one of his own grease spots."

From disgruntled oilmen, Miss Tarbell received a great volume of tips to look into, but her distaste for hearing their woes accumulated with the success of her series. Rogers introduced her to Henry Flagler, Rockefeller's scandal-prone business partner (who later became known as a key developer of Miami), who let her know in an off-the-record conversation that Rockefeller was "the biggest little man and the littlest big man he ever knew. . . . He would do me out of a dollar today—that is, if he could do it honestly." It quickly became clear that Flagler was more interested in clawing back a respectable image for himself than in supplying Miss Tarbell with actual insight.

At least she wasn't alone in the monumental task of sifting through rumors and deciding what to believe. She found a brilliant lieutenant, a young writer with a nose for investigative work whose bubbling energy bolstered her enthusiasm as she trudged through her interviews and reading. She had been hiring local assistants in Cleveland, Rockefeller's home base, since early in her research, but hadn't seen particular promise in many of them. All were young men: the first two were courteous and competent but inclined to check off the tasks she had assigned and go quiet. The third, John Siddall, was a different breed. Miss Tarbell wrote that he was "short and plump, his eyes glowing with excitement. He sat on the edge of his chair. As I watched him I had a sudden feeling of alarm lest he should burst out of his clothes. I never had the same feeling about any other individual except Theodore Roosevelt . . . so steamed up, so ready to go, attack anything, anywhere."

Like Miss Tarbell, Siddall was a former editor at *The Chautauquan*. He was naturally curious and persistent, unafraid to prod and question his redoubtable boss. He wrote such animated, entertaining letters that the rest of the *McClure's* staff petitioned Miss Tarbell to bring him to New York after the Standard series was through. But as long as he was assigned to her, he pursued her story with dedication equal to her own.

Although she investigated Standard Oil over a period of four years, she missed other sources much closer to her quarry. Siddall had assumed Rockefeller's father, a con artist and bigamist who had never been close to his eldest son, was long since dead, and had not looked into the particulars. When it turned out he was alive and well in Illinois, Siddall wrote, shocked and penitent, to Miss Tarbell in late April 1903, "I am startled almost beyond expression to learn, as I have through the telephone within the last five minutes, that the old man is living."

He was convinced that John D. Rockefeller had conspired to hide the existence of his disreputable father. Siddall was not the only one who was fooled; William Rockefeller Sr. had lived a double life under an alias complete with a bogus medical title, Dr. William Levingston, for years. Dr. Levingston himself was elusive, ninety-three years old, deaf, and in his own world. But Siddall found the one photographer in Cleveland who admitted to having a confidential file of Rockefeller plates, including images of John D.'s father; at first the man refused to let Siddall see them, but with the lubrication of fifty dollars, *McClure's* was able to print the images in later installments of the series.

More fruitful was a teenaged clerk at Standard Oil, who by chance one day noticed that the papers he'd been given to burn bore the name of an independent oil refiner who had been his Sunday school teacher. He started a habit of looking for the name on all of the paperwork he was given for the incinerator, and pieced together what was happening: Standard Oil was issuing orders that amounted to "Stop that shipment—get that trade," diverting its competitor's business with collusion from the railroad companies.

The clerk discreetly passed the documents to his former teacher, who knew of the *McClure's* series and shared the evidence with Miss Tarbell. With this nameless insider's help, she confirmed the truth of a charge that others had suggested to her, but that she had considered little more than a conspiracy theory. Standard Oil was spying on independent oil refiners and manipulating distribution through a byzantine system of railroad rebates.

She was electrified by the scoop, and the next installment in the series drew heavily from it. Rogers was "white with rage" in their next interview. "Where did you get that stuff?" he demanded. When Miss Tarbell refused to give away her source's identity, the ensuing conversation brought a curt, angry end to their collaboration. With Siddall's help, she would have to finish her research completely shut out of the Standard itself.

# 13

## *You Have the Moon Yet, Ain't It?*

L incoln Steffens, looking out his train window as Manhattan's sprawl
fizzled into pastureland, mulled over his latest order from McClure.
He was to travel—free of menial and managerial tasks at last—and, in
theory, this would result in a story.

It was daunting. Ever since he had returned from Europe and started
his career as a journalist, Steffens had been either a city reporter or a city
editor. New York, overflowing with stories of crime, graft, black markets,
and powerful characters, was his professional home. Now, going on tips and
skill alone, he would have to start from scratch in a strange new landscape.

He quickly got a long-haul ticket in hand. *McClure's* was owed an advertising fee from the Lackawanna Railroad, so in the summer of 1902
Steffens boarded a westbound train on that line, thinking he might disembark in either Cleveland or Chicago. The Midwest, after all, was exotic to a
Californian-turned-expatriate-turned–New Yorker.

As the sky dimmed and he was pulled ever deeper into the heartland,
Steffens hopped on and off around a dozen trains, stopping not just in Cleveland and Chicago, but also taking in Kansas City, Topeka, Minneapolis,
St. Paul, Duluth, Louisville, and Cincinnati. He began to pursue ideas for
features, going through jotted lists of topics and power brokers from other

*McClure's* staffers, working his way through other people's address books. His targets were "writers, editors, leading citizens" who would connect him to promising material as yet unknown back east. This line of questioning eventually took him to St. Louis, and it was there that a path finally took shape. Rather than trailing after his colleagues and reporting on the trusts, or on labor, Steffens turned his eye on another rapidly changing and much-reviled hotbed of wrongdoing: the looming, festering American city. "I started something," Steffens later wrote, claiming somewhat justifiable credit for himself, "which did 'make' not one but several magazines. I started our political muckraking."

When he moved from the *Advertiser* to *McClure's*, Steffens had hoped to finally get beyond the rhythm of the newspaper world. As long as he was confined to the daily news cycle, he knew that whatever he published today would be crumpled up to wrap fish tomorrow. In St. Louis, and in his mandate from McClure, he found the first opportunity to make the leap from daily news to something more substantial.

St. Louis was the fourth-largest American city, and one of the fastest growing. Between the Civil War and the turn of the century, the population rose from 160,000 to 600,000; city government could not scale up so fast. Instead, a rogue administration controlled by mob bosses stepped into the void and seized control. Shortly before Steffens's arrival, the streetlamps of St. Louis were dark for a stretch of several weeks. Mayor "Uncle Henry" Ziegenhein ignored the dilapidated streets and left the "new" city hall unfinished as the money dedicated to the building was funneled to private interests. He famously scolded a group of citizens protesting the prolonged lack of street lighting by saying, "You have the moon yet, ain't it [*sic*]? Well, what more do you want?"

Long before the cinematic conventions of noir were created, Steffens managed to find the hard-bitten, dogged hero whose righteous zeal was set to collide with the leaders of the protection racket in place. He focused his keen eye on the unlikely, unsmiling figure of circuit attorney Joseph Folk.

Folk swept into the circuit attorney's office on a miscalculation. A local

Democrat power broker had stuffed the ballot boxes in his favor, assuming the newcomer would understand his obligation to them once in office. When that mob began trying to dictate the appointments in Folk's office, Folk instead began the intricate and hazardous task of reforming the city through the courts. "I'll have to do my duty," Folk warned his superiors, and from late 1902 onward he amassed incontrovertible evidence of corporate and municipal bribery, commonly called "boodling" in the press. He started to indict witnesses—who eventually numbered in the hundreds—and bring agents of corruption to court.

The scourge delighted newspapermen, who jostled in the public gallery to see what came to light. But when some of St. Louis's most prominent and respected citizens trudged up to the stand, reporters who had initially enthused over Folk's escapades began to draw back in alarm. No one could be certain Folk would succeed, and newspaper editors were reluctant to bring trouble upon their own heads. Steffens was one of the few newsmen in the gallery without a Missourian's stake in the game. Here, at last, was his story.

The drama of Folk's reforms had many elements Steffens liked and McClure encouraged. Most crucially, it was already the talk of the town. Everyone in St. Louis was aware that their elections were controlled by one mob boss or another. For months before Steffens's arrival, Folk had rarely been out of the local papers. This gave Steffens a chance to take "confused, local, serial news of the newspapers and [report] it all together in one long short story for the whole country"—and this solidified into a cornerstone of *McClure's* investigative style.

Steffens worked with what was already there and presented it in a re-combined, value-added form: a comprehensive, in-depth piece that joined old testimony with audacious new interviews and facsimiles of bribe records. He hired a St. Louis journalist, Claude Wetmore, to write up the story from Steffens's reporting and stop him from making any blunders about local society.

At long last, Steffens began having fun. He wrote home to *McClure's* that if the magazine was open to a series on corruption in cities, he wanted to have a leading role. "If I should be trusted with the work," he said, "I think I could make my name."

Steffens had landed on a true match between subject and skill, even though he delved into St. Louis as a cultural outsider. Steffens himself knew his greatest assets were interested eyes and an omnivorous brain. As his friend Brand Whitlock later wrote, "in Steffens's case a lack of [local] knowledge was in itself a qualification, since he had eyes, like the old sailor, and, like Joseph Conrad, the power to tell what he saw. That is, Steffens had vision, imagination, and if the history of the city in America is ever written he will fill a large place on its page." When Whitlock wondered aloud to his face what, precisely, Steffens knew about municipal government to qualify him for the job, Steffens replied, "Nothing. That's why I'm going to write about it."

As he began to outline the material for his *McClure's* report, Steffens found it impossible to cast the St. Louis scandal as an isolated event. Instead, he argued in his narrative, it was a flare-up of a widespread, national-scale infection. He decided to write the struggle in St. Louis as a microcosm of flawed American politics, a case study for a grand theory of boodling. "Bribery," he decided, "is not a mere felony, but a revolutionary process which [is] going on in all our cities. . . . [I]f I could trace it to its source, I might find the cause of political corruption and—the cure." Claude Wetmore, his cowriter, was perturbed by Steffens's excitement about the boldness and bigness of the story. Wetmore lived and worked in St. Louis, and was equally determined to tread lightly in portraying his hometown as the focal point for disease. He turned in a smoothly diplomatic draft, protesting, "Why should [I] be a pariah in [my] own city?" In summer 1902, after Steffens rewrote the piece, Wetmore insisted that they should share a byline—and the anticipated blame. Steffens agreed, thinking that he could never work with someone as lily-livered as Wetmore again. He landed on a title that suited his own purpose: "Tweed Days in St. Louis." Then he presented his piece to McClure.

The Chief was excited by the story's potential, but he had a bone to pick with the writer. The theoretical, sociological strand in "Tweed Days" was out of line. "I wanted to study cities scientifically," Steffens wrote in his memoirs. "[McClure] would not have it. Science did not interest the readers, except as a source of wonders." McClure insisted on keeping to the most outrageous facts of the case, aiming for an emotional reaction from readers, not enlarging the story to actually naming causes or solutions to boodling as a larger phenomenon. After a bitter editorial tussle, "Tweed Days" was published in the October 1902 issue of *McClure's,* alongside an article about a coal strike in Pennsylvania by Baker and the first announcement of Miss Tarbell's Standard Oil series.

McClure and Steffens could not see eye to eye on the magazine's purpose. The Chief was eager to restrain Steffens's growing sense of vision and agency—a liking for power that agitated McClure. "All tyrants have short necks," S. S. would mutter, eyeing Steffens, though the two men were proportionally similar. The reporter, meanwhile, saw McClure as the would-be dictator. He balked at being told what to write. The fiercely independent-minded, "little keen-faced gentleman with a string tie" had proven himself, believed in his own ideas, and insisted he should have earned his editor's trust by now. "We had a pretty hot fight," Steffens remembered. "McClure won." McClure, to Steffens's bitter dismay, preferred to cover the seamy underside of powerful institutions without venturing theories toward a solution, or, when pushed, a vague and simplistic answer. "[T]he dictatorship of one strong, wise man (like Sam McClure . . .) would abolish our political evils and give us a strong, wise administrator of cities," Steffens put it, drolly but not incorrectly.

As the reporter prepared to return to the Midwest, McClure exhorted Steffens to trust the Chief's instinct above his own: "if you [like a thing], then I know that, say, ten thousand readers will like it. If Miss Tarbell likes a thing, it means that fifty thousand readers will like it. . . . But I go most by myself. For if I like a thing, then I know that millions will like it. My mind and taste are so common that I'm the best editor."

Readers, meanwhile, leapt on Steffens's St. Louis article. The office began receiving excited letters from cities and towns across America, inviting the journalist to come and expose them, too. For this, the Chief naturally credited himself. McClure soon assigned Steffens to another "Shame of the Cities" piece. To circumvent any freewheeling big ideas, the Chief gave him the title of the next article before Steffens even left New York. It was to be "The Shame of Minneapolis."

\* \* \*

**STEFFENS HAD LITTLE OPPORTUNITY** to hash out his editorial differences with McClure, whose adventures that year nearly led to his abdication. The Chief, sinking into yet another dark phase, fled New York yet again. He went to Salonika in Turkey in early 1902 to organize the rescue of kidnapped missionary Ellen Stone.

He was chasing a story that was both the first international crisis featuring an American hostage and a notable case of Stockholm syndrome. The abductees were Miss Stone, a middle-aged missionary, and her colleague, the pretty, pregnant Katerina Tsilka. The kidnappers were Bulgarian revolutionaries who doted on their captives, even killing a turkey for them at Thanksgiving. The women in turn admired their "handsome brigands" and became fervent believers in their cause. But tension ratcheted up as Miss Stone harangued them about the evils of smoking and alcohol and insisted on calling them by unmanly nicknames.

The men negotiated a colossal ransom with the U.S. government, and the case had lurid headlines covering newspapers in the United States and Europe for the better part of a year. The ransom was finally paid and the women released; McClure wasted little time in soliciting a blurb from the newly notorious Miss Stone, who complied: "*McClure's* has become a part of my home life with its brightness and life and fearless stand for the right in our land." He barreled back to Manhattan against Hattie's pleading and his doctor's stern warning that "[w]ith Mr. McClure's history and temperament it would be absolutely foolhardy for him to live in New York City."

When he got back to the office, McClure exploded the peace that his staff had grown used to in his absence. He started by firing Jaccaci. The art director had helped start *McClure's,* left temporarily to work at *Scribner's,* and had returned to an increasingly impossible relationship with the Chief. To Phillips, McClure claimed Jaccaci lacked originality and was "loyal only to his emotions," but he privately wrote to Hattie: "I do not like the way he keeps a diary of all I say to him in our personal relations." He was touch- ily self-aware, perhaps out of a realization his frailty was more and more obvious.

Later the same year, and in private, McClure offered the editor-in-chief post to Baker. He wanted to launch another magazine and to be free from his obligation to run every idea past Phillips and the rest of the staff. Baker was stunned. McClure had always insisted, "Always remember that I am not simply an editor, but that I have a feeling of jealousy for *McClure's Magazine* very much like what the lioness has for her cubs." Though he considered it and held a flustered conference with Phillips, Baker declined the offer. He recognized the opportunity as the fruit of an irrational mind, and that if he accepted he would have a kind of bogus leadership, with McClure holding tight to his namesake. To Phillips, he wrote, "I feel deeply for Mr. McClure: he was so much in earnest in his talk with me and he seemed to feel so keenly his own physical limitations & the impossibility of doing things as he once did. . . . [T]he circumstances of the office & the personality of the man behind it are sure as to make the position one of great difficulty."

Ruefully, McClure set aside the idea of moving on to a second mag- azine. He and Baker then set off together to the pit-scarred hills around Wilkes-Barre, Pennsylvania. A coal miners' strike created bitter opposi- tion between union men and nonstrikers, who reported their houses being stoned and burned, physical assaults, and several murders. The unions, meanwhile, claimed to be nonviolent victims of the "coal and iron police . . . city thugs with orders to shoot and kill."

Baker strung together powerful interviews with a community bitterly split by labor disputes, complete with sobering pictures of hungry families and scenes of action. "They hung me in effigy," the anthracite miner had told him. Another man had his eyes put out by blows from a stone. "Every night," confided one nonunion miner's wife, "I was afraid to go to bed for fear they would blow up my home with dynamite. They did dynamite three houses in the same neighborhood." The article's gritty details harked back to Baker's early work for Chicago newspapers. As he had during the Pullman strike, he wanted to broadcast what a struggling people were living through, to close the distance between reader and subject. As long as the conflict was written up with as much color as possible, McClure rarely disputed with Baker.

He could not muster the same level of trust in Steffens. The Chief wrote to Phillips, "In any event, the editorial policy of the magazine belongs to you and me. . . . Steffens is not getting at the cause of the trouble. . . . He must disabuse himself of any predilections in the matter and write up things as they are." Steffens's perception of "things as they are" would never match McClure's, but the younger journalist kept quiet his disdain that McClure was solely "interested in facts, startling facts." He turned his focus to corruption in Minneapolis, and what he found was startling indeed.

* * *

DESCRIBING MINNEAPOLIS AS "A YANKEE" with a small Puritan head, an open prairie heart, and a great, big Scandinavian body," Steffens made vivid a city that generally obeyed the rule of law without paying too much attention to politics, until the regime of Albert Alonzo "Doc" Ames, a physician and four-term mayor, began. Then "slot machines . . . opium joints and unlicensed saloons, called 'blind pigs,'" sprang up. Ames made his brother Fred chief of police and promptly dismissed 107 officers from a force of 225. Those who remained were in on the game, and looked away from the criminal system flexing its muscles, starting with the ransacking of the Pabst Brewing Company—helped along by an employee who helped shuttle the takings back to Ames's cronies. The ensuing struggle between a municipal jury and the leaders of the racket made for one of the most popular pieces Steffens ever published in *McClure's*.

"The Shame of Minneapolis: The Ruin and Redemption of a City That Was Sold Out" appeared in the January 1903 issue, alongside a piece by

Baker about labor disputes in Pennsylvania and the third installment of Ida Tarbell's Standard Oil series. By that time, a grand jury had already gone after Ames. The jury foreman was angry citizen Hovey Clarke, who confronted his quarry on the steps of City Hall in a tableau now part of Minneapolis legend: "Yes, Doc Ames, I'm after you," Clarke hissed at the mayor, who seemed unfazed. "I've been in this town for seventeen years, and all that time you've been a moral leper. . . . Now I'm going to put you where all contagious things are put—where you cannot contaminate anybody else." Steffens included this scene as a centerpiece of his article, which undercut Ames's notion of himself as an accomplished gangster or well-loved man, if he'd held on to one. Instead, although he was "amiable" and "cheerful" enough, he was also bad at running a hustle. "Even lawlessness must be regulated," Steffens wrote. Instead, "Dr. Ames, never an organizer, attempted no control, and his followers began to quarrel among themselves." Rather than a tight web of loyalties, it was every man for himself. "There was not left even the traditional honor among thieves," Steffens concluded. Doc Ames was not only a rotten apple—a man whose dying wife tried to summon him from the saloon where he was drinking, and who dictated an obscene reply—but a failure as a mob patriarch, too.

A month after the *McClure's* article on Minneapolis was published, Doc Ames was arrested while trying to elude the authorities in New Hampshire. While his brother Fred went to prison, Doc Ames's own multiple trials for running protection rackets ended in mistrials; when the state finally dropped charges against him, he returned to practicing medicine.

Steffens's work in Minneapolis garnered awe and excitement from the public, transforming McClure's level of trust in the reporter. "I ought to write to you that you have made a marvelous success of your Minneapolis article," the Chief wrote, in a rare note of unqualified praise. "I think it will probably arouse more attention than any article we have published for a long time." Steffens's dissection of the city's criminal underworld revealed the "big mitt ledger," the accounts kept between the police and the criminals they directed. Again, he had not uncovered much that hadn't already been reported in the local papers. Instead he enlivened the story for a national audience: the rise and fall of a mayor who structured his rule around a protection racket that consumed the city.

Steffens's methods gradually settled into a pattern, one that always began with a key individual who unlocked the city's particular brand of corruption and ended with an argument with McClure. He would land in a city, hoping to proceed anonymously—something that got harder by the time his Pittsburgh story got under way, as his photograph had been published and he was sometimes recognized in the street. He started by asking strangers point-blank about who really decided things in their neighborhood, and often found that people told him right away. He would then inquire into "how the game was worked"—what were the typical prices for public jobs, and what about the profit-sharing systems? He read the local papers for clues, visited the city's newspaper office, and asked an office boy repeatedly who was in charge—not by title, but by the way the paper actually operated. That person would point Steffens toward the right subject to shadow, someone on the front line of either the machine or the anticorruption campaign in that particular city who had the most explosive facts and evidence at their disposal.

His report on Philadelphia, published in July 1903, added a new magnitude to Steffens's fame and to the murky implications of his work. Until then, northeastern states had been able to blame the lawless western territories for shoddy government. Long-settled communities scapegoated immigrants, especially Catholics, the Irish, and southern Europeans, while old cities pointed at newer, rougher, merchant-driven ones without a patrician past. Steffens's Philadelphia piece could not silence those pernicious arguments, but they lost some traction after *McClure's* looked at them.

Philadelphia had more open and ingrained organized crime than any other city yet covered by *McClure's*, all conducted within a mostly white, Anglo-Saxon, Protestant society. Philadelphia was "corrupt and content," in Steffens's view, and it was easy to find witnesses who vociferously agreed—and gave evidence. The manager at Steffens's hotel told of going to the polls on Election Day only to be told that he had "voted already." "Lots of my friends had the same experience," he told Steffens. "I kicked so hard that they let me vote, but they called in a couple of gangsters to offset my ballot by voting the other way—in the names of George Washington and Benjamin Franklin." It was in Philadelphia that Steffens first saw a citizens' vigilance committee driven from outrage to action, threatening councilmen with lynching if they gave the city's gasworks to a single powerful fixer.

One of his readers was President Theodore Roosevelt. In October 1903, he invited McClure and Steffens to the White House. Over dinner, he proposed a series of articles, written by none other than himself, that would follow his own battle against big business. The president, the editor-in-chief, and the journalist talked until well past midnight. The new series could not fail to be the sensation of 1904. And yet, two or three weeks later, McClure withdrew from the project. Roosevelt had a way of monopolizing any story that touched on him—he was too energetic and extraordinary not to. But McClure was wary of being seen as anyone's mouthpiece, and he wanted Steffens to investigate cities independently of the president's preferred narrative.

Steffens's own acquaintance with Roosevelt waxed and waned in closeness, as the president contended, with increasing ambivalence, with the deep-rooted political wrongdoings brought to light by the media. It was never easy to communicate with Roosevelt in the traditional sense—as Steffens wrote, "It was hard to tell him anything; it was easy to make him talk, even about a State secret, but to reverse the process and make him listen was well-nigh impossible."

The reporter and the president exchanged letters that were alternately warm and miffed. In the fall of 1903, writing to his father, Steffens seemed poised for recognition as a formative man of his time: "The President, who had resented my impersonal attitude toward him, has come around. The articles did that too. He has asked me to write the most important things that are to be said next year; the account of his fight with capital and with labor. It will make a sensation. . . . The President thanked me for bringing Folk to his notice. 'Indeed,' he said, 'I have read your articles for men, real men.'"

As he peeled back the wholesome façades of "his" cities, Steffens cemented his reputation as investigator-in-chief. Increasingly, much of the mail delivered to *McClure's* was from Steffens's fans; one cable from Cleveland read, "OHIO RECOGNIZES YOUR MESSAGE, CINCINNATI RESPONDS TO IT, CLEVELAND VINDICATES IT, WE ALL APPRECIATE IT." Steffens became a household name, discussed as much in the White House as in the steel plants of Pittsburgh.

His articles brought in fabulous profits for the magazine. One afternoon McClure surprised him with the thank-you gift of a brand-new, twenty-foot sailboat. A son who compulsively tried to impress his father throughout his life, the younger Steffens wrote to the elder in late 1903 to announce, "Last week a cigar manufacturer asked permission to name a cigar after me. . . . If I wished money, I could turn from what I am doing and make it in piles. Offers of amazing rates are made to me for articles on any subject; but I do nothing that does not contribute directly to the thing I am working for, and I let pass the best-paying offers."

One of Steffens's great gifts was that he was equally at ease with sources from every walk of life. He listened to reformers but often developed a personal affinity for "bad" people. Israel Durham, the Republican boss of Philadelphia, saw in Steffens "a born crook that's gone straight," and, to the astonishment of his men, often stopped by the reporter's hotel room "just to chew the rag." "Iz" Durham was, Steffens claimed, "the best man I met in that town, the best for mental grasp, for the knowledge of life and facts in his line," and for honesty at least with himself. In theory, Durham was excited at the idea of turning reformer after Steffens's story broke, but ultimately, pleading his frail health, he quietly went west in 1905.

Criminals and reformers, fixers and presidents, all attracted Steffens's sincere and almost anthropological writerly interest. By what moral codes did they operate? How did they justify themselves, and who was most susceptible to believing them? His years as a student of ethics and philosophy in Berlin made him quick to brush aside any simplistic opposition between good and evil, a concept that the more stridently Christian Progressive writers relied on. "[T]here is so much good in bad people, there must be some good in good people," Steffens liked to joke. Faith in a single system never appealed to him much. "Dogmas do so obstruct the vision," he wrote. "How much better it is to read men than books!"

\* \* \*

**AFTER HIS INVESTIGATIONS OF CITIES,** Steffens turned his attention to the states: Missouri, Illinois, Wisconsin, Rhode Island, Ohio, and New Jersey were all called to account. Steffens described his purpose with these articles, "I would aim [libelous, dangerous, and explosive facts] and the whole story, like a gun, at the current popular theories (including Mr. McClure's). . . . I was a good shot in those days. I could write to the understanding and hit the convictions of the public because I shared or had so recently shared them."

The gunshot metaphor was also favored by Upton Sinclair, interviewed in *The Cosmopolitan* in 1906 about his novel set in Chicago's stockyards and meatpacking plants, *The Jungle*: "I aimed for the public's heart, and by accident I hit it in its stomach." Sinclair's novel, following in the wake of the *McClure's* exposés, had started as a commission from the socialist magazine *Appeal to Reason*. Stockyard workers went on strike in September 1904 in protest against the exploitative and otherwise unlivable conditions of their lives—awaking in sheds along the stockyards, crowded with sick hogs and goats that were often sold as lamb, and spending long hours in the packing plants, where men had died after getting tangled in the enormous sausage mixers. The writer immersed himself in their world, which was governed by meat-industry behemoth Armour & Company: he woke, wrote, and slept in "a strange, pungent odor. . . . You could literally taste it, as well as smell it—you could take hold of it, almost."

The result was a brilliant, indelible, genre-defining activist novel, admired by Churchill and Theodore Roosevelt alike and selling upwards of five thousand copies per day at its peak. (The president entered into an enthusiastic correspondence with Sinclair, until the author began to step on his toes; Roosevelt finally wrote Frank Doubleday, who had published *The Jungle*, "Tell Mr Sinclair to go home and let me run the country for a while.")

Sinclair himself scolded Steffens for his reluctance to embrace socialism, asking him, "But don't you *see* what you are seeing?" Steffens liked to reiterate the question with a chuckle, though in later years he would grow closer to the same perspective.

The *McClure's* group were not revolutionaries. The Chief and his staff had a firm underlying agreement with the social status quo that helped secure their popularity as "safe," consensus-oriented voices. All three writers examined problems but stopped short of offering action. Their readers—ranging from the working class to power brokers—liked *McClure's* for the way it mingled the known and the new. They were compelled by exposés aimed at disasters within the system, not the potential of pulling apart the system itself. As Steffens wrote of Miss Tarbell, she was an "unconscious politician," "not a radical at all," but "a nice person with a lot of power."

McClure's own heady awareness of that power reached beyond the clattering presses above Madison Square and soirées at Delmonico's. In the *McClure's* office, the Chief saw enough of himself in Steffens to include him in his increasingly grand vision of the magazine. "I believe," McClure wrote him, "we can do more toward making a President of the United States than any other 20 organs." Together they looked at the troubled American horizon and saw their chance to be arbiters of the future.

# 14

## *The Cleveland Ogre*

I n January 1903, Miss Tarbell felt her usual cheerful stamina wearing thin. She began to long for escape from the subject of Standard Oil. Not content with monopolizing the oil industry, it had swallowed her life, too. "It has become a great bugbear to me," she told Siddall, longing for a trip to Europe. "I dream of the octopus by night and think of nothing else by day, and I shall be glad to exchange it for the Alps." Instead, her work plunged her into reliving one of the most fearful chapters of her own past: the Oil War of 1872. *McClure's* published her piece on the independent refiners' war with Rockefeller, a work suffused with all the anger she had felt since experiencing it at fifteen.

It is a passionate piece of writing, balanced tightly between investigation and the vivid force of memory. The *New York Times* said the series was "[a]s readable as any 'story' with rather more romance than the usual business novel," while the *Boston Globe* called it a work "of unequalled importance as a 'document' of the day." The review concluded, "The results are likely to be far-reaching; she is writing unfinished history."

McClure crowed victory. "You cannot imagine how we all love & reverence you. You are the real queen of the establishment," he wrote from Divonne. He wrote to Richard Watson Gilder, editor of *The Century,* that the investigative turn of *McClure's* reflected a new social responsibility that now belonged to the magazines. McClure's hope, he told Gilder, was to "get the people to see that we have been left simply the husks of liberty while the real substance has been stolen from us." Magazines, he posited, had a better chance of waking up their readership than any other medium: "it evidently is up to the magazines to arouse this public opinion, for the newspapers have forfeited their opinion by sensationalism and by selling their opinions to a party."

Miss Tarbell described the Oil War from the perspective of the Pennsylvania oilmen, and it was in this installment that she pointed at her villain in no uncertain terms: "It was inevitable that under the pressure of their indignation and resentment some person or persons should be fixed upon as responsible, and should be hated accordingly. . . . It was the Standard Oil Company of Cleveland, so the Oil Regions decided, which was at the bottom of the business, and the 'Mephistopheles of the Cleveland Company,' as they put it, was John D. Rockefeller."

The tinge of biblical language in her lines wasn't accidental. At a moment when inequality of wealth and the rise of a few industrial giants seemed irreversible, *McClure's* Standard Oil story assigned a face to a phenomenon that many saw as outright evil. Christian metaphor pervaded Progressive Era reform writing, and in time, *McClure's* investigations were painted in newspaper cartoons and the popular imagination as spearheading a cleansing crusade against the mendacious rule of robber barons.

Despite high praise in the papers and McClure holding her up as an avenging angel of liberty, one of the final pieces in the series was giving her trouble. She was determined to write a character profile of Rockefeller himself—believing the epigraph she had taken from Emerson's "Self-Reliance," "An Institution is the lengthened shadow of one man"—but had no access to him. Her subject had been completely walled off from her ever since her rupture with Rogers.

She had no way to construct Rockefeller's character from direct experience, so instead she worked from documentary sources and interviews, just as when she wrote about Lincoln. Initially she let his publicly documented actions speak for his character. Then, as she gleaned more from records and witnesses, she began to get personal.

This yielded surprising sympathies. John's estranged brother, Frank Rockefeller, tried to influence her portrait, offering "the most unhappy and the most unnatural" of the grievances she'd heard levied against the tycoon. Miss Tarbell went to Frank's office in Cleveland, entering the building in disguise so word could not leak out. She found him "excited and vindictive," listened to him, and came away with a sad impression of Frank's free spending and love of good horses, and John's consequent disapproval and withdrawal of Standard stock from his brother during the Panic of 1893. Miss Tarbell found herself appreciating John's hard wisdom and strict morals, rather than Franklin Rockefeller's sense of entitlement, which she would try to convey in her profile. Her colleagues, though, insisted that grudge-driven anecdotes weren't enough. She had to find a way to portray Rockefeller the man for the readers.

It took nearly a year to find the right time and place to see him with her own eyes. The mission tested Siddall's sleuthing abilities. He finally laid a plan after a sympathetic reader divulged the tycoon's churchgoing schedule. During summers at his Forest Hill home in Cleveland, Rockefeller rarely emerged in public—except for Sundays, when he would join the congregation at Euclid Avenue Baptist Church. Miss Tarbell's series had turned this weekly outing into an ordeal; crowds would gather outside the church to catch a glimpse of him, and Rockefeller had to be sure that Pinkerton detectives were on hand for security. It became his habit to greet a church attendant before the service with the query "Are there any of our friends, the reporters, here?"

On Sunday, October 11, 1903, they were indeed. After considerable reconnaissance by Siddall, three newcomers slid into the pews. Miss Tarbell, Siddall, and illustrator George Varian sat, tense and perspiring, to hear Rockefeller speak at a Sunday school rally. Miss Tarbell was agitated by the dark, stuffily decorated room, the covertness, and the physical presence of the man she had portrayed as a tyrant. The Sunday school room was "dismal . . . barbaric . . . so stupidly ugly." Next to her, Siddall, she noted, was visibly triumphant, "nearly choking with glee. . . . I feared a scene on the spot." Varian seated himself apart and tried to sketch the scene without attracting notice.

Rockefeller, Miss Tarbell noted, repeatedly glanced at the gallery area where she was sitting, and she wondered whether he knew she was there. Feeling "a little mean," she gathered her impressions of "the oldest man I had ever seen . . . but what power!" At the time, Rockefeller was sixty-four and she was forty-six. She saw a man with a large, clear yet deeply lined face, a thin nose "like a thorn," and "no lips." She noted his uneasiness, the darting of his eyes, and the sincerity of his voice. His fellow parishioners seemed to admire him, and Miss Tarbell was surprised by the emotion that took hold of her as she took in the scene: "I was sorry for him. . . . Mr. Rockefeller, for all the conscious power written in face and voice and figure, was afraid, I told myself, afraid of his own kind."

When it came time in the service to shake hands, she and Siddall went down to join the throng around Rockefeller. He looked Miss Tarbell "fully in the face" before she quickly moved away. A blazing current of revulsion ran through her. "It was too awful," she recorded just after the fact. In her loose handwritten notes from the morning, she wrote wildly of Rockefeller's "colorless" eyes and, under them, "the puffiness I have long associated in men and women with sexual irregularity . . . Great power written on his mummy-like head and lust and death." As if describing a Dickensian villain, she embedded her impression of Rockefeller's morals into his physical features. His church, too, struck her as repugnant in atmosphere, filled with "stupid," "stolid faces."

She and Siddall did not linger, and Siddall tentatively suggested that they get drunk to relieve the stress of the morning. Instead Miss Tarbell sought out some hotel stationery and began to write.

* * *

**WRITING ABOUT ROCKEFELLER HIMSELF** was an ordeal for reasons that ran deeper than the lines of his features. As a journalist, she was tasked with being a watchdog rather than an activist; the idea of a wholehearted character assassination made her pause. She knew she could not in good faith base her reportage on her feelings alone, but still that antipathy refused to subside.

Miss Tarbell recognized her obligation to impartiality. She saw there was authentic industriousness, skill, and intelligence in the organization Rockefeller had assembled, and titled one of her chapters "The Legitimate Greatness of the Standard Oil Company." She searched newspaper archives and set Siddall to searching for reports of Rockefeller's professional deals, charitable gifts, and personal anecdotes; she asked Standard Oil competitors if they would be willing to share any letters or memos they had received from Rockefeller or his men. When it came to reporting on Standard Oil, "I never had an animus against their size and wealth, never objected to their corporate form," she claimed.

Every word of this statement is worthy of interrogation, for she did have an animus against Rockefeller, a rancor that seemed to gather force as the series drew to a close. She knew there was little intellectual justification for hating a wealthy man for his wealth, even if much of the evidence she had painstakingly gathered bore out her suspicions of Rockefeller as an embodiment of a ruthless fortune hunter. Confirmation bias, or the application of newly discovered evidence to back up an existing frame of mind, undoubtedly figured into her skewering final profile of Rockefeller and his career. Her finished narrative sketched a bloodless tycoon, a parasite bent on bringing financial and moral disaster upon his host.

Even in the early installments of the series, her far-from-neutral feelings about Rockefeller were already palpable. As one perceptive historian said of the character who emerged, "a reptilian John D. Rockefeller slither[ed] into view." Her opinion became the hinge on which the narrative turned, gave it an activist quality, and extended it into a larger argument about society. As she argued, it was the perception and evidence that "they had never played fair" that turned Standard Oil from a company into a cause, a symbol of all that was wrong with big business's scant regard for the individuals who fed it. "Human experience," in Miss Tarbell's words, "long ago taught us that if we allowed a man or a group of men autocratic power . . . they used that power to oppose or defraud the public." From her initial perception of the Standard as voracious and sly, the facts she reported and the way she framed them smoldered with judgment.

She tried with varying degrees of persuasiveness to assign her anger to causes that were objective and quantifiable. Her conclusion was that "[Standard Oil] had never played fair, and that ruined their greatness for me." Yet all she had seen at fifteen provided a bitter seed for the investigation. In a draft for an early article in the series, she even wrote, "A young Iowa school teacher and farmer, visiting at his home in Erie County, saw his chance to invent a receptacle which would hold oil in quantities." This character, written into the story as an example of hardworking entrepreneurship, was Franklin Tarbell.

Much later, as she neared eighty, Miss Tarbell told a friend that Standard Oil had cast a permanent sense of tragedy over her Oil Region home. She wrote, "This district saw and lived through the mad search for petroleum and the long labor to make it fit to give men more light, more power and heat. And along with it went the struggle of a few to get all that was in it for themselves. It was enough to curse the land forever." The Standard was always, for her, the destroyer of home and hope.

The story of Standard Oil came to represent America's moral fitness moving into the new century. "What I most feared," Miss Tarbell later wrote in her memoir, "was that we were raising our standard of living at the expense of our standard of character." In the mythology of her own family's struggles, the Standard's scale had allowed it to suppress healthy individualism. In Titusville, she had seen what selling out to Rockefeller could do to a man's place in society. "The most tragic effect I had seen in my girlhood," she recalled, "was partial ostracism of the renegade . . . a man's old associates crossed to the other side of the street rather than meet him." As for herself, she wrote, "In those days I looked with more contempt on the man who had gone over to the Standard than on the one who had been in jail."

*McClure's* gave readers startling photographic portraits of Rockefeller to illustrate Miss Tarbell's narrative. One was taken after a bout of alopecia—for which, some said, her articles were at least partially to blame—had left him without any hair at all, not even brows or lashes. In another version he wore a black skullcap, provoking a wave of Rockefeller-as-Shylock caricatures. Through 1905, newspaper cartoons showed Rockefeller in a variety of wigs—some shaped like devil horns, others like octopus tentacles, still others like a forest of dollar signs. (A Detroit magazine, *The Gateway*, demonstrated the injustice of this editorial decision by hiring an artist to doctor a selection of portraits of great Americans—beginning, of course, with Lincoln—removing hair, eyebrows, and beard, to bizarre and uncanny effect.)

Rockefeller, an intensely private man, was no miserly hermit. He has been called "the greatest philanthropist in American history." Rockefeller put his charity toward causes that Progressives might have applauded, had the source and size of his wealth not gotten in the way. The University of Chicago exists largely thanks to him, and he championed the cause of public health, funding schools at Johns Hopkins and Harvard. He funded a clinic for low-income women, and he also answered a plea from a school for black women in Georgia, becoming a major funder for what would later be Spelman College. Rockefeller himself was a devoted family man and churchgoer. He and his wife avoided high society in favor of playing with their children and landscaping their property, often rode the elevated train between home and the office, and built a public ice-skating rink next to the family home.

All this beneficence was turned against Rockefeller in *McClure's*. Miss Tarbell described his faith as "ignorant superstition." Of his tightly budgeted household, she noted that "parsimony . . . [was] made a virtue." She frankly disdained his home in aesthetic terms, putting bad taste on the same moral plane as monopolizing a natural resource. She called Forest Hill, the Rockefeller manse outside Cleveland, "a monument of cheap ugliness." About his legacy she wrote, "Our national life is on every side distinctly poorer, uglier, meaner for the kind of influence he exercises." She concluded that he was a calculating master of compartmentalization; there was a dual personality at work, she wrote, capable of corruption and bullying on a grand scale and clean, simple living in private.

As one of Miss Tarbell's own biographers has noted, her slant on Rockefeller is nearly as revealing of the author as the subject. Her tentative boundary between the professional and personal spheres of life was being dismantled. More and more, it seemed her heart itself hung in the balance.

* * *

AFTER CLEVELAND, Miss Tarbell returned to New York subdued by her sneaky encounter with Rockefeller, yet driven to finish what she had started. Emotion began to drain from her, and she had some trepidation about her character study being read by an attentive critical audience, as she wrote Siddall in early December 1903: "I think I shall watch the effect this article produces on the press more anxiously than any other. . . . I feel sometimes that my judgment of these papers is all raveled out; by the time I get to the end of one I cease to have any feeling about it at all."

She underestimated her own ability to convince readers. The Chicago *Inter-Ocean* called her series "one of the most stirring in our commercial history," an endeavor that "illustrates most strikingly the strange new conditions of business life in America." Perhaps most complimentary to her scientist's heart, the New York *World* said her work "gives us the same insight into the nature of trusts in general that the medical student gains of cancers from a scientific description of a typical case." "WOMAN DOES MARVELOUS WORK" exclaimed another paper, while the New York *Globe* called the series "so thrilling and dramatic that even those superior people whose boast is that they never read a serial made an exception for this one." One day a determined man appeared in the *McClure's* office and asked Miss Tarbell to get her hat: he intended to marry her and take her out west.

Miss Tarbell kept a scrapbook of all her reviews, including one announcement that S. S. McClure had been rejected from Westchester County's Ardsley Country Club by Standard supporters. One club member wrote to the Chicago *Examiner* to explain the decision, signing himself "A Gentleman": McClure, he wrote, "has forfeited his right to associate with millionaires, with gentlemen. He is the publisher of a magazine, and to that magazine he has admitted a history of the Standard Oil Company which is to the last degree offensive, not only to the Rockefeller family, but to all safe, sane and conservative citizens. I do not assert that the history is untrue; my point is that it discloses to the public in the most daring and reckless way the methods by which giant fortunes are accumulated." He concluded, with foot-in-mouth earnestness, "it is high time for the higher orders to assert themselves."

Despite Rockefeller's work as a philanthropist, his money was now seen as contaminated. Increasingly, politicians and institutions turned away gifts from the nation's richest man, whose net worth was around 1.5 percent of the country's total economic output—roughly equivalent to triple the wealth held by Bill Gates. Starting in 1904, Theodore Roosevelt declined campaign donations from Standard Oil, keenly aware that public image, once compromised, rarely recovers. A newspaper cartoon showed the harried, top-hatted tycoon asking a newsstand merchant, "Have you any reading matter that isn't about me?" Mark Twain wrote a satirical "Letter from Satan" to *Harper's Weekly,* protesting the new vogue of rejecting Rockefeller's contributions: "In all the ages," he wrote, "three-fourths of the support of the great charities has been conscience-money, as my books will show."

After Miss Tarbell's write-up from the church, arguments and counterarguments about Rockefeller's ethics, and hers, ricocheted through the media, from the *Newark News* to the *Sacramento Bee* and abroad, to Canada, Germany, and France. *The Nation* printed a scornful review, which cut Miss Tarbell deeply. In its view, *McClure's* betrayed serious naïveté about the reality of big business, singling out normal competitive practices as illegal and immoral when they were nothing of the kind. Several papers called out what they saw as "yellow magazinism," citing what they saw as the gratuitous, vindictive negativity of the series. The *Denver Republican* predicted that Miss Tarbell's reputation would endure as "the greatest of all literary vivisectionists." One of the most partisan attacks came from a small newspaper, the *Derrick,* of Oil City, Pennsylvania, under the head-line "Hysterical Woman Versus Historical Fact." The *Derrick* was faithful to the Standard, accusing Miss Tarbell of being "venomous," proving herself a "literary pervert," producing "history made to order," and single-handedly discrediting the literature of exposure.

Gender was a frequent theme among critical letters and reviews. In the near-universal acclaim for her Lincoln series, the fact that she was a woman was rarely mentioned as a factor behind any guiding quality of the work. The Rockefeller profile provoked a very different reaction, one that derided a "nagging," "scolding" Miss Tarbell for seeing her subject through the blurry lens of unchecked subjectivity. The *Derrick* did not mince words when it accused her of "shameless audacity and feminine mendacity," rail-ing that as a woman, Miss Tarbell "accepts half truths for whole facts . . . perverts facts to suit her own peculiar ideas of circumstances and distorts everything in her effort to be sensational and maintain her reputation as a 'yellow' writer." In the words of one Detroit-based critic, "it should not be forgotten that Miss Tarbell, as her name implies, is a woman . . . [w]ith all a woman's weakness of will, ideals of manly beauty, desire for showy entertainment, magnificent dinners, [and] personal adornment." In sketch-ing a monster, the writer argued, Miss Tarbell had shown herself as being monstrous. She was, like all women, "ruled by her sympathies," and should be pitied.

A diverging but equally reductive tack painted Miss Tarbell as robotic and merciless—unnatural qualities for a woman. One Los Angeles reporter, comparing her to her colleague William Allen White, wrote that while White was bubbling and exuberant, "Miss Tarbell's wonderful intellect is a pitiles [*sic*], disinterested, white light." She would long be seen as a fascinating enigma; twenty years later, as she toured the Midwest on the speaking circuit and sat by the stage as local luminaries introduced her, she would hear herself described as a "notorious woman" and the subject of long musings as to why she had never married.

One of the more in-depth efforts at discrediting the series, *A Study of John D. Rockefeller,* was produced in 1905 by a Cleveland businessman and fellow congregation member of the Euclid Avenue church, a man named Marcus Brown. "It is not surprising that Mr. Rockefeller suffers a good deal of criticism, and even worse," wrote Brown, "from poisonous seed sown in the popular mind by persons craving notoriety. . . . This is only what the best and truest characters have always suffered." Brown's book had a second purpose, as an oddly packaged personal ad. His wife had died less than a year before the book's publication, leaving him with four children; Brown included a photograph of his palatial home as well as testimonials to his character in the book's preface, hoping suitable unmarried women might take interest.

The best-known rebuttal started as a Harvard senior thesis. Gilbert Holland Montague, with the collaboration of Standard Oil's in-house lawyer, hastily finished *The Rise and Progress of the Standard Oil Company* in 1903. Montague's book was, in Miss Tarbell's view, "not exactly a best seller but certainly a best circulator"—and deliberately so. Public libraries were sent generous stock by an anonymous funder, and ministers, teachers, and politicians similarly received free copies from the publisher. She read Montague's account as soon as she could, noting that it "separated business and ethics in a way that must have been a comfort at 26 Broadway."

When Rockefeller was questioned about Miss Tarbell's series, he remained tight-lipped, saying only that her claims were "without foundation" and that "it has always been the policy of Standard Oil to keep silent under attack and let our acts speak for themselves." The idea of directly rebutting *McClure's* struck him as "unstatesmanlike." When allies of the Standard urged him to respond, he answered, "Gentlemen, we must not be entangled in controversies. If she is right we will not gain anything by answering, and if she is wrong time will vindicate us." He had decided to play the long game, but could not have known how long it would remain in the forefront of public consciousness. Miss Tarbell had not yet finished her series, which would be compiled and released as a book two years later.

Rockefeller even once claimed not to have read *McClure's,* but his wife's amanuensis accidentally broke his cover when remembering a long trip she took with the family in the spring of 1903. "He liked to have things read to him, and during these months I read aloud Ida Tarbell's diatribes," she recalled. "He listened musingly, with keen interest and no resentment." When prodded, he said that Tarbell made "a pretense of fairness" but "like some women, she distorts facts, states as facts what she must know is untrue, and utterly disregards reason."

Rockefeller refused to budge from his decision to remain silent. One day, walking near his Forest Hill estate, a friend questioned this policy. Rockefeller told him, gesturing toward a worm in their path, "If I step on that worm I will call attention to it. If I ignore it, it will disappear." But to those in his circle, he showed a flinching resentment against Ida Tarbell and her story. Her perspective seemed to fit in with his sense that the world turned against true greatness and leadership. "Not a word about that misguided woman," he said when he heard her name. To one acquaintance, he remarked, "Things have changed since you and I were boys. The world is full of socialists and anarchists. Whenever a man succeeds remarkably in any particular line of business, they jump on him and cry him down."

The concerted PR campaign to counteract Miss Tarbell's influence was quietly sustained for years. Rockefeller himself never directly denied her findings, though with age, he warmed very slightly to publicity and occasionally allowed himself to be photographed on the golf course. Sympathetic reporters focused on Rockefeller the family man and philanthropist.

In 1910, Standard Oil funded the distribution of a pamphlet that gave Miss Tarbell her first chance at reading her own biography. It was written by Elbert Hubbard, the socialist founder of an Arts & Crafts movement commune in western New York. Far from an obvious admirer of Rockefeller, Hubbard was a self-identified anarchist who published a satirical magazine. Ida thought Hubbard was "entertaining" and looked forward to reading his piece, only to be gravely disappointed. Throughout his article, Hubbard was alternately sorrowful and hostile. He called her "an honest, bitter, talented, prejudiced and disappointed woman" burdened by resentment since her father's business failure, a ruthless "bushwhacker" who "shot from cover, and she shot to kill." He concluded that her "method of inky warfare is quite as unethical as the alleged tentacle-octopi policy" that was the object of her attack. Her chagrin was compounded by the fact that the pamphlet seemed constantly pushed her way—"some waggish member of the McClure group" would inevitably give her another copy around her birthday or Christmas.

Miss Tarbell was never much for gossip, but getting to the bottom of grudges, feuds, and rumors had become her life's work. By now, the bulk of new information about the company had been reported and published, and she had assessed the man himself as best she could, through infiltrating his church—she did not quickly forgive herself for spying. "No achievement on earth could justify those methods," she felt.

As her name became practically synonymous with her fearsome, interminable *History of Standard Oil,* mental exhaustion overwhelmed her. She longed intensely to put it all behind her. "The more intimately I went into my subject, the more hateful it became to me," she wrote. Unfortunately, it seemed to raise its head wherever she looked.

Other writers stepped in to supply readers with derivative stories on Rockefeller. There was even a play inspired by Miss Tarbell's series. In *The Lion and the Mouse,* heroine Shirley Rossmore determines to expose the man who betrayed her father; she claims to be a biographer to gain access to John S. Ryder, the world's richest man. But he falls in love with her, and makes an offer she cannot refuse. Miss Tarbell herself was offered the starring role for a fee of $2,500 per week for twenty weeks—the highest offer yet made to an American theater actress—but she declined.

Writing about the dead seemed much easier than trying to deliver a fair and accurate picture of the living. She yearned to return to writing about history long past. "There would be none of these harrowing human beings confronting me, tearing me between contempt and pity, admiration and anger, baffling me." Her brain was "fogged," hastening her desire to put the story behind her and start something new.

Instead, she would become mired in a new calamity—one that would lead to the dissolution of *McClure's* at the very height of its power and prestige.

*Part III*

---

# FALL

# 15

# The Shame of S. S. McClure

Theodore Roosevelt turned the final page of the January 1903 issue of *McClure's,* then sent McClure a letter inviting him to the White House. Newsstands sold out, and the Chief exulted. The Cleveland *Plain Dealer* announced, *"McClure's* is edited with clairvoyance." "I doubt whether any other magazine published in America ever achieved such sudden and overwhelming attention," wrote Ray Stannard Baker. "We put our finger upon the sorest spots in American life."

As McClure paged through the proof or "dummy" version of the magazine, it struck him that the feature stories were all, at their base, about the same thing—the high-stakes dysfunction in industry and politics. Alongside Miss Tarbell's Oil War chapter and Steffens's exposé of corruption in Minneapolis, Baker published his fourth dispatch from the labor unrest in Pennsylvania coal country.

Just before the issue went to press, McClure himself contributed an editorial that pointed out the intersections between their pieces, which together made "such an arraignment of American character as should make every one of us stop and think." His final words were a portentous warning against apathy: "We forget that we are all the people; that while each of us in his group can shove off on the rest of the bill to-day, the debt is only postponed. . . . We have to pay in the end, every one of us. And in the end the sum total of the debt will be our liberty."

The crux of the magazine's message at the start of 1903 was a sober challenge to the ascending power of business in politics, which, as *McClure's* saw it, were learning "to hunt together." The focus of that particular issue may not have been deliberate, and there were few clear answers to be found in its pages, but it nevertheless sounded a hectoring alarm bell.

Meanwhile, as McClure's rival editors readied their own sensational investigative stories, he abandoned New York and moved restlessly between London, France, and the Italian lakes. The magazine approached its tenth birthday having attained unhoped-for fame, but just as it seemed its star couldn't rise higher, its Chief looked determined to tear it down.

\* \* \*

**IN THE SAME LANDMARK ISSUE,** a singsong poem appeared. It contrasted bafflingly with the in-depth reporting and sophisticated flair of the rest of the magazine. The title was "A Boy's Point of View," and it went:

> Sometimes the road to Sunday School
> Drags out so hot and dreary,
> But that same road to go trout-fishing,
> It springs along so cheery.
>
> I get so tired running errands
> I'd almost like to drop;
> But when I'm playing hare-and-hounds
> I never want to stop.

The author was twenty-five-year-old Florence Wilkinson, from Tarrytown, New York. McClure had insisted on publishing Miss Wilkinson over the wishes of Witter Bynner, who had first read the poem after it was submitted, and Viola Roseboro, who was certain they should reject it.

Miss Tarbell noted this editorial dustup with concern, though on the surface it was ordinary enough. In McClure's attitude this time, however, she sensed a submerged danger. It had been nearly a decade since Ida Tarbell and S. S. McClure had first met in Paris, and she was surprised to find herself, despite the demands of the Standard series and discomfort with fame, fulfilled. "Here was a group of people I could work with, without sacrifice or irritation," she wrote. "Here was a healthy growing undertaking which excited me, while it seemed to offer endless opportunity to contribute to the better thinking of the country." Her future at *McClure's* looked "fair and permanent." But in the clash of opinions over Florence Wilkinson's verse she saw the seeds of something that would threaten that permanence: scandal.

In the spring after the January 1903 issue, as Miss Tarbell looked ahead to another year's worth of Standard Oil articles, McClure boarded a steamer for Europe. He was accompanied by Hattie and their son Robby, as well as Florence Wilkinson, who bore a startling resemblance to Hattie in her college days. Hattie herself, plagued by ill health, frequently felt too unwell to socialize and stayed in her stateroom, but a friend who had joined the trip, rising novelist Alice Hegan Rice, wrote of "starry nights on the boat deck when we lay in steamer chairs and listened by the hour to Mr. McClure's fascinating reminiscences. . . . He held us enthralled."

The phases of the trip seemed designed to give McClure time away from his wife's frailty and Miss Tarbell's beady eye. Once in London, McClure packed Hattie off to France and threw himself into a social whirl. Bram Stoker invited him to his theater box. The following night brought a long lunch and more calls, and the night after that another literary debauch at the Vagabond Club; otherwise, McClure wrote breezily and inaccurately to Hattie, "I am doing very little."

Miss Wilkinson joined the party going from London to France. Then, leaving Hattie to buy clothes and knickknacks in Paris, she and McClure withdrew to the mountain resort of Chamonix, where the affair likely began in earnest. Ida Tarbell arrived on the Continent for a vacation and found herself assigned to keep Hattie company, waiting for word from McClure, who had decided to throw a veil over his flirtation by inviting Miss Tarbell and the Rices to hike with him in Italy. Alice Hegan Rice and her new husband, oblivious to the rumblings of crisis, delighted in tramping through the Alps with their belongings in rucksacks—"a rollicking adventure as conducted by our buccaneer leader," wrote Rice, rhapsodizing about the cowbells and sunshine of Switzerland, the bemused hausfraus who allowed McClure to poke around their kitchens as he cooked dinner for the group, and the way the Chief "went through life like a tornado carrying everything in his wake."

Once the Rices had gone, McClure abruptly rejoined Miss Wilkinson in Lake Como. Hattie and Miss Tarbell were flummoxed by their boldness. In late August 1903, the young poet sent a chatty, impressionistic letter to Hattie from Lake Como, writing how, with McClure by her side, "The days pass quietly, dreamily." She described the heavenliness of evenings gazing at "the lake in a bath of opal lights," and expressed hopes that Hattie was enjoying an extended Parisian shopping trip. The same day, McClure wrote his wife and Miss Tarbell that he had reserved their steamer tickets from France to New York, and that "you had better go Saturday." If he was trying to get rid of them, he was foiled by their swift protest. In the end, they all sailed back together, with McClure in appeasement mode: the McClures' twentieth wedding anniversary fell while they were at sea, and McClure gave Hattie a dazzling marquise ring, with three large diamonds set among eighteen smaller stones. Unwilling to face her husband's betrayal head-on, Hattie drew instead on her deep faith—in both God and her husband—and landed in New York with all her suspicions repressed.

McClure accepted another Wilkinson verse for the October 1903 issue, in which the biggest feature was Lincoln Steffens's report from Chicago. This poem was titled "Naughtiness," with the apt starting verse:

Why am I sometimes naughty
And sometimes very good?
What makes me act so different?
I never understood.

The catchy, juvenile rhythm of Miss Wilkinson's poetry grated on Miss Tarbell, who was once again in demand as a counselor for the staff. Once home, McClure did not take long to sow further unrest at the office. Against the advice of the other directors—Phillips, Robby McClure, and the surviving Brady brothers, Curtis and Oscar—he hired two new journalists to work on his idea for a new weekly magazine. Then, announcing he wanted to pursue a new story on crime in Europe and needed to gather his own statistics, he sailed—alone, apparently—for England in November.

There he threw himself once more into deal making and fun, though this time he traveled alone. An assistant tasked with informing Hattie of his movements gave a snapshot of that season's social whirl: "I have just left Mr McClure at Charing Cross where he was leaving for Mr. Kipling's home in Sussex. He is spending the night there, and is coming up to town some time during the morning, for he has an engagement to lunch with Conan Doyle, and also appointments in the afternoon with Mr Heinemann and Mr. Anthony Hope Hawkins. . . . On Thursday he has planned to lunch with Mr. Conrad and Mr. Hueffer [Ford Madox Ford]."

McClure claimed the bustle made him young again. "My mind is clearing up in many matters," he wrote Hattie; "I feel *sure* of myself as I haven't for many years." She, who had seen these "sure" phases come and go over the past thirty years, no doubt took the transformation with a grain of salt and hoped the subsequent crash would not be too steep.

Miss Tarbell had become so close to McClure and Hattie that she had her own bedroom in their home in Ardsley, the Westchester village on the Hudson where they had bought a large house. In a melodramatic moment of fearing for his health, McClure had even written his wife, "In case of my death [Miss Tarbell] would be your mainstay," and he encouraged Hattie to decorate the room with every consideration of Miss Tarbell's character and comfort. Conscious of the intimacy between McClure and Miss Wilkinson, and the volatility of the Chief's sudden good cheer, Miss Tarbell could not have slept well at Ardsley despite her elegantly appointed suite. Her alarm only grew when McClure disappeared on yet another holiday in spring

1904, supposedly hiking the Appalachian Mountains alone, a story that no one could verify.

The intrigue put not just McClure's marriage and editorial authority at risk, but also the magazine's hard-earned reputation. The senior staff knew that once S. S. began to sink under the wave of scandal, the value of *McClure's* would do the same. Any discussion of *McClure's* would inevitably drift to gossip, and McClure himself would be vulnerable to blackmail. No matter how they might strive to produce groundbreaking, substantial work, if William d'Alton Mann, editor of the *Town Topics* gossip sheet, were to write about the salacious rumors swirling around the Chief, *McClure's* would no longer be taken seriously.

Mann's weekly "Saunterings" column, a precursor to *The New Yorker's* "Talk of the Town" with a dash of *National Enquirer* thrown in, was read with bated breath at genteel breakfast tables from Manhattan to Newport. Juicy blind items abounded, with harmless gossip jostling alongside scathing allegations of high-society adultery and crookedness. (Among many others, the column was responsible for the divorce of a young Emily Post, future arbiter of etiquette, from her husband, Edwin, who was maintaining a secret apartment with a chorus girl.) Mann had an army of spies to supply him with these secrets, mainly in the servants' quarters of the very rich, but extending to telegraph operators, hotel employees, and disgruntled aspirants like the struggling young literary men out of the Midwest who were continually hired and forgotten by McClure.

At the same time, the magazine was doing important and original work. In January 1904, McClure assigned Carl Schurz to write "Can the South Solve Its Negro Problem?" and then published Thomas Nelson Page's reply, "The Negro: The Southerner's Problem." It was the first open discussion of the racial divide in a major magazine read by those in power, a debate that had long been under moratorium by editorial gatekeepers who worried about alienating readers. McClure was jeopardizing his name at a time when he was responsible for an essential national conversation.

Miss Tarbell called on Phillips to help. Motivated by both mercenary and moral instincts—each owned 16 percent of the S. S. McClure Company, and both felt personally bound to McClure—the two joined forces in trying to make S. S. realize the weight of his actions.

When McClure dispatched Witter Bynner to deliver a note and a box of flowers to Miss Wilkinson, their suspicions that the affair was still happening were confirmed. Miss Tarbell intercepted Bynner on his return and angrily accused him of acting as an accomplice. The young man promised he would never run such an errand again; the note, he summarized for his colleagues, was a letter of acceptance for "some very bad lines by a most incompetent young lady," handwritten by McClure. Later Bynner saw Miss Tarbell and Phillips cornering their editor-in-chief. McClure sat quiet and seemingly abashed as his closest allies scolded, pleaded, and negotiated with him to refrain from making a fool of himself.

Now that his secret life was a topic of office strife, McClure found his sleep troubled by suffocating dreams. By the start of June 1904, his mental health had disintegrated. He joined Hattie at Divonne, where he told her of a vivid dream that their contemporary Freud would have chewed over with appetite: "I dreamt last night I was sleeping under the mattress with a couple on the mattress." He was trapped, he seemed to be saying, and constitutionally unable to wake up and change direction.

An intervention proceeded outside the office. Phillips himself went alone to meet Miss Wilkinson, urged her to stop writing to McClure, and asked her to return all the love letters she had from him. She asked for time to think it over and later sent a response that bewildered Miss Tarbell and Phillips: she would continue to write to McClure, but she assured them that future letters would be sent care of Hattie. "The Lord keep us! I'm too small for this!" Miss Tarbell scribbled to Phillips. "Letters under her convoy! He can persuade her to *anything* and if in the end we see a ménage à trois, I shall not be greatly surprised. . . . He's a Mormon, an uncivilized, unmoral, untutored natural man with enough canniness to keep himself out of jails and asylums."

Despite Miss Wilkinson's bohemian leanings, Miss Tarbell thought the woman was probably still the more reasonable party. She suggested to Phillips that they hasten her disenchantment with McClure by telling her that the Chief had other flirtations. "It may be cruel to tell her this," wrote Miss Tarbell, "but we seem to be the only ones to use the knife and someone must do it."

In the March 1904 issue, another few verses by Miss Wilkinson appeared, titled "Genius." It is tempting to conjecture the poet was thinking of McClure as she wrote:

> What seest thou in yonder human face,
>     Pale, frail, and small?
> I see a soul by tragedy worn thin;
> I read a page of poetry and of sin.
>     What seest thou?
> I see a human face,
>     Pale, frail, and small.

It must have been infuriating for Miss Tarbell to see this glaze of romance applied to McClure's breakdown. But she had to keep her sharp words sheathed in velvet, at least for now. Miss Wilkinson was starting to bristle at being scolded like a child. "My Dear Miss Wilkinson," Miss Tarbell wrote on May 28, 1904, in a tone that betrays pursed lips and a frown. "Neither Mr. Phillips nor I have the . . . inclination to judge the hearts of other men and women. Both of us deplored from the first the intimacy between you and Mr. McClure because we believed that in the nature of things nothing but pain and moral disintegration could come from it—but we have not judged."

The assurance was unconvincing. Miss Tarbell was a practiced diplomat, but Miss Wilkinson sensed she was seen as a liability by the magazine staff, and she resented it. The younger woman was caught up in the experience of being loved by S. S. McClure, and that heady sense of power was as yet undimmed by the knowledge that Miss Tarbell, Hattie, and others assumed "pain and moral disintegration" would be quick to follow.

Miss Tarbell needed to muster a stronger campaign. An ally presented herself in the form of Mary Bisland, originally of New Orleans, who had worked her way up the staff and was then managing the London office. Miss

Bisland radiated fierce propriety; always stiffly corseted, she rarely removed her gray suede gloves in the office. After their rest cures in Divonne, S. S. and Hattie liked to linger in London before heading back to work. As she got to know her employer better, Miss Bisland watched McClure with steely judgment, and she was appalled when Hattie began openly discussing her husband's antics.

Through the summers of 1903 and 1904, Miss Bisland and Miss Tarbell sketched out the dire situation in their letters. "Imagine my surprise on meeting them at the Bedford hotel to have Mrs McClure pour out the odious story in all its base & squalid details," wrote Miss Bisland. "She told me he was already tired of her & was using every artifice to persuade her to return to New York, while swearing that he was having no communications with his light o' love. I knew he was constantly sending letters & cables."

Furthermore, Miss Bisland reported—gloves off, when it came to this topic—that "he & that female beast took an apartment & lived together" briefly in Paris. McClure, far from being abashed, seemed to relish having a frank and listening ear and mischievously confided in Miss Bisland. "His poor wife does swallow his falsehoods & he chuckled in telling me of the way she believed him," Miss Bisland wrote Miss Tarbell. "He never even speaks of his children, grew impatient if I mentioned the magazine or business & wanted to talk of nothing but his relations with Miss Wilkinson." She found even McClure's face "bloated & disfigured with vice," and in an effort to throw cold water on his infatuation she gave him a piece of her mind. "Mr M'Clure said no one had used such language to him," she wrote, "but pshaw! It was breath wasted."

McClure continued to insist that, though he and Miss Wilkinson had briefly shared an apartment in Paris, nothing immoral had taken place between them. Phillips was willing to believe him, but Tarbell and Bisland were not. The two women knew their livelihood was potentially at risk, given the frenzied popularity of the gossip pages in New York, and they were growing exasperated—though, as the tone of their letters indicates, also fascinated—by their Chief's astoundingly public dalliance.

Both women were appalled at Hattie's lack of gumption. But by late

May 1904, Hattie faced the seriousness of the situation. To Phillips and Miss Tarbell, Hattie wrote assuaging letters; she told them she intended to take charge of McClure's recovery, both mental and moral. Her new, crisp tone of high dudgeon put some heart into Miss Tarbell, who applauded the letter as being "a great satisfaction. . . . You must take the upper hand for Mr. McClure's sake as well as your own." She tried to emphasize the high stakes of the matter: "I feel the office and business cannot endure permanently the strains which have been put upon it in the past and which to my consternation seem to me we are about to have to endure again. Mr. McClure *must* get well."

That rush of hope was short-lived. If Hattie had any real sway over McClure's compulsions, she found she could only exert it through tender persuasion, not by assertively taking charge. McClure himself turned the tables on the situation by wooing her for the duration of a steamer voyage. Afterward, Hattie credulously cabled Miss Tarbell that all was once again harmonious between them. Miss Tarbell was at her wit's end. She vented to Phillips, "Isn't he the most amazing creature the Lord ever made! And is there any bottom to the trustfulness of such a woman! . . . [H]e has evidently been *making love to his wife*! But if I were she I'd watch him!"

For Miss Tarbell, standing by patiently and watching the McClures' bogus reconciliation felt nearly as disreputable as spying on Rockefeller in church. She found herself repelled by McClure's lies, Hattie's passivity, and Miss Wilkinson's air that she was the aggrieved heroine of a great and misunderstood romance.

It was painful enough to read Florence's work in a magazine that published William Butler Yeats and A. E. Housman; ultimately, *McClure's* would publish more titles by Miss Wilkinson than any other poet.

* * *

**AFTER MONTHS OF CAMPAIGNING** by Phillips and Miss Tarbell, Miss Wilkinson capitulated. She wrote to Phillips that she still cared for McClure, but the affair was over, and the love letters were returned to McClure in France. The contentious packet arrived on June 27, 1904, and later that week, Hattie wrote to Miss Tarbell, "The suspense and anxiety are all over now, and Sam has nothing to do but recover."

The Chief himself wrote to Phillips from his rest cure, "I've done some squirming & squealing, but I'm all right. . . . I've been an awful fool. My desires & my duties again jump together." He was in reality exhausted and guilty, and in worse health than ever. Doctors prescribed endless esoteric cures, including one that required him to eat nothing but broiled squab twice a day. Periodically, he retired to bed for days on end, consuming nothing but milk. But nothing assuaged McClure's anxiety that he and his magazine were deteriorating irrevocably. He obsessed over the rise of *Everybody's Magazine,* whose investigative series "Frenzied Finance" won a circulation of more than 500,000 readers.

It was now clear—and painfully public—that his and Hattie's relationship had permanently passed beyond the intensity he craved. The couple's friend Frances Hodgson Burnett noted Hattie's confession that S. S. was her "youngest, my most cherished babe." Since before the launch of the magazine, when Hattie went to her family in Galesburg to recover from the lingering pain that dogged her after the birth of their four children, she recognized their relationship had settled into a pattern that she had never anticipated during their fevered courtship at Knox.

McClure, though he loved and enjoyed his family, was single-minded about the magazine. He was a nineteenth-century husband and father; his *McClure's*-era letters to Hattie have a tone of paternalistic tenderness rather than partnership. Frequently he extended trips without telling her, forgot to leave her a copy of his itinerary, or reunited with her only to dash off traveling with friends immediately. After the revelation of his affair, Hattie relied on her faith to sustain her. "Our life has a deep wound," she wrote Miss Tarbell from France, "but it is all given to God."

Her renewed wifely sympathy was again shaken at the end of July, when she received a vengeful missive from Florence Wilkinson. It appeared McClure had, with stunning speed and secrecy, acquired another mistress: Miss Wilkinson's close friend, the writer Edith Wherry.

McClure again denied everything. Hattie, worried that tough love would lead to his complete nervous breakdown, decided to put on a show of believing him and dedicate herself to improving his health. "I find myself tempted to fling back at him his promises, but I have seen how disastrous that would be, and I tenderly accept all he offers," Hattie wrote to Phillips. McClure's clouded thinking worried his family and staff alike, and Hattie wrote to Miss Tarbell that their doctor thought her husband "quite ill in the mind."

McClure's return to New York in late 1904 found his staff tense and skeptical. "Mrs. McC is radiant and full of confidence," Miss Tarbell wrote Phillips. "He has persuaded her he never saw Miss W[herry] but three times in Geneva and that all the suspicion about her is of Miss W's creation, a work of jealousy and spite." Miss Tarbell thought she saw McClure clearly: he was "the same canny, scheming, unstable soul. . . . He is not changed." Beneath her exasperation with him, she must have been deeply saddened. McClure had inspired her and believed in her. If he changed or fell apart, she would be losing much more than an employer.

Edith Wherry was not as retiring or understanding as Florence Wilkinson had been. In the summer of 1905, after nearly a year of increasingly erratic behavior by her husband, Hattie McClure opened a manuscript packet that turned out to be "The Shame of SS McClure, Illustrated by Letter and Original Documents," a tell-all written by Miss Wherry, with the direction that McClure should "publish it in the magazine with other important revelations." There was a needling, sarcastic echo between her title and Steffens's "The Shame of Minneapolis," published two years previously. The timing was absurd: in August, McClure was prominently featured in the press as a voice for reform, an intellectual "pioneer" advocating that "the press is the Republic's hope," and that "with one honest newspaper . . . the battle will be won."

A line from one of Miss Wherry's letters survives; she wrote, "I have decided to live henceforth in truth and honor. . . . But to carry out my intention it is necessary that your wife know the truth. . . . [She] should know that after your 'conversion' you returned to me with the same ardor as before." Her manuscript was quietly disposed of.

Now desperate, Hattie turned to Miss Tarbell, who sent an urgent telegram to McClure, who was now off apparently researching a story in Chicago. He missed it but was back in New York the next day and repented to Hattie yet again. "My precious wife," he effused after they had reconciled. "I believe I am wholly well mentally, morally and physically. Thank God and thank you wife of my heart and of my youth!"

Hattie had few choices. She was, as was expected from a traditional Christian wife, the moral compass of the household, but she could not really influence her husband's thinking on any significant point. Instead she wielded her power over domestic matters and raised children. When their middle daughter, Elizabeth, in the midst of the upheaval of 1904, unexpectedly asked her mother if they could adopt a three-year-old boy she had met on a chance charitable visit to an impoverished Italian immigrant family in New York, Hattie quickly accepted him. She threw herself into caring for Enrico, or Henry as he was later called.

Even after the revelation of the second affair, Hattie could only respond with a muddle of submissive devotion and pious watchfulness. As she went to meet S. S. for a late summer rest cure, she wrote her husband: "You may think of me as the faithful dog, lying before your door, waiting to hear sounds of your stirring in your chamber, ready to spring up when your door opens, reaching for a caress from your beloved hand, and closely following the steps of your dear feet wherever they may go."

At the end of her letter, Hattie attempted to change tack. She emphasized her own frayed sense of dignity and encouraged him to think of his, too. "You may think of me also more highly than that," she wrote, and warned him not to indulge in "buying the personal honor of women, corrupting their consciences and staining their reputations. Watch and pray, that ye enter not into temptation." But temptation was not finished with McClure.

# 16

# More Sinister and Painful

I n March 1905, grieving from the death of her much-loved father and tired of Rockefeller and public attention alike, Miss Tarbell decided to go west. The loss of Franklin "darkened my world," she later wrote. It prompted a period of angry bereavement, self-preservation, and rethinking her obligations to the magazine. This withdrawal, just after the completion of *The History of Standard Oil,* reverberated through the foundations and buttresses of *McClure's.*

Blessedly, her expense account gave her the leeway to take some distance after Franklin's funeral. She spent ten days riding across the Kansas prairie in between dust storms, bumping along on a horse-drawn buckboard, going without a bath for the duration because the drought had sucked out the water supply. She was too exhilarated to care. Here was a setting far from the intrigues of home, with the vitality and fresh promise that had never been part of the Standard Oil story, with its fait-accompli dominance. Taking notes for a story on young western fortune hunters, she wrote, "I had joined an eager, determined, exultant procession of wildcatters and promoters, of youths looking for their chance or seeking adventure for the first time, tasting it to the full."

The concluding piece in her Standard Oil series had been published in October 1904, and the articles were collected and published as a book the same year. In the final chapters, she was staunch in her condemnation of Rockefeller and his empire, but her disenchantment with her own work seeped through. She even suspected that her dismembering of the Standard Oil Company and its predatory ways would be read in the future as a guide to wily business practices, instead of a shocking exposé. "The history of the organization is studied as a practical lesson in money-making," she wrote. "More than once the writer of these articles, in talking with business men, has had the uncomfortable feeling that the chief result of her work as far as these persons were concerned, was to give them pointers!" Everyone, it seemed, was awed by Miss Tarbell's work, with the exception of the author herself.

McClure gloried in her achievement as if it were his own. "The way you are generally esteemed and reverenced pleases me tremendously," McClure wrote her. "You are today the most generally famous woman in America. . . . People universally speak of you with such a reverence that I am getting sort of afraid of you." His joking tone clothed a real anxiety. As Miss Tarbell became the subject of admiring talk in smoky club rooms across the nation, McClure began to realize she no longer depended on his authority and pocketbook as she had ten years previously.

Ida Tarbell had supposed that by avoiding intimate relationships with men, she would be protected from the burdens of the average woman who kept to her "place" as the anchor of family life. It was disturbing to find she was still vulnerable, and still obliged to be a man's helpmeet. Mitigating public disaster from McClure's affairs was now one of her primary concerns. When she heard that Florence Wilkinson had written yet again to McClure to invite him for a visit—accompanied by Hattie, for propriety's sake—Miss Tarbell was quick to secure a promise from all parties that it would be the last meeting.

There was nothing interesting now about chaperoning these misbehaving adults, all of whom thought themselves socially superior to their hawk-eyed spinster friend, Miss Tarbell. She wrote to Bert Boyden, "She [Miss Wilkinson] has become simply impossible & fancy. Too exacting &

unreasonable for even the General [McClure] who is in a wild state of excitement." Miss Tarbell keenly missed the ideas and enthusiasm she had formerly drawn from her Chief, but still, she exhorted her colleagues to have faith in the genius of McClure, who, she wrote Boyden, "has done some really wonderful work—if we can only carry it out. I believe he's tired of the girl." As if trying to convince herself, she ended with the hopeful thought that McClure's philandering was simply a midlife phase.

Meanwhile, McClure himself began to worry that one of his foundational relationships was in flux. When Miss Tarbell, tired out by grief and unsavory responsibilities, turned inward, he quickly felt the cold. He wrote and reminded her, almost pleadingly, of the history and love between them. Who else, he seemed to ask in these letters, truly *saw* her the way he did? "There are times when your face expresses a singular pathos & sense of suffering," he wrote from Lausanne. "With regret & infinite longing I recall the many years of your singular kindness & devotion to me. I have no right ever again to command them." Experiencing something like withdrawal, McClure wooed her earnestly, regretfully. "I have always cared for you in a special manner, as much as a man can care for a woman without loving her," he wrote. "What a pearl of great price to throw away in losing you!"

The Chief sensed Miss Tarbell's sharp and inexorable judgment in her silence, and appealed to her to soften. "I am now at the bottom. I can go no farther or feel any sadder," he wrote her, in the midst of the Wilkinson affair. Even if her personal sympathies were now unavailable to him, he couldn't quite believe that Miss Tarbell had run out of excitement for their shared work. "We have the greatest & most splendid achievements in front of us than any living people have," he wrote in the same letter. Then, concluding on a note of mournful vanity, he implied that he felt the burden of his troubles more acutely than anyone: "My face *looks* strong in determination & force, but it is getting terribly lined, & I shall be gray when I return."

As he had while courting Hattie, and while patching over his marriage after the revelations of Florence Wilkinson and Edith Wherry, McClure made sweeping assurances of present and future devotion. "Dearest & dearest & best friend," he scribbled from Paris. "You have saved me & now I am very happy in my new life. . . . I shall never again be first in your affections as I once was, that will be a punishment, but I want your perfect esteem & confidence. . . . I am yours as in all the dear years." His soaring words did not have the effect of renewing their closeness, however, for his reader was jaded by the time she read these lines.

Miss Tarbell generally found reserve more effective than intimacy, at least in her friendships at work, but she had allowed herself to grow close with her General. Now she began to withhold more of herself. It didn't come naturally. She was by reflex solicitous, raised with the notion that members of her sex were programmed to care for others. "I always feel brutal when I don't do what the other person wants," she once remarked. But with her trust in McClure eroded and her patience with melodrama exhausted, she reverted to a pattern of behavior that Viola Roseboro had long noticed. "[H]er life largely consisted in holding people off," Miss Roseboro recalled, and this total absence of "coquettries" seemed to fan the interest and admiration of others. The Chief hadn't realized how she had privileged him until that closeness was taken away.

Though S. S. now grasped after affection and reassurance—"To me you are the soul & solace & substance of our whole enterprise," he insisted—he could not help himself. As much as he clung to memories of Miss Tarbell's warmth and loyalty, he itched to deploy her toward a story that would make *McClure's* the talk of Washington. He concluded his letter after Franklin Tarbell's death by suggesting she return to the office and begin a piece on the U.S. Senate, "what seems to me to be the most important piece of work to be done for a magazine in America." He was certain that in her hands, the story couldn't fail to bring further fame and profit. The thought that investigative assignments did not have a place in a condolence letter did not occur to him.

In addition to fielding McClure's aggrieved letters, Miss Tarbell found fame increasingly disagreeable. Though she sought a change of scene, she was recognized everywhere she went, even in the West. "It brought fantastic situations where I was utterly unfit to play the part," she recalled. Once, in the then-small, uncouth town of Tulsa, Oklahoma, a band serenaded her and she was called upon to make an impromptu speech to her fans. "I was horrified at the idea," she wrote, and distracted her audience by buying them all cigars. "A woman of twenty-five, fresh, full of zest, only interested in what was happening to her, would have reveled in the experience," she knew. Ida Tarbell, meanwhile, was "fifty, fagged, wanting to be let alone while I collected trustworthy information for my articles."

It was all a distraction from the work of researching a new article, though she begrudgingly admitted to enjoying the "prima donna" feeling of her send-off from Tulsa, laden with candy and flowers. In time, she managed to poke fun at her own notoriety. She relished her readers' lively recognition more than the partisan press response to her articles, taking both critiques and adulation with a large helping of salt. "The conservatives tell me I'm uprooting society, and the radicals all call me a prophet!" she wrote Phillips.

Hailed as the Joan of Arc of the oil industry, she could not deliver on her audience's expectations of a ramrod-stiff firebrand, aligned with the popular conception of a "muchly masculinized old maid." Coverage of Miss Tarbell's persona typically included coded references to her probable identity as a barely closeted and therefore dangerous influence. As one reporter put it, "She was regarded as a raging, rampant suffragette, and the chances are, as a freak. Therefore, it was especially interesting to me to meet [Miss Tarbell] and to learn, first hand, that she is 'just the same as other folks.'" Another reporter observed her as "well-dressed, serene of face, quiet in manner . . . she is exceedingly feminine." Yet another returned repeatedly to her large gray eyes, describing them as "soft and eloquent . . . wonderfully sincere and really beautiful," casting her as more of a tragic heroine than the mannish figure they had expected.

The Knife and Fork Club of Kansas City, Missouri, which had never invited a woman to speak before, was taken aback by Miss Tarbell's choice of a low-cut mauve gown for the evening. The Paris, Missouri, *Herald* described the event: "Instead of sober garb, straight lines and stern simplicity expected . . . the lines were circles! Above all, imagine a woman, hated and feared by John D. Rockefeller and his fellow oligarchs, being so feminine as to appear décolleté in order to make her assault more effective!" The crowd had invited a battle-ax, but a woman had shown up instead.

\* \* \*

**MEANWHILE, IN NEW YORK,** the *annus horribilis* between the summers of 1904 and 1905 dragged further. Fine cracks in the loyalty of the staff began to show more boldly, especially as Phillips's authority grew in proportion to McClure's wildness. McClure himself was unable to stay still longer than a couple of weeks. In February 1905, he was a guest of the American consul at the Kremlin. Then he was in the fishing village of Nervi, Italy, opening prickly letters from Phillips. He fired his Johns Hopkins doctors and replaced them with Europeans who recommended that his disposition required work to be well, so he called an end to his rest cure and came home.

The staff began holding secret sessions in hotel rooms to figure out a way to circumvent McClure's orders—as well as to finish their articles ahead of deadline. He nevertheless found a way to manipulate them when needed. One day he sent for Miss Tarbell urgently and ordered her to Germany to research a series on exotic animals. Complying, she "spent a lively month visiting zoos, interviewing animal trainers and hunters and keepers, buying books and photographs." She sent her work to McClure, and it was never seen again. The thought must have crossed her mind that McClure was thinking up ways to monopolize her attention and foil her surveillance of his personal life.

Facing distasteful work wherever she turned, she began to feel estranged from the office that had become her home. Her colleagues, especially Phillips, intervened with the Chief and encouraged her where they could. Everyone hoped that McClure would show a new flash of energy and inspiration for the magazine he already had, and that he would at the same time grow bored of his experiments in seduction. As Bert Boyden wrote to Miss Tarbell, "I hope these two women will scare him as I'm satisfied that the only hope lies in his being a coward." In the same letter, Boyden regrets that the burden of keeping scandal at bay and the magazine afloat had fallen on her shoulders, expressing sincere exasperation that no one else was able to manage the Chief with her tact and persuasion. "I wish sometimes it weren't so—this always putting it up to you to do everything because you can do it best only piles more responsibility on you who should be freer. But it's your own fault!" Wanting nothing more than to be left alone, Miss Tarbell could not escape the fact that she had become both the Chief's conscience and the staff's best hope to right the ship.

It was then that McClure landed anew on a long-favored ambition of his antic mind. He was once again set on the idea of a new magazine, though the precise details of how it could improve on *McClure's* without competing with it, and who would read it, were undetermined. At first Miss Tarbell hoped it was a passing madness—she had successfully ignored these rumblings before. McClure's method of realizing his visions, Miss Tarbell thought, "had the character of improvisation . . . [of] gay spurts of fancy." She kept quiet and hoped it would soon be replaced by another figment.

The idea of a second publication had manifested many times before over the years, but now it was evolved enough in his mind that he slipped it into flattering notes to Miss Tarbell: "I feel heart-sore to leave you. I feel, that after all, personally you are the most important to me. . . . I look forward with eagerness to the time when you & I & Boyden & Baker will start our new magazine." Even as Miss Tarbell's Standard Oil success was on the rise in the spring of 1903, he was writing to her: "we will side by side found McClure's Review, which I have just fully invented, business scheme & everything. I have a splendid program & we can make absolutely the greatest monthly in the world." To Steffens, he put the idea of a second publication in terms of a daily paper: "[A]ll my life I have in editorial matters acted instinctively," he told Steffens. "I think we have entered upon the greatest campaign that any periodical has ever undertaken. I think it will develop into both a political and business field that we hardly now suspect. It may be the route by which I shall get to a daily newspaper. I cannot tell."

When McClure returned to New York in June 1905, he was brought face-to-face with unwilling troops. Phillips was away, but he heard the upshot from Miss Tarbell. "Mr McClure arrived yesterday. . . . I had a long talk with him and it left me with an impression of his condition more sinister and painful than I can express." She intended to openly disagree with the Chief and try to forge a compromise, though she would have to do so without Hattie's help. "Of course Mrs McClure is stone blind and deaf and dumb. She makes me wild," continued Miss Tarbell's blunt report. She now felt herself solely answerable to Phillips. He was a welcoming, generous, and calm listening ear on the rare occasions her rage erupted into language. The two shared a wearied affection for S. S., tied to a professional and financial stake in the magazine.

It would be McClure's attempt at launching a grand new enterprise—not just a second magazine—that firmly turned the staff from frazzled allies to mutineers. By late November 1905, he put his vision into a more definite—and startling—form. "I am going to reward you by confiding in you a tremendous secret," he wrote Miss Tarbell—though he shared the same information with Phillips. "I enclose a prospectus of a little scheme I have for the founding of the magazine." The magazine would be edited "upon the same general principles as *McClure's Magazine*. . . . It would be managed by members of the staff of *McClure's Magazine*. . . . I believe that this has in it the germ of the greatest periodical ever published in America."

His lengthy prospectus started with a new magazine, *McClure's Universal Journal*. This time McClure envisioned the second magazine in granular detail: it was another general, investigative publication, only 64 pages long, but printed in small type so that the content would equal *The Century*'s 160 pages. He would sell it for five cents a copy, or fifty cents a year. McClure may have thought that a new enterprise was the only way to reclaim some of the energy and urgency of the early days. But none of the numbers that the scheme relied upon were real or justifiable: *McClure's,* despite its success on the newsstands, had lost money in 1904 due to rising manufacturing costs. To compensate for the new magazine's ultracheap price, he would print it on low-quality paper and expect a monthly circulation of one million, although *McClure's* had never reached half that number of assured subscribers.

As Phillips and Miss Tarbell paged through his proposal, it was with disbelief that they found this new magazine was only part of a larger family of new McClure institutions: these included a bank, insurance company, and "McClure's Ideal Settlement"—a community, not unlike Pullman's model town, dedicated to the mission that people should be able to have low-cost homes on their own terms. The new prospectus also included "McClure's People's University," which would provide a curriculum via mail and publish its own textbooks.

As he had with his syndicate, McClure was enlarging on experiments that had borne fruit for other magazine innovators. He had doubtless tracked the *Ladies' Home Journal*'s savvy inclusion of neat, modern, reasonably priced architectural plans for small houses in its ad pages, and *The Cosmopolitan*'s efforts to launch the Cosmopolitan University, which was quickly overloaded by subscriptions and failed in the late 1890s. He was certain that the *McClure's* brand was strong enough to build on these models and succeed. By the time he circulated the proposal at the office, McClure had already begun writing to shareholders of the S. S. McClure Company, including Arthur Conan Doyle, suggesting that they buy shares in his new company—and omitting any mention of the bank, insurance company, university, textbooks, or model town. He hired an art director for the as-yet-theoretical magazine, prominent illustrator Howard Pyle, at an extravagant salary.

After reading his empire-building plan, Miss Tarbell was, for once, too angry to tell the Chief what was on her mind. "I am not fit to write to him," she claimed, writing to Boyden from a mule-riding holiday in Arizona with Phillips and William Allen White. "Mr. P[hillips] as usual is an angel and has written him a beautiful letter which *ought* to show him what an inferior creature [he] is but which probably he will consider as someway a consent to his scheme. . . . I am sure it can be fixed . . . if not we *can* secede."

She tersely told McClure that she would "never have anything to do with such a scheme." Steffens saw it as not only "fool," but "not quite right"—implying it was not just addled, but in fact dishonest. When Miss Tarbell confided the situation to her brother William, now an attorney for the Pure Oil Company, he replied with a smile. "His new proposition, it seems to me, would make another excellent scoop for you to let him go ahead with it and then write it up."

The staff was losing the will to "temper his wilder impulses," as they had always done in the past. Boyden tentatively raised the idea of negotiating— could they agree to a new magazine, so long as the model settlement and other schemes were dropped? Phillips tried another tack: if McClure needed to dedicate his attention to these new ventures, would he agree to relinquish direct control of the original *McClure's*?

The Chief would not negotiate. He was, instead, astonished at his staff's doubts. Strenuously defending himself against Phillips's implication that he couldn't do it all, McClure questioned his partner's perception of reality, projecting his own confusion onto Phillips. "This new magazine is no more alien here than the July number of *McClure's* compared with the June number," the Chief argued. "I notice how unessentials and imaginary things have loomed up and filled your mind." Phillips's counterproposal, while entirely logical from a business perspective, struck McClure as the work of a delusional mind. "Your suggestion of a compromise whereby I should withdraw from the active control of *McClure's Magazine* is just as possible as suggesting to a mother that she may have a second child if she will surrender her rights in the first, and yet retain a kind of consulting mothership." He scoffed at any suggestion that he should set down his work and rest, insisting his mind had never been clearer, telling Miss Tarbell, "I am unusually vigorous in every way, more so than I have been for years."

McClure's plan "seemed to possess him like a religious vision which it was blasphemy to question," noted Miss Tarbell. "Human reason has little influence on one who believes he is inspired." Alongside her, Phillips stood firm that *McClure's* was made up of journalists, not insurance agents or real estate developers. To the staff, McClure's scheme was "suicidal." They hoped against expectations that he would come into the office one day having changed his mind so they could finally turn the page on this long, strange season.

# 17

# The Ear of the Public

On February 9, 1906, President Theodore Roosevelt asked Ray Stannard Baker to visit him at the White House and keep him company during his morning shave. This was one of Washington's most coveted invitations. Though it wasn't his first time in the halls of power, Baker arrived keyed up with wonder and trepidation.

The barber had little opportunity to complete his task, for the president's jaw was in constant motion as the razor hovered around him. Roosevelt told Baker that his idea for the government to take ownership of the railroads was "a disaster." Although he was determined to bring forward legislation that would give the government oversight of the railroads—and did so with the Hepburn Act, later in 1906—Roosevelt dismissed the reporter's suggestion that taking the railroads out of private hands was the only way to correct the current state of completely unregulated freight rates, which favored industrial monopolists like Armour and Rockefeller. But as Baker warned the president, "The people out there are getting beyond you on these questions."

Baker's brand of ambition puzzled Roosevelt and McClure alike. The midwestern reporter was discreet and disciplined, and genuinely preferred spending time with his family in Michigan to glittering evenings in

Manhattan. His reporting, too, was a meld of fact and opinion, scrupulously researched yet reliant as much on the writer's impressions as on documentary evidence. He was more apt than Miss Tarbell—who used "the reporter" when compelled to refer to herself in writing—to use the first person in his dispatches. Unlike Steffens, he rarely ventured deep into social science theory in the drafts he sent to Phillips and McClure. Now thirty-five, bearing more the manner of a college professor than a fiery interrogator of the nation's ills, Baker had begun to chafe against his obligations at *McClure's*. He still mulled over the prospect of novel writing; about journalism, he reflected, "I have felt myself a gadabout cackling a great deal about things of which I know very little." However, his natural tendency was to be interested in the people and events around him, and he was susceptible to the charms of regular attention from the president. Journalism left him no opportunity to write for himself, and little time to sit and think, but he wasn't ready to give it up.

McClure once swiped an envelope from the White House off Baker's desk and opened it despite the mail boy's protests because, as he said, "I happen to know what this is. Baker sent proofs of his first article on the railroads to the President. . . . Let's see what Teddy had to say." What McClure actually found was something like the reverse: Roosevelt had sent Baker an advance proof of the president's message to Congress because he wanted the journalist's comments. Roosevelt cared what Baker thought. He considered Baker one of the more ethical and least sensational of the investigative set. The president intended to keep him close—whether as an ally or adversary was still to be determined.

As early as July 1903, the president invited Baker to his "Summer White House" estate in Oyster Bay, on the north shore of Long Island, to talk about a recent corruption case in Arizona. Though he had prepared for a private conversation, Baker arrived to find a large party in progress. Roosevelt quickly approached the reporter, only to digress vigorously from the subject he'd been summoned to discuss. Baker did not have a chance to get a word in edgewise or open his briefcase, which was weighed down with memos and evidence he'd painstakingly compiled for their meeting. He caught the late train back to Manhattan and began the hot, dusty journey home bewildered by the experience. The incident was an early clue that the president was more interested in keeping an eye on Baker than engaging him in a meaningful exchange of ideas.

In late 1904, Baker embarked on a six-part series titled "The Railroads on Trial." His research started with a visit to Roosevelt, who was struck by Baker's thoughtful lines of questioning—though he righteously opposed any verdict that hinted at the shortcomings of his administration. From that point onward, the president made a point of courting him. He wrote Baker in September 1905, "I have learned to look to your articles for real help. You have impressed me with your earnest desire to be fair, with your freedom from hysteria, and with your anxiety to tell the truth rather than to write something that will be sensational." The first article on the railroads in November 1905 had earned a comradely letter from Roosevelt, who told Baker after reading the proofs, "I haven't a criticism to suggest about the article. You have given me two or three thoughts for my own message."

As the series progressed, however, the malfeasance of the railroad leadership proved overwhelming even for the warrior president. Baker exposed the machinations that had won corporate giant Armour & Company tacit rule over the nation's railroad system. His explanations were detailed yet riveting; his readers' lives intersected with Armour several times a day. Armour, Baker wrote, was "peculiarly the autocrat of the American breakfast table." It manufactured meat and its derivatives, including sausages, lard, eggs, soup, soap, bones for bone china, hooves for glue making, and fertilizer. More surreptitiously, railroads exclusively used the Armour Company's own refrigerated railroad cars and charged fruit producers to use them.

Baker emphasized the parallels between Miss Tarbell's perspective on Standard Oil and his own study of Philip Danforth Armour: "Armour was exactly like Rockefeller," he wrote, saying both allowed rivals to spring up so long as they test-drove new technologies for manufacture and transport, "until they were proved practicable; then [Armour] quietly gobbled them up." Like Rockefeller's control of both oil and pipelines, Armour not only

made every livestock-derived product in American homes but also monopo-
lized the only feasible means of transport for perishables, from pineapples
brought in via the Gulf of Mexico to California oranges to Michigan cher-
ries. Armour himself was no minor mob boss, but rather a wily and highly
connected kingpin.

Ahead of Upton Sinclair's treatment of Armour's empire in his novel
*The Jungle,* Baker roused readers to take up the pen themselves. They
sent bagfuls of letters to the White House, demanding that the railroads
be wrested from the control of a single giant company. Roosevelt was, as
he made clear during his morning shave in Baker's company, growing en-
raged with these calls to action. He still hoped to steer Baker back to writing that reflected better on his own leadership.

When at last Baker and *McClure's* decisively ran afoul of Roosevelt,
the repercussions were severe. The clash accelerated the outbreak of war
between the presidency and the media, and it sowed a new uncertainty in
readers' minds: between the president and the publishers, whose truth mat-
tered?

\* \* \*

**THE BLIND SPOT THAT BAKER DECIDED TO EXPOSE,** against all known
trends and tendencies of his readership, was racial injustice. The Fifteenth
Amendment, ratified in 1870, had given black men the vote, but the policies
that came soon afterward took another direction.

The Supreme Court had affirmed *Plessy v. Ferguson* and the "separate but equal" doctrine in 1896—mere months after the death of Frederick
Douglass—but just as many southern states passed statutes effectively dis-
enfranchising African Americans. The same year, W. E. B. Du Bois became
the first African American to be awarded a Harvard doctorate. North and
South remained at odds in theory but not so much in practice, as landlords,
business owners, and white citizens on both sides of the divide reacted with
fear, denial, and violence to the equal distribution of basic civil rights.

The summer of 1900 was especially tense in New York. On August 15, a "Negro Hunt" was set off by the death of a policeman who had been wounded in a confrontation with a black man. White men roamed the avenues southwest of Central Park looking for an opportunity to retaliate. The most liberal city in the union was host to murderous violence that night. The *New York Times* reported that "every trolley car passing up or down 8th Avenue was stopped and every negro on board was dragged out, and beaten." A lynching near Union Square was interrupted by police.

At the peak of the great boom in the literature of exposure, publishers of national papers and magazines glossed over the national issue of racial hatred—even as it manifested itself in its most horrific form, lynching. Thousands died by the noose during the heyday of *McClure's*.

Ida Bell Wells, a contemporary of the *McClure's* group who was born a slave in Mississippi, rose from teaching in rural schools and helping to raise her siblings to become a pioneering journalist and voice for racial equality. Her writing and lectures, stark and compelling in their portrayal of local courts easily toppled by lynch mobs, fueled her pursuit of justice in a nation startled—and, in large part, incensed—by her audacity. By 1892, the year before *McClure's* was launched, she was perceived by white neighbors as enough of a threat that her office at the *Memphis Free Speech and Headlight* was destroyed by a mob. The following year, she protested the exclusion of African Americans from the Chicago World's Fair, and the year after that, she crossed the Atlantic to found the British Anti-Lynching Society, figuring it would ballast her cause back home. But through the rise of *McClure's* and its rivals, her writing was primarily published in newspapers aimed at African American readers and did not deeply stir readers at the White House breakfast table.

The national press, by contrast, condemned social injustice so long as the victims were delineated by features other than race, which, a half century after the Civil War, was deemed too personal and inflammatory. The plight of the poor, the overworked, the slum-trapped, those preyed upon by quacks and fraudsters—these were proper subjects.

After the turn of the century this definition began, very slowly, to widen. More than other magazines, *Collier's* from 1901 onward ran unsigned comments decrying lynchings and noting the intensifying "race problem," but concluded, "The Negro is a being apart from the whites—a creature of incomprehensible morals and practices." When the magazines did make an African American the subject of a profile, it was nearly always a "safe" subject, such as Booker T. Washington, emphasizing his message of hard work and self-help. Even in popular fiction, this had become provocative territory; it had been a half century since *Uncle Tom's Cabin,* twenty years since *The Adventures of Huckleberry Finn.*

Baker decided that the continued phenomenon of lynching was noteworthy. He traveled to see Jim Crow laws in effect for himself, report on mob violence, and bear witness. In early 1905, his two-part "What Is a Lynching? A Study of Mob Justice, South and North" covered lynchings in Statesboro, Georgia, and Springfield, Ohio.

Reading "What Is a Lynching?" now, one senses Baker's judgment as both an eyewitness and an analyst; morality and drama are woven into a carefully observed encounter. He begins, perhaps addressing his closest readers in the Northeast, "You and I imagine that a lynching somehow could not possibly take place in our town; our people are orderly and law-abiding; our officials, whatever may be said of their politics, may be depended upon to do their duty; you and I are truly civilized. And conversely, we imagine that the people in towns where lynchings occur must be somehow peculiarly barbarous, illiterate, lawless. A lynching, like death, is a great way off until it strikes us." Baker visited sites of recent lynchings in both North and South and was struck by their "homely familiarity," the church bells each Sunday, fraternal societies, women's clubs, and the absence of obvious unrest in the streets.

In landscapes that otherwise held sparkling rivers, dignified steeples, and industrious merchant districts, Baker had little trouble discovering where socially sanctioned murders took place. "In each successive place," he wrote, "they pointed out the telegraph-pole or tree from which the mob's victim had dangled, or the stake at which he was burned to death; they showed me the jails which had been broken open; they told me the awful and gruesome details of the crimes committed." He was struck by how unreal these stories seemed. "Yet they have happened, both in the North and in the South," he wrote, ". . . and they will happen again—next time, perhaps, in your town or mine. No, lynching is not a crime of barbarians; it is not a Southern crime, nor a Western crime, nor a Northern crime; it is an American crime."

Baker saw that the homely innocence and dignity of the small town was a pernicious myth. He took the risky stance that the steady procession of murders was nationally significant, that a happy conclusion aligned with America's ideal of itself was unlikely. In Statesboro, he saw two men who had been burned alive. In Springfield, he wrote, "This jail is said to be the strongest in Ohio, and having seen it, I can well believe that the report is true. But steel bars have never yet kept out a mob; it takes something a good deal stronger: human courage backed up by the consciousness of being right."

His coverage of the Ohio events curdled the complacency of northern readers who previously ascribed racial violence to a backward South:

Well, on Monday afternoon the mob began to gather. At first it was an absurd, ineffectual crowd, made up largely of lawless boys of sixteen to twenty—a pronounced feature of every mob—with a wide fringe of more respectable citizens, their hands in their pockets and no convictions in their souls, looking on curiously, helplessly. They gathered hooting around the jail, cowardly, at first, as all mobs are, but growing bolder as darkness came on and no move was made to check them. . . . [I]t was a mob from the back rooms of the swarming saloons of Springfield; and it included also the sort of idle boys "who hang around cigar stores," as one observer told me. The newspaper reports are fond of describing lynching mobs as "made up of the foremost citizens of the town." In no cases that I know of, either South or North, has a mob been made up of what may be called the best citizens; but the best citizens have often stood afar off "decrying the mob"—as a Springfield man told me piously—and letting it go on.

Baker blamed the town government's reluctance to intercede and law enforcement's deliberate inertia. "A sort of dry rot, a moral paralysis, seems to strike the administrators of law in a town like Springfield. What can be expected of officers who are not accustomed to enforce the law, or of a people not accustomed to obey it—or who make reservations and exceptions when they do enforce it or obey it?"

The question seemed designed to inflame the president. Roosevelt mistrusted Baker's view of racial injustice as a problem worthy of presidential notice. He wrote to Baker that he opposed "interference in every state where a Negro is lynched . . . at this moment . . . most of the Southern states." At the same time, he was receptive to a larger, inchoate danger murmured in Baker's article. That suggested wider civic unrest was gathering momentum despite a "reform president" with overwhelming energy and charisma. Compounded with his railroad corruption articles and imperviousness to Rooseveltian torrents of animated speech, Baker and his resonant stories became a public-image liability to be dealt with.

To those already in power, the rise of long-silenced voices provoked quick and brutal suppression as few other threats did. W. E. B. Du Bois would write in *The Atlantic* ten years later: "All over the world there are leaps to articulate speech and ready action [on] that singular assumption that if white men do not throttle colored men, then China, India, and Africa will do to Europe what Europe has done and seeks to do to them."

Building on "What Is a Lynching?," Baker traveled extensively in the South for his book *Following the Color Line*. In it he reported on what he saw of the African American experience in cities, on farms, and in politics. In Baker's words, "My purpose . . . has been to make a clear statement of the exact present conditions and relationships of the Negro in American life." His work formed part of the documentation used as a basis for the founding of the National Association for the Advancement of Colored People and the Urban League. To many in the halls of power, this alone marked Baker as a traitor. As Du Bois warned him, "you may not find as cordial a welcome from the white brothers the next time you come South."

However many enemies he made among whites, Baker was not a transcendent champion of the oppressed. His mind was inquisitive and his writing vivid, but Baker's stories came from the White Man's Burden–bearing view typical of privileged voices of the time. In his view, "Nearly all the crimes committed by negroes are marked with almost animal-like ferocity." He suggested that crimes committed by African Americans should be seen in a more forgiving light, but his reasoning was based in white superiority and the assumption that criminal justice would always be a predominantly white system. "[W]e execute the law, and if we are too bad or too lazy to do our work properly, let us in all honesty take the blame—and not shoulder it on the irresponsible negro."

In his letters to his father back in Wisconsin, Baker wrote rather that "it seems almost as though I had a mission to perform—to talk straight out on a difficult subject." He was convinced that the *McClure's* investigations and exposés did "more for stirring up the American people than any other publication ever did before." He ended his letter uplifted by certainty, saying, "I think we have struck the right Grail."

It was an idea that he would hold tight even when he yearned to abandon the hectic machine of *McClure's,* move to the country, and write a novel: that reporting from America's social and industrial conflicts would grant him more drama than the richest wells of his imagination.

* * *

**McCLURE'S NOW HAD** a downright intimidating hold on readers across America. In William James's view, it was "one of the best forums in the country." In the eyes of President Roosevelt, initially a supporter of the magazine, that influence was increasingly and exasperatingly outside his control. He was beginning to find, as Samuel Johnson had, that the liberty of the press was a fickle asset: "a blessing when we are inclined to write against others, and a calamity when we find ourselves overborne by the multitude of our assailants."

Roosevelt had always been canny in courting the press and using it to broadcast his voice and build his persona. But once he was president,

Roosevelt became thin-skinned to any suggestion that he was not the nation's savior. On March 15, 1906, he wrote to Secretary of War William Howard Taft: "I do not at all like the social conditions at present. . . . The corruption in business and politics, have tended to produce a very unhealthy condition of excitement and irritation in the popular mind."

Just one year into his second administration, Roosevelt was angered by the constant hammering at corruption sustained by progressive-minded writers in all-too-popular magazines like *McClure's*. As one midwestern mayor observed, "Reform is popular so long as some one else is to be reformed."

The magazines' clamor felt unjust. The president, though undeniably patrician himself, claimed an exceptional and sincere personal sympathy for economically squeezed Americans. The wealthy men and women who surrounded him, he argued, were simply "friends of my father's," well-intentioned people who, unlike the president, preferred not to dwell upon "the great mass of the people who work with their hands." Unfortunately for the president, the splashy amusements of old and new money bolstered the theory that inequality had gotten out of control. In 1905, James Hazen Hyde, twenty-three-year-old heir to an insurance fortune, gave a French-themed masquerade ball for six hundred in a restaurant transformed to look like the gardens of Versailles, which seemed almost to invite a public reaction against such excess.

Roosevelt set himself apart, and asked citizens to believe in his exceptionalism. Under his leadership, American business was held to a stricter moral standard. Roosevelt's Congress forbade railroad rebates, passed a meat-inspection act and a pure food and drug law, and forced big business into arbitration during a national coal strike. Yet instead of recognition, the president faced an exasperating, continued focus on corruption in the pages of the popular magazines. Roosevelt confided in *Ladies' Home Journal* editor Edward Bok, "When do I get the ear of the public? In its busiest moments. My messages are printed in the newspapers and read hurriedly, mostly by men in trolleys or railroad-cars." He regretted that women readers seemed disinterested in him, and that "in the evening by the fireside or under the lamp, when the day's work is over and the mind is at rest"—during readers' most receptive moments—they chose to pick up a magazine.

After Baker's railroad series and reports on lynching, *McClure's* was a thorn in his side, perhaps even an existential threat to his popularity. The magazine, compared to its rivals, had disturbing and persistent ambitions beyond popular entertainment. This was foreshadowed during a comic speech at the Periodical Publishers' Association on April 7, 1904, a rollicking Washington evening at which President Roosevelt was the guest of honor. Speaker Henry Van Dyke's joking words of advice to a young writer suggested a reframing of the same subject—the Clam—for each of the prominent magazines. For *Harper's,* the subject would need to be treated with some scholarly rigor; for *The Atlantic,* it would need a New England angle; *The Century* would want classical allusions. For example:

*Harper's* (scholarly yet humorous): "The Standard Pronunciation of the Word Clam"

*The Atlantic Monthly* (published in New England): "The Causes of Superiority of the Cod to the Clam"

*Scribner's* (just then focused on realist fiction): "The Under-Clam"

*The Century* (leaned toward classical culture and tenement house reform): "Il Mercatore della Clamma," a poem

*Outlook* (marketed as a healthy diversion): "Quatrain to a Recreant Clam"

*The Smart Set* (frivolous and tending toward the romantic): "A Little-Neck Love Lyric"

But, the speaker went on, suppose the piece should be rejected by each of these editors—what then? "Naturally you would turn to *McClure's Magazine.* In order to succeed with that periodical, you must expose the corruption of the trusts, and strike the note of American democracy, and strike it hard! Be Virile now, if you have any virility concealed about you; and come as near as you can to profanity without being actually profane. . . . Write an Ode on 'The Fettered Clam.'" The choice of metaphor made sense, in a way. Suddenly readers were hyperaware that, in the magazines they devoured daily, events were not merely reported but mediated into a narrative, filtered through a reporter's mind like brackish water through a bivalve.

Reading outrage-provoking journalism was, for many, a substitute for meaningful action. One urban myth in New York magazine offices told of a well-to-do Alaskan who walked into an editor's office, clamoring that the time had come for the people to rise up:

"Well!" replied the editor, "you certainly are a progressive, aren't you?"

"Progressive!" the man cried. "Progressive! I tell you I'm a full-fledged insurgent. Why, man, I subscribe to thirteen magazines."

A remarkably prolific writer during his presidency, Roosevelt first attempted to change the tone of *McClure's* by pitching his own articles on reform. McClure didn't want his magazine to become the president's mouthpiece, but the president nevertheless published in *Scribner's* and elsewhere, producing a steady churn of articles on bear hunting, wolf coursing, and maintaining the ever-expanding publication of *The Works of Theodore Roosevelt,* which had begun to come out in 1900.

One day the president opened a strongly worded letter of sympathy from humorist Finley Peter Dunne, famous for his *Doonesbury*-like creation of the credulous Irish barkeep Mr. Dooley. Dunne's letter was to provide a crucial seed of inspiration for his public blow against the journalists. "I am so tired of the perpetual scolding in the newspapers and magazines," Dunne wrote the President. "Whenever I see the worst of these rascals marking through *McClure's* or *Collier's,* I feel like saying, 'But for the grace of God, there goes John Bunyan.'" Dunne didn't mean to preach, he told Roosevelt, and instead he'd taken action by talking it over with his friend William Allen White, who "promised to take up the 'merry sunshine' work. . . . I look to him to save our countrymen from the suicide which is the logical consequence of believing all we read now-a-days."

(Oddly, the Mr. Dooley of his cartoons was more complacent, reassuring his friends in Old Country accents, "Th' noise ye hear is not th' first gun iv a revolution. It's on'y th' people iv th' United States batin' a carpet.")

From the White House, however, it was impossible to tell whether this armchair insurgency was all bluster. Roosevelt's postmaster general George B. Cortelyou warned in a Lincoln's Birthday speech at Grand Rapids, Michigan: "Of late years there has developed a style of journalism, happily as yet limited in its scope, whose teachings are a curse and whose influence is a blight upon the land. Pandering to unholy passions, making the commonplace to appear sensational, fanning the fires of sectionalism and class hatred, invading the privacy of our firesides, it presents one of the most important of our present-day problems."

Meanwhile, Finley Peter Dunne's reference to Bunyan, author of *Pilgrim's Progress,* stuck with the president. He decided that if Dunne wouldn't preach on the subject, he would do so himself.

Roosevelt first struck back on March 17, 1906, after a sumptuous white-tie dinner of chestnut-stuffed squab at Washington's Gridiron Club. Earlier that month, author David Graham Phillips had debuted a series in *Cosmopolitan* titled "The Treason of the Senate," denouncing Nelson Aldrich and other U.S. senators who served big business rather than the people. Thus inspired, Roosevelt stood before the Gridiron Club audience and gave a spontaneous talk that, according to a fellow guest, "sizzled" with stinging rebuke. It turned out to be a rehearsal for a far more public and damning performance one month later.

Baker heard about the Gridiron speech when he crossed paths with a friend on the street in New York. "Hello, Muckraker," the man said with a smile. Baker was nonplussed; when he heard Roosevelt's speech had equated truth-telling gadfly reporters with "muckrakers," alluding to the character of the man with the muck-rake in *Pilgrim's Progress,* he was gravely concerned. He wrote to Roosevelt, trying to dissuade him from encouraging a backlash against exposures "which may prevent the careful study of modern conditions and the presentation of the facts in a popular form."

Roosevelt's speech at the laying of the cornerstone of the House of Representatives on April 14, 1906, was the formal, public evolution of the Gridiron Club talk. The president had disregarded Baker's letter, replying that he would make a clear distinction between the "light and air" of reputable magazines like *McClure's* and the "sewer gas" of publications like *The Cosmopolitan*. Indeed, William Randolph Hearst, then both publisher of that magazine and congressman, was Roosevelt's true and admitted target, called out by the president as an "influence for evil upon the social life of this country." No one who heard or read about the speech afterward noted that distinction at all.

The president painted a dark picture of the nation's prospects: "At this moment we are passing through a period of great unrest—social, political, and industrial unrest," he said. But he warned against narratives that looked too closely at "a line of cleavage . . . which divides those who are well off from those who are less well off," in other words "a mere crusade of appetite against appetite." There would always be an "inevitable inequality of conditions," he said, and journalists as well as readers needed to accept that. He concluded, "The men with the muckrakes are often indispensable to the well-being of society; but only if they know when to stop raking the muck, and to look upward to the celestial crown above them, to the crown of worthy endeavor."

In other words, the muckrakers were barraging the nation with so much bad news that readers came away with all useful energy, all motivation to improve themselves and the world around them, beaten out of them. That kind of depressed apathy, Roosevelt indicated, was in itself evil, and its source needed to be routed.

After the speech, aware that many listeners immediately assumed the president meant to discredit journalists in general, Roosevelt wrote directly to Baker and Steffens to deny it. This was disingenuous. With William Howard Taft, he shared his overweening desire to put the press in its place. "Nothing effective . . . is being done to combat the great amount of evil which, mixed with a little good, a little truth, is contained in the outpourings of the *Cosmopolitan,* of *McClure's,* of *Collier's* . . . ," said the president. "Some of these are socialists; some of them merely lurid sensationalists; but they are all building up a revolutionary feeling which will most probably take the form of a political campaign." Roosevelt was prepared to absorb the superficial jabs of "a little truth," but instead he found himself contending with an onslaught. He treated it as he would have any other barbarous enemy.

The damage spread. Steffens, who was in Cleveland, was quickly buttonholed by reporters who wanted to know what he thought of the speech. On the spot, he replied that the president's message had been misunderstood. The only truly contentious point, he continued, was Roosevelt's refusal to acknowledge that the essence of the problem was the system itself, which "rewards an honest man with a mere living and a crook with all the magnificence of our magnificent modern life."

The attack on the muckrakers made headlines across the country and even in Europe. The *New York Times* printed a song about the journalists' downfall, calling out Ida Tarbell and Lincoln Steffens by name, with the chorus,

> *They're exposin' the exposers, they're callin' of 'em down,*
> *They are huntin' of 'em hotly from New York to Packin'town,*
> *They will chuck 'em in a lake o' ink an' let 'em swim or drown;*
> *They're exposin' the exposers in the mornin'.*

It took little time for rival magazines to chime in with the new antiexposure sentiment, which blurred true investigative journalism with personally motivated hatchet jobs. *The Atlantic* cautioned that journalism had overstepped its bounds—"Men are tried and found guilty in magazine counting rooms before investigation is begun"—while *Collier's* ironically asked, "Why listen to facts when diatribes are at hand?" The press seemed to be taking a cue from the president, turning fiercely on the mingling of facts and values churned out by magazines like *McClure's,* and hailing the advent of a period of self-censorship.

The stinging *Nation* review of Miss Tarbell's Standard Oil series concisely captured the new feeling about investigative journalism: "To stir up envy, to arouse prejudice, to inflame passion, to appeal to ignorance, to magnify evils, to charge corruption—these seem to be the methods in favor with too many writers who profess a desire to reform society. They will not accomplish reform in this way, but they may conceivably bring on revolution." What Roosevelt called "torrential journalism" overpowered the reader with its depth of research, adept storytelling, and underlying chord of moral disdain.

The power of journalism over public opinion surprised and dismayed those who either inherited political leadership or were elected to it. It complicated the business of political deal making and placed heavy stakes on what kind of public image a politician could gin up and maintain. A month after his speech, Roosevelt wrote to a friendly newspaperman, George Horace Lorimer of *The Saturday Evening Post,* that he was acting in the interests of national security as well as moral judgment. The muckrakers' articles, and particularly the *Cosmopolitan* series, he wrote, "excite a hysterical and ignorant feeling against everything existing, good or bad; the kind of hysteria which led to the 'red fool fury of the Seine,' the kind of hysteria which renders it so difficult for the genuine reformers in Russia to secure reform in the teeth of those who mix up reform and destruction." Roosevelt discerned an actual threat in such a muscular press.

As the *McClure's* group saw it, the president was driven by fear. "He was afraid that they were adding to the not inconsiderable revolutionary fever," Miss Tarbell wrote. She rightly understood that the validity of her work, at least in the eyes of the public, was in jeopardy.

After the shock of the "Muckraker" speech sank in, Steffens took a bleak view: "Well, Mr. President," he wrote, "you have put an end to all these journalistic investigations that have made you." He may have had a warning of Roosevelt's new views since October 4, 1905, when the president advised Steffens, via a letter to McClure, to "put more sky in his landscape. I do not have to say to you that a man may say what is absolutely true and yet give an impression so one-sided as to represent the whole truth." The following month, the president obliquely warned Baker, "In social and economic, as well as political, reforms, the violent revolutionary extremist is the worst friend of liberty, just as the arrogant and intense reactionary is the worst friend of order." Baker, who had carefully stressed "evolution rather than revolution" when it came to reform, was surprised and hurt. He privately wrote that he "could never again give [Roosevelt] . . . full confidence nor follow his leadership."

Baker would later write that although the president did much good, he'd been too determined to shackle the press to his own ends. In his words, "Latterly I believe Roosevelt did a disservice to the country in seizing upon a movement that ought to have been built up slowly and solidly from the bottom with much solid thought and experimentation, and hitching it to the cart of his own political ambitions. He thus short-circuited a fine and vigorous current of aroused public opinion into a futile partisan movement."

The president seemed changed by his rise to power, disillusioning those who had known him as New York City's zealous police commissioner. He had, in Miss Tarbell's opinion, "a good deal of the usual conviction" of a man grown territorial of his place in public life, "that correction should be left to him," and a "resentment that a profession outside his own should be stealing his thunder." McClure wrote to the president to protest that *McClure's* should not be scapegoated with the rest, because the magazine printed only the truth. A rumor started that McClure had muzzled his staff and ordered an end to their investigations, but in fact, apart from this letter, the Chief was uncharacteristically silent, at a loss as to what the president's words meant for the future.

The White House's decree against the muckrakers echoed the conundrum of the Wizard in L. Frank Baum's *The Wonderful Wizard of Oz,* published in September 1900. In the fairy-tale land of Oz, Baum created a utopian vision that was quickly read as a biting allegory of Progressive Era America. Standing in for the president is the Wizard, who is forced to admit to being a "humbug." "How can I help being a humbug," he asks, ". . . when all these people make me do things that everyone knows can't be done?"

# 18

# A Momentous Decision

I n later years, McClure wrote of March 21, 1906, as the day that precipi-
tated the end of his dearest ambitions. McClure's writers had always
believed in him, or at least believed his genius outran his madness—until
now. The Chief had started *McClure's* when he was twenty-six. Now he was
forty-nine, a time of life when men were supposed to ascend to their professional prime. But instead his staff had succumbed to what McClure could
only think of as "a malignant wave of hysteria." The mutiny blindsided him
despite the long-standing fissures that had already threatened his rickety
empire.

The day marked McClure's return from another European trip. Upon
his arrival at the office, a tempestuous conversation with Phillips began
behind closed doors. Phillips hoped that by now, McClure would have let
go of the idea of *McClure's Universal Journal,* but when it became clear that
McClure still held fast to the plan, Phillips resigned immediately.

Immediately the magazine's center of gravity changed. Phillips described his emotions in an unpublished memoir: "It was a momentous decision for a man of forty-five to make. The impelling reasons were personal,
almost spiritual. . . . As soon as the decision was made, there was a great
calm, a serene contentment." McClure could not believe he really meant

it. At first he tried to conciliate Phillips, offering terms that showed how little he grasped of his magazine's existential crisis. He offered his partner three years of paid vacation, which were declined. When he then called in Miss Tarbell and asked if he could count on her to stay, she said Phillips's decision had made up her mind: "I can't stay without him or some one like him. . . . [I s]hall go."

Miss Tarbell and Phillips laid out their litany of reasons in blisteringly frank language: McClure was too controlling, spent too much time abroad, and had lost the knack for managing a working magazine. Sobered, McClure asked who else on the staff was considering resigning; Miss Tarbell knew that Boyden would go. Baker threw his name in, feeling "that the very earth was dropping out from under me," as did Steffens.

Steffens's unhappiness at work was recent. He had enjoyed having success, regardless of the editorial and personal scuffles that had entailed. As he wrote, "In the building up of that triumph we had been happy, all of us; it was fun, the struggle." He was often away on reporting trips that saved him from enduring McClure's temperamental variability face-to-face. Of the more desperate moments, he wrote, "I heard about them after they were over, and they were amusing; other people's tragedies are our comedies." McClure's "outrageous" moments, he thought, were comparable to the mob's rule in the cities and states Steffens investigated: "they were funny, except when they affected me."

Then, in New York for an investigation into the life insurance industry, Steffens had a change of heart. "I realized that those who had to live and work every day with him were learning to hate him," he wrote. "I got more of his variability, temperament and extravagance, both in ideas and in expenditures. . . . The editor had to be edited."

McClure began to flail. He made a spontaneous offer to buy all of Phillips's stock, then retracted it. He argued that since the staff were leaving, the shares would doubtless be worth much less than the current $1,000-per-share valuation. Phillips pushed back, making a speech about the "only fair and manly thing" being for S. S. to buy out his staff—but the Chief suggested that they buy *him* out instead, and stretched out his hand.

"Mr. P shook it," wrote Miss Tarbell, "and flew from the room." The break had been formalized, and for McClure, the nightmare became real.

It was a terrible awakening. In the late afternoon, Miss Tarbell went in to see S. S. again. She found him "putting on his coat, his eyes red from weeping. I gave him my hand and he said—'It's all right. I am at peace for the first time in days.'" He remained in "broken talk for a half hour." He focused his emotions on Ida Tarbell, telling her he had always loved her—"said it was all which had saved him in *l'affaire* Wilkinson." At the end of thirty minutes, he "sprang up and flung his arms around me and kissed me—left weeping."

As soon as she was alone, she gave in to tears. It was a scene characteristic of their relationship: he was emotional, and she was steady; he confessed, and she soothed him. In her journal, she wrote, "Awful for me. Could not talk. He referred to his love for me. . . . Feel he is not wholly sincere yet thinks he is—am not cured yet. I ache dreadfully."

Miss Tarbell went home to the silence of her Greenwich Village apartment and tried to make sense of the day's events. She could not yet see a future outside *McClure's,* but she knew she would write her way there. In the small, leather-bound journal she had bought in the wake of *l'affaire* Wherry, she wrote: "There has come a point where it is life or death-in-life—and I am not willing to give up life. If the innermost recesses are to be entered I must go there alone. I am conscious so much of myself is evading me. And this poor little book is a feeble prop in my effort to reach the land I've never explored." For the past twelve years, she had made her home at the magazine, but now she felt the ground shift beneath her as, for once, she refused to rally behind McClure. She had imperiled the source of her income and independence and had alienated herself from her greatest professional supporter. What could come next?

When it came time to compose her memoir, she betrayed little of what she must have felt on that wrenching day. Instead she reported the facts: Phillips decided to resign, and she followed because, as she wrote, she "could not see the magazine without him." She admitted there was a "tragedy" in McClure's ultimate failure in judgment and chalked it up to his long mental and physical exhaustion. Then she allowed herself a paragraph or two of eulogy, first for McClure as the most generous and encouraging editor in the field, and then for the magazine, which had woven itself into the life of the country.

Immediately after their embrace, McClure found himself bereft of her gimlet gaze for the first time in more than a decade. He boarded a train up the Hudson to his wife and home, then returned to the office the following week to face Phillips's plans for the buyout. Hattie, meanwhile, sent Miss Tarbell a letter stuffed with Bible verses and affectionate sympathy: "I love and pray for you daily. . . . I forget not the love and firmness of your relation to me in my deep distress."

By nightfall of March 24, McClure had changed his position twice. He didn't know whether to buy out his staff or give up on the magazine and force them to buy him out. Finally, McClure bought out Miss Tarbell's shares as well as Phillips's. One morning during this period, he walked into Curtis Brady's office "looking like a whipped dog" and announced he was leaving, "like a clerk who had lost his job." When asked what he meant, he sat down across the desk, "laid his head on his arms and sobbed."

He continued this way for weeks. In mid-April 1906, just as Roosevelt delivered his "muckraker" speech that all but pointed at *McClure's* and named it one of the "potent forces for evil" in America, McClure changed his mind one more time. To Miss Tarbell, he wrote, "I cannot leave the magazine. *I simply cannot.* I would soon lose my mind with unavailing regret. I can master all other matters. . . . My interest in the magazine surpasses all other interests. . . . I am sorry, sorry." At last, the storm of emotion had given way to the realization that he must reinvent himself in midlife.

McClure wrote privately to his illustrious friends, seeking sympathy and renewed investment. He railed about the situation to Kipling, and the author wrote him, "Dear McClure . . . Don't have *too* many magazine children. It's weakening to the system and confusing to the public." At home, McClure turned to his one source of ever-giving support and asked Hattie to take on the role of his editorial and business partner.

He was still hoping to win back Phillips, but unfortunately, his ability to woo had worn thin. In letters from this period, his tone with Phillips turned out more supercilious than he intended or realized. "I felt awfully sorry for you yesterday morning. . . . Your leg shook in a manner that indicated serious nervous strain," McClure wrote. "I believe I am more competent to edit *McClure's* than if I had been here all the time. My facilities for getting to know public opinion and the opinion of able thinkers is vastly greater than it was ten years ago." He turned dismissive, telling Phillips the "democratization of the office" was not only "mischievous" but impossible, and that a rest cure in France would be the only remedy for his—that is, Phillips's—mental disturbance.

The Chief's most overwrought letter to Phillips concluded on a note worthy of a brainwashed Shakespearean monarch: "When you read history you find that kings who have come to the end of their tether, as a rule, suffer death rather than give up part of their power. . . . I shall have to make considerable changes in the editorial staff, for I cannot work with people who have exhibited such lack of confidence in me and what I regard as disloyalty." If his goal was to make Phillips question his own grip on reality and rationality, he failed miserably.

The mercurial McClure soon realized what the loss meant to him. In mid-April he wrote to a board trustee of the break and his plans to launch a new publication, emphasizing what an emotionally significant deal it was. "I think I may say that it is the greatest tragedy thus far of my life to lose them," he wrote. "I am extremely sorry that in the course of negotiations there were harassing hours, but my continued wavering was caused by my utter inability to face the separation." On April 27, Ida Tarbell formally resigned, requesting six months' salary as severance pay. She too was flattened by the breakup, but she was eager to dispel McClure's lingering disbelief that she would really go.

By the first week of May, word of the staff breakup got out to the rest of the media. Curtis Brady groaned, "It is doubtful that a single publisher or advertising man had not heard of the McClure trouble." One newspaper confidently reported that McClure had fired them all; most conjectured that Roosevelt's "muckraker" speech had had a rapid effect on the magazine's

editorial policy. *McClure's,* the press suggested, had been "spoiled by notoriety." "MUCK RAKE SPEECH SCARES M'CLURE," blared a *Cleveland News* headline.

Once those outside the *McClure's* group heard what happened, many
were titillated rather than surprised. Among them was Ellery Sedgwick,
who remarked, "[I]t was miraculous how in the incandescent office the
forces of attraction and repulsion were kept so nearly in balance; that with
all the subterranean rumblings and occasional little spurts of flame, the explosion was so long in coming."

McClure was quick to deny that the presidential message against muckraking had influenced events. He agitated less against reports that there
had been strife over who was the real editor of the magazine, and that it had
been McClure's decision to reorganize the staff, who had amiably "retired"
from his employ. The Chicago *Journal* ignored this version and drew a direct line between Roosevelt's speech and muckraking's demise, with Mc-
Clure as an instrumental actor: "No man in this country is a shrewder judge
of the state of public sentiment than the publisher of McClure's Magazine.
Therefore the news that he has rid himself of Muck Raker Lincoln Steffens
and Muck Raker Ray Stannard Baker is important, for it shows that public
sentiment has turned at last against muck-raking."

Fewer, quieter voices pointed out the irony—and the danger—of the
president's turn against the magazines. If it hadn't been for McClure and his
reporters, "he would not have the power he is using so well. . . . [W]ho has
been and would still be the people's informers?" Baker himself, when put
to the question, emphasized that the president's speech had been an "ir-
ritant," and nothing more, as far as the staff of *McClure's* was concerned.

On May 10, 1906, Tarbell, Phillips, and Boyden cleaned their desks and
left. Siddall followed. Steffens and Baker were out of town, but voiced their
intentions as well. Harry McClure, the cousin in charge of the syndicate,
also defected. Together they closed the office door behind them, descended
to the street, and sat together on a bench on Madison Square, trying to
make sense of what had happened. "We were derelicts without a job," wrote
Miss Tarbell.

At the end of the day, poetry editor Witter Bynner found McClure sitting alone in the editorial department. "Bynner," he said, "are you leaving me too?" Bynner could not speak, but watched as McClure again buried his face in his arms and broke down. In advanced age, Bynner would recall, "The most vivid and the saddest memory I have of Mr. McClure remains his face on the grim day . . . when almost his entire staff left him." Bynner equivocated, unable to break the news that he had in fact planned to leave, and stayed several months longer.

The legacy of the original *McClure's* group would be long—many more magazines, investigations, and visionaries would follow—but just then, each member sat in shock, wondering what had so swiftly broken up the deep attachment and monumental stories that had grown up between them.

* * *

**A SMALL, INTERESTING CORPS STAYED AT *McCLURE'S*.** Bynner was promoted to managing editor, replacing Boyden; Viola Roseboro stayed, too, as did the remaining Brady brothers. McClure recruited Will Irwin and Willa Cather, whose stories, after they were noticed by Miss Roseboro, he had published. Steffens remained on the payroll as he finished a series on Denver; McClure began to refer to the writer as "our friend, the enemy."

As the terrible days receded in time, McClure finally felt the panic starting to ebb. He was even able to spin the outcome to others—and perhaps to himself, as well—into a long-desired personal autonomy. As he began to tell people, "I am a free man at last."

A new magazine, resembling *McClure's* in form and authorship, soon arose. Within weeks of the final walkout, Phillips was approached by the owner of *The American,* a magazine that had started as *Frank Leslie's Popular Monthly* and was now trying to move into a more investigative direction. The old *McClure's* group convened and reached a decision quickly; they incorporated the Phillips Publishing Company and bought *The American.* Each contributed what they could to the purchase, and the rest of the stock was easily sold to friends. William Allen White and Finley Peter Dunne both joined as contributors. In Miss Tarbell's opinion, Dunne, who had helped gin up Roosevelt's anti-media sentiment, was "the greatest satirist . . . the country has yet produced." Less than six months later, in October 1906, the first issue appeared.

The new dynamic was humbling for Ida Tarbell. She had been Mc-Clure's confidante and lieutenant, his most valued writer, but the *American* group had other luminaries, urbane men comfortable with public adulation. Dunne was one of Miss Tarbell's harshest critics at a point in her career when few were curtailing her work. He rejected one of her editorials, saying "You sputter like a woman"—and Miss Tarbell, even years later, suspected he was right.

She threw herself into the mission of re-creating a magazine as lively and fearsome as *McClure's,* but it often felt like she was working twice as hard for half the satisfaction. She had never been lonesome at work before. Through her career, the fact that she was a woman sometimes excluded her from the more clubby aspects of reporters' society, but she'd never cared much. Now Phillips, Dunne, and the other men occasionally gathered at a bar on the northeast corner of Broadway and Twenty-Seventh Street for a snifter of whiskey. Once, Miss Tarbell confided in a letter, "The whole office goes on Thursday to the publishers' dinner—that is, everybody but myself. It is the first time since I came into the office that the fact of petticoats has stood in my way, and I am half inclined to resent it."

On evenings when she needed some good talk, Miss Tarbell dined out or went to Boyden's. A sprightly bachelor not long out of Harvard, Boyden was everybody's friend. "One can have friends, one can have editors," noted Baker, "but Bert was both." Though he was the youngest of the colleagues, he often hosted teas or dinners in his fourth-floor walk-up on Stuyvesant Square. Miss Tarbell paged through his guestbook from those evenings and noted some of the names there: "Booth Tarkington, Edna Ferber . . . politicians, scientists, adventurers. What talk went on in that high-up living room! What wonderful tales we heard!" The regular congenial gatherings lent the *American* group an intermittent "gay unity" that inspired their days and nights.

McClure, meanwhile, got to know the everyday workings of an office again. Despite the publicity over the break, he still had support in respectable circles. Conan Doyle sent cheering words after the schism. "You are the root of the business & it is bad when the branches quarrel with the root," he wrote, praising McClure's "energy and genius." Without Phillips and Miss Tarbell, though, McClure found himself in need of an editorial surrogate who could make the magazine work and preserve its spark while he traveled to gather ideas.

Willa Cather was living in Pittsburgh and had had two stories accepted into *McClure's* by the time of the staff walkout. McClure met her and saw potential; he hired her, inviting her first to visit him and Hattie at Ardsley. After a day in their home, Cather found herself "in a state of delirious excitement, his captive for life."

Their connection gave Cather an entrée to New York publishing. Over four years at *McClure's,* he trained her into a satisfactory substitute for Ida Tarbell. Fifteen years younger than her predecessor, Cather also settled in Greenwich Village. She had left behind her relationship with Isabelle McClung in Pittsburgh, and had not yet met Edith Lewis, with whom she would spend the latter four decades of her life.

Through 1906, though, completely at the disposal of McClure and his storms of ideas, Cather felt her initial idealization of her new boss rapidly diminish. As she got more familiar with the Chief and the relentless flow of pages to fill and temperamental authors to be managed, Cather felt increasingly disoriented. The pace of a monthly magazine was dizzyingly fast and stultifying at the same time. She was compelled to edit a great deal of passable writing that made her feel awash in a "tepid bath." Cather was vocal with her friends about her life of always-mounting tasks, and she confided to author Sarah Orne Jewett, "I live just about as much during the day as a trapeze performer does when he is on the bars—it's catch the right bar at the right minute, or into the net you go. I feel all the time so dispossessed and bereft of myself."

Office obligations interfered with her true calling. Echoing Ida Tarbell's early battle to transition from editor to writer, Cather wrote to Jewett, "Mr. McClure tells me that he does not think I will ever be able to do much at writing stories, that I am a good executive and I had better let it go at that. I sometimes, indeed I very often think that he is right." She broke away in September 1911, returning the following year to ghostwrite his autobiography.

Cather and McClure had an enduringly warm relationship thereafter, but her story "Ardessa," published in *The Century* in 1918, gives an unvarnished idea of her more critical impressions of S. S. It also came bitingly close to confirming rumors of McClure's personal scandal. Her narrator is an indolent staffer for magazine editor Marcus O'Mally, of *The Outcry,* come to New York out of the rural West. O'Mally had "built up about him an organization of which he was somewhat afraid and with which he was vastly bored"; he made his name exposing vice and was temporarily "amused" by turning run-of-the-mill reporters into famous ones. But as years passed, he resented how he had become "constrained by these reputations that he had created out of cheap paper and cheap ink. . . . He left his office to take care of itself for a good many months of the year while he played about on the outskirts of social order."

Outside of work, McClure, Miss Tarbell, and the old guard eventually managed a friendly reconciliation. Their work suffered from the separation. Under McClure's hodgepodge new regime, his one notable journalistic coup was a series on Maria Montessori that started in 1911, the same year the first Montessori school opened in Tarrytown, New York. McClure was instrumental in bringing Montessori from Italy to America and advocating her teaching methods, still in widespread use today. Generally, after the walkout, *McClure's* leaned more heavily on fiction.

As he himself admitted, McClure's attention lingered too much on past glories. He mulled over Kipling's advice, "It takes the young man to find the young man." It was true, he realized. McClure would dictate to Cather these lines for his autobiography: "No man's judgment retains that openness for very many years. His successes become his limitations. He is influenced by the development of his own tastes, by the memory of past pleasures, by the great personalities who have made the most interesting chapters of his life."

Practical matters tended to stump him. He hadn't given much thought to money for many years. When he needed it, he got it from the *McClure's* office cash box. Whenever he went abroad, the ticket was purchased under his expense account, by an assistant. At each year's end, if it turned out he had overdrawn for household expenses, travel, or anything else beyond his salary, the board of directors had always given him a bonus that precisely canceled out the debit.

At long last, there was a reckoning. Enormous debts from the ill-advised construction of a new production plant forced McClure to turn to an ever-more-controlling board of trustees—for a time directed by Frank "Effendi" Doubleday, McClure's old partner-adversary—to manage business affairs. They kept McClure as a desk editor but restricted his salary and expense account. He did not take well to being made a figurehead. When the trustees began interfering in editorial decisions, McClure was shocked and humiliated. *"No one is to be trusted,"* he hissed at Hattie, more insulted than he could express. Until he was ousted from his namesake magazine by creditors in 1911, he insisted a comeback was imminent.

\* \* \*

**A PORTRAIT OF IDA TARBELL** done in 1907 shows her looking down at something just out of frame. Her mouth is set in a firm line, but her expression is gentle, the default "benign, searching look" leaning more toward the former than the latter. She has a heavy brow, and her glossy hair is pulled straight back and up from a widow's peak. She is simply posed in a high-necked dress. The only signs that she is fifty and not thirty-five are the shadowy lines around her mouth and a near-smiling crinkle around her eyes. A weariness set in after the move to *The American.*

She was still, on some level, unmoored. New York was her writing headquarters, but it had grown to feel unhomelike. Titusville still held a claim on her, but Titusville was five hundred miles away, and most weekends she stayed in New York, often thinking that she was frittering much of that time away on aimless walks, matinee shows, and other "makeshifts of a homeless person in a city." She told a fellow reporter, "I am an optimist. My great ambition is to have a house in the country where I can write in the garden."

In the turbulent months of 1906, with revenue from the two-volume book edition of *The History of the Standard Oil Company,* she realized that dream and bought a small farm among the clear rolling hills of Easton, Connecticut. She named it Twin Oaks for the two graceful trees that bracketed the house from the road, and perhaps in homage to Gardiner Greene Hubbard's manse in Washington, D.C. It was already an old house, begun in the late 1700s, but it was far from a grand country estate: Miss Tarbell "had no stomach, or money, for a 'place.'"

The white-clapboard farm in the hills was, however, magnetic and energizing to her. She was irresistibly drawn to the project of making it a working farm again, planting an orchard and acquiring chickens, horses, a cow, and a pig. Country life gave her a sense of belonging that even Bert Boyden's intellectual salons could not conjure.

Possibly it brought back some of her earliest memories, of her grandparents' log house in Erie County, before the move to Oil Creek. Her closest neighbor at Twin Oaks was an antiques dealer who charmed her into buying highly impractical things. Typically she skimped on her clothing budget to be able to afford fertilizer for her orchard, but her first purchase for the house was from the antiquarian's store: an old melodeon, a little concert-hall organ.

There were other journalists in the area, too. Miss Tarbell knew and admired her "lively" neighbor Jeannette Gilder, editor of *The Critic* (and sister to *Century* editor Richard Watson Gilder), and together they caught the rumor that Mark Twain was building a place close by. News of the celebrity in their midst traveled fast, thanks in part to Twain's sociable nature. He threw large parties, giving the invitations to the butcher to distribute among all of the neighbors along with their meat deliveries, and now and then he had Tarbell and Gilder over for tea.

Miss Tarbell shared the refuge with her fellow *American* staffers. Boyden first visited before she had even signed the deed. He "had banged down an over-crowded desk" and tagged along because "I was not fit to be trusted to buy property," she recalled affectionately. The house was heated by actual fires, the old-fashioned way. "Of course you are an idiot," Boyden kidded her, "and of course you cannot be cured." In fact, they were both charmed. He advised her to buy the place immediately and involved himself in everything from the wallpaper—inspired by the Parisian styles Miss Tarbell had known in her youth—to the larder. When he arrived on a cold evening he would barrel into the cellar, fill his arms with apples, and "himself made the hot apple-sauce, without which he always declared no winter house party was tolerable." Phillips came out and rested. Baker and Siddall and their families visited when they could. Frank Norris and his wife, Kathleen, came out and named her pig Juicy. (Miss Tarbell used her own middle name for her steady workhorse, Minerva.) On the farm, her sadness after the break faded into the background. She created a home for herself.

The rub was that writing was more difficult on the farm than in New York, and personal woes pursued her. Her first major project for *The American* was a history of the tariff system from the Civil War onward. She already had a friendly acquaintance with Grover Cleveland, whose two tariff-reform bills had failed. During her last two years at *McClure's* she had written to him regularly to encourage him to publish his memoirs in the magazine, and to offer herself as a ghostwriter if he felt he needed one. And yet, despite Cleveland's approachability and her dutiful examination of the *Congressional Record,* her narrative felt devoid of life.

The men she had most admired had grown small and sad. She deeply felt the loss of the symbiosis she had shared with McClure, and her work at *The American* felt faded compared to the lively writing the Chief had inspired. She stopped writing disruptive exposure stories. One November day in 1907, she and Rockefeller's PR strongman Henry Rogers met by chance. Miss Tarbell was waiting at a crosswalk on Fifth Avenue when she noticed an open-topped car rolling slowly past, and Rogers smiling and waving at her from within. He received her at his house, where she discovered he had had a stroke and that his recovery was bedeviled by guilt and uncertainty about the future.

Rockefeller himself faced worse problems than bad press. Prospectors struck oil in Texas, Oklahoma, and Kansas. Abroad, Britain and Russia had started drilling for oil in Iran. New sources dwarfed the wells of Pennsylvania and Ohio, the Standard's stronghold. In September 1907, the trial of the *United States of America v. the Standard Oil Company of New York et al.* began. It had been seven years since Miss Tarbell first outlined the series with McClure; she decided not to attend the hearings. On May 5, 1911, the Supreme Court affirmed a judgment that dissolved the monopoly. Instead of one corporation that controlled nearly all the oil in America, thirty-seven small companies emerged. Miss Tarbell read the trial transcripts but remained in the background as Rockefeller and his empire were finally called to account. She turned down reporters' requests for comment, admitting "I had no stomach for it."

After the dissolution, Rockefeller's wealth actually multiplied. He kept his shares in the new companies and his net worth rose with the advent of the motorcar, eventually making Rockefeller America's first billionaire. In 1917, Rockefeller sat for a series of interviews with biographer William O. Inglis, who read aloud part of the series. Three facts were immediately clear: Rockefeller was unfamiliar with much of the material, he grudgingly admired it, and beneath his determined air of calm, he remained angry. He was certain that Miss Tarbell was "animated more with jealousy begotten by the inability of her father and her brother and some of her neighbors to do as well as the Standard Oil Company." At the same time, he remarked, "How clever she is, compared with poor [Henry Demarest] Lloyd, who was always hysterical! She makes her picture clear and attractive, no matter how unjust she is. She really could write."

*The American* never aimed to change the world. If the voice at the heart of *McClure's* was a voraciously curious and idealistic citizen, wild-eyed S. S. himself, the one that spoke for *The American* was a genteel dinner guest reluctant to offend. The new magazine "had little genuine muckraking spirit," wrote Miss Tarbell, but perhaps they were all better, more impartial journalists for it. "[I]t sought to present things as they were, not as somebody thought they ought to be. We were journalists, not propagandists; and as journalists we sought new angles on old subjects." The shift in reporting agenda troubled Steffens. Increasingly passionate about socialism and frustrated by his colleagues' editorial feedback on his work—they discouraged his desire to editorialize on the facts he was reporting—he left the new magazine less than a year after joining it.

The technological marvels of the future, at least, retained some excitement for *The American,* as they had buoyed *McClure's.* While reporting for *The American,* Miss Tarbell became the first woman to fly in an airplane and write about it, a tremor-inducing experience that left her "lost in the amazement at the suddenness and ease of it," and predicting that "possibly before we die we may both be traveling back and forth to business from country to city in an airplane!" The assignment gave her a glimpse of a coming era much changed from her own coming-of-age, when the telephone had instilled the same skepticism and wonder.

She needed another great undertaking. In 1912, Miss Tarbell decided to embark on a wholly different kind of story: she would travel across America and report on the improvements she saw in industry and quality of life. Instead of driving change through exposure and rallying cries for reform, she would inspire others with good examples that they might follow. She took to the road to talk to mill owners, miners, shoemakers, railroaders, factory owners—including Henry Ford in Detroit—and others. Executives were reluctant to talk to her, until she managed to soften them with promises that she only wanted to listen and observe; reminding them of her Lincoln series also seemed to help. For four years, she crisscrossed the country to gather material, her finances stretched thin by her modest salary, scarce savings, and shares in *The American,* which was not a commercial success.

The reasons for *The American*'s lackluster performance were hard to pin down from within the magazine. Phillips felt they were lacking "a quality of effort"; William Allen White thought they were too serious, telling Phillips that readers had come to expect "the pale drawn face; the set lips and a general line of emotional insanity." Miss Tarbell decided, "We always have lacked it: a certain hustle, ingenuity, a general energizing effect such as we used to get out of S.S." In later years, she told Miss Roseboro that she and Phillips missed McClure and "a certain radiance he gave to work." She saw their problem as an internal one, but circumstances beyond the office walls were driving it, too.

Print was no longer the world's only mass medium. Motion pictures broadcast the news now, with "actuality" films projected in nickelodeon theaters. In 1900, Thomas A. Edison Inc. produced a short film of McKinley's assassin's death by electric chair. Three years later, mass entertainment caught up: *The Great Train Robbery,* a silent, twelve-minute western, was released to enormous popular acclaim. The effect on magazines was one of displacement, especially for the general-interest genre that encompassed *McClure's* and *The American.* The magazines that survived tended to become increasingly specialized, or were acquired by deep-pocketed investors who were often less inclined to support muckraking.

Ironically, a blow to investigative stories came from within the ranks of prominent publishers. In 1910, Will Irwin undertook an exposé of Hearst's dealings with advertisers for *Collier's.* When he got wind of this, Hearst lashed out with a $500,000 civil libel lawsuit. Libel suits had long been a meddlesome hazard of muckraking, but this set a precedent for how expensive it could get, and made editors more likely to kill or avoid commissioning investigative projects.

Despite her renown, Miss Tarbell lived practically from story to story, or lecture to lecture. In addition to difficult reminders of her *McClure's* days, family worries followed her up to Twin Oaks. In the late 1910s, her brother Will suffered a nervous breakdown likely brought on by a pileup of debts. He turned to his sisters for help, but the disaster went beyond financial concerns. Sarah Tarbell closed her painting studio in Titusville and learned bookkeeping, while Ida looked to make quick money from a speaking tour. She moved Will into Twin Oaks and opened both her farm and her New York apartment to his children, despite episodes of paranoid despair where Will held her at gunpoint as they argued.

To her benefit, Miss Tarbell had plenty of steel left in her. When any-one asked how she could bear Will's behavior, she replied that she found it "terribly interesting." Her view of Will was that he was "a remarkable person, great possibilities combined with irresponsibility, immense ego-tism, charm, gaiety, but in money matters incapable of holding on to any-thing, generous, indifferent to accumulation, quick to sacrifice if irritated or stirred to pity, an amazing creature." Her close-range alliance with Mc-Clure had prepared her for life with a much-loved but volatile and rapidly, reluctantly aging man.

When she returned from her reporting trip and lecture tour, a world war had broken out, *The American* had to be sold, and Miss Tarbell was, at nearly sixty, scanning the horizon for her next career. Who knows how many times she sifted through her letters from the old *McClure's* days and reread this one from her old and best editor:

*July 1, 1907*

*My dear Miss Tarbell—*

*I am so starved to see you! . . .*

*I dreamed of you a day or two ago. I often dream of you.*

*I thought I was telling you how I found out that by speaking slowly & calmly & acting calmly I found I had much greater influence on people (I am actually doing this) & I thought that I was standing by your chair & you drew me down & kissed me to show your approval.*

*When you disapproved of me it nearly broke my heart. . . .*

*I never cease to love you as I have for many, many years.*

*I wish you had not turned away.*

*With great esteem & affection*

*Very sincerely yours*
*SSMcClure*

# Epilogue

Sunset and evening star,
　　And one clear call for me!
And may there be no moaning of the bar,
　　When I put out to sea [. . .]

*—from "Crossing the Bar" by Alfred, Lord Tennyson*

S. McClure, Ida Tarbell, and their colleagues broke apart, but the craft they invented and the stories they aimed at the troubles of their day have stayed with us. *Forbes* has described journalists like Tarbell as "the Ralph Naders and Jack Andersons of their time." Judges convened by New York University's journalism department listed Ida Tarbell's *The History of the Standard Oil Company* in the twentieth century's top five works of journalism, alongside John Hersey, Rachel Carson, Bob Woodward and Carl Bernstein, and Edward R. Murrow. Today we might see the spirit of the *McClure's* group in journalists across a range of media sources characterized by deep reporting, at publications like *The New Yorker* and *ProPublica,* in documentary film and investigative podcasts, and in any telling of a true story that allows us to see our society and political leadership more clearly.

The parallels between the Gilded Age and today are not neat enough to draw easy lessons from the rise and fall of *McClure's,* but there are clues worth dwelling on. For the most part, the *McClure's* group believed they had far more foresight regarding the trajectory of the culture around them and their own careers than they truly did. Beyond a parable of hubris falling hard, though, is a case study of communal endeavor toward truth and profit together. Through open-minded collaboration between the various thinkers of *McClure's,* the magazine succeeded in creating a whole that was greater than the sum of its parts: it revealed how wealth and power in America worked. Their editorial disagreements were as vital to this undertaking as the idealism that lay beneath, but survival was threatened the moment one of its leaders lost his hold on his underlying moral compass.

A great magazine makes culture, and it is also made by it. As much as the *McClure's* group had drive, they were also products of the time and place they were so vocal about changing. Out of all of them, only S. S. McClure had known real hunger and hardship. His writers for the most part strove to report facts without advocating for a specific solution. Upton Sinclair once teased Ray Stannard Baker that he "beat even the rest of the folks on *McClure's* for getting together facts minus conclusions"—a remark that Baker regarded as high praise. It was a literature of exposure largely produced by individuals who had only theoretically considered what it might be to experience oppression due to race, poverty, lack of education, or dearth of opportunity. Perhaps this distance was a fundamental flaw, and no such group, no matter how brilliant, can keep pace with the "pulse of the nation" around them without the background noise of their competing passions and ambitions growing too loud for the collective to function.

The bitterness between politicians and the press weighs on us now, too, more than a century after the "muckrake" speech and mutiny at *McClure's.* Now, at a time when powerful voices question the value and validity of a free press every day, the story of *McClure's* illuminates both what can happen when investigative journalism is able to thrive and the consequences that come when it is deliberately torpedoed. It also shows the pitfalls of a media world whose major currency is outrage, a dynamic that can jeopardize the integrity of investigative work and seems certain to set readers on a path to apathy.

When he launched the magazine, McClure could not foresee the embattled days that lay ahead, nor did he suspect that the seeds of its collapse lay within its starting strength: himself. *McClure's* likely would have changed tack even without rising acrimony between politics and press, as McClure pushed those closest to him beyond their limits. But his decision to fund and publish revelatory investigations was like a flag planted on a peak half-accidentally. It pitted the written word against the growing alliance between politics and business and redefined what ambitious, thoughtful, time- and money-intensive journalism could do.

\* \* \*

**SOON AFTER THE BREAK AT *McCLURE'S*,** several forces came together to push muckraking into sharp decline. With the advent of World War I, patriotism gained a stronger hold over readers' imaginations than everyday injustice—allowing realities like Jim Crow, eugenics advocacy, and immigration restriction to flourish in the mainstream without substantial debate in the press. "Two hateful world wars will leave little, I am afraid, of the spirit we knew in those days," Baker reflected.

As reforms such as the dissolution of Standard Oil and the Pure Food and Drug Act passed into law, there was also a sense that the mission had been accomplished, that everyone could move on. In 1909, *Everybody's Magazine* summed up this sense of complacency:

Wall Street cannot gull the public as it once did. . . . Banking is adding new safeguards. Advertising is nearly honest. . . . Food and drug adulteration are dangerous. Human life is more respected by common carriers. The hour of the old-time political boss is struck. . . . The people are naming their own candidates. . . . Our public resources are being conserved. The public health is being considered. . . . It is a new era. A new world. Good signs, don't you think? And what had brought it about? Muckraking. Bless your heart, just plain muckraking. By magazine writers and newspapers and preachers and public men and Roosevelt.

The magazine as the dominant vehicle for information and entertainment gradually lost its singular hold on the public. First Edison's moving pictures captured the popular imagination, and then in the 1920s, radio rose up as the new mass medium, eating away at advertising revenues that had once kept magazines flush. A generation later, radio, too, would fade in relevance with the explosion of network television in the 1950s.

McClure left his namesake magazine when he was forcibly bought out by the board in 1911. His autobiography, ghostwritten by Willa Cather, began to be serialized in the magazine the same year. McClure, much reduced in finances and fame, became a full-time philosopher, publishing three books on politics, world peace, and human nature. The books made little impression, but he became a regular on the lecture circuit at clubs and universities. Regardless of the topic at hand, he steered his talks toward the one he loved best. "The subject of my lecture involves the five greatest problems of our civilization," he mused in 1910, "but it really involves the making of a magazine, as well." His highest praise for up-and-coming reporters was that they demonstrated an instinct for capturing the great figures and events of their particular time—as he put it, a true journalist always kept "an eye on the squirrel."

To many, he continued to embody the golden age of the magazine, and periodically speculators tried to resurrect that era by resurrecting its General. McClure was briefly reinstated as editor of *McClure's* when the magazine came under new ownership in 1928, and his first move was to hire Ida Tarbell to write an update to her *History of the Standard Oil Company*. She plunged in, eager to taste once more "the gaiety and excitement Mr. McClure gave to work," but this second tenure lasted barely a year before finances failed once more. The magazine was eventually sold to Hearst, who drastically altered its focus and added a new subtitle, "The Magazine of Romance." Hearst could not make it work, either, and in 1929, *McClure's* was combined with *Smart Set;* both ceased publication just over two years later.

Without careful management, he struggled to make ends meet. McClure and Hattie had drifted between rented homes and an apartment at the Majestic Hotel near Central Park, and in the mid-1920s, he had written her regarding money, "I tell you I have got to the point of breaking. I wake up in the night in despair. I don't wonder at what my brother Robert did." (Robby, the youngest of the McClure brothers, had shot himself in a spell of depression in 1914.)

After Hattie's final illness and her death in 1929, McClure moved into a small room at the Murray Hill Hotel and spent much of his time at the Union League Club. He used the club's library as his personal office until formally barred from doing so, for he could never pay his dues as regularly as they were charged. In the fall of 1933, Miss Tarbell wrote to the inner *McClure's* circle campaigning to raise money for a near-broke McClure. Miss Cather, now a Pulitzer-winning novelist, quickly sent a check. She was perhaps thinking of McClure when she described her character Oswald Henshaw in later years as "an old man, a gentleman, living in this shabby, comfortless place, cleaning his neckties of a Sunday morning and humming to himself."

He continued to pursue castles in the sky, or rather, on riverbank mud. On the verge of the Great Depression, S. S. grasped at what appeared to be a delayed fulfillment of his McClure's Ideal Settlement. He was appointed chairman of the board, alongside wealthy midwestern real estate investors and lawyers, to develop a model industrial city on the grounds of an old estate along a stretch of the Savannah River, extending from South Carolina to Georgia. He seems to have achieved the position by charisma alone. S. S. told reporters he meant to make it his "life's work" going forward, but the development fell through before it had broken ground.

Preoccupied by what the future might hold in an increasingly crowded and bellicose world, McClure chose a path that would seem to contradict his earlier career. He fell under the spell of Benito Mussolini and defended the fascist leader in public lectures and debates, praising the Italian dictator as having "solved the problem of democracy." At one event at a New York theater, newspapers reported that McClure was "Taken from Theatre on Cheering Fascisti Shoulders." Coincidentally, Miss Tarbell went to Italy for an assignment and was, like McClure, utterly charmed by Mussolini; "a fearful despot," she judged, "but he had a dimple." She came home seriously wondering if a dictator might someday seize the government of Washington and Lincoln. Where McClure exalted the prospect of a fascist America, however, Miss Tarbell grimly steeled herself against it.

Periodically, reporters sought him out for a dose of colorful nostalgia. "MAGAZINE TITAN OF YESTERYEAR," read one caption in 1943, beneath a photograph of a dark-suited McClure looking up from his book, his deep-set eyes slightly perturbed, his mouth open as if he's about to speak. New Yorkers learned to look out for his slight figure, sometimes lost in thought but always with something to say. Younger magazine men tended to find him a "garrulous old bore," but to those forewarned about his tendency to monologue, he was voluble good company. His usual corner newsboy told a reporter in 1940, when asked who was his most interesting customer, "[It's] a toss-up between Mr. McClure of magazine fame and a beautiful blonde who looks soulfully into my eyes each morning and asks for The News."

McClure was awarded the Order of Merit of the National Institute of Arts and Letters on May 19, 1944, alongside Willa Cather and Paul Robeson. Write-ups noted his bearing, "a slender, gray man with stooped shoulders, whose speech and movement are still precise and quick," and who claimed to have entirely stopped reading magazines a decade earlier. As he presented the award to S. S., writer Arthur Train said, "The American people owe a great debt to this man, once famous, now almost forgotten." It must have smarted to hear it announced to the crowd.

The other men of *McClure's* pursued substantial careers, emblematic of the way wartime eventually defined every journalist's livelihood. John Phillips was an advisory editor for other publishers and edited the widely read *Red Cross Magazine* during World War I. Ray Stannard Baker began a second career as a humorist and chronicler of cozy family life under the pen name David Grayson, until he met Woodrow Wilson in 1910. Baker then became press director at the Versailles Conference following the war, and earned the Pulitzer Prize in 1940 for his eight-volume *Woodrow Wilson: Life and Letters*. The hazards of reporting events as they happen continued to be a theme in his more reflective writing. "How our life has been warped by books!" he wrote in his David Grayson compendium *Adventures in Contentment*. "We are not contented with realities: we crave conclusions. With what ardour our minds respond to real events with literary deductions. Upon a train of incidents, as unconnected as life itself, we are wont to clap a booky ending."

Lincoln Steffens became passionately procommunist, saying of the Soviet Union, "I have seen the future, and it works." He moved to an artist colony in California and founded the San Francisco Workers' School, an ideological training center for the American Communist Party. His *Autobiography,* published in 1931, was a bestseller that earned Steffens acclaim as the major chronicler of muckraking. His razor-sharp mind and dedicated work toward a better future continued through the rest of his life. When a young reporter teased him for being a "tired liberal," he shot back, "Do not think that I believe this work is done. I do have faith in your generation."

Ida Tarbell shared that view. She was constitutionally an optimist, despite circumstances that turned her from a scourge of industry to an itinerant scrapper. She left *The American* in 1915, when precarious finances pushed the group to sell. She moved to a studio near Gramercy Park and spent more and more time, as well as she could afford, at Twin Oaks. She and Phillips struck up a routine of getting together every Sunday evening. Her family relied on her for financial support, especially after Will's breakdown. Her mother moved up to Twin Oaks, too; her sister, Sarah, built a painting studio up the hill, and her nieces took refuge there. To drum up cash, Ida periodically went on the national lecture circuit, training her body and voice to withstand stretches of forty-nine nights in forty-nine different places. When she wasn't living in train berths, she published more than twenty books, including her autobiography, *All in the Day's Work;* a novel, *The Rising of the Tide;* and, at last, in 1916, *Madame Roland*. She picked up her Lincoln research again, seeking the balm of working on a subject who was both dead and good.

Through her post-*McClure's* career, Ida Tarbell's stance on feminism gradually shifted. She trained her reporter's eye on the subject starting in 1909, with the series *The American Woman,* and continued with *The Ways of Woman* in 1913. She argued for women to take Abigail Adams as an ideal model: turning her talents to a revolutionary cause, without trying to claim a public role. This position, broadcast so publicly by a woman writer of such stature, was disruptive enough to the suffragist cause to inspire a rally, on April 15, 1912, when Charlotte Perkins Gilman and other thinkers assembled at the Metropolitan Temple in New York. No one was quite ready to give up on Miss Tarbell. Gilman's speech refuted the articles while affirming "the ability and dignity and power of the woman who writes them."

During World War I, President Wilson appointed Miss Tarbell to the eleven-member Woman's Committee of the Council of National Defense. The group also included several prominent feminists, some of whom resented Miss Tarbell's antisuffrage position. It was likely through getting to know one of these women, Anna Shaw, the president of the National American Woman Suffrage Association, that Miss Tarbell's views began to change. "She was so able, so zealous, so utterly given to her cause," wrote Miss Tarbell admiringly. "[M]ost warm-hearted . . . as well as delightfully salty in her bristling against men and their ways." In the course of her conversion, meeting Miss Shaw was the tip of the spear.

For the October 1924 edition of *Good Housekeeping,* Miss Tarbell wrote a long investigation provocatively titled "Is Woman's Suffrage a Failure?" It had been four years since women had gained the right to vote. She traveled across the country to research the story and enthusiastically reported on the women she met who held public office. She argued that a woman could lead a nation just as well as a man: "Consider Catherine of Russia . . . Elizabeth of England, Catherine de Medici. And it was of Marie Antoinette that Mirabeau said she was the only man the king had about him." Women's suffrage had once struck her as unnatural; even as she became a feminist symbol, she had resisted supporting the movement in word or deed. But after others had fought and won the battle, its rightness had become self-evident.

Relieved of being den mother at *McClure's,* Ida Tarbell remade her bond with McClure as one of warm friendship. She was always willing to read his latest draft and relive their indelible years together over lingering lunches. "I have never known anybody that was ever to collect about him for so long a period so devoted a group as you," she wrote him when they were both in their eightieth year. "And that devotion certainly as far as I am concerned has never faltered, even though the very qualities that inspired it made the relation in the end impractical." He had, years earlier, told her he cared for her "in a special manner, as much as a man can care for a woman without loving her"; after a long silence, Miss Tarbell replied that she would always care for him, too, in her way, though she would never try to be his better half again.

To Baker, she confided that the *McClure's* days still preoccupied her. "Was there ever a group like it? Was there ever so much fun in work?" she wrote him—"Or ever so much anguish of spirit when the thing exploded?" That rift haunted her. "Somebody," she wrote her old colleague, "should go to work analyzing the reasons for the explosions of our fine idealistic undertakings."

No one who fell into McClure's entourage and later broke away managed to permanently maintain that separation. When Frank Doubleday bumped into the Chief one day on Fifth Avenue, the former mentioned he was going to Europe the next morning. "I think I will go with you," McClure answered, and without looking for an enthusiastic assent he showed up with wife and luggage on the gangplank the next morning. He and Hattie were lively members of the dozen or so travelers in the Doubleday party, requesting songs from the band at dinnertime and standing to toast the musicians whenever he caught a strain of Wagner.

Doubleday never forgot the sight of McClure raising his glass with the words, "Ah, Wagner! He was the McClure of music." To his listeners, that line alone perfectly encapsulated "the inside of Sam's mind concerning himself." There was an infuriating poignancy to S. S. in these moments. Just after Bert Boyden bumped into the Chief in post–World War I Paris, Boyden wrote Miss Tarbell in amazement, "He is still talking about starting a new magazine."

McClure, meanwhile, felt the loss of Ida Tarbell keenly. Their mutual friend Jeannette Gilder wrote, "The discovery that Mr. McClure was the most proud of, if I may take his own words for it, was Miss Ida Tarbell." Through the 1930s, the *McClure's* group gathered to celebrate each of their birthdays, with McClure taking up the role of lead raconteur and narrating with great verve memories dear to all of them—of a time when they had together tried "to do something in reporting and interpretation of what was good and sound and progressive." For Miss Tarbell, these reunions were "the most beautiful personal demonstrations I have had of this unbreakable quality in friendship." Even while they were together, she seemed to sense that their collaboration belonged to another time, and to hold tight to the bond that remained, as though it could still be tested and broken.

That sense of pathos intensified with time. At one gathering for his seventy-eighth birthday, McClure trotted out all the old stories, about being the "honest little peddler," winning Hattie's hand against the odds, and "storming the citadels in the publishing business." His friends listened as though hearing these worn tales for the first time. "The quality in him which I think we all found so marvelous flared like a torch," Ida Tarbell wrote Miss Roseboro later, "but I could see a flicker at the end."

After months of feeling unwell, S. S. McClure died on a quiet Monday evening, March 21, 1949, aged ninety-two, just one month after John Phillips. The *New York Herald Tribune* called him "extraordinary," and began the obituary, "Everything about him was phenomenal," while acknowledging his faded name: "To many he is only a memory, but this man was probably America's greatest magazine editor. . . . The McClure genius for being lively and interesting, along with an almost inexhaustible energy, awakened Americans to their possibilities, inspired political conscience, spread improved taste in literature, and generally pointed the way to magazines as we know them." His loved ones bid him farewell at St. Barnabas' Hospital in the Bronx, where the chaplain read Tennyson's "Crossing the Bar." He is buried in Galesburg.

Reporters sometimes sought out Ida Tarbell, too, for profiles that gaped at her unapologetically independent, modest life. Setting her up as the "Terror of the Trusts," they marveled at the dissonance between her formidable reputation and actual demeanor. "When she isn't writing on public questions," one reporter noted, "she is raising prize dahlias, making apple jelly or collecting old pewter." Idealized in older age as a "tall, stalwart-looking woman in white" who called to mind "your favorite aunt, and Jo March grown up," Miss Tarbell oscillated between enjoying society and shunning it. For more than thirty years she was president of the Pen & Brush Club in New York, directing a convivial gathering place for women artists and writers. She also relished evenings when no one was there to question her equal enjoyment of Disney cartoons, Dorothy Sayers novels, Virginia Woolf essays, and the occasional solitary cigarette and nip of whiskey.

Ida Tarbell took ill with pneumonia and died in 1944. She had lived with Parkinson's disease for years, continuing to write via Dictaphone and secretary. To readers she was a figure of admiration, fascination, and bafflement to the end. When a *Cosmopolitan* reporter approached her about participating in a panel on the question "What Interests You Most in This Cosmopolitan World of Today?" Miss Tarbell did not hesitate to reply, "Work." Her purpose had not faded, though her hand had started to shake. In work, she wrote, comes "the consciousness that you are growing, the realization that gradually there is more skill in your fingers and your mind. . . . You do more. By giving yourself freely to your work you become a creator suggesting new techniques, new machines, finding new magic in words, new arrangement of facts and thoughts."

Frail in body, she had held on to one satisfaction: that she had led an original life, not driven by a superficial desire for originality, but fueled by a true intrinsic curiosity. Not only had she survived by her pen, but she had been an integral part of the Progressive experiment. In a commencement speech she gave at Allegheny College in 1913, she exhorted graduates to take visionary leaps of faith as she had, saying, "The greatest service of the imagination to the average girl is saving her from an imitative life. . . . Imagination is the only key to the future. Without it none exists—with it all things are possible."

Before giving that speech, she had wondered at the renewed landscape around the college, now cheerful and green with little trace of the Oil Region's oil-smeared beginnings. A bright-eyed new generation of men and women looked to her for wisdom, and she liked what she saw. "I believe," she wrote to a friend, "that we are passing on in all this jumbled effort of ours, a better equipped youth than we have ever had before."

Above all, Ida Tarbell urged her young listeners to be open to the world around them and throw their whole selves into their work. She finished the lecture with words that may well have guided her own decisions. "Nothing," she concluded, her voice grave and sure, "comes from the mind or heart which has not gone in."

# Acknowledgments

This book would not have been completed without generous support from many quarters.

Relatives of several major characters contributed time, sources, and encouragement to the project. Frederick Dodds McClure and Diane McClure opened their home and archives, which were invaluable. I am similarly grateful to Peter Price, Caroline Tarbell Tupper, Nancy Huntington, and Daneet Steffens. Wendy Chaix graciously walked me through her home in Easton, Connecticut, formerly Ida Tarbell's Twin Oaks, and shared photographs of the landscape as it was in Ida's time.

Librarians, archivists, and curators opened new doors into the story and allowed the characters to speak for themselves. In particular I thank Jane Westenfeld at the Pelletier Library, Allegheny College; Marilyn Black at the Oil Region Alliance; Susan Beates at the Drake Well Museum; Isabel Planton and Emily Grover at the Lilly Library, Indiana University, Bloomington; Meredith Mann at the New York Public Library; Cynthia Harbeson at the Jones Library, Amherst; and Maryjo McAndrew at Knox College. I did most of my secondary-source research at Brown University's John D. Rockefeller Library and came to appreciate a philanthropist whose legacy furnishes writers with resources even when the result doesn't reflect rosily on him. Thanks are also due to the Harvard Houghton Library and Wisconsin Historical Society.

Authors and historians with deep knowledge of journalism and the Progressive Era made themselves and, in some cases, their unpublished works available to me in support of this book. In particular I thank Kathleen Brady, Jessica Dorman, and Steve Weinberg for leading the way.

At the extraordinary Goucher College Creative Nonfiction MFA program, I benefited from the mentorship of Suzannah Lessard, Jacob Levenson, Diana Hume George, Philip Gerard, Patsy Sims, and Leslie Rubinkowski. Memsy Price, Neda Toloui-Semnani, Ginny McReynolds, Kristina Gaddy, and Rachel Dickinson, among others I was fortunate to meet at Goucher, are invaluable to my work and life as readers and friends. Thanks always to Kelsey Osgood and Carrie Hagen for putting me on the path. Colleagues and friends near and far "got" the book from the outset and generously cheered it on. When I broke from working on it around the birth of a child, Dan Crissman gave my first draft a thorough and transformative edit.

Amelia Atlas at ICM is a masterful literary agent. With patience, wisdom, and excellent instincts in all things, she coaxed a proposal into being and found this book a home. Sincere and everlasting thanks are due to Katherine Marino, who made the connection.

At Ecco I am indebted to Emma Dries, who acquired the book and had an excellent vision for it; Emma Janaskie, who edited it beautifully; and Sara Birmingham, a true pleasure to work with. I also wish to thank copy editor Tom Pitoniak, proofreader Chloe Bollentin, designer Michelle Crowe, publicist Martin Wilson, and marketer Meghan Deans.

I am immeasurably privileged in several ways, but none more so than being part of the Gorton and Murphy families. I'm glad to have the opportunity to thank them here for support far beyond the limits of this book. From my parents, Andrée Feghali Gorton and Ted Gorton, as well as my siblings, Haig, Maya, and Alex Gorton, I have long been graced with inspiration, understanding, and love. The Murphy family, including my own Josephine, offered open arms and a new sense of home.

Deepest thanks go to Paul Jarod Murphy, who made this book possible and who brings his complete, brilliant self to our Full Catastrophe every day. This book is dedicated to Paul, with love.

# Notes

### Preface

x    *The two friends*: Charles W. Calhoun, ed., *The Gilded Age: Essays on the Origins of Modern America* (Wilmington, DE: Scholarly Resources, 1996), xi.

x    *the frontier vanished*: Jack Beatty, *The Age of Betrayal: The Triumph of Money in America, 1865–1900* (New York: Knopf, 2007), 4.

xi    *"fairies and angels" to instead "flesh and blood"*: Cecelia Tichi, *Exposés and Excess: Muckraking in America, 1900–2000* (Philadelphia: University of Pennsylvania Press, 2004), 69.

xi    *Actors might have been known*: Robert Ernest Christin, "McClure's Magazine, 1893–1903: A Study of Popular Culture" (Ph.D. diss., Ohio State University, 1958), 146–47.

xi    *"the pulpit, the press, and the novel"*: Frank Norris, *The Responsibilities of the Novelist, and Other Literary Essays* (New York: Doubleday, Page, 1903), 10.

xi    *"the real governing classes"*: Jessica Dorman, "'Deliver Me from This Muck-Rake': The Art and Craft of Progressive Era Journalism" (Ph.D. diss., Harvard University, 1996), 28–29.

xii    *"this people shall possess"*: Theodore Roosevelt, "Remarks at the Dinner of the Periodical Publishers Association of America," April 7, 1904, the Almanac of Theodore Roosevelt, http://www.theodore-roosevelt.com/trspeechescomplete .html (accessed March 18, 2019).

xii    *"nobody's hand has been more perceptible"*: E. S. M., "Notes on the Periodicals," *Life* 63, no. 1645 (March 12, 1914): 444.

xii    *"a queer bird"*: Mark Sullivan, *The Education of an American* (New York: Doubleday, Doran, 1938), 196.

xii  *"cyclone in a frock-coat"*: Peter Lyon, *Success Story: The Life and Times of S. S. McClure* (Deland, FL: Everett/Edwards, 1967), 146–47.

xii  *"the most brilliant staff"*: Ibid., 295.

xiii  *"like a gun"*: Lincoln Steffens, *The Autobiography of Lincoln Steffens* (Berkeley, CA: Heyday Books, 2005), 394.

xiii  *"lively, friendly, aggressive, delightful"*: Ida M. Tarbell, *All in the Day's Work: An Autobiography* (New York: Macmillan, 1939), 145.

## Prologue

1  *"I suppose there is no place"*: Letter, S. S. McClure to Granville Hicks, May 6, 1933, McClure mss, Lilly Library, Indiana University, Bloomington.

1  *a reporter, crossed*: Gove Hambidge, "Ida Tarbell—a Spirited 76," *New York Herald Tribune*, February 25, 1934, Ida Tarbell papers, Sophia Smith Collection, Smith College. In this scene, details of Ida Tarbell's apartment and an often-referenced quote about her reputation are drawn from the article "A Talk with Miss Tarbell . . ." by James Creelman, as cited below. These details are further corroborated in other sources. All interview quotes are drawn from the Hambidge article alone.

1  *his eyes scanned*: James Creelman, "A Talk with Miss Tarbell . . ." New York *World*, undated, Drake Well Museum collection.

2  *"grown around her"*: Hambidge, "Ida Tarbell—a Spirited 76."

2  *A colleague had warned him*: Creelman, "A Talk with Miss Tarbell."

2  *Instead, Miss Tarbell*: Ibid.

2  *Evenings were usually quiet*: Hambidge, "Ida Tarbell—a Spirited 76."

2  *Among her favorites*: Kathleen Brady, *Ida Tarbell: Portrait of a Muckraker* (Pittsburgh: University of Pittsburgh Press, 1989), 240.

2  *"I am a student of events and men"*: Hambidge, "Ida Tarbell—a Spirited 76."

3  *At seventy-seven*: Richard H. Waldo, "The Genius of S. S. McClure," *Editor & Publisher*, July 21, 1934, McClure Publishing Company collection, University of Delaware.

3  *"Merchant of Men's Minds"*: Galesburg *Post* clipping, June 7, 1929, McClure mss, Lilly Library.

3  *"Active does not begin"*: Boston *Post* clipping, December 9, 1923, McClure mss, Lilly Library.

3  *"on the top of his mind and heart"*: Waldo, "The Genius of S. S. McClure."

4  *"concatenation of unusualness"*: Mark Sullivan quoted in Alice Hegan Rice, *The Inky Way* (New York: Appleton-Century, 1940), 59–60.

4  *"They became presses"*: Sullivan, *The Education of An American*, 197–98.

## 1: *A Country for Youth*

8   *"well-to-do poor"*: S. S. McClure and Willa Cather, "My Autobiography, Part 1," *McClure's Magazine* 41, no. 6 (October 1913), http://cather.unl.edu/index.mcclure .html (accessed October 6, 2017).

8   *"It was then"*: Ibid.

8   *"Opening those boxes"*: Ibid.

9   *Later in life*: Ibid.

9   *Spirited and stocky*: Ibid.

9   *Back near Drumaglea*: Undated typed memo, McClure mss, Lilly Library.

9   Samuel, your da is deid: McClure and Cather, "My Autobiography, Part 1."

10  *Much later, keeping the brothers together*: Harold S. Wilson, *McClure's Magazine and the Muckrakers* (Princeton, NJ: Princeton University Press, 1970), 25.

11  *He recalled sitting*: McClure and Cather, "My Autobiography, Part 1."

11  *"Here was a young country"*: Ibid.

12  *"I lay on the carpet"*: S. S. McClure and Willa Cather, "My Autobiography, Part 2," *McClure's Magazine* 42, no. 1 (November 1913), http://cather.unl.edu /index.mcclure.html (accessed October 6, 2017).

12  *They crowded in*: Ibid.

12  *All were so malnourished*: Lyon, *Success Story*, 8–9.

12  *"Something had to be done"*: McClure and Cather, "My Autobiography, Part 2."

13  *"It seemed to me"*: Ibid.

13  *"Here were good stories"*: Ibid.

13  *Sam gratefully*: Archibald McKinlay, "After Humble Beginnings, Valpo's Mc-Clure Led Nation's Muckrakers," *Northwest Indiana Times,* April 22, 1999, http:// www.nwitimes.com/uncategorized/after-humble-beginnings-valpo-s-mcclure -led-nation-s-muckrakers/article_54538d7f-5dfa-566b-97e5-13f8d49c5dd2.html (accessed June 25, 2018).

14  *"[L]ike most things"*: McClure and Cather, "My Autobiography, Part 2."

14  *A classmate recalled*: Letter, Rachel Wilson Van Ness to S. S. McClure, February 20, 1905, McClure mss, Lilly Library.

14  *Other boys mocked*: Lyon, *Success Story*, 11.

14  *Much later, an up-and-coming*: Alice Hegan Rice, *Sandy* (New York: Century, 1905), http://www.classicreader.com/book/2479/ (accessed October 13, 2017).

15  *"I escaped being a tramp"*: McClure and Cather, "My Autobiography, Part 2."

15  *With Sam, Jack, Tom, and Robby*: Lyon, *Success Story*, 12–13.

## 2: *Oildorado*

17  *Classification, not fratricide*: Tarbell, *All in the Day's Work*, 7.

17 *Ida later wrote*: Ibid.

18 *A local observer reported*: Brady, *Ida Tarbell*, 11–12.

19 *Separately, in New Hampshire*: Dan Yergin, "The Pennsylvania Start-Up that Changed the World," *Forbes* (September 3, 2009), https://www.forbes.com/2009/09/03/oil-daniel-yergin-business-energy-oil.html (accessed October 16, 2017).

19 *In the window*: Charles Austin Whiteshot, *The Oil-Well Driller: A History of the World's Greatest Enterprise, the Oil Industry* (self-published in 1905), 39.

19 *Among the words*: Shawn Macomber, "Oil City Is Well Again," *The American Spectator*, January 26, 2009, https://spectator.org/42535_oil-city-well-again/ (accessed June 25, 2018).

20 *Silliman told him*: Yergin, "The Pennsylvania Start-Up That Changed the World."

21 *He filled an unprecedented*: "Early Oil in Pennsylvania," Eno Petroleum Corporation, 2018, http://www.enopetroleum.com/earlyoilpennsylvania.html (accessed June 25, 2018).

21 *Witnesses dashed off*: Yergin, "The Pennsylvania Start-Up That Changed the World."

21 *As Ida Tarbell would later report*: Tarbell, "The History of the Standard Oil Company—Chapter 1," *McClure's Magazine* 20, no. 1 (November 1902): 6.

21 *A contemporary of Drake*: Macomber, "Oil City Is Well Again."

21 *The strip of petroleum-rich land*: Sean Dennis Cashman, *America in the Age of the Titans: The Progressive Era and World War I* (New York: NYU Press, 1988), 16.

21 *"Ile, or Vay Down in Bennsylvany"*: Hans Schmidt, "Ile, or Vay Down in Bennsylvany" (New York: William A. Pond, 1865), https://www.loc.gov/resource/ihas.100008837.0/?sp=1 (accessed June 18, 2018).

22 *Daily work schedules stretched*: Charles R. Morris, *The Tycoons: How Andrew Carnegie, John D. Rockefeller, Jay Gould, and J. P. Morgan Invented the American Supereconomy* (New York: Times Books, 2005), 150.

22 *Clemenceau wrote to President Wilson*: Clemenceau quoted in Tarbell, *All in the Day's Work*, 362.

22 *suddenly oil was as necessary*: More recently (January 2009), the Venango Museum of Art, Science & Industry in Oil City, Pennsylvania, featured a twenty-minute spoof of the film *Clueless*. Titled *Fuel-less*, the film follows a spoiled high school girl who loses all oil-based products (makeup, aspirin, stylish clothes, functioning car) until she takes the time to appreciate fractional distillation, upon which her oil-rich life is restored. (Macomber, "Oil City Is Well Again.")

22 *At the peak*: Elliott H. Gue, "Oil Demand: Emerging Markets Follow the American Roadmap," *Investing Daily*, August 2, 2010, https://www.investingdaily.com/13503/oil-demand-emerging-markets-follow-the-american-roadmap (accessed November 7, 2015) and Eno Petroleum Corporation, "Early Oil in Pennsylvania."

22 *The rise of "Oildorado"*: Steve Weinberg, *Taking On the Trust: How Ida Tarbell Brought Down John D. Rockefeller and Standard Oil* (New York: Norton, 2009), 55.

22 *The land became so densely settled*: Brian Black, "Oil Creek as Industrial Apparatus: Re-Creating the Industrial Process through the Landscape of Pennsylvania's Oil Boom," *Environmental History* 3, no. 2 (April 1998): 213.

22 *"a collection of pine shanties"*: Brady, *Ida Tarbell*, 15.

22 *"It aroused me to a revolt"*: Tarbell, *All in the Day's Work*, 5.

23 *"creek rushing wildly"*: Ibid., 5–6.

23 *"No industry of man"*: Ibid., 9.

23 *"a cast-iron still"*: Tarbell, "The History of the Standard Oil Company—Chapter 1," 11.

23 *"Anybody who could get the apparatus"*: Ibid.

23 *As a child, Ida witnessed*: Brady, *Ida Tarbell*, 13.

23 *"vindicate her sex"*: Tarbell, *All in the Day's Work*, 3, 30–31.

23 *She and Franklin were staunch*: Weinberg, *Taking on the Trust*, 61.

24 *"I saw from the corner"*: Tarbell, *All in the Day's Work*, 15.

24 *She never forgot*: Ibid., 11.

24 *"Keeping a child busy'"*: Tarbell, *The Ways of Woman* (New York: Macmillan, 1915), 128.

24 *A sharp-eyed girl*: Ibid., 122.

24 *"more enticing, far lovelier"*: Ibid., 123.

24 *"There are still family storeroom copies"*: Tarbell, *All in the Day's Work*, 13.

25 *"notion of elegance"*: Ibid., 22.

25 *"I must be free"*: Ibid., 36.

26 *"I'd rather be a free spinster"*: Alcott quoted in Joan Acocella, "How 'Little Women' Got Big," *The New Yorker* (August 27, 2018), https://www.newyorker.com/magazine/2018/08/27/how-little-women-got-big (accessed October 26, 2018).

26 *It was far from revolutionary*: Stacy A. Cordery, "Women in Industrializing America," in Calhoun, ed., *The Gilded Age*, 125.

26 *"Ours was a yeasty time"*: Tarbell, *All in the Day's Work*, 30–31.

26 *The Seneca Falls Convention*: Paul Foley, "Whatever Happened to Women's Rights," *The Atlantic Monthly* (March 1964), https://www.theatlantic.com/past/docs/issues/64mar/6403rights.htm (accessed June 25, 2018).

27 *"for the first time introducing the word 'male'"*: Tarbell, *All in the Day's Work*, 31.

27 *"first intellectual passion"*: Ibid., 30.

28 *"blow between the eyes"*: Ibid., 23.

28 *In Rouseville, oilmen*: Ibid., 24.

28 *Franklin Tarbell*: Ibid., 24.

29 *"silent and stern"*: Ron Chernow, *Titan: The Life of John D. Rockefeller, Sr.* (New York: Random House, 1998), 436.

**29**  *"the sly, secret, greedy way"*: Tarbell, *All in the Day's Work,* 26.

**29**  *"There was born"*: Ibid., 26.

**29**  *"much elated"*: Ibid., 203.

**29**  *"Often I wish"*: Yergin, *The Prize: The Epic Quest for Oil, Money, and Power* (New York: Free Press, 2011), Kindle ed.

### 3: *A Garibaldi Type of Mind*

**31**  *To reach the hastily built*: Quoted on Knox College website, "Knox College & Lincoln," https://www.knox.edu/about-knox/lincoln-studies-center/knox-and-lincoln (accessed May 30, 2018).

**32**  *"There are few feelings"*: McClure and Cather, "My Autobiography, Part 2."

**32**  *"Everything of any importance"*: Handwritten undated note, McClure mss, Lilly Library.

**32**  *"In seven years"*: Lyon, *Success Story,* 16.

**33**  *To keep body and soul*: McClure and Cather, "My Autobiography, Part 2."

**33**  *In the wintertime*: Wilson, *McClure's Magazine and the Muckrakers,* 15.

**33**  *Crawling between ultrachilled*: S. S. McClure and Willa Cather, "My Autobiography, Part 3," *McClure's Magazine* 42, no. 2 (December 1913), https://cather.unl.edu/nf006_03.html (accessed June 25, 2018).

**33**  *"the honest little peddler"*: Undated McClure memo on autobiography, McClure mss, Lilly Library.

**33**  *"I have seldom seen"*: Lyon, *Success Story,* 13.

**33**  *"Be idle"*: Ibid., 14.

**34**  *"hasn't an overplus"*: Letter, S. S. McClure to Harriet Hurd, May 20, 1882, McClure mss, Lilly Library.

**34**  *"I once ate"*: S. S. McClure and Willa Cather, "My Autobiography, Part 4," *McClure's Magazine* 42, no. 3 (January 1914), https://cather.unl.edu/nf006_04.html (accessed June 25, 2018).

**34**  *"He is a genius"*: Lyon, *Success Story,* 14.

**35**  *"Sam had a powerful effect"*: Ibid., 16–17.

**35**  *"Don't cry for the moon"*: Ibid.

**35**  *Regardless, on May 30, 1876*: Ibid., 18.

**36**  *Using cash from the recent sale*: McClure and Cather, "My Autobiography, Part 3."

**36**  *Sam finally worked*: Lyon, *Success Story,* 19–20.

**37**  *"[He] just assumes"*: Ibid., 20.

**37**  *"outside powers can intervene"*: McClure and Cather, "My Autobiography, Part 3."

**37**  *"I leave forever"*: Lyon, *Success Story,* 22.

**37**  *For more than two years*: Ibid., 23.

37    *Being jilted*: Ibid., 26–27.

37    *"Social intolerance"*: S. S. McClure, "Intolerance," essay, March 17, 1880, Mc-Clure mss, Lilly Library.

38    *"buttonholed almost everybody"*: Robert Stinson, "S. S. McClure and His Magazine: A Study in the Editing of McClures, 1893–1913" (Ph.D. diss., Indiana University, 1971), 5.

38    *"tried to get him to work"*: Letter, Fanny Hague to Hattie Hurd, undated (probably June 1882), McClure mss, Lilly Library.

38    *One of Hattie's friends*: Ibid.

39    *"the readiest and easiest"*: Letter, S. S. McClure to Harriet Hurd, May 20, 1882, McClure mss, Lilly Library.

39    *"killing off"*: Ibid.

39    *"Everything hums"*: Letter, S. S. McClure to Harriet Hurd, May 29, 1882, McClure mss, Lilly Library.

39    *"[I]t is agony to me"*: Letter, Hattie Hurd to S. S. McClure, undated February 1882, McClure mss, Lilly Library.

39    *"To tell you the real real truth"*: Letter, S. S. McClure to Harriet Hurd, April 4, 1881, McClure mss, Lilly Library.

39    *"nothing but weakness"*: Letter, S. S. McClure to Harriet Hurd, May 7, 1882, McClure mss, Lilly Library.

40    *"cursed mediocre versatility"*: Letter, S. S. McClure to Harriet Hurd, June 1, 1882, McClure mss, Lilly Library.

40    *"the insatiable desire"*: Letters from S. S. McClure to Hattie Hurd, McClure mss, Lilly Library.

40    *"Nobody dreams"*: Letter, Hattie Hurd to S. S. McClure, undated February 1882, McClure mss, Lilly Library.

40    *"There are very few men"*: Letters between Hattie Hurd and S. S. McClure, October 15, 1881, McClure mss, Lilly Library.

40    *"just the same boy"*: McClure and Cather, "My Autobiography, Part 4."

41    *He shuffled*: Lyon, *Success Story*, 29.

41    *As a finale to his tenure*: Ibid., 30.

41    *"Many of my friends"*: Letters, S. S. McClure to Harriet Hurd, April 10 and 13, 1882, McClure mss, Lilly Library.

41    *"I can't imagine"*: Letter, S. S. McClure to Harriet Hurd, February 6, 1882, McClure mss, Lilly Library.

42    *Just in case*: Lyon, *Success Story*, 31–32.

42    *He didn't yet know*: S. S. McClure and Willa Cather, "My Autobiography, Part 5," *McClure's Magazine* 42, no. 4 (February 1914), https://cather.unl.edu/index.mcclure.html (accessed June 25, 2018).

42   *"I do not love you"*: Lyon, *Success Story,* 33.

42   *Uncharacteristically quiet*: Ibid., 33.

42   *"for a moment"*: McClure and Cather, "My Autobiography, Part 5."

42   *McClure waited*: Lyon, *Success Story,* 34.

42   *"in a terrible storm"*: Undated McClure memo on autobiography, McClure mss, Lilly Library.

43   *Pope's classic Columbia Roadster*: Lyon, *Success Story,* 34.

43   *"in the predicament"*: McClure and Cather, "My Autobiography, Part 5."

43   *"weave the bicycle"*: Lyon, *Success Story,* 36.

44   *"You always alight"*: Letter, John S. Phillips to S. S. McClure, July 18, 1882, McClure mss, Lilly Library.

44   *The three men shared*: Stephen B. Goddard, *Colonel Albert Pope and His American Dream Machines: The Life and Times of a Bicycle Tycoon Turned Automotive Pioneer* (Jefferson, NC: McFarland, 2008), 79.

44   *In the words of a later colleague*: Curtis P. Brady, *The High Cost of Impatience,* 118, McClure mss, Lilly Library.

44   *"Up to this time"*: McClure and Cather, "My Autobiography, Part 5."

44   *On the threshold*: Ibid.

44   *McClure was inspired*: In 1881, *Scribner's Monthly* was renamed *The Century,* and it ran under this title until 1930. Confusingly, the popular *Scribner's Magazine* ran at the same time. References to *Scribner's* in these pages are to the latter.

44   The Century, *in the eyes*: "An English View of Roswell Smith," *New York Times,* June 12, 1892, https://timesmachine.nytimes.com/timesmachine/1892/06/12/104135232.html?action=click&contentCollection=Archives&module=LedeAsset&region=ArchiveBody&pgtype=article&pageNumber=5 (accessed March 28, 2018).

45   *Holmes obliged*: Lyon, *Success Story,* 123–24.

45   *He gave it the long-winded title*: Ibid., 40.

45   Topics of the Time: Ibid., 42.

46   *"It seems so strange"*: Ibid., 39.

46   *"[McClure's] personal appearance"*: Ibid., 42.

46   *A dean at Knox wrote*: Dean Willard's address in the Knox *Student,* McClure mss, Lilly Library.

46   *"I shall be married"*: Lyon, *Success Story,* 81.

46   *The romance and its hard-won culmination*: Charles Johanningsmeier, "Unmasking Willa Cather's 'Mortal Enemy,'" *Cather Studies* 5 (2003), https://cather.unl.edu/cs005_johanningsmeier.html (accessed June 13, 2018).

46   *During the ceremony*: McClure and Cather, "My Autobiography, Part 5."

47   *"indignant and wicked"*: Lyon, *Success Story,* 45.

47   *Though Hattie didn't instinctively*: Letters between S. S. McClure and Professor Anderson, November 1883, McClure mss, Lilly Library.

## 4: *Among the Furies*

49   *"rebelling, experimenting child"*: Tarbell, *All in the Day's Work*, 35.

49   *Another Allegheny girl*: Brady, *Ida Tarbell*, 28.

50   *Tingley then gathered*: Tarbell, *All in the Day's Work*, 43–44.

50   *She resolved*: Ibid., 44.

50   *"Nature always brings"*: Ibid., 42–43.

51   *She scolded herself*: Ibid., 46.

51   *Ida had never*: Mary Caroline Crawford, "The Historian of Standard Oil," *Public Opinion*, May 27, 1905, Drake Well Museum collection.

51   *"You see such countenances"*: Creelman, "A Talk with Miss Tarbell."

51   *When she wore*: Tarbell, *All in the Day's Work*, 46.

51   *"possibly some day"*: Ibid., 47.

51   *Her male classmates*: Ibid., 40.

51   *More than fifty years later*: Ibid.

52   *"I was learning"*: Brady, *Ida Tarbell*, 30.

52   *"It was my first look"*: Tarbell, *All in the Day's Work*, 43.

52   *Ida's peak moment*: Brady, *Ida Tarbell*, 29.

52   *Forced into selling*: Ibid., 34.

52   *He grieved that Rockefeller*: Ibid., 94.

53   *"They believed in independent effort"*: Tarbell quoted in Chernow, *Titan*, 444.

53   *Ida puzzled*: Brady, *Ida Tarbell*, 31.

53   *Missionary work was impossible*: Ibid., 29.

53   *"If I had been going on my honeymoon"*: Ibid., 31.

53   *She abandoned*: Tarbell, *All in the Day's Work*, 48.

54   *"with more or less"*: Ibid., 51.

54   *It was a "killing" workload*: Ibid., 53.

54   *Ida and Dot took drives*: Brady, *Ida Tarbell*, 32.

54   *"I learned the meaning of Maenads"*: Tarbell, *All in the Day's Work*, 57.

55   *"This was a stop-gap"*: Brady, *Ida Tarbell*, 35–36.

55   *"where I learned my trade"*: Robert C. Kochersberger, ed., *More Than a Muckraker: Ida Tarbell's Lifetime in Journalism* (Knoxville: University of Tennessee Press, 1994), xxviii.

55   *"college outlook"*: "Chautauqua Movement History," https://www.chautauqua.com/about-us/history/chautauqua-movement-history/ (accessed October 5, 2017).

55   *"Sobriety and industry"*: William James quoted in Brady, *Ida Tarbell*, 41.

55   *James concluded*: Ibid.

56 *"as informal . . . as non-committal"*: Brady, *Ida Tarbell*, 40.

56 *"A woman is a natural executive"*: Tarbell, *All in the Day's Work*, 73.

56 *"The editor-in-chief knows"*: Brady, *Ida Tarbell*, 37.

56 *"She must not put forward"*: Ibid.

56 *"Queen of the Gironde"*: Ibid., 44.

57 *"I had never wanted things"*: Tarbell, *All in the Day's Work*, 78.

57 *"fresh attempts"*: Ibid., 79.

57 *"dripped with blood"*: Ibid., 82.

57 *At one point, she stood*: Ibid., 80.

57 *One Sunday she was taken aback*: Ibid., 79.

58 *"doormat, toy, and tool"*: Ibid., 84.

58 *"Why must I persist"*: Ibid., 85.

58 *"I at last knew"*: Ibid., 80.

58 *"Poor stuff"*: Ibid., 84.

58 *"There were friends"*: Ibid., 87.

59 *"You'll starve"*: Ibid.

59 *"puzzled and fearful"*: Ibid., 88.

59 *"It was not to be"*: Ibid.

59 *"Harry's escapades"*: Letter, Ida Tarbell to family, undated May 1893, Ida M. Tarbell Collection, Pelletier Library, Allegheny College, Meadville, Pennsylvania.

59 *"worry you into any kind"*: Letter, Ida Tarbell to family, September 9, 1891, Tarbell mss, Pelletier Library.

59 *the "Meadville matter"*: Ibid.

59 *"Gyascutus"*: Letter, Ida Tarbell to family, undated May 1893, Tarbell mss, Pelletier Library.

60 *"I esteem you"*: Letter, Dr. Flood to Ida Tarbell, March 19, 1891, Tarbell mss, Pelletier Library.

## 5: *New York*

61 *"Just before dawn"*: Lyon, *Success Story*, 48.

61 *New York was*: Esther Crain, *The Gilded Age in New York, 1870–1910* (New York: Black Dog & Leventhal, 2016), 279.

62 *"I think you told me"*: Letter, Harriet McClure to Professor Anderson and wife, November 6, 1883, McClure mss, Lilly Library.

62 *"the uttermost limit"*: McClure and Cather, "My Autobiography, Part 5."

62 *McClure had absorbed*: The Century archive, https://babel.hathitrust.org/cgi/pt?id=hvd.hnyb7t;view=1up;seq=62 (accessed April 3, 2018).

62 *McClure resolved*: McClure and Cather, "My Autobiography, Part 5."

63 *"Everything about the work"*: Ibid.

63    *He freely admitted*: Undated McClure memo on autobiography, McClure mss, Lilly Library.

63    *A friend noted*: Jeannette Gilder, "How McClure's Began," *McClure's Magazine* (August 1913): 69.

63    *"huge transparent globes"*: Wilson, *McClure's Magazine and the Muckrakers*, 38.

63    *"I saw it"*: McClure and Cather, "My Autobiography, Part 5."

64    *An article or short story*: "Newspaper Syndicates," Encyclopedia.com, https://www.encyclopedia.com/history/culture-magazines/newspaper-syndicates (accessed April 4, 2018).

64    *"To be sure, the thing"*: McClure and Cather, "My Autobiography, Part 5."

64    *Roswell Smith advised*: Lyon, *Success Story*, 49.

64    *"Everyone with whom"*: McClure and Cather, "My Autobiography, Part 5."

64    *"I surmise that many"*: Wilson, *McClure's Magazine and the Muckrakers*, 55–56.

65    *"A Woman Who Commits Bigamy"*: "And McClure Tells How He Did It," *Editor & Publisher*, July 21, 1934, McClure Publishing Company mss, University of Delaware.

65    *The novelist Ouida*: Pseudonym of English writer Maria Louise Ramé.

65    *"precisely as the Chicago killing"*: Ouida, "Letter to the Editor," London *Times*, May 22, 1891, quoted in "Newspaper Syndicates," Encyclopedia.com, https://www.encyclopedia.com/history/culture-magazines/newspaper-syndicates (accessed April 4, 2018).

65    *He was an admitted monomaniac*: McClure and Cather, "My Autobiography, Part 5."

65    *"My blood [is] like champagne"*: Wilson, *McClure's Magazine and the Muckrakers*, 55.

65    *He believed in his scheme*: Lyon, *Success Story*, 58.

66    *"This method of publication"*: "And McClure Tells How He Did It," *Editor & Publisher*.

66    *"[T]he men who wrote for me"*: McClure and Cather, "My Autobiography, Part 5."

66    *"if I do any more work"*: Lyon, *Success Story*, 66.

66    *Each morning's mail*: Ibid., 59.

66    *He got into the habit*: Undated McClure memo on autobiography, McClure mss, Lilly Library.

66    *"trotting his foot"*: Gilder, "When McClure's Began," 72.

66    *He took a temporary job*: Lyon, *Success Story*, 60.

67    *When he returned*: Ibid., 61.

67    *"It was a business"*: Undated McClure memo on autobiography, McClure mss, Lilly Library.

67    *He made a smart purchase*: Lyon, *Success Story*, 64.

67   *The couple worked together*: Ibid., 64.

68   *"Some of the daily stories"*: Ibid., 71.

68   *Newsprint was cheap*: Ibid., 73.

68   *For the McClure Syndicate*: Ibid., 61.

68   *McClure wrote to his in-laws*: Wilson, *McClure's Magazine and the Muckrakers,* 43.

69   *For the next twenty years*: Stinson, "S. S. McClure and His Magazine," 24.

69   *"His job as partner"*: Ibid.

69   *Journalist William Allen White*: White quoted in Weinberg, *Taking On the Trust,* 171.

69   *"the kindest man alive"*: Letter of introduction from Munsey Company, December 29, 1919, Phillips mss, Lilly Library.

69   *"nothing flamboyant"*: Ray Stannard Baker, *American Chronicle: The Autobiography of Ray Stannard Baker* (New York: Charles Scribner's Sons, 1945), 98.

69   *"He was no easy editor"*: Tarbell, *All in the Day's Work,* 157.

69   *"Be not deceived"*: Letter of introduction from Munsey Company, December 29, 1919, Phillips mss, Lilly Library.

69   *He had known tragedy*: Brady, *Ida Tarbell,* 112.

69   *By July 1887*: Lyon, *Success Story,* 73–74.

70   *"To find the best authors"*: J. L. French, "The Story of McClure's," *Profitable Advertising,* October 5, 1897, 140.

70   *Whisking Hattie along*: Edward Bok, *The Americanization of Edward Bok: An Autobiography* (New York: Pocket Books, 1965), 81.

71   *McClure quickly proved*: Lyon, *Success Story,* 87.

71   *Stevenson and his wife*: Typescript titled "Tusitala," McClure mss, Lilly Library.

71   *"If Mr. McClure's generosity"*: Ibid.

71   *"John, I want the syndicate"*: S. S. McClure and Willa Cather, "My Autobiography, Part 6," *McClure's Magazine* 42, no. 5 (March 1915), https://cather.unl.edu/nf006_06.html (accessed June 25, 2018).

71   *"The Outlaws of Tunstall Forest"*: Ibid.

72   *While he considered*: Typescript titled "Tusitala," McClure mss, Lilly Library.

72   *Habitually forgetful*: McClure and Cather, "My Autobiography, Part 6."

72   *McClure advertised*: Lyon, *Success Story,* 90.

72   *Stevenson referred*: Ibid., 92.

72   *He took further vengeance*: Ibid., 108.

72   *To save face*: Rice, *The Inky Way,* 61–62.

73   *Together they worked out a plan*: Lyon, *Success Story,* 92.

73   *"South Sea Letters"*: In 1896, these were collected and published in book form under the title *In the South Seas.*

73   *"it was the moralist"*: McClure and Cather, "My Autobiography, Part 6."

73    *"song, flowers and hula stuff"*: "Famous Writers in Britain and America Introduced First by SS McClure," New York *World-Telegram*, 1944, McClure Publishing Company mss, University of Delaware.

73    *"I never got ideas"*: McClure and Cather, "My Autobiography, Part 6."

73    *"Whatever work I have done"*: Ibid.

73    *An author in South Carolina*: Lyon, *Success Story,* 96.

73    *"The restlessness"*: McClure and Cather, "My Autobiography, Part 6."

74    *The next morning*: Lyon, *Success Story,* 83.

74    *McClure wrote Hattie*: Ibid., 79.

74    *"I found," McClure noted*: Mike Delahant, "A Gift for Henry James," *Adirondack Daily Enterprise,* March 30, 2018, http://www.adirondackdailyenterprise.com /opinion/columns/2018/03/a-gift-for-henry-james/ (accessed April 4, 2018).

74    *"My main success was this"*: Lyon, *Success Story,* 79.

74    *"a very uneducated"*: Ibid., 81.

74    *"I was the limit"*: Delahant, "A Gift for Henry James."

74    *"There was never any haggling"*: "Famous Writers in Britain and America Introduced First by SS McClure," New York *World-Telegram*.

75    *Robert Louis Stevenson complained*: Quoted in Christin, "McClure's Magazine, 1893–1903," 176–77.

75    *Henry James wrote*: Wilson, *McClure's Magazine and the Muckrakers,* 50.

75    *Messrs. Hodder and Stoughton*: Rice, *The Inky Way,* 64.

75    *At lunch with a curator*: McClure and Cather, "My Autobiography, Part 6."

75    *"The coming man"*: Ibid.

75    *"literary sensation"*: Lyon, *Success Story,* 98.

75    *Soon after, he started touting*: Wilson, *McClure's Magazine and the Muckrakers,* 53.

76    *He sold "Esther"*: Ibid., 44.

76    *And he grasped*: Letters from William Morris to S. S. McClure, June 19, 1892, and from Charles Darwin to McClure, July 12, 1892, McClure Publishing Company mss, University of Delaware.

76    *On the home front*: Wilson, *McClure's Magazine and the Muckrakers,* 45.

76    *McClure contended*: "Famous Writers in Britain and America Introduced First by SS McClure," New York *World-Telegram*.

76    *"wild over Sherlock Holmes"*: Letter, S. S. McClure to Harriet McClure, April 9, 1894, McClure mss, Lilly Library.

77    *"I suppose I am completely wedded"*: Lyon, *Success Story,* 76.

77    *"By studying the present"*: Ibid.

77    *In many offices*: Bok, *The Americanization of Edward Bok,* 117.

77    *"I could never believe"*: McClure and Cather, "My Autobiography, Part 6."

77    *He set a rule*: Ibid.

77  *On very good days*: Wilson, *McClure's Magazine and the Muckrakers*, 55.

77  *McClure's roving eye*: Lyon, *Success Story*, 92.

78  *"This revolution, this discovery"*: Ibid., 74.

78  *He had learned the business*: Undated McClure memo on autobiography, Mc-Clure mss, Lilly Library.

78  *"I would rather edit"*: Lyon, *Success Story*, 109.

## 6: *"I Fall in Love"*

79  *"dewy parting"*: Letter, Ida Tarbell to family, August 5, 1891, Tarbell mss, Pelletier Library.

79  *Ida was "Mammy"*: Ibid.

80  *"look exactly like Standard Oil tanks"*: Letter, Ida Tarbell to family, August 16, 1891, Tarbell mss, Pelletier Library.

80  *"obvious fleas"*: Tarbell, *All in the Day's Work*, 92.

80  *Most mornings*: Brady, *Ida Tarbell*, 55.

80  *She passed the house*: Tarbell, *All in the Day's Work*, 124.

80  *"The roofs of Paris"*: Tarbell, "The Queen of the Gironde," *The Chautauquan*, no. 12 (March 1891), quoted in Kochersberger, *More Than a Muckraker*, 18.

81  *"You mustn't think"*: Letter, Ida Tarbell to family, September 9, 1891, Tarbell mss, Pelletier Library.

81  *"They were quite"*: Tarbell, *All in the Day's Work*, 104.

81  *"children's parties"*: Ibid., 104.

81  *"It is remarkable"*: Letter, Ida Tarbell to family, June 17, 1892, Tarbell mss, Pelletier Library.

82  *"charm, beauty"*: Brady, *Ida Tarbell*, 60.

82  "femme travailleuse": Tarbell, *All in the Day's Work*, 103.

82  *"Things aren't so good"*: Letter, Ida Tarbell to family, September 20, 1891, Tarbell mss, Pelletier Library.

82  *On occasion, Ida dressed*: Weinberg, *Taking On the Trust*, 138.

82  *"those whom we call"*: Tarbell, *All in the Day's Work*, 93.

83  *She backed into a corner*: Ibid., 118.

83  *When she could*: Letter, Ida Tarbell to family, March 1, 1893, Tarbell mss, Pelletier Library.

83  *"There was nothing"*: Tarbell, *All in the Day's Work*, 133.

83  *"They can't get used"*: Brady, *Ida Tarbell*, 71.

84  *"Five hundred years"*: Tarbell, *All in the Day's Work*, 134.

84  *"a high broad country"*: Ibid., 137.

84  *"a steady, intuitive"*: Ibid., 143.

84  *Before the revolution*: Brady, *Ida Tarbell*, 76.

**84**  *Roland was also*: Ibid., 77.

**84**  *"[clear] up my mind"*: Tarbell, *All in the Day's Work*, 145.

**85**  *"This girl can write"*: S. S. McClure and Willa Cather, "My Autobiography, Part 7," *McClure's Magazine* 42, no. 6 (April 1914), https://cather.unl.edu/nf006_07 .html (accessed June 25, 2018).

**85**  *"No idea"*: Lyon, *Success Story*, 117.

**85**  *"possessed exactly the qualities"*: McClure and Cather, "My Autobiography, Part 7."

**85**  *"in the meteoric fashion"*: Tarbell, *All in the Day's Work*, 118.

**85**  *"a slender figure"*: Lyon, *Success Story*, 117.

**85**  *"[h]e stood at my door"*: Tarbell, undated memo on "S.S. McClure—Introduction," from notes on *All in the Day's Work*, Tarbell mss, Pelletier Library.

**86**  *"always John this"*: Tarbell, *All in the Day's Work*, 119.

**86**  *"It would be a good joke"*: Brady, *Ida Tarbell*, 67.

**86**  *"my natural enthusiasm"*: Tarbell, *All in the Day's Work*, 120.

**86**  *"inconsolable"*: Brady, *Ida Tarbell*, 73.

**86**  *"a rather small man"*: Ibid., 82.

**87**  *"something startling"*: Letter, Ida Tarbell to family, August 22, 1892, Tarbell mss, Pelletier Library.

**87**  *McClure wrote her*: Letter, S. S. McClure to Ida Tarbell, February 6, 1894, Tarbell mss, Pelletier Library.

**87**  *"marvelous fellow"*: Letter, Ida Tarbell to family, February 26, 1893, Tarbell mss, Pelletier Library. Also: Brady, *Ida Tarbell*, 103 (pronunciation).

**87**  *Gossip had it*: Brady, *The High Cost of Impatience*, 180–81.

**87**  *"It raised my interest"*: Tarbell, *All in the Day's Work*, 122.

**87**  *When McClure's first came off press*: Ibid., 159.

**88**  *"I've just received"*: Letter, Ida Tarbell to family, March 16, 1894, Tarbell mss, Pelletier Library.

**88**  *First, she pawned*: Tarbell, *All in the Day's Work*, 141.

**88**  *"It seems my articles"*: Letter, Ida Tarbell to family, undated 1893 or 1894 from London, Tarbell mss, Pelletier Library.

**88**  *"She could endure"*: Tarbell story quoted in Brady, *Ida Tarbell*, 79–80.

**89**  *"I tell you loneliness"*: Caroline Moorehead, *Gellhorn: A Twentieth-Century Life* (New York: Henry Holt, 2004), 88.

**89**  *"I know I was never meant"*: Letter, Ida Tarbell to family, April 24, 1894, Tarbell mss, Pelletier Library.

## 7: *The Moving Spirit of the Time*

**93**  *"[McClure] entered"*: Lyon, *Success Story*, 123.

**94**  *"whirled round"*: Ibid., 146–47.

94 *"[McClure] is a great man"*: Lyon, *Success Story*, 147.

94 *"liked and admired"*: Ibid., 123.

94 *In the author's depiction*: This idea is suggested in Sue Walsh's *Kipling's Children's Literature* (46) and Philip Mason's *Kipling* (168).

94 *McClure offered*: Rudyard Kipling, *Something of Myself: For My Friends Known and Unknown,* Project Gutenberg edition, http://gutenberg.net.au /ebooks04/0400691.txt (accessed November 8, 2015).

94 *"made good dependence"*: Ibid.

95 *"Money?"*: McClure and Cather, "My Autobiography, Part 7."

95 *"masses of people"*: Ibid.

96 *"The doors of the Union"*: *Rock Island Daily Argus,* May 13, 1893, https:// chroniclingamerica.loc.gov/lccn/sn92053945/1893-05-13/ed-1/seq-2/ (accessed June 25, 2018).

96 *McClure realized*: McClure and Cather, "My Autobiography, Part 7."

96 *By 1899, the public*: Baker quoted in Justin Kaplan, *Lincoln Steffens: A Biography* (New York: Simon & Schuster, 1974), 115.

96 *"Were it left to me"*: Thomas Jefferson quoted in Matthew Felling, "Best. Journalism Quotes. Ever," CBS News, July 3, 2007, https://www.cbsnews.com/news /best-journalism-quotes-ever/ (accessed March 8, 2018).

97 *"Nothing can now be believed"*: Jefferson quoted in Michael Knigge, "Presidents Always Rail Against the Press, but Not Like Trump," DW.com, https:// www.dw.com/en/presidents-always-rail-against-the-press-but-not-like -trump/a-38629072 (accessed October 10, 2018).

97 *The word "magazine"*: Richard Ohmann, *Selling Culture: Magazines, Markets, and Class at the Turn of the Century* (New York: Verso, 1996), 224–25.

97 *The word was first*: Kirstin Fawcett, "The Bitter Race to Publish America's First Magazine," Mental Floss, February 13, 2017, https://mentalfloss.com /article/92095/bitter-race-publish-americas-first-magazine (accessed June 25, 2018).

97 *The concept took*: James Playsted Wood, *Magazines in the United States: Their Social and Economic Influence* (New York: Ronald Press, 1949), ix, 10.

97 *Though neither Franklin's*: Fawcett, "The Bitter Race to Publish America's First Magazine."

97 *Hale is also credited*: Wood, *Magazines in the United States,* 56.

98 *They had gained*: Christin, "McClure's Magazine, 1893–1903," 8.

98 *Their only rival*: Greene, *America's Heroes,* 63.

98 *Edgar Allan Poe*: Wood, *Magazines in the United States,* 64.

99 *"What I have"*: French, "The Story of McClure's," *Profitable Advertising,* 140.

99 *"is able to feel"*: Arlo Bates quoted in Frank Luther Mott, *A History of Ameri-*

*can Magazines,* vol. 4, *1885–1905* (Cambridge, MA: Belknap Press of Harvard University Press, 1957), 122.

99    *"a powerful agency"*: Stinson, "S. S. McClure and His Magazine," 28.

99    *His guidelines:* Ibid.

99    *"[H]is exposures of the depravities"*: Ibid., 29.

99    *"Now I'll tell you"*: Poole's *The Bridge, My Own Story,* quoted in Stinson, "S. S. McClure and His Magazine," 212.

99    *"uttered a low cry"*: Stinson, "S. S. McClure and His Magazine," 48.

100   *Magazines began to position themselves:* Ohmann, *Selling Culture,* 284.

100   *"what it was all about"*: Will Irwin, *Propaganda and the News: or, What Makes You Think So?* (New York and London: McGraw-Hill, 1936), 68.

100   *"The reader who skimmed"*: Irwin, *Propaganda and the News,* 68.

100   *Between 1870 and 1903:* Beatty, *Age of Betrayal,* 25.

100   *"The police in the United States"*: Ibid., 25.

100   *The protest ended:* Lyon, *Success Story,* 115.

101   "McClure's Magazine *is designed"*: Theodore P. Greene, *America's Heroes: The Changing Models of Success in American Magazines* (New York: Oxford University Press, 1970), 72.

101   *"the human struggle"*: Waldo, "The Genius of S. S. McClure."

101   *"[i]t seemed to be"*: Stinson, "S. S. McClure and His Magazine," 51–52.

101   *Another critic:* Ibid., 52.

101   *Munsey then started:* "Frank A. Munsey," Argonotes: The Readers' Viewpoint, February 22, 2011, https://argonotes.blogspot.com/2011/02/frank-munsey.html (accessed May 31, 2018).

102   *Both he and McClure embraced:* Ohmann, *Selling Culture,* 25, 224.

102   *"magazine to suit"*: Frank A. Munsey, "The Making and Marketing of Munsey's Magazine," *Munsey's Magazine* 22, no. 3 (December 1899), https://books .google.com/books?id=irsmAQAAIAAJ&pg=PA323&lpg=PA323&dq=%22the +making+and+marketing+of+munsey%27s+magazine%22&source=bl&ots=d_ FkVGqW5B&sig=q4U8AIZu6F8se-SnVvh0UA5lfM0&hl=en&sa=X&ved=0ahU KEwjeq_Kz9LLbAhUSEqwKHflWCGYQ6AEILzAB#v=onepage&q=%22the%20 making%20and%20marketing%20of%20munsey's%20magazine%22&f=false (accessed June 1, 2018).

102   *"The magazine, then"*: Munsey, "The Making and Marketing of Munsey's Magazine."

102   *"The* Century Magazine": McClure and Cather, "My Autobiography, Part 7."

102   *Immediately after the Civil War:* Wilson, *McClure's Magazine and the Muckrakers,* 30.

102   *By 1900:* Ibid.

103 *Its pages featured*: A startling proportion—upwards of 20 percent—of these interviews focused on writers. *McClure's* explained this by noting that "men of letters are perhaps interested in each other, and they are numerous enough to constitute an audience by themselves; unhappily, but not necessarily, a critical audience" (quoted in Christin, "McClure's Magazine, 1893–1903," 186).

103 *Theodore Roosevelt*: Letter, Theodore Roosevelt to S. S. McClure, May 29, 1893, McClure mss, Lilly Library.

103 *"It throbs"*: Mott, *A History of American Magazines*, vol. 4, 596.

103 *"He is a rash man"*: "Literary Novelties That No One Else Possesses," Albany *Argus*, June 11, 1893.

103 *"How often does this happen"*: "Literary Notes," *The Outlook*, June 15, 1893.

103 *"Will there never come a season"*: James Kenneth Stephen, "Lapsus Calami," in Edmund Clarence Stedman, ed., *A Victorian Anthology, 1837–1895* (Cambridge, MA: Riverside Press, 1895), http://www.bartleby.com/246/1065.html (accessed November 8, 2015).

104 *McClure's model*: Ohmann, *Selling Culture*, 25.

104 *"If he had been a woman"*: Lyon, *Success Story*, 119.

105 *"We are nearly"*: Letter, S. S. McClure to Harriet McClure, June 9, 1893, McClure mss, Lilly Library.

105 *the magazine shrank*: McClure and Cather, "My Autobiography, Part 7."

106 *"I felt, day after day"*: Ibid.

106 *"The telegraph ties together"*: Edwin J. Houston, "The Edge of the Future in Science," *McClure's Magazine* (January 1894), McClure mss, Lilly Library.

107 *"labor pass[ing] into the brutalizing stage"*: Hamlin Garland, "Homestead and Its Perilous Trades: Impressions of a Visit," *McClure's Magazine* (June 1894), https://ehistory.osu.edu/exhibitions/Steel/June1894-Garland_Homestead (accessed September 8, 2017).

107 *The "squalid and unlovely" town*: Garland, "Homestead and Its Perilous Trades: Impressions of a Visit."

107 *"I'd as soon go to hell"*: Ibid.

107 *"town and its industries"*: Ibid.

107 *McClure hired young people*: Christin, "McClure's Magazine, 1893–1903," 27.

107 *There was a thin*: Lyon, *Success Story*, 153.

108 *When Norris resigned*: Letter, Frank Norris to John S. Phillips, January 9, 1900, Phillips mss, Lilly Library.

108 *Theodore Dreisser*: Lyon, *Success Story*, 157.

108 *"every man who had graduated"*: Wilson, *McClure's Magazine and the Muckrakers*, 25.

108   *"The very name* McClure's Magazine*"*: Ellery Sedgwick quoted in Gerald L. and Patricia A. Gutek, *Bringing Montessori to America: S. S. McClure, Maria Montessori, and the Campaign to Publicize Montessori Education* (Tuscaloosa: University of Alabama Press, 2016), 20.

108   *"You often thought"*: Letter, Willa Cather to S. S. McClure, May 26, 1933, quoted in Andrew Jewell and Janis Stout, eds., *The Selected Letters of Willa Cather* (New York: Knopf, 2013), 485–86.

108   *By its third birthday*: French, "The Story of McClure's," 139.

109   *"These offices"*: "The Third Anniversary of the Founding of *McClure's Magazine*," *McClure's Magazine* (June 1896), https://babel.hathitrust.org/cgi/pt?id=mdp.39015030656154;view=1up;seq=105 (accessed June 7, 2018).

109   *Crossing the short couple of blocks*: William Allen White, *The Autobiography of William Allen White*, 2nd ed. revised and abridged, edited by Sally Foreman Griffith (Lawrence: University Press of Kansas, 1973), 200.

109   *"bristling and busy"*: Baker, *American Chronicle*, 144.

109   *"My God!" cried Twain*: Lyon, *Success Story*, 138.

109   *McClure was proud*: "The Third Anniversary of the Founding of *McClure's Magazine*."

110   *Then to the bindery*: Munsey, "The Making and Marketing of Munsey's Magazine."

110   *"Rosey" kept up the unusual habits*: Lyon, *Success Story*, 141.

110   *she rolled herself*: William Irwin quoted in Jane K. Graham, *Viola: The Duchess of New Dorp: A Biography of Viola Roseboro* (Danville: Illinois Printing Co., 1955), 121.

110   *She presided*: Wilson, *McClure's Magazine and the Muckrakers*, 77.

110   *She was "fidgity"*: Stinson, "S. S. McClure and His Magazine," 140.

110   *Most evenings*: Brady, *Ida Tarbell*, 117.

110   *Shortly afterward, he was imprisoned*: Irwin, *The Making of a Reporter* (New York: G. P. Putnam's Sons, 1942), 149–50.

110   *She picked out*: Lyon, *Success Story*, 157–58.

110   *When McClure tried*: Wilson, *McClure's Magazine and the Muckrakers*, 118.

110   *"The McClure group"*: White, *The Autobiography of William Allen White*, 157.

111   *"They were at heart Midwestern"*: Ibid.

111   *Brands still sold*: *McClure's Magazine* (July 1898).

111   *Patent filings multiplied*: Scott Miller, *The President and the Assassin: McKinley, Terror, and Empire at the Dawn of the American Century* (New York: Random House, 2013), 19.

111   *"applied intelligence"*: *McClure's Magazine* (July 1898).

## 8: *The Uneasy Woman*

113 *In the steamy July*: Weinberg, *Taking On the Trust*, 169.

113 *"stripped fields"*: Tarbell, *All in the Day's Work*, 205.

113 *They searched*: Ibid.

114 *"The success of a feature"*: Ibid., 155.

114 *She offered him a beer*: Brady, *Ida Tarbell*, 112–13.

114 *A graceful country estate*: Tarbell, *All in the Day's Work*, 149.

114 *"the handsomest"*: Notes on chapter 10 of *All in the Day's Work*, Tarbell mss, Pelletier Library.

114 *"accustomed to geniuses"*: Tarbell, *All in the Day's Work*, 149.

114 *"horrified"*: Ibid.

115 *At the start of the series*: *McClure's Magazine* (December 1894): 3.

115 *He joined a select crowd*: Lyon, *Success Story*, 138.

115 *"the whippy little Irishman"*: Lemuel F. Parton column, New York *Sun*, May 23, 1939, McClure mss, Lilly Library.

115 *Given license*: Crawford, "The Historian of Standard Oil."

116 *The Scranton* Tribune *noted*: Quote taken from *McClure's Magazine* (June 1896), 5.

116 *"McClure's got a girl"*: Brady, *Ida Tarbell*, 105.

116 *When she sent word*: Tarbell, *All in the Day's Work*, 164.

116 *"she could mobilize"*: Brady, *Ida Tarbell*, 95.

116 *"never seemed to get tired"*: Notes from Ada McCormick-Steffens interview, 1933, Tarbell mss, Pelletier Library.

117 *Taken when he was*: Mary E. Tomkins, *Ida M. Tarbell* (New York: Twayne, 1974), 46.

117 *From that article*: Brady, *Ida Tarbell*, 98.

117 *McClure later claimed*: Undated McClure typed memo on autobiography, McClure mss, Lilly Library.

117 *Their partnership*: Ohmann, *Selling Culture*, 288.

117 *The staff writer*: Typescript "On the Making of McClure's Magazine," McClure mss, Lilly Library.

117 *he was "lonesome"*: Letter, S. S. McClure to Ida Tarbell, December 13, 1899, Phillips mss, Lilly Library.

117 *"I lean on you"*: Letter, S. S. McClure to Ida Tarbell, December 30, [1901], Tarbell mss, Pelletier Library.

118 *"noble woman"*: Letter, Harriet McClure to her mother, February 18, 1895, McClure mss, Lilly Library.

118 *"Chiefly, it was the sense"*: Brady, *Ida Tarbell*, 94.

118  *Ida Tarbell lived alone*: Ibid., 114–15.

118  *"There are in the city"*: Tarbell quoted in Tomkins, *Ida M. Tarbell*, 93.

119  *"a species of big sister"*: Notes on chapter 10 of *All in the Day's Work*, Tarbell mss, Pelletier Library.

119  *They had the habit*: Ada McCormick notes on "Ida Tarbell's Student Days in France," February 24, 1931, Tarbell mss, Pelletier Library.

119  *"[s]he could change him"*: Ada McCormick interview with Steffens, 1933, Tarbell mss, Pelletier Library.

119  *"Whereas S. S."*: Bynner quoted in Brady, *Ida Tarbell*, 119.

119  *"The main staff"*: John S. Phillips review of Tarbell's *All in the Day's Work* in the *Independent Republican*, undated, Tarbell mss, Pelletier Library.

120  *"to belong to the human race"*: Rheta Childe Dorr, *A Woman of Fifty*, 2nd ed. (New York: Funk & Wagnalls, 1924), 101.

120  *"Of all the tawdry"*: Crain, *The Gilded Age in New York, 1870–1910*, 246.

120  *In Ruskin's quintessentially Victorian words*: John Ruskin, "Of Queen's Gardens," quoted in *The Norton Anthology of English Literature: Norton Topics Online*, https://www.wwnorton.com/college/english/nael/victorian/topic_2/ruskin .htm (accessed October 5, 2017).

121  *"The Wail of the Male"*: Lorna Shelley, "Female Journalists and Journalism in fin-de-siècle Magazine Stories," *Nineteenth-Century Gender Studies* 5, no. 2 (Summer 2009), https://www.ijpc.org/uploads/files/Female%20Journalists%20 Lorna%20Shelley.pdf (accessed June 26, 2018).

121  *evolutionary biologist George Romanes*: George Romanes, "Mental Differences of Men and Women," *Popular Science* 31 (July 1887), https://en.wikisource.org /wiki/Popular_Science_Monthly/Volume_31/July_1887/Mental_Differences_ of_Men_and_Women (accessed October 6, 2017).

121  *"Lastly, with regard to judgment"*: Ibid.

121  *"[A] female"*: Quoted in Crain, *The Gilded Age in New York, 1870–1910*, 241.

121  *"[T]hey can write for children"*: Constance Fenimore Woolson, "In Sloane Street," originally published in *Harper's Bazaar*, June 11, 1892, http://www.lehigh .edu/~dek7/SSAWW/writWoolsonSloane.htm (accessed October 21, 2017).

122  *"Personally, I believe"*: Charlotte Perkins Gilman, "The Yellow Wall-Paper," originally published in *The New England Magazine* (January 1892), https://www .gutenberg.org/files/1952/1952-h/1952-h.htm (accessed November 2, 2017).

122  *"written intelligently"*: Norris, *The Responsibilities of the Novelist* (London: Grant Richards, 1903), 302–3.

122  *"bachelor soul"*: Tarbell, *The Business of Being a Woman*, ch. 4, originally published 1912, http://www.gutenberg.org/files/16577/16577-h/16577-h.htm (accessed September 11, 2017).

**123** *"I grew up among people"*: Letter "To the Editor-in-Chief of The American Magazine," Ida Tarbell to John S. Phillips, undated, Tarbell mss, Pelletier Library.

**123** *"To go to a man's college"*: Letter "To the Editor-in-Chief of The American Magazine," Ida Tarbell to John S. Phillips.

**123** *"The most conspicuous occupation"*: Tarbell, *The Business of Being a Woman*.

**123** *The ballot*: Letter "To the Editor-in-Chief of The American Magazine," Ida Tarbell to John S. Phillips.

**123** *"Radical and conservative"*: Ibid.

**124** *"The central fact"*: Tarbell, *The Business of Being a Woman*.

**124** *"I confess I've always pitied"*: Letter "To the Editor-in-Chief of The American Magazine," Ida Tarbell to John S. Phillips.

**124** *"Madame Curie"*: Tarbell, *All in the Day's Work*, 405.

**124** *Miss Tarbell liked to quote*: Tarbell, *The Business of Being a Woman*.

**125** *She confided*: Letter "To the Editor-in-Chief of The American Magazine," Ida Tarbell to John S. Phillips.

**125** *"aroused my flagging sense"*: Tarbell, *All in the Day's Work*, 179.

**125** *"The stories are intended"*: *McClure's Magazine* 15 (August 1900): 356.

**125** *Science was, in the beginning*: Christin, "McClure's Magazine, 1893–1903," 45–46.

**126** *"What a play-ball"*: Judy Crichton, *America 1900: The Turning Point* (New York: Henry Holt, 2000), 5.

**126** *"How could any sensible man"*: Baker, *American Chronicle*, 148.

**126** *Reporting from the army*: Tarbell, *All in the Day's Work*, 189.

**126** *"Theodore had a clear idea"*: Notes on Theodore Roosevelt for *All in the Day's Work*, undated, Tarbell mss, Pelletier Library.

**126** *"thought him a delight"*: Roseboro quoted in Brady, *Ida Tarbell*, 142.

**127** *"I could not run away"*: Tarbell, *All in the Day's Work*, 195.

**127** *"no name is more familiar"*: McClure quoted in Weinberg, *Taking On the Trust*, 186.

**127** *"architectural incentive"*: Edith Wharton, *The Age of Innocence*, Kindle ed.

**127** *"The war had done something"*: Tarbell, *All in the Day's Work*, 195.

**128** *"was a citizen"*: Ibid., 196.

## 9: *Facts Properly Told*

**129** *"And I say"*: Walt Whitman quoted in Baker, *American Chronicle*, 179.

**129** *His father, Joseph Stannard Baker*: John E. Semonche, *Ray Stannard Baker: A Quest for Democracy in Modern America, 1870–1918* (Chapel Hill: University of North Carolina Press, 1969), 5.

**129** *Five years later*: Ibid., 7.

130  *"half Indian and half river-driver"*: Ray Stannard Baker, *Native American: The Book of My Youth* (New York: Charles Scribner's Sons, 1941), 4.

130  *Stannard framed his hikes*: Semonche, *Ray Stannard Baker*, 15.

130  *Even the walls of their privy*: Baker, *Native American*, 153.

130  *"this age of machinery"*: Ibid., 71.

130  *"I know you pioneers!"*: Ibid., 10.

131  *"it was writing or nothing"*: Baker, *American Chronicle*, 53.

131  *Because of a slight*: Semonche, *Ray Stannard Baker*, 54.

131  *"My ignorance"*: Baker, *American Chronicle*, 1.

131  *The formidable* News-Record: The paper was later renamed *The Record*.

131  *independent in politics*: Semonche, *Ray Stannard Baker*, 54.

132  *He lived off heaps*: Baker, *Native American*, 276.

132  *Stannard replied*: Ibid., 288.

132  *"glimpses, street scenes"*: Semonche, *Ray Stannard Baker*, 57.

132  *"After she had fallen dead"*: Ibid.

132  *By early autumn*: Ibid.

133  *"all the evils"*: Baker, *American Chronicle*, 2.

133  *A cigar maker*: Miller, *The President and the Assassin*, 35.

133  *In New York, Rahel Golub*: Michael McGerr, *A Fierce Discontent: The Rise and Fall of the Progressive Movement in America* (New York: Oxford University Press, 2003), 19.

133  *The inventions unveiled*: Barbara Maranzani, "Chicago Was Home to a Serial Killer During the 1893 World's Fair," History.com, May 1, 2013, http://www .history.com/news/7-things-you-may-not-know-about-the-1893-chicago-worlds -fair (accessed October 5, 2017).

134  *"the plateau of mediocrity"*: Baker, *American Chronicle*, 46.

134  *"I wish I could feel"*: Baker, *Native American*, 312.

134  *"fresh and strong"*: Baker, *American Chronicle*, 77–78.

135  *"a great, big strong fellow"*: Nell Irvin Painter, *Standing at Armageddon: A Grassroots History of the Progressive Era* (New York: Norton, 2008), 118.

135  *"Bums, tramps!"*: Baker, *American Chronicle*, 2.

135  *Coxey's teenaged son*: Painter, *Standing at Armageddon*, 119.

136  *"I had seen groups"*: Baker, *American Chronicle*, 26.

136  *Other writers observed*: Ranjit S. Dighe, ed., *The Historian's Wizard of Oz: Reading L. Frank Baum's Classic as a Political and Monetary Allegory* (Westport, CT: Praeger Publishers, 2002).

136  *"town from which"*: Ibid., 35.

137  *The company deducted*: Painter, *Standing at Armageddon*, 122.

137  *"gift of explosive profanity"*: Baker, *American Chronicle*, 37.

137 *"If I rise"*: Ibid., 38.

137 *On the scale of strikes*: Miller, *The President and the Assassin,* 108.

137 *"I can hire one half"*: Ibid., 36.

137 *In the spring of 1894*: Ibid., 247.

137 *Tourists avoided Paris*: Ibid., 248.

138 "Les anarchistes! Une bombe!": Ibid., 248.

138 *On July 2*: Painter, *Standing at Armageddon,* 123.

138 *"[all] southern Chicago"*: Baker, *American Chronicle,* 38.

138 *Baker's first bulletin*: Ibid., 39.

138 *A moment later*: Ibid., 40.

138 *The battle broke the strike*: Painter, *Standing at Armageddon,* 123.

139 *"I can recall"*: Baker, *American Chronicle,* 42.

139 *"What crowds gathered"*: Ibid., 43.

139 *For Baker*: Ibid., 44.

140 *"My soaring fancies"*: Ibid., 65.

140 *"I am trying"*: Ibid., 67.

140 *"Would it be"*: Ibid., 79.

140 *His anticipation mounted*: Letter, Ray Stannard Baker to Jessie Baker, April 3, 1897, Baker mss, Jones Library.

140 *"Mr. McClure had suddenly dashed off"*: Baker, *American Chronicle,* 79.

140 *"marvelous new world"*: Ibid.

141 *"a quality of enthusiasm"*: Ibid., 79–80.

141 *He kept quiet*: Semonche, *Ray Stannard Baker,* 83.

141 *"Our baby herself"*: Baker, *American Chronicle,* 81.

141 *"Mr. Phillips says"*: Letter, Ray Stannard Baker to Jessie Baker, May 21, 1898, Baker mss, Jones Library.

142 *"good long hour"*: Letter, Ray Stannard Baker to Jessie Baker, June 10, 1898, Baker mss, Jones Library.

142 *"I've rubbed up"*: Semonche, *Ray Stannard Baker,* 80.

142 *Over the next*: Stinson, "S. S. McClure and His Magazine," 180.

142 *Many articles in* McClure's: Baker, *American Chronicle,* 94.

142 *"[W]hat a boon"*: Letter, Ray Stannard Baker to Jessie Baker, June 10, 1898, Baker mss, Jones Library.

142 *Most pieces were edited*: Brady, *Ida Tarbell,* 133.

142 *"We maintained no society"*: Baker, *American Chronicle,* 94.

142 *One assistant reported*: Letter, Joseph Rogers to Ida Tarbell, April 16, 1900, Phillips mss, Lilly Library.

143 *"all intuition and impulse"*: Baker, *American Chronicle,* 95.

143 *Baker's origin myth*: Ibid., 96.

143   *McClure demanded articles*: Lyon, *Success Story*, 148.

143   *"Everything with him"*: Baker, *American Chronicle*, 96.

143   *"flashes of extraordinary penetration"*: Ibid.

143   *Ellery Sedgwick wrote*: Sedgwick quoted in Lyon, *Success Story*, 304.

143   *"[W]ith all his pokings and proddings"*: Sedgwick quoted in Arthur and Lila Weinberg, eds., *The Muckrakers*, 2.

143   *He funded Stephen Crane's tour*: Lyon, *Success Story*, ix.

143   *"We are greatly interested"*: Ibid., 158.

143   *"Did I tell you"*: London quoted in Earle Labor, *Jack London: An American Life* (New York: Farrar, Straus & Giroux, 2013), 146.

143   *"a failure"*: Labor, *Jack London*, 146.

144   *"preposterous, untrue"*: Labor, *Jack London*, 235, and Lyon, *Success Story*, ix, 190.

144   *"Making war number"*: Letter, Ray Stannard Baker to Jessie Baker, April 27, 1898, Baker mss, Jones Library.

144   *"there is not the slightest chance"*: Ibid.

144   *"to a sense of a swiftly expanding world"*: Baker, *American Chronicle*, 85.

144   *"vultures" hovering*: *McClure's* June 1898 quoted in Stinson, "S. S. McClure and His Magazine," 162.

145   *"the Americans being the chosen people"*: Beatrice Webb quoted in Ray Ginger, *Age of Excess: The United States from 1877 to 1914*, 2nd ed. (New York: Macmillan, 1975), 211.

145   *In 1893, Wellesley professor Katharine Lee Bates*: Miller, *The President and the Assassin*, 119.

145   *Three years later*: Miller, *The President and the Assassin*, 120.

145   Youth's Companion *coordinated*: Ibid., 121.

145   *The circulation*: Mott, *A History of American Magazines*, vol. 4, 596.

146   *"Flags were flying"*: Letter, Ray Stannard Baker to Jessie Baker, April 29, 1898, Baker mss, Jones Library.

146   *"Crowds have been standing"*: Letter, Ray Stannard Baker to Jessie Baker, May 5, 1898, Baker mss, Jones Library.

146   *He was swept up*: Ibid.

146   *"was rising on the journalistic horizon"*: Baker, *American Chronicle*, 93.

146   *Pulitzer, a Hungarian immigrant*: Painter, *Standing at Armageddon*, 194.

146   *After the sinking*: "Yellow Journalism," PBS, Crucible of Empire, 1999, http://www.pbs.org/crucible/frames/_journalism.html (accessed June 4, 2018).

147   *"Click! Click! Click!"*: Mott, *A History of American Magazines*, vol. 4, 148–49.

147   *"[I]t was not the evils"*: Baker, *American Chronicle*, 96.

147   *"banal stand-bys"*: Ibid.

147   *"interesting" and "best"*: Ohmann, *Selling Culture*, 290.

147 *"The proper policy"*: Lyon, *Success Story*, 201.

148 *"A marksman"*: S. S. McClure, "A Platform for Editors," *America's Future* (October 1938), McClure Publishing Company mss, University of Delaware.

148 *"Everything I am"*: Baker, *American Chronicle*, 66.

## 10: *The Brilliant Mind*

149 *"I proceed on the theory"*: Elizabeth Lee, "Ida M. Tarbell: Biographer and Historian," *Topeka State Journal*, June 11, 1904.

150 *"Cleveland ogre"*: Tarbell, *All in the Day's Work*, 206.

150 *"catch it, fix it"*: Ibid., 203.

151 *The other risk*: Kathleen Brady, "Madame Muckraker," PBS, November 2017, https://www.pbs.org/wgbh/americanexperience/features/ida-tarbell-pioneering-journalist/ (accessed June 12, 2018).

151 *"I shy a little"*: Lyon, *Success Story*, 191.

151 *"McClure method"*: Tarbell, *All in the Day's Work*, 24.

151 *"deteriorating social order"*: Booth Tarkington's *The Turmoil*, quoted in Robert G. Barrows, "Urbanizing America," in Calhoun, ed., *The Gilded Age*, 91.

151 *Corporate stakeholders*: Tarbell, *All in the Day's Work*, 202.

151 *"Nature was, then"*: Frank Norris, *The Octopus: A Story of California* (Minneapolis: Filiquarian, 2007), 566.

152 *The farsighted, high-quality science*: Letter, A. Hurd to S. S. McClure, February 3, 1896, McClure mss, Lilly Library.

152 *"From 1890 on"*: McClure quoted in Gutek, *Bringing Montessori to America*, 21.

152 *in hotel bathtubs*: Witter Bynner, "Bynner reads between Lyon's lines in recording S. S. McClure's success story," Santa Fe *New Mexican* magazine *Pasatiempo*, undated, Witter Bynner Collection, Harvard Houghton Library.

153 *"Everyone about him"*: Ellery Sedgwick, *The Happy Profession* (New York: Little, Brown, 1946), 139.

153 *A rising journalist*: Sullivan, *The Education of an American*, 195.

153 *One of McClure's quixotic*: Ibid., 195.

154 *"attractive and agreeable"*: Brady, *The High Cost of Impatience*, 44.

154 *"Effendi"*: F. N. Doubleday, *The Memoirs of a Publisher* (Garden City and New York: Doubleday, 1972), 69.

154 *"He was erratic"*: Ibid., 45.

154 *"very warm heart"*: Ibid.

154 *"I do not like"*: Letter, Ida Tarbell to S. S. McClure, Dec 13, 1899, McClure mss, Lilly Library.

155 *When the company*: Lyon, *Success Story*, 161.

155 *"like the intoxicated rabbit"*: Brady, *The High Cost of Impatience*, 46.

155  *His symptoms matched*: Julie Beck, "'Americanitis': The Disease of Living Too Fast," *The Atlantic* (March 11, 2016), https://www.theatlantic.com/health/archive/2016/03/the-history-of-neurasthenia-or-americanitis-health-happiness-and-culture/473253/ (accessed June 4, 2018).

155  *Neurologist George Beard*: Ibid.

155  *Like its elder cousin*: Ibid.

155  *As the weather grew warm*: Lyon, *Success Story,* 164.

156  "I do not understand it": Letter, S. S. McClure to John S. Phillips, October 30, 1900, Phillips mss, Lilly Library.

156  *"Destroy the Paris letter"*: Ibid.

156  *"I am sure"*: Letter, Ida Tarbell to Harriet McClure, June 27, 1899, McClure mss, Lilly Library.

156  *He couldn't sink*: Undated McClure typed memo on his autobiography, McClure mss, Lilly Library.

157  *"not very saleable"*: Letter, Robert McClure to T. C. McClure, March 6, 1899, McClure mss, Lilly Library.

157  *"He has at last concluded"*: Lyon, *Success Story,* 194.

157  *On a later trip*: Ibid., 256.

157  *The novel was* Kim: Ibid., 182.

157  *"There will, under no circumstances"*: Ibid., 183.

158  *"intimate physical contact"*: Letter, S. S. McClure to Mark Twain, February 28, 1900, McClure mss, Lilly Library.

158  *White explained his refusal*: Walter Johnson, *William Allen White's America* (New York: Henry Holt, 1947), 122.

158  *Reporter Samuel Hopkins Adams*: Baker, *American Chronicle,* 97.

158  *When he and Hattie emerged*: Brady, *Ida Tarbell,* 122.

158  *"mud baths and steam soaks"*: Tarbell, *All in the Day's Work,* 206.

159  *In June 1901, Baker wrote*: Baker quoted in Stinson, "S. S. McClure and His Magazine," 242.

159  *"He is a very extraordinary creature"*: Letter, Ida Tarbell to Albert Boyden, April 26 [no year], Phillips mss, Lilly Library.

159  *She assured him*: Ibid.

160  *"How kind it was of you"*: Letter, Ida Tarbell to Harriet McClure, November 8, 1902, McClure mss, Lilly Library.

## 11: *The Gentleman Reporter*

162  *Spiritualism and thought transference*: Kaplan, *Lincoln Steffens,* 29.

163  *"a rather pessimistic vein"*: "Sad Experiences in a Story," *New York Times,* August 19, 1899, https://timesmachine.nytimes.com/timesmachine/1899/08/19

/issue.html?action=click&contentCollection=Archives&module=ArticleEndCT A&region=ArchiveBody&pgtype=article (accessed March 8, 2019).

163 *In her own married life*: Peter Hartshorn, *I Have Seen the Future: A Life of Lincoln Steffens* (Berkeley, CA: Counterpoint Press, 2012), 78.

163 *"My dear son"*: Kaplan, *Lincoln Steffens*, 52.

164 *Responding to a timber baron*: Steffens, *Autobiography*, 366.

164 *Steffens became known*: Hartshorn, *I Have Seen the Future*, 34.

165 *"There is more law"*: Ralph Blumenthal, "The City's Rough Past, Frighteningly Familiar," *New York Times*, August 26, 1990, https://www.nytimes .com/1990/08/26/weekinreview/the-region-the-city-s-rough-past-frighteningly -familar.html (accessed June 7, 2018).

165 *"My present contentment"*: Ella Winter, Introduction to Lincoln Steffens, *The Letters of Lincoln Steffens*, ed. Ella Winter and Granville Hicks (New York: Harcourt Brace, 1938), xii.

165 *"More horrible"*: Mott, *A History of American Magazines*, vol. 4, 195.

165 *"multitudinous skyscrapers"*: James quoted in Crain, *The Gilded Age in New York, 1870–1910*, 283.

165 *In New York City*: Glenn Porter, "Industrialization and Big Business," in Calhoun, *The Gilded Age*, 5.

165 *"What I want"*: Ella Winter introduction to Steffens, *Letters*, xi.

166 *"To my generation"*: Kaplan, *Lincoln Steffens*, 54–55.

166 *The Anti-Saloon League*: Crain, *The Gilded Age in New York, 1870–1910*, 228.

166 *While the Irish*: Ibid., 109.

167 *"charging . . . dashing"*: Hartshorn, *I Have Seen the Future*, 57.

167 *"a personal friend"*: Ibid., 58.

167 *Riis, whose camera philosophy*: Jacob Riis, *The Making of an American* (New York: Macmillan, 1901), 42. Also: Edmund Morris, *The Rise of Theodore Roosevelt* (New York: Modern Library, 2001), 512.

167 *"Dr. Parkhurst on the floor"*: Crain, *The Gilded Age in New York, 1870–1910*, 213.

168 *Throughout Steffens's career*: Morris, *The Rise of Theodore Roosevelt*, 502.

168 *"Don't you dare"*: Hartshorn, *I Have Seen the Future*, 62.

169 *"Care like hell!"*: Ella Winter introduction to Steffens, *Letters*, xv.

169 *now McClure looked*: Lyon, *Success Story*, 251.

170 *"A jim-dandy"*: Ibid., 157.

170 *"He could not be a friend"*: Stinson, "S. S. McClure and His Magazine," 121.

170 *Then Phillips took Steffens*: Steffens, *Autobiography*, 357.

170 *There were some news stories*: Ibid., 358.

171 *As he recalled*: Ibid.

171 *In May 1901*: Kaplan, *Lincoln Steffens*, 95.

171   *"We've got out"*: Ibid.
171   *"used up"*: Steffens, *Autobiography*, 358.
171   *"rather encouraged [him]"*: Ibid.
172   *"an author or a journalist"*: Ella Winter introduction to Steffens, *Letters*, xiv.
172   *"It was just like springing"*: Steffens, *Autobiography*, 359.
172   *He could see why*: Ibid.
172   *"As I wandered"*: Ibid., 360.
173   *"my job, the job of all of us"*: Ibid., 362–63.
173   *"We had to unite"*: Hartshorn, *I Have Seen the Future*, 90.
173   *"Sometimes he had"*: Greene, *America's Heroes*, 82–83.
173   *"like terrible summer thundershowers"*: Stinson, "S. S. McClure and His Magazine," 121.
173   *"devoted friend of S.S."*: Steffens, *Autobiography*, 264.
173   *Miss Tarbell seemed exempt*: Ibid., 392.
173   *"She would pick out"*: Ibid., 392–93.
174   *"incredibly outspoken"*: Hartshorn, *I Have Seen the Future*, 87.
174   *"Nobody will remain long"*: Ibid., 89.
174   *"the most brilliant addition"*: Ibid., 87.
174   *"I knew our excited discussions"*: Tarbell, *All in the Day's Work*, 200.
175   *Able to nimbly move*: Wilson, *McClure's Magazine and the Muckrakers*, 124.
175   *McClure and Steffens*: Steffens, *Autobiography*, 392.
175   *"the only great editor"*: Ibid., 364.
175   *"[P]olitics is a business"*: Lyon, *Success Story*, 216.
176   *McClure decided to reorganize*: Ibid., 175.
176   *"You can't learn"*: Steffens, *Autobiography*, 364.
176   *Then he sprang*: Ibid., 364.
176   *"Go to Washington"*: Steffens, *Letters*, 154–55.

## 12: *Big Game*

177   *Writing about architecture*: Walt Whitman, "Tear Down and Build Over Again," *American Whig Review* (November 1845): 536.
177   *"I think we have nothing to fear"*: Baker quoted in Semonche, *Ray Stannard Baker*, 97.
178   *"no amount of charities"*: Weinberg, *Taking on the Trust*, 211.
178   *"had a glint"*: Ibid.
178   *Since the 1870s*: Ibid.
178   *"practicing methods"*: Tarbell, *All in the Day's Work*, 207.
178   *The typed covering letters*: Letters, Tarbell mss, Sophia Smith Collection, Smith College.

179   *"These experiences had exactly"*: Tarbell, *All in the Day's Work,* 208.

179   *"Don't do it, Ida"*: Chernow, *Titan,* 440.

179   *Some fellow journalists*: Tarbell, *All in the Day's Work,* 207.

180   *"Mr. McClure dashed into the office"*: Ibid., 212.

180   *"as fine a pirate"*: Ibid., 10.

180   *It was a chance to repaint*: Richard Digby-Junger, *The Journalist as Reformer: Henry Demarest Lloyd and* Wealth Against Commonwealth (Westport, CT, and London: Greenwood Press, 1996), 127.

180   *"the handsomest"*: Tarbell, *All in the Day's Work,* 212.

180   *Rogers, she thought*: Notes on Rogers for *All in the Day's Work,* January 8, 1902, Tarbell mss, Pelletier Library.

180   *"She got in the habit"*: Roseboro quoted in Brady, *Ida Tarbell,* 150.

180   *"Men were as impersonal"*: Tarbell quoted in Brady, *Ida Tarbell,* 151.

181   *"Probably I've seen you"*: Tarbell, *All in the Day's Work,* 212.

181   *"an outrageous business"*: Ibid., 214.

181   *"He's a liar"*: Ibid., 218.

181   *In her sessions*: Weinberg, *Taking On the Trust,* 215.

182   *"Mr. Rogers," she would say*: Notes on interview with Rogers, undated, Tarbell mss, Pelletier Library.

182   *Her efforts at verification*: Weinberg, *Taking On the Trust,* 180–81.

182   *"caught him looking at me"*: Notes on interview with Rogers, undated, Tarbell mss, Pelletier Library.

182   *Rogers was her only key*: Dinitia Smith, "From Dimes to Millions and Mystery," *New York Times,* July 13, 1998, http://www.nytimes.com/1998/07/13 /books/from-dimes-to-millions-and-mystery.html (accessed June 26, 2018).

182   *"a little doubtfully"*: Tarbell, *All in the Day's Work,* 215.

182   *"If I hinted"*: Ibid., 220.

183   *"It looks as if something"*: Ibid., 215.

183   *The recent Spindletop*: Sean Dennis Cashman, *America in the Age of the Titans: The Progressive Era and World War I* (New York: NYU Press, 1988), 17.

183   *The streets and homes*: Miller, *The President and the Assassin,* 73.

183   *"When you get through"*: Letter, H. D. Lloyd to Ida Tarbell, April 11, 1903, McClure mss, Lilly Library.

183   *"the biggest little man"*: Weinberg, *Taking on the Trust,* 216.

184   *"short and plump"*: Tarbell, *All in the Day's Work,* 211.

184   *"I am startled"*: Ibid., 224.

185   *Dr. Levingston himself*: Chernow, *Titan,* 460.

185   *But Siddall found*: Stinson, "S. S. McClure and His Magazine," 214–15.

185  *More fruitful*: Tarbell, *All in the Day's Work*, 217.

185  *"Stop that shipment"*: Ibid., 226.

185  *"white with rage"*: Ibid., 227.

185  *"Where did you get"*: Chernow, *Titan*, 442.

## 13: *You Have the Moon Yet, Ain't It?*

187  *As the sky*: Hartshorn, *I Have Seen the Future*, 91.

188  *"writers, editors, leading citizens"*: Steffens, *Autobiography*, 365.

188  *"I started something"*: Ibid., 264.

188  *Between the Civil War*: Kaplan, *Lincoln Steffens*, 104.

188  *Shortly before Steffens's arrival*: Ibid.

188  *"You have the moon"*: Ibid., 105.

189  *"I'll have to do my duty"*: Louis Filler, *The Muckrakers*, new and enlarged edition of *Crusaders for American Liberalism* (University Park and London: Pennsylvania State University Press, 1976), 97.

189  *This gave Steffens*: Steffens, *Autobiography*, 368.

190  *"If I should be trusted"*: Steffens quoted in Tarbell, *All in the Day's Work*, 200–201.

190  *"in Steffens's case"*: Brand Whitlock, *Forty Years of It* (New York: Appleton, 1914), 163.

190  *When Whitlock wondered*: Hartshorn, *I Have Seen the Future*, 96.

190  *"Bribery," he decided*: Steffens, *Autobiography*, 373.

190  *"Why should [I] be a pariah"*: Kaplan, *Lincoln Steffens*, 106–7.

190  *In summer 1902*: Ibid., 107.

191  *"I wanted to study cities"*: Steffens, *Autobiography*, 375.

191  *"All tyrants"*: Sullivan, *The Education of An American*, 200.

191  *"little keen-faced gentleman with a string tie"*: Frederic Howe quoted in Filler, *The Muckrakers*, 90.

191  *"We had a pretty hot fight"*: Steffens, *Autobiography*, 375.

191  *"[T]he dictatorship of one"*: Ibid.

191  *"if you [like a thing]"*: Ibid., 393.

192  *He went to Salonika*: Lyon, *Success Story*, 197.

192  *"McClure's has become*: Typescript for *McClure's*, May 1904, McClure mss, Lilly Library.

192  *"[w]ith Mr. McClure's history"*: Letter, John S. Phillips to Harriet McClure, March 14, 1902, McClure mss, Lilly Library.

193  *"loyal only to his emotions"*: Letter, S. S. McClure to Harriet McClure, April 24, 1902, McClure mss, Lilly Library.

193  *"I do not like the way"*: Lyon, *Success Story*, 200.

193 *"Always remember"*: Ibid., 221.

193 *"I feel deeply"*: Letter, Ray Stannard Baker to John S. Phillips, April 13, 1902, Phillips mss, Lilly Library.

193 *A coal miners' strike*: Lyon, *Success Story,* 203.

193 *"coal and iron police"*: Ibid.

193 *"They hung me"*: Baker, "The Right to Work," *McClure's Magazine* 20, no. 3 (January 1903): 326.

193 *"Every night"*: Ibid., 334.

194 *"In any event"*: Kaplan, *Lincoln Steffens,* 109.

194 *"interested in facts, startling facts"*: Steffens, *Autobiography,* 393.

194 *Describing Minneapolis*: Lincoln Steffens, "The Shame of Minneapolis: The Ruin and Redemption of a City That Was Sold Out," reprinted by the Minnesota Legal History Project, 2011, http://minnesotalegalhistoryproject.org/assets /Steffens%20Shame%20of%20Mpls.pdf (accessed November 8, 2015).

194 *"slot machines"*: Ibid.

194 *Ames made his brother*: Lyon, *Success Story,* 218.

194 *Those who remained*: Ibid.

195 *"Yes, Doc Ames"*: Steffens, "The Shame of Minneapolis."

195 *"Even lawlessness"*: Ibid.

195 *Steffens's work in Minneapolis*: Kaplan, *Lincoln Steffens,* 112.

195 *Steffens's dissection*: Filler, *The Muckrakers,* 99.

196 *"how the game was worked"*: Steffens, *Autobiography,* 401.

196 *Philadelphia had more open*: Ibid., 410.

197 *It was in Philadelphia*: Filler, *The Muckrakers,* 100.

197 *But McClure was wary*: Lyon, *Success Story,* 222.

197 *"It was hard to tell him anything"*: Steffens, *Autobiography,* 509.

197 *"The President, who had resented"*: Steffens, *Letters,* 158.

198 *"OHIO RECOGNIZES"*: Lyon, *Success Story,* 228.

198 *One afternoon McClure*: Steffens, *Autobiography,* 442.

198 *"Last week a cigar manufacturer"*: Steffens, *Letters,* 161.

198 *"just to chew the rag"*: Steffens, *Autobiography,* 414, 416.

198 *"the best man I met"*: Ibid., 417.

198 *"[T]here is so much good"*: Winter introduction to Steffens, *Letters,* xv.

199 *"Dogmas do so obstruct"*: Ibid., xvi.

199 *"I would aim"*: Steffens, *Autobiography,* 394.

199 *"I aimed for the public's heart"*: Eric Schlosser, "'I Aimed for the Public's Heart, and . . . Hit It in the Stomach," *Chicago Tribune,* May 21, 2006, http:// articles.chicagotribune.com/2006-05-21/features/0605210414_1_upton-sinclair -trust-free (accessed June 26, 2018).

199 *Sinclair's novel*: Lyon, *Success Story,* 244.

199 *"a strange, pungent odor"*: Ibid., 237.

199 *admired by Churchill and Theodore Roosevelt*: Gary Younge, "Blood, Sweat, and Fears," *Guardian,* August 5, 2006, https://www.theguardian.com/books/2006/aug/05/featuresreviews.guardianreview24 (accessed May 1, 2018).

199 *"Tell Mr Sinclair"*: Ibid.

200 *"But don't you* see": Winter introduction to Steffens, *Letters,* xv.

200 *They were compelled*: Kaplan, *Lincoln Steffens,* 120.

200 *"unconscious politician"*: Ada McCormick interview with Steffens, 1933, Tarbell mss, Pelletier Library.

200 *"we can do more"*: Lyon, *Success Story,* 220.

## 14: *The Cleveland Ogre*

201 *"It has become a great bugbear"*: Chernow, *Titan,* 440.

201 *The* New York Times *said: McClure's,* December 1902.

201 *The review concluded*: Ibid.

201 *"You cannot imagine"*: S. S. McClure to Ida M. Tarbell, July 20, [1903], Ida M. Tarbell Collection, Pelletier Library, Allegheny College, Meadville, PA.

202 *McClure's hope*: Letter, S. S. McClure to Richard Watson Gilder, December 31, 1902, Richard Watson Gilder Papers, New York Public Library.

202 *"It was inevitable"*: Tarbell, "The Oil War of 1872," *McClure's Magazine* (January 1903).

202 *She was determined to write*: Chernow, *Titan,* 445.

203 *"the most unhappy and the most unnatural"*: Tarbell, *All in the Day's Work,* 237.

203 *"excited and vindictive"*: Ibid.

203 *"Are there any of our friends"*: Chernow, *Titan,* 451.

203 *"dismal . . . barbaric"*: Tarbell, *All in the Day's Work,* 234.

204 *"nearly choking"*: Notes and sketch for Rockefeller character study, Tarbell mss, Pelletier Library.

204 *Feeling "a little mean"*: Tarbell, *All in the Day's Work,* 235.

204 *She saw a man*: Ibid.

204 *"I was sorry for him"*: Ibid., 236.

204 *"written in face and voice and figure"*: It was then an accepted convention of journalism that physical features could be interpreted on a moral level. In a profile of Beef Trust baron Philip D. Armour in *McClure's* of February 1894, the reporter notes, "Armour is in every way a large man—large in build, in mind, in nature. . . . He moves easily, but he thinks in flashes. He has a big powerful head, broad over the eyes . . . a head that is full of character and determination. He has the strongest, and at the same time, the sweetest, face that I have ever

seen in a man. It is the face of one who is so much the master of himself that he can afford to be gentle. His voice is kindly in its tone and low; and while the eyes twinkle and around them are the lines of good humor. There is in them all the shrewdness, all the searching quality that you can imagine a man of his record to possess. They are the eyes of an analyst of human nature." Noted in Christin, "McClure's Magazine 1893–1903," 81–82.

204  *"colorless" eyes*: Notes and sketch for Rockefeller character study, Tarbell mss, Pelletier Library.

204  *His church, too*: Ibid.

205  *"I never had an animus"*: Tarbell, *All in the Day's Work,* 230.

205  *"a reptilian John"*: Tomkins, *Ida M. Tarbell,* 55.

205  *"Human experience"*: Ida Tarbell, *The History of the Standard Oil Company,* edited by David Chalmers (New York: Harper & Row, 1966), 48.

206  *"[Standard Oil] had never played fair"*: Tarbell quoted in Chernow, *Titan,* 443.

206  *"A young Iowa school teacher"*: Brady, *Ida Tarbell,* 130.

206  *"This district saw and lived"*: Letter, Ida Tarbell to Gertrude Hall, May 25, 1939, Phillips mss, Lilly Library.

206  *"What I most feared"*: Tarbell, *All in the Day's Work,* 407.

206  *"The most tragic effect"*: Ibid., 230.

206  *"In those days"*: Ibid., 83.

207  *A Detroit magazine*: John H. Hogan, "A Plea for Fair Play," *Gateway,* Drake Well Museum.

207  *He has been called*: Ron Chernow quoted in John Steele Gordon, "John Rockefeller Sr.," Philanthropy Roundtable, 2018, https://www.philanthropyroundtable .org/almanac/people/hall-of-fame/detail/john-rockefeller-sr (accessed May 31, 2018).

207  *He funded a clinic*: Weinberg, *Taking On the Trust,* 107.

207  *He and his wife*: Ibid., 127.

207  *"ignorant superstition"*: Tarbell quoted in Weinberg, *Taking On the Trust,* excerpted in *Wall Street Journal,* https://www.wsj.com/articles /SB120663481864568879 (accessed June 12, 2018).

207  *"parsimony"*: Tarbell quoted in Weinberg, *Taking On the Trust,* 236.

207  *"Our national life"*: Tarbell quoted in Weinberg, excerpted in *Wall Street Journal.*

208  *her slant on Rockefeller*: Weinberg, *Taking on the Trust,* 229.

208  *"I think I shall watch"*: Letter, Ida Tarbell to John Siddall, December 10, 1903, Tarbell mss, Pelletier Library.

208  *"one of the most stirring"*: *McClure's Magazine* (December 1902).

208  *"gives us the same insight"*: Lyon, *Success Story,* 213.

208 "WOMAN DOES MARVELOUS WORK": "Story of Standard Oil," undated New York *Globe*, Drake Well Museum.

208 *"so thrilling and dramatic"*: Chicago *Examiner*, September 17, 1904, Drake Well Museum.

208 *One day a determined man*: Brady, *Ida Tarbell*, 148.

208 *Miss Tarbell kept a scrapbook*: Ibid., 152.

209 *"has forfeited his right"*: "'A Gentleman' Denounces Millionaire M'Clure," undated Chicago *Examiner*, Drake Well Museum.

209 *Despite Rockefeller's work*: Gordon, "John Rockefeller Sr."

209 *Starting in 1904*: Letter, Theodore Roosevelt to George Cortelyou, October 26, 1904, Tarbell mss, Pelletier Library. Also: Morris, *Theodore Rex*, 206.

209 *A newspaper cartoon*: *Daily Tribune*, June 27, 1905, Drake Well Museum.

209 *Mark Twain wrote*: Twain, "A Humane Word from Satan," undated *Harper's Weekly*, Drake Well Museum.

209 The Nation *printed*: Brady, *Ida Tarbell*, 153.

209 *In its view,* McClure's: Tarbell, *All in the Day's Work*, 240.

209 *"the greatest of all literary vivisectionists"*: Undated Denver *Republican*, Drake Well Museum.

209 *One of the most partisan attacks*: Undated Oil City *Derrick*, Drake Well Museum.

210 *"shameless audacity"*: "Ida's Idee," undated Oil City *Derrick*, Drake Well Museum.

210 *"it should not be forgotten"*: Hogan, "A Plea for Fair Play."

210 *"ruled by her sympathies"*: Ibid.

210 *"Miss Tarbell's wonderful intellect"*: Unknown Los Angeles paper dated February 14 [no year], Drake Well Museum.

210 *She would long be seen*: Kochersberger, *More Than a Muckraker*, xxxv. Also: Brady, *Ida Tarbell*, 225 ["notorious"].

211 *"It is not surprising"*: Marcus Monroe Brown, *A Study of John D. Rockefeller: The Wealthiest Man in the World* (Cleveland: Marcus M. Brown, 1905), 14.

211 *Public libraries*: Tarbell, *All in the Day's Work*, 241.

211 *She read Montague's account*: Weinberg, *Taking On the Trust*, 240.

211 *When Rockefeller was questioned*: Tarbell, *All in the Day's Work*, 225.

211 *"unstatesmanlike"*: Digby-Junger, *The Journalist as Reformer*, 101.

211 *When allies of the Standard*: John D. Rockefeller quoted in Chernow, *Titan*, 442.

211 *"He liked to have things"*: Adella Prentiss Hughes quoted in Chernow, *Titan*, 457.

212 *"a pretense of fairness"*: Rockefeller quoted in Weinberg, *Taking On the Trust*, 258.

212 *"If I step on that worm"*: Chernow, *Titan*, 456.

212 *"Things have changed"*: Tarbell, *All in the Day's Work*, 225.

212 *"an honest, bitter, talented"*: Kochersberger, *More Than a Muckraker,* 66.

213 *"some waggish member"*: Tarbell, *All in the Day's Work,* 241.

213 *"No achievement"*: Brady, *Ida Tarbell,* 238–39.

213 *There was even a play*: Ibid., 169.

213 *Miss Tarbell herself was offered*: Ibid., 170.

213 *"There would be none"*: Tarbell, *All in the Day's Work,* 239.

## 15: *The Shame of S. S. McClure*

217 "McClure's *is edited"*: *McClure's Magazine* (January 1903), typescript in McClure mss, Lilly Library.

217 *"I doubt whether"*: Kaplan, *Lincoln Steffens,* 114.

217 *"such an arraignment"*: *McClure's Magazine* (January 1903), typescript in McClure mss, Lilly Library.

217 *"We forget that we are"*: Ibid.

218 *"to hunt together"*: Kaplan, *Lincoln Steffens,* 114.

219 *"Here was a group"*: Tarbell, *All in the Day's Work,* 254.

219 *"starry nights"*: Rice, *The Inky Way,* 61.

219 *The following night*: Letter, S. S. McClure to Harriet McClure, June 15, 1903, McClure mss, Lilly Library.

220 *"a rollicking adventure"*: Rice, *The Inky Way,* 65.

220 *"The days pass"*: Letter, Florence Wilkinson to Harriet McClure, August 26, 1903, McClure mss, Lilly Library.

220 *"the lake in a bath"*: Ibid.

220 *"you had better go"*: Letter, S. S. McClure to Harriet McClure, August 26, 1903, McClure mss, Lilly Library.

220 *a dazzling marquise ring*: Lyon, *Success Story,* 257.

220 *"Why am I sometimes naughty"*: *McClure's Magazine* 21, no. 6 (October 1903): 577.

221 *"I have just left Mr McClure"*: Letter, N. W. Gillespie to Harriet McClure, quoted in Martin Bock, "S. S. McClure, the Conrad Circle, and the Messy Season of '09," *The Conradian* 40, no. 1 (Spring 2015), Frederick Dodds McClure collection.

221 *"My mind is clearing"*: Letter, S. S. McClure to Harriet McClure, November 21, 1903, McClure mss, Lilly Library.

221 *"In case of my death"*: Lyon, *Success Story,* 257.

221 *Her alarm only grew*: Ibid., 259.

222 *No matter how they might strive*: Ibid., 259.

222 *Mann's weekly "Saunterings" column*: Mark Caldwell, excerpt from *A Short History of Rudeness: Manners, Morals, and Misbehavior in Modern America* (New

York: Picador, 1999), http://movies2.nytimes.com/books/first/c/caldwell-rude
ness.html (accessed October 8, 2018).

**222** *It was the first*: Ohmann, *Selling Culture,* 266.

**223** *"some very bad lines"*: Bynner, "Bynner Reads Between Lyon's Lines in Recording S. S. McClure's Success Story."

**223** *McClure sat quiet*: Lyon, *Success Story,* 260.

**223** *"I dreamt last night"*: Letter, S. S. McClure to Harriet McClure, June 8, 1904,
McClure mss, Lilly Library.

**223** *"The Lord keep us!"*: Letter, Ida Tarbell to John S. Phillips, June 1904, Phillips
mss, Lilly Library.

**224** *"It may be cruel"*: Ibid.

**224** *"What seest thou"*: Florence Wilkinson, "Genius," *McClure's Magazine* 22, no. 5
(March 1904): 547.

**224** *"My Dear Miss Wilkinson"*: Greg Gross, "The Staff Breakup of *McClure's
Magazine,* Ch. 3," Allegheny College website, 1997, https://sites.allegheny.edu
/tarbell/mcclurestaff/chapter-iii/ (accessed June 26, 2018).

**224** *An ally presented herself*: Brady, *Ida Tarbell,* 117.

**225** *"Imagine my surprise"*: Letter, Mary Bisland to Ida Tarbell, July 7, 1904, from
Tarbell mss, New York Public Library.

**225** *"Mr M'Clure said no one"*: Ibid.

**225** *Phillips was willing*: Lyon, *Success Story,* 266.

**226** *"a great satisfaction"*: Letter, Ida Tarbell to Harriet McClure, July 12, 1904,
McClure mss, Lilly Library.

**226** *She vented to Phillips*: Letter, Ida Tarbell to John S. Phillips, May 27, 1904,
Phillips mss, Lilly Library.

**226** *She wrote to Phillips*: Gross, "The Staff Breakup of *McClure's Magazine,* Ch. 3."

**227** *The contentious packet*: Letter, Harriet McClure to Ida Tarbell, July 2, 1904,
Tarbell mss, Pelletier Library.

**227** *"I've done some squirming"*: Lyon, *Success Story,* 263.

**227** *But nothing assuaged*: Ibid., 269.

**227** *The couple's friend Frances Hodgson Burnett*: Ibid., 264.

**227** *"Our life has a deep wound"*: Letter, Harriet McClure to Ida Tarbell, June 1,
1904, Tarbell mss, Pelletier Library.

**228** *"I find myself tempted"*: Letter, Harriet McClure to John S. Phillips, July 30,
1904, Tarbell mss, Pelletier Library.

**228** *McClure's clouded thinking*: Lyon, *Success Story,* 264.

**228** *"He has persuaded her"*: Ibid., 264.

**228** *"the same canny"*: Letter, Ida Tarbell to John S. Phillips, undated September
1904, Phillips mss, Lilly Library.

**228**  *In the summer of 1905*: Gross, "The Staff Breakup of *McClure's Magazine,* Ch. 3."

**228**  *The timing was absurd*: Merrill Teague, "Likening Boodlers to Sneak Thieves, S. S. McClure Says Press is the Republic's Hope," *North American* newspaper (Philadelphia), August 14, 1905.

**228**  *"I have decided to live"*: Gross, "The Staff Breakup of *McClure's Magazine,* Ch. 3."

**229**  *"My precious wife"*: Letter, S. S. McClure to Harriet McClure, July 5, 1905, McClure mss, Lilly Library.

**229**  *"You may think"*: Letter, Harriet McClure to S. S. McClure, September 1, 1904, McClure mss, Lilly Library.

### 16: *More Sinister and Painful*

**231**  *The loss of Franklin*: Tarbell, *All in the Day's Work,* 245.

**231**  *"I had joined"*: Ibid., 246.

**232**  *"The history of the organization"*: Tarbell, "The History of the Standard Oil Company: Conclusion," *McClure's Magazine* 23, no. 6 (October 1904): 670.

**232**  *"The way you are generally esteemed"*: Lyon, *Success Story,* 213.

**232**  *She wrote to Bert Boyden*: Ibid., 277.

**233**  *she exhorted her colleagues*: Ibid.

**233**  *"There are times"*: Letter, S. S. McClure to Ida Tarbell, March 29, 1905, Tarbell mss, Pelletier Library.

**233**  *"I have always cared"*: Letter, S. S. McClure to Ida Tarbell, undated Saturday [1905], Tarbell mss, Pelletier Library.

**233**  *"I am now at the bottom"*: Letter, S. S. McClure to Ida Tarbell, June 22, [1904], Tarbell mss, Pelletier Library.

**233**  *"My face* looks *strong"*: Ibid.

**233**  *"Dearest & dearest"*: Letter, S. S. McClure to Ida Tarbell, undated [1904], Tarbell mss, Pelletier Library.

**234**  *"I always feel brutal"*: Tarbell quoted in Brady, *Ida Tarbell,* 115.

**234**  *this total absence of "coquettries"*: Roseboro quoted in Brady, *Ida Tarbell,* 115.

**234**  *"To me you are the soul"*: Letter, S. S. McClure to Ida Tarbell, undated, Tarbell mss, Pelletier Library.

**234**  *He concluded his letter*: Letter, S. S. McClure to Ida Tarbell, March 29, 1905, Tarbell mss, Pelletier Library.

**234**  *"It brought fantastic situations"*: Tarbell, *All in the Day's Work,* 248.

**235**  *"fifty, fagged"*: Ibid.

**235**  *"prima donna"*: Ibid., 249.

235  *"The conservatives tell me"*: Letter, Ida Tarbell to John S. Phillips, March 28, 1905, Tarbell mss, Pelletier Library.

235  *"muchly masculinized old maid"*: "Scrap-Bag," undated Paris, Missouri, *Herald*, Drake Well Museum.

235  *"She was regarded"*: Helen Douglas, "Ida M. Tarbell 'Just Folks,' Girl Finds," Atlanta *Georgian*, February 26, 1923, Lilly Library.

235  *"well-dressed, serene"*: Crawford, "The Historian of Standard Oil."

235  *"soft and eloquent"*: Creelman, "A Talk with Miss Tarbell."

235  *"Instead of sober garb"*: Tarbell, *All in the Day's Work*, 157.

236  *He fired his Johns Hopkins doctors*: Ibid., 274.

236  *The staff began holding*: Brady, *Ida Tarbell*, 135.

236  *"spent a lively month"*: Tarbell, *All in the Day's Work*, 255.

236  *"I hope these two women"*: Letter, Albert Boyden to Ida Tarbell, dated Thursday the 11th, [1905], Tarbell mss, Pelletier Library.

237  *"I wish sometimes"*: Ibid.

237  *"had the character of improvisation"*: Tarbell, *All in the Day's Work*, 255.

237  *"I feel heart-sore"*: Letter, S. S. McClure to Ida Tarbell, December 30, [1901], Tarbell mss, Pelletier Library.

237  *"we will side by side"*: Letter, S. S. McClure to Ida Tarbell, March 18, [1903], Tarbell mss, Pelletier Library.

237  *"[A]ll my life"*: Lyon, *Success Story*, 220.

237  *"I think we have entered"*: Ibid.

237  *"Mr McClure arrived"*: Letter, Ida Tarbell to John S. Phillips, undated June 1903, Tarbell mss, New York Public Library.

238  *"Of course Mrs McClure"*: Tarbell, *All in the Day's Work*, 275.

238  *"I am going to reward you"*: Letter, S. S. McClure to Ida Tarbell, November 27, 1905, Tarbell mss, Pelletier Library.

238  *The magazine would be edited*: S. S. McClure, "Proposition for Founding of a Magazine," November 27, 1905, Tarbell mss, Pelletier Library.

238  *This time McClure envisioned*: Gross, "The Staff Breakup of *McClure's Magazine*, Ch. 3."

238  *To compensate*: Tarbell, *All in the Day's Work*, 251, 280.

238  *As Phillips and Miss Tarbell*: Ibid., 256.

239  *The new prospectus also included*: Gross, "The Staff Breakup of *McClure's Magazine*, Ch. 3."

239  *He had doubtless tracked*: Bok, *The Americanization of Edward Bok*, 172–73; and Matthew Schneirov, *The Dream of a New Social Order* (New York: Columbia University Press, 1994), 109.

239   *By the time he circulated*: Lyon, *Success Story,* 284.

239   *"I am not fit"*: Ibid., 285.

239   *"Mr. P[hillips] as usual"*: Letter, Ida Tarbell to Albert Boyden, undated February 1906, McClure mss, Lilly Library.

239   *She tersely told McClure*: Tarbell, *All in the Day's Work,* 256.

239   *"not quite right"*: Steffens, *Letters,* 173.

239   *"His new proposition"*: Gross, "The Staff Breakup of *McClure's Magazine,* Ch. 3."

240   *"temper his wilder impulses"*: Ibid.

240   *Boyden tentatively raised*: Letter, Albert Boyden to John S. Phillips, February 6, 1906, Tarbell mss, Pelletier Library.

240   *"This new magazine"*: Letter, S. S. McClure to John S. Phillips, February 17, 1906, Tarbell mss, Pelletier Library.

240   *"I am unusually vigorous"*: Letter, S. S. McClure to Ida Tarbell, November 27, 1905, Tarbell mss, Pelletier Library.

240   *"seemed to possess him"*: Tarbell, *All in the Day's Work,* 256.

240   *"Human reason has little influence"*: Ibid., 257.

240   *"suicidal"*: Ibid.

## 17: *The Ear of the Public*

241   *Roosevelt told Baker*: Morris, *Theodore Rex,* 434.

241   *"The people out there"*: Ibid.

242   *He still mulled*: Letter, Ray Stannard Baker to John S. Phillips, April 13, 1902, Phillips mss, Lilly Library.

242   *"I happen to know"*: Lyon, *Success Story,* 230.

242   *What McClure actually found*: Ibid.

242   *Roosevelt quickly approached*: Baker quoted in Morris, *Theodore Rex,* 257–58.

243   *His research started*: Lyon, *Success Story,* 236.

243   *he righteously opposed*: Letter, Theodore Roosevelt to Ray Stannard Baker, September 8, 1905, quoted in Semonche, *Ray Stannard Baker,* 132.

243   *"I haven't a criticism"*: Roosevelt quoted in Weinberg, eds., *The Muckrakers,* 298.

243   *"peculiarly the autocrat"*: Ray Stannard Baker, "Railroads on Trial," *McClure's Magazine* 26, no. 4 (February 1906): 398.

243   *Baker emphasized*: Ibid., 399.

245   *On August 15, a "Negro Hunt"*: Judy Crichton, *America 1900: The Turning Point* (New York: Henry Holt, 2000), 187

245   *"every trolley car"*: Crichton, *America 1900,* 187.

245   *A lynching near Union Square*: Ibid.

245   *More than other magazines*: Maurice H. Beasley, "The Muckrakers and Lynch-

ing: A Case Study in Racial Thinking," paper presented at the 66th Annual Meeting of the Association for Education in Journalism and Mass Communication (August 6–9, 1893, Corvallis, Oregon), 8, http://files.eric.ed.gov/fulltext /ED229769.pdf (accessed October 2, 2017).

246   *"You and I imagine"*: Ray Stannard Baker, "What Is a Lynching?" *McClure's Magazine* 24, no. 3 (January 1905): 299.

246   *"In each successive place"*: Ibid., 300.

247   *"This jail is said"*: Ray Stannard Baker, "Lynching in the North," *McClure's Magazine* 24, no. 4 (February 1905): 426.

247   *"Well, on Monday afternoon"*: Ibid., 425.

248   *"A sort of dry rot"*: Ibid.

248   *"interference in every state"*: Theodore Roosevelt quoted in Beasley, "The Muckrakers and Lynching," 21.

248   *"All over the world"*: W. E. Burghardt Du Bois, "The African Roots of War," *The Atlantic Monthly* 115, no. 5 (May 1915): 707–14.

248   *"My purpose"*: Baker, *Following the Color Line* (New York: Doubleday, Page, 1908), Project Gutenberg ebook edition, https://www.gutenberg.org/files /34847/34847-h/34847-h.htm (accessed October 8, 2018).

248   *His work formed*: Beasley, "The Muckrakers and Lynching," 24.

248   *As Du Bois warned*: Ibid.

249   *His mind was inquisitive*: Lyon, *Success Story,* 233.

249   *He suggested that crimes*: Ibid.

249   *"[W]e execute the law"*: Ibid.

249   *In his letters to his father*: Baker quoted in Chalmers, "Ray Stannard Baker's Search for Reform," *Journal of the History of Ideas* 19 no. 3 (June 1958): 423.

249   *"I think we have struck"*: Baker quoted in Chalmers, "Ray Stannard Baker's Search for Reform," 424.

249   *"one of the best"*: Semonche, *Ray Stannard Baker,* 119–20.

249   *"a blessing when we are inclined"*: Samuel Johnson, quoted in Felling, "Best. Journalism Quotes. Ever."

250   *"I do not at all like"*: Lyon, *Success Story,* 207–8.

250   *Just one year*: Morris, *Theodore Rex,* 195.

250   *"Reform is popular"*: Whitlock, *Forty Years of It,* 164.

250   *The wealthy men*: Letter, Theodore Roosevelt to Justice Moody, September 21, 1907, Tarbell mss, Pelletier Library.

250   *Roosevelt's Congress forbade*: Eric F. Goldman, *Rendezvous with Destiny: A History of Modern American Reform* (New York: Knopf, 1952), 163.

250   *Roosevelt confided*: Bok, *The Americanization of Edward Bok,* 196.

251   *Speaker Henry Van Dyke's joking words*: Brady, *The High Cost of Impatience,* 196.

252  *One urban myth*: Filler, *The Muckrakers,* 357–58.

252  *McClure didn't want*: Morris, *Theodore Rex,* 419.

252  *"I am so tired"*: Dunne quoted in Elmer Ellis, *Mr. Dooley's America: A Life of Finley Peter Dunne* (Hamden, CT: Archon Books, 1969), 216.

252  *"promised to take up"*: Ibid.

253  *"Th' noise ye hear"*: Goldman, *Rendezvous with Destiny,* 175.

253  *"Of late years"*: David Graham Phillips, *The Treason of the Senate,* edited with an introduction by George E. Mowry and Judson A. Grenier (Chicago: Quadrangle Books, 1964), 33.

253  *Roosevelt first struck*: Morris, *Theodore Rex,* 439.

253  *Earlier that month*: McGerr, *A Fierce Discontent,* 175.

253  *Thus inspired, Roosevelt stood*: Morris, *Theodore Rex,* 440.

253  *He wrote to Roosevelt*: Mowry and Grenier introduction to *The Treason of the Senate,* 34.

254  *an "influence for evil"*: Morris, *Theodore Rex,* 437.

254  *"At this moment"*: McGerr, *A Fierce Discontent,* 176.

254  *"inevitable inequality of conditions"*: Ibid.

254  *"The men with the muckrakes"*: Roosevelt quoted in Chalmers, *The Social and Political Ideas of the Muckrakers,* iv.

254  *After the speech*: Lyon, *Success Story,* 209.

255  *"a little truth"*: Roosevelt quoted in Dorman, "'Deliver Me from This Muck-Rake,'" 21.

255  *"rewards an honest man"*: Hartshorn, *I Have Seen the Future,* 142.

255  *The attack on the muckrakers*: John E. Semonche, "Theodore Roosevelt's 'Muck-Rake' Speech: A Reassessment," *Mid-America* 46, no. 2 (April 1964): 124.

255  *"They're exposin' the exposers"*: W. D. Nesbit, *New York Times,* April 17, 1906, reprinted in the *Seaside Times,* April 26, 1906, clipping in McClure mss, Lilly Library.

255  *"Why listen to facts"*: Brady, *Ida Tarbell,* 175.

256  *mingling of facts and values*: Michael Schudson quoted in Robert Miraldi, *Muckraking and Objectivity* (New York: Greenwood Press, 1990), 32.

256  *"To stir up envy"*: "A Review of Miss Tarbell's Famous Book," unsigned in *The Nation,* January 5, 1905, Drake Well Museum.

256  *"torrential journalism"*: Morris, *Theodore Rex,* 195.

256  *The muckrakers' articles*: Letter, Theodore Roosevelt to George Horace Lorimer, May 12, 1906, *The Letters of Theodore Roosevelt,* vol. 5, *This Big Stick, 1905–1907,* selected and edited by Elting E. Morrison (Cambridge, MA: Harvard University Press, 1952), 269.

256  *"He was afraid"*: Tarbell, *All in the Day's Work,* 241.

256   *"Well, Mr. President"*: Gross, "The Staff Breakup of *McClure's Magazine,* Ch. 3."

257   *"put more sky"*: Letter, Theodore Roosevelt to S. S. McClure, October 4, 1905, quoted in Mowry and Grenier introduction to Phillips, *The Treason of the Senate,* 31–32.

257   *"In social and economic"*: Mowry and Grenier introduction to Phillips, *The Treason of the Senate,* 31–32.

257   *"evolution rather than revolution"*: Semonche, "Theodore Roosevelt's 'Muck-Rake' Speech," 116–17.

257   *He privately wrote*: Gross, "The Staff Breakup of *McClure's Magazine,* Ch. 3."

257   *"Latterly I believe"*: Baker 1910 comments on Theodore Roosevelt quoted by John Simkin, "Ray Stannard Baker," Spartacus Educational, April 2013, http://spartacus-educational.com/JbakerR.htm (accessed October 1, 2017).

257   *"a good deal of the usual conviction"*: Gross, "The Staff Breakup of *McClure's Magazine,* Ch. 3."

257   *McClure wrote to the president*: Stinson, "S. S. McClure and His Magazine," 252.

## 18: *A Momentous Decision*

259   *In later years*: Gross, "The Staff Breakup of *McClure's Magazine,* Ch. 3."

259   *"a malignant wave"*: Ibid.

259   *"It was a momentous decision"*: Phillips quoted in Lyon, *Success Story,* 286.

260   *"I can't stay"*: Journal entry, March 22, 1906, transcribed by Kate Wayland-Smith, Tarbell mss, Pelletier Library.

260   *"that the very earth"*: Baker, *American Chronicle,* 211.

260   *"In the building up of that triumph"*: Steffens, *Autobiography,* 535.

260   *"they were funny"*: Ibid.

260   *"I realized that those who had to live"*: Ibid.

260   *He argued*: Gross, "The Staff Breakup of *McClure's Magazine,* Ch. 3."

261   *"Mr. P shook it"*: Journal entry, March 22, 1906, transcribed by Kate Wayland-Smith, Tarbell mss, Pelletier Library.

261   *She found him*: Journal entry, March 22, 1906, transcribed by Kate Wayland-Smith, Tarbell mss, Pelletier Library.

261   *He focused his emotions*: Ibid.

261   *At the end of thirty minutes*: Ibid.

261   *"Awful for me"*: Brady, *Ida Tarbell,* 173.

261   *"There has come a point"*: Journal entry, May 5, 1905, transcribed by Kate Wayland-Smith, Tarbell mss, Pelletier Library.

262   *Then she allowed herself*: Tarbell, *All in the Day's Work,* 258.

262   *"I love and pray"*: Letter, Harriet McClure to Ida Tarbell, March 23, 1906, Tarbell mss, Pelletier Library.

262 *By nightfall*: Lyon, *Success Story,* 288.

262 *"laid his head"*: Brady, *The High Cost of Impatience,* 226.

262 *"potent forces for evil"*: Gross, "The Staff Breakup of *McClure's Magazine,* Ch. 3."

262 *"I cannot leave"*: Note, S. S. McClure to Ida Tarbell, handwritten on Waldorf-Astoria stationery, undated, Tarbell mss, Pelletier Library.

262 *"Dear McClure"*: Letter, Rudyard Kipling to S. S. McClure, June 3, 1906, McClure mss, Lilly Library.

263 *"I felt awfully sorry"*: Letter, S. S. McClure to John S. Phillips, April 5, 1906, McClure mss, Lilly Library.

263 *"When you read history"*: Ibid.

263 *"I think I may say"*: Letter, S. S. McClure to Robert Mather, April 14, 1906, McClure mss, Lilly Library.

263 *On April 27*: Lyon, *Success Story,* 293.

263 *"It is doubtful"*: Brady, *The High Cost of Impatience,* 227.

264 *"spoiled by notoriety"*: Clippings on staff breakup, McClure mss, Lilly Library.

264 *"MUCK-RAKE SPEECH SCARES M'CLURE"*: Cleveland *News,* May 7, 1906, McClure mss, Lilly Library.

264 *Sedgwick*: Quoted in Brady, *Ida Tarbell,* 135–36.

264 *"retired"*: "M'Clure Editors at Outs," Topeka *Capital,* May 6, 1906, McClure mss, Lilly Library.

264 *"No man in this country"*: "The End of Muck-Raking," Chicago *Journal,* May 5, 1906, McClure mss, Lilly Library.

264 *"he would not have the power"*: Grand Rapids *News,* May 10, 1906, untitled, McClure mss, Lilly Library.

264 *Baker himself*: Baker, *American Chronicle,* 211.

264 *"We were derelicts"*: Tarbell, *All in the Day's Work,* 258.

265 *"Bynner," he said*: Lyon, *Success Story,* 294.

265 *"The most vivid"*: Bynner, "Bynner Reads Between Lyon's Lines in Recording S. S. McClure's Success Story."

265 *"our friend, the enemy"*: Lyon, *Success Story,* 299.

265 *"I am a free man"*: Ibid.

266 *"the greatest satirist"*: Tarbell, *All in the Day's Work,* 260.

266 *"You sputter"*: Ibid.

266 *Now Phillips, Dunne*: Brady, *The High Cost of Impatience,* 233.

266 *"Booth Tarkington, Edna Ferber"*: Tarbell, *All in the Day's Work,* 262.

267 *"You are the root"*: Letter, Arthur Conan Doyle to S. S. McClure, September 10, 1906, McClure mss, Lilly Library.

267 *"in a state of delirious excitement"*: James Woodress quoted in Johannings-

meier, "Unmasking Willa Cather's 'Mortal Enemy,'" *Cather Studies* 5, no. 1 (January 2003), https://cather.unl.edu/cs005_johanningsmeier.html (accessed June 13, 2018).

267  *"tepid bath"*: Cather quoted in Woodress, *Willa Cather: A Literary Life* (Lincoln: University of Nebraska Press, 1987), https://cather.unl.edu/life.woodress.html (accessed June 27, 2018).

267  *"Mr. McClure tells me"*: Cather to Sara Orne Jewett, *The Selected Letters of Willa Cather*, 119.

268  *"He left his office"*: Cather quoted in Brady, *Ida Tarbell*, 163.

268  *"No man's judgment"*: McClure and Cather, "My Autobiography, Part 7."

269  *At each year's end*: Brady, *The High Cost of Impatience*, 227.

269  "No one is to be trusted": Letter, S. S. McClure to Harriet McClure, September 15, 1906, McClure mss, Lilly Library.

269  *"benign, searching look"*: Bynner, review of three Willa Cather biographies in *New Mexico Quarterly* (Autumn 1953): 332.

270  *"makeshifts of a homeless person"*: Tarbell, *All in the Day's Work*, 262.

270  *"I am an optimist"*: Crawford, "The Historian of Standard Oil."

270  *"had no stomach"*: Tarbell, *All in the Day's Work*, 263.

270  *Typically she skimped*: Ibid., 265.

270  *There were other journalists*: Ibid.

271  *"I was not fit"*: Tarbell in *Albert Boyden, April 10, 1875–May 21, 1925: Reminiscences and Tributes by His Friends* Tarbell mss, Pelletier Library.

271  *"Of course you are an idiot"*: Ibid.

271  *When he arrived*: Ibid.

271  *Frank Norris and his wife, Kathleen*: Tarbell, *All in the Day's Work*, 266.

271  *Miss Tarbell used*: Brady, *Ida Tarbell*, 181.

271  *despite Cleveland's approachability*: Tarbell, *All in the Day's Work*, 271.

272  *"I had no stomach for it"*: Ibid., 253.

272  *After the dissolution*: Weinberg, *Taking on the Trust*, 257.

272  *"animated more with jealousy"*: Chernow, *Titan*, 457.

272  *"How clever she is"*: Ibid.

272  *The new magazine*: Tarbell, *All in the Day's Work*, 281.

272  *"[I]t sought to present things"*: Ibid.

273  *While reporting for* The American: Tarbell, "Flying—A Dream Come True," *The American* (November 1913), quoted in Kochersberger, *More Than a Muckraker*, 186–87.

273  *Phillips felt*: Letter, Ida Tarbell to Albert Boyden, July 1, 1907, McClure mss, Lilly Library.

273  *William Allen White thought*: Johnson, *William Allen White's America*, 159.

273  *Miss Tarbell decided*: Letter, Ida Tarbell to Albert Boyden, July 1, 1907, Mc-Clure mss, Lilly Library.

274  *In later years*: Letter, Ida Tarbell to Viola Roseboro, September 14, 1938, Roseboro mss, Pelletier Library.

274  *Ironically*: Miraldi, *Muckraking and Objectivity,* 70–71.

275  *Her view of Will*: Brady, *Ida Tarbell,* 215, 236.

275  *"My dear Miss Tarbell"*: Letter, S. S. McClure to Ida Tarbell, July 1, [1907], Tarbell mss, Pelletier Library.

## Epilogue

277  *the craft they invented*: Dorman, "'Deliver Me from This Muck-Rake,'" 8.

277  Forbes *has described*: "Have We Been Here Before?" *Forbes* (May 15, 1972), Frederick Dodds McClure collection.

277  *Judges convened*: Felicity Barringer, "Journalism's Greatest Hits: Two Lists of a Century's Top Stories," *New York Times* (March 1, 1999), Frederick Dodds McClure collection.

278  *Upton Sinclair once teased Ray Stannard Baker*: Ray Stannard Baker, *American Chronicle: The Autobiography of Ray Stannard Baker* (New York: Scribner's, 1945), 195.

279  *With the advent*: Beverly Gage, "More 'Progressive' Than Thou," *New York Times,* January 12, 2016, https://www.nytimes.com/2016/01/17/magazine/more-progressive-than-thou.html (accessed June 27, 2018).

279  *"Two hateful world wars"*: Baker, *American Chronicle,* 227.

279  *"Wall Street cannot gull"*: C. C. Regier, *The Era of the Muckrakers* (Gloucester, MA: Peter Smith, 1957), 204–5.

280  *"The subject of my lecture"*: Letter, S. S. McClure to Lee Keedick, January 27, 1910, McClure mss, Lilly Library.

280  *"an eye on the squirrel"*: St. Louis *Democrat,* April 12, 1914, McClure mss, Lilly Library.

280  *She plunged in*: Tarbell, *All in the Day's Work,* 363.

280  *Hearst could not make it*: Mott, *A History of American Magazines,* vol. 4, 607.

281  *"I tell you I have"*: Letter of July 28, 1924, quoted in Johanningsmeier, "Unmasking Willa Cather's 'My Mortal Enemy.'"

281  *In the fall of 1933*: *The Selected Letters of Willa Cather,* 491.

281  *"an old man"*: Cather quoted in Johanningsmeier, "Unmasking Willa Cather's 'My Mortal Enemy.'"

281  *S. S. told reporters*: Abbeville *Press & Banner* clipping, October 4, 1928, McClure mss, Lilly Library.

281 *He fell under the spell*: "Mussolini Debate Turns into Cash," *New York Times* clipping, March 12, 1928, McClure mss, Lilly Library.

281 *At one event*: Ibid.

281 *Coincidentally, Miss Tarbell*: Tarbell, *All in the Day's Work*, 383.

282 *Younger magazine men*: Bynner, "Bynner Reads Between Lyon's Lines in Recording S. S. McClure's Success Story."

282 *His usual corner newsboy*: New York *Daily News* clipping, November 6, 1940, McClure Publishing Company mss, University of Delaware.

282 *Write-ups noted*: "S.S. M'Clure, 87, Pioneer Editor, to Be Honored," unknown newspaper, April 19, 1944, McClure mss, Lilly Library.

282 *"The American people"*: "Famous Writers in Britain and America Introduced First by SS McClure," undated *New York World-Telegram* 1944, McClure Publishing Company mss, University of Delaware.

282 *Baker then became*: Wood, *Magazines in the United States,* 139.

283 *"a booky ending"*: Baker quoted in Dorman, "'Deliver Me from This Muck-Rake,'" 73.

283 *His razor-sharp*: F. A. Gutheim, "Steff," *Survey Graphic* (December 1936), Tarbell mss, Pelletier Library.

283 *She moved to a studio*: Brady, *Ida Tarbell*, 219.

283 *She argued for women*: Tomkins, *Ida M. Tarbell*, 101.

284 *"the ability and dignity"*: Gilman quoted in Brady, *Ida Tarbell*, 202.

284 *"She was so able"*: Tarbell, *All in the Day's Work*, 328.

284 *"Consider Catherine of Russia"*: Tarbell quoted in Weinberg, *Taking on the Trust*, 262.

284 *"I have never known"*: Letter, Ida Tarbell to S. S. McClure, October 15, 1937, Tarbell mss, Pelletier Library.

285 *Miss Tarbell replied*: Letter, S. S. McClure to Ida Tarbell, undated Saturday [1905], Tarbell mss, Pelletier Library.

285 *"Was there ever a group"*: Letter, Ida Tarbell to Ray Stannard Baker, October 17, 1939, Tarbell mss, Pelletier Library.

285 *When Frank Doubleday*: Doubleday, *Memoirs of a Publisher,* 100–101.

285 *Just after Bert Boyden*: Letter, Albert Boyden to Ida Tarbell, January 10, 1921, Tarbell mss, Pelletier Library.

285 *Their mutual friend*: Jeannette Gilder, "When McClure's Began," *McClure's Magazine* (August 1913): 72.

285 *Through the 1930s*: Phillips quoted in Doris Kearns Goodwin, *The Bully Pulpit: Theodore Roosevelt, William Howard Taft, and the Golden Age of Journalism* (New York: Simon & Schuster, 2013), 750.

**286** *For Miss Tarbell*: Tarbell, *All in the Day's Work,* 406.

**286** *McClure trotted out*: Goodwin, *The Bully Pulpit,* 750.

**286** *"The quality in him"*: Letter, Ida Tarbell to Viola Roseboro, November 6, 1937, Roseboro mss, Pelletier Library.

**286** *"To many he is only"*: New York Herald Tribune clipping, March 23, 1949, McClure mss, Lilly Library.

**286** *His loved ones*: New York Journal-American clipping, March 23, 1949, McClure Publishing Company mss, University of Delaware.

**286** *"When she isn't writing"*: Mary Day Winn, "The Terror of the Trusts," *New York Herald Tribune,* April 1, 1928, Tarbell mss, Sophia Smith Collection, Smith College.

**287** *Idealized in older age*: Ada McCormick quoted in Brady, *Ida Tarbell,* 237.

**287** *She also relished*: Brady, *Ida Tarbell,* 245, 248.

**287** *When a* Cosmopolitan *reporter*: Tarbell quoted in Kochersberger, *More Than a Muckraker,* 205.

**287** *In a commencement speech*: Tarbell, "What I Should Like to Tell June Graduates," 1913, http://sites.allegheny.edu/tarbell/fromtarbell/junegrads/ (accessed October 5, 2017).

**288** *"I believe"*: Letter, Ida Tarbell to Gertrude Hall, May 25, 1939, Phillips mss, Lilly Library.

**288** *She finished the lecture*: Tarbell, "What I Should Like to Tell June Graduates."

# Bibliography

## ARCHIVES

S. S. McClure Manuscripts, Lilly Library, Indiana University, Bloomington

McClure Publishing Company Archives, University of Delaware Library

John S. Phillips Manuscripts, Lilly Library, Indiana University, Bloomington

Ida M. Tarbell Collection, Pelletier Library, Allegheny College

Ida M. Tarbell Papers, Drake Well Museum, Titusville, PA

Ida Tarbell Papers, Sophia Smith Collection, Smith College

Ida M. Tarbell Collection, New York Public Library

Ray Stannard Baker Papers, Manuscript Division, Library of Congress

Ray Stannard Baker ("David Grayson") Papers, Jones Library, Amherst, MA

Lincoln Steffens Papers, Rare Book & Manuscript Library, Columbia University in the City of New York

Witter Bynner Papers, Houghton Library, Harvard University

Richard Watson Gilder Papers, New York Public Library

Chronicling America, the digital collection of historic American newspapers at the Library of Congress

## BOOKS

Aaron, Daniel. *Men of Good Hope: A Story of American Progressives.* New York: Oxford University Press, 1951.

Aucoin, James L. *The Evolution of American Investigative Journalism.* Columbia and London: University of Missouri Press, 2005.

Baker, Ray Stannard. *American Chronicle: The Autobiography of Ray Stannard Baker.* New York: Charles Scribner's Sons, 1945.

———. *Following the Color Line: An Account of Negro Citizenship in the American Democracy.* New York: Doubleday, Page, 1908.

———. *Native American: The Book of My Youth.* New York: Scribner, 1941.

Beatty, Jack. *Age of Betrayal: The Triumph of Money in America, 1865–1900.* New York: Vintage, 2007.

Bok, Edward. *The Americanization of Edward Bok: An Autobiography.* 1920; reprint, New York: Pocket Books, 1965.

Brady, Kathleen. *Ida Tarbell: Portrait of a Muckraker.* Pittsburgh: University of Pittsburgh Press, 1989.

Caldwell, Mark. *A Short History of Rudeness: Manners, Morals, and Misbehavior in Modern America.* New York: Picador, 1999.

Calhoun, Charles W., ed. *The Gilded Age: Essays on the Origins of Modern America.* Wilmington, DE: Scholarly Resources, 1996.

Camhi, Jane Jerome. *Women Against Women: American Anti-Suffragism, 1880–1920.* Brooklyn: Carlson, 1994.

Cashman, Sean Dennis. *America in the Age of the Titans: The Progressive Era and World War I.* New York and London: New York University Press, 1988.

Cather, Willa. *The Selected Letters of Willa Cather.* Edited by Andrew Jewell and Janis Stout. New York: Knopf, 2013.

Chalmers, David Mark. *The Muckrake Years.* New York: Van Nostrand, 1974.

———. *The Social and Political Ideas of the Muckrakers.* New York: Citadel Press, 1964.

Chernow, Ron. *Titan: The Life of John D. Rockefeller, Sr.* New York: Vintage, 2004.

Crain, Esther. *The Gilded Age in New York, 1870–1910.* New York: Black Dog & Leventhal, 2016.

Crichton, Judy. *America 1900: The Turning Point.* New York: Henry Holt, 1998.

Digby-Junger, Richard. *The Journalist as Reformer: Henry Demarest Lloyd and* Wealth Against Commonwealth. Westport, CT, and London: Greenwood Press, 1996.

Dorr, Rheta Childe. *A Woman of Fifty.* 2nd ed. New York: Funk & Wagnalls, 1924.

Doubleday, F. N. *The Memoirs of a Publisher.* Garden City, NY, and New York: Doubleday, 1972.

Edel, Leon. *Henry James, The Master: 1901–1916.* Philadelphia and New York: Lippincott, 1953.

Ellis, Elmer. *Mr. Dooley's America: A Life of Finley Peter Dunne.* Hamden, CT: Archon Books, 1969.

Filler, Louis. *The Muckrakers*: New and enlarged edition of *Crusaders for American Liberalism.* University Park and London: Pennsylvania State University Press, 1976.

Ginger, Ray. *Age of Excess: The United States from 1877 to 1914*. 2nd ed. New York: Macmillan, 1975.

Gissing, George. *The Odd Women*. Amazon Digital Services e-book edition, 2013.

Goddard, Stephen B. *Colonel Albert Pope and His American Dream Machines: The Life and Times of a Bicycle Tycoon Turned Automotive Pioneer*. Jefferson, NC: McFarland, 2008.

Goldman, Eric F. *Rendezvous with Destiny: A History of Modern American Reform*. New York: Knopf, 1952.

Goodwin, Doris Kearns. *The Bully Pulpit: Theodore Roosevelt, William Howard Taft, and the Golden Age of Journalism*. New York: Simon & Schuster, 2013.

Graham, Jane K. *Viola, The Duchess of New Dorp: A Biography of Viola Roseboro*. Whitefish, MT: Kessinger, 2006.

Greene, Theodore P. *America's Heroes: The Changing Models of Success in American Magazines*. New York: Oxford University Press, 1970.

Gutek, Gerald L., and Patricia A. Gutek. *Bringing Montessori to America: S. S. McClure, Maria Montessori, and the Campaign to Publicize Montessori Education*. Tuscaloosa: University of Alabama Press, 2016.

Hardy, Stephen. *How Boston Played: Sport, Recreation, and Community, 1865–1915*. Knoxville: University of Tennessee Press, 2003.

Hartshorn, Peter. *I Have Seen the Future: A Life of Lincoln Steffens*. Berkeley, CA: Counterpoint Press, 2012.

Hofstadter, Richard. *The Age of Reform: From Bryan to FDR*. New York: Knopf, 1961.

Hubbard, Elbert. *Selected Writings of Elbert Hubbard: His Mintage of Wisdom, Coined from a Life of Love, Laughter, and Work*. Vol. 1. New York: Wise, 1922.

Irwin, Will. *The Making of a Reporter*. New York: G. P. Putnam's Sons, 1942.

———. *Propaganda and the News: or, What Makes You Think So?* New York and London: McGraw-Hill, 1936.

Johanningsmeier, Charles. *Fiction and the American Literary Marketplace: The Role of Newspaper Syndicates in America, 1860–1900*. New York: Cambridge University Press, 1997.

Johnson, Walter. *William Allen White's America*. New York: Henry Holt, 1947.

Kaplan, Justin. *Lincoln Steffens: A Biography*. New York: Simon & Schuster, 1974.

Kipling, Rudyard. *Something of Myself: For My Friends Known and Unknown*. New York: Cambridge University Press, 1991. Accessed November 8, 2015. http://gutenberg.net.au/ebooks04/0400691.txt.

Kochersberger, Robert C., ed. *More than a Muckraker: Ida Tarbell's Lifetime in Journalism*. Knoxville: University of Tennessee Press, 1994.

Labor, Earle. *Jack London: An American Life*. New York: Farrar, Straus & Giroux, 2013.

Lefevre, Edwin. *Reminiscences of a Stock Operator*. Larchmont, NY: American Research Council, 1923.

Leonard, Thomas C. *The Power of the Press: The Birth of American Political Reporting*. New York and Oxford: Oxford University Press, 1986.

Lloyd, Henry Demarest. *Wealth Against Commonwealth*. New York: Harper & Brothers, 1894.

Lyon, Peter. *Success Story: The Life and Times of S. S. McClure*. Deland, FL: Everett/Edwards, 1967.

Martin, Justin. *Rebel Souls: Walt Whitman and America's First Bohemians*. New York: Da Capo, 2014.

McClure, S. S., and Willa Cather. *My Autobiography*. Lincoln: University of Nebraska Press, 1997. Accessed November 14, 2018. https://cather.unl.edu/index.mcclure.html.

McGerr, Michael. *A Fierce Discontent: The Rise and Fall of the Progressive Movement in America*. New York: Oxford University Press, 2003.

Miller, Scott. *The President and the Assassin: McKinley, Terror, and Empire at the Dawn of the American Century*. New York: Random House, 2011.

Miraldi, Robert. *Muckraking and Objectivity: Journalism's Colliding Traditions*. New York: Greenwood Press, 1990.

Morris, Charles R. *The Tycoons: How Andrew Carnegie, John D. Rockefeller, Jay Gould, and J. P. Morgan Invented the American Supereconomy*. New York: Times Books, 2005.

Morris, Edmund. *The Rise of Theodore Roosevelt*. 1979; reprint, New York: Modern Library, 2001.

———. *Theodore Rex*. New York: Random House, 2001.

Mott, Frank Luther. *A History of American Magazines*. Vol. 4, *1885–1905*. Cambridge, MA: Belknap Press of Harvard University Press, 1957.

Norris, Frank. *The Octopus: A Story of California*. Minneapolis: Filiquarian, 2007.

———. *The Responsibilities of the Novelist*. London: Grant Richards, 1903. Accessed November 14, 2018. https://archive.org/stream/responsibilities00norruoft#page/n7/mode/2up.

Ohmann, Richard. *Selling Culture: Magazines, Markets, and Class at the Turn of the Century*. London and New York: Verso, 1996.

Painter, Nell Irvin. *Standing at Armageddon: The United States: 1877–1919*. New York: Norton, 1987.

Peterson, Theodore. *Magazines in the Twentieth Century*. Champaign: University of Illinois Press, 1956.

Phillips, David Graham. *The Treason of the Senate*. Edited with an introduction by George E. Mowry and Judson A. Grenier. Chicago: Quadrangle Books, 1964.

Phillips, John S., ed. *Albert A. Boyden, April 10, 1875–May 2, 1925: Reminiscences and Tributes by his Friends.* New York: privately published, 1925.

Piott, Steven L. *Daily Life in the Progressive Era.* Westport, CT: Greenwood Press, 2011.

Regier, C. C. *The Era of the Muckrakers.* Gloucester, MA: Peter Smith, 1957.

Rice, Alice Hegan. *The Inky Way.* New York and London: Appleton-Century, 1940.

———. *Sandy.* New York: Century, 1905. Accessed October 13, 2017. http://www.classicreader.com/book/2479/.

Rice, Cale Young. *Bridging the Years.* New York: Appleton-Century, 1939.

Riis, Jacob A. *The Making of an American.* New York: Macmillan, 1901.

Rockefeller, John D. *Random Reminiscences of Men and Events.* New York: Doubleday, Page, 1909.

Roosevelt, Theodore. *The Letters of Theodore Roosevelt.* Vol. 5, *The Big Stick, 1905–1907.* Selected and edited by Elting E. Morrison. Cambridge, MA: Harvard University Press, 1952.

Schneirov, Matthew. *The Dream of a New Social Order: Popular Magazines in America.* New York: Columbia University Press, 1994.

Sedgwick, Ellery. *The Happy Profession.* New York: Little, Brown, 1946.

Semonche, John E. *Ray Stannard Baker: A Quest for Democracy in Modern America, 1870–1918.* Chapel Hill: University of North Carolina Press, 1969.

Steffens, Lincoln. *The Autobiography of Lincoln Steffens.* New edition with foreword by Thomas C. Leonard. Berkeley, CA: Heyday Books, 2005.

———. *The Letters of Lincoln Steffens.* Vol. 1, *1889–1919.* Edited with introductory notes by Ella Winter and Granville Hicks, with a Memorandum by Carl Sandburg. New York: Harcourt Brace, 1938.

Stein, John M., and Harry H. Harrison, eds. *Muckraking: Past, Present, and Future.* University Park: Pennsylvania State University Press, 1973.

Sullivan, Mark. *The Education of an American.* New York: Doubleday, Doran, 1938.

Tarbell, Ida M. *All in the Day's Work: An Autobiography.* New York: Macmillan, 1939. Accessed November 14, 2018. https://babel.hathitrust.org/cgi/pt?id=mdp.39015003448555;view=1up;seq=9.

———. *The Business of Being a Woman.* New York: Macmillan, 1921. Accessed November 14, 2018. https://www.gutenberg.org/files/16577/16577-h/16577-h.htm.

———. *The History of the Standard Oil Company.* Edited by David M. Chalmers. New York: Dover, 2013.

———. *The Ways of Woman.* New York: Macmillan, 1915.

Tassin, Algernon. *The Magazine in America.* New York: Dodd, Mead, 1916.

Tichi, Cecelia. *Exposés and Excess: Muckraking in America, 1900–2000.* Philadelphia: University of Pennsylvania Press, 2004.

Tomkins, Mary E. *Ida M. Tarbell*. New York: Twayne, 1974.

Traxel, David. *Crusader Nation: The United States in Peace and at the Great War, 1898–1920*. New York: Knopf, 2006.

Weinberg, Arthur, and Lila Weinberg, eds. *The Muckrakers*. 1961; reprint, Urbana and Chicago: University of Illinois Press, 2001.

Weinberg, Steve. *Taking On the Trust: How Ida Tarbell Brought Down John D. Rockefeller and Standard Oil*. New York: Norton, 2009.

Weisberger, Bernard A. *The American Newspaperman*. Chicago and London: University of Chicago Press, 1961.

Wharton, Edith. *The Age of Innocence*. New York: Vintage Classics, 2012.

White, Richard. *The Republic for Which It Stands: The United States During Reconstruction and the Gilded Age, 1895–1896*. New York: Oxford University Press, 2017.

White, William Allen. *The Autobiography of William Allen White*. 2nd edition, revised and abridged, edited by Sally Foreman Griffith. Lawrence: University Press of Kansas, 1973.

Whiteshot, Charles Austin. *The Oil-Well Driller: A History of the World's Greatest Enterprise, the Oil Industry*. Self-published in 1905.

Whitlock, Brand. *Forty Years of It*. New York and London: Appleton, 1914.

Wilson, Harold S. *McClure's Magazine and the Muckrakers*. Princeton, NJ: Princeton University Press, 1970.

Wood, James Playsted. *Magazines in the United States: Their Social and Economic Influence*. New York: Ronald Press, 1949.

Woodress, James. *Willa Cather: A Literary Life*. Lincoln: University of Nebraska Press, 1987.

Yergin, Daniel. *The Prize: The Epic Quest for Oil, Money, and Power*. New York: Free Press, 2011.

## DISSERTATIONS

Christin, Robert Ernest. "McClure's Magazine, 1893–1903: A Study of Popular Culture." Ph.D. diss., Ohio State University, 1958.

Dorman, Jessica. "'Deliver Me from This Muck-Rake': The Art and Craft of Progressive Era Journalism." Ph.D. diss., Harvard University, 1996.

Gross, Greg. "The Staff Breakup of *McClure's Magazine*: 'The Explosions of Our Fine Idealistic Undertakings,'" Thesis, Allegheny College, 1997. Accessed November 14, 2018. http://sites.allegheny.edu/tarbell/mcclurestaff/.

Stinson, Robert. "S. S. McClure and His Magazine: A Study in the Editing of McClure's, 1893–1913." Ph.D. diss., Indiana University, 1971.

## ARTICLES AND SHORT STORIES

Acocella, Joan. "How 'Little Women' Got Big." *The New Yorker,* August 27, 2018. Accessed October 26, 2018. https://www.newyorker.com/magazine/2018/08/27/how-little-women-got-big.

Beasley, Maurice H. "The Muckrakers and Lynching: A Case Study in Racial Thinking." Paper presented at the 66th Annual Meeting of the Association for Education in Journalism and Mass Communication, August 6–9, 1893, Corvallis, OR, 8. Accessed October 2, 2018. http://files.eric.ed.gov/fulltext/ED229769.pdf.

Beck, Julie. "'Americanitis': The Disease of Living Too Fast." *The Atlantic,* March 11, 2016. Accessed June 4, 2018. https://www.theatlantic.com/health/archive/2016/03/the-history-of-neurasthenia-or-americanitis-health-happiness-and-culture/473253/.

Black, Brian. "Oil Creek as Industrial Apparatus: Re-Creating the Industrial Process through the Landscape of Pennsylvania's Oil Boom." *Environmental History* 3, no. 2 (April 1998): 213.

Brady, Kathleen. "Madame Muckraker." PBS *American Experience,* November 2017. Accessed June 12, 2018. https://www.pbs.org/wgbh/americanexperience/features/ida-tarbell-pioneering-journalist/.

Chalmers, David Mark. "Ray Stannard Baker's Search for Reform." *Journal of the History of Ideas* 19, no. 3 (June 1958): 422–34.

Cruea, Susan M. "Changing Ideals of Womanhood During the Nineteenth-Century Woman Movement." Bowling Green State University, General Studies Writing Faculty Publications. Paper 1 (2005). Accessed November 16, 2018. https://pdfs.semanticscholar.org/78a3/4b180d4d91559fdcb46b44275d52ca387e16.pdf.

Du Bois, W. E. Burghardt. "The African Roots of War." *The Atlantic Monthly* 115, no. 5 (May 1915): 707–14.

Foley, Paul. "Whatever Happened to Women's Rights." *The Atlantic Monthly,* March 1964. Accessed June 25, 2018. https://www.theatlantic.com/past/docs/issues/64mar/6403rights.htm.

French, J. L. "The Story of McClure's." *Profitable Advertising,* October 5, 1897.

Gilder, Jeannette L. "Some Women Writers." *New Outlook* 78 (1904): 281–89.

———. "When McClure's Began." *McClure's* (August 1913): 69–77.

Gilman, Charlotte Perkins. "The Yellow Wall-Paper." *The New England Magazine,* January 1892. Accessed November 2, 2017. https://www.gutenberg.org/files/1952/1952-h/1952-h.htm.

Gue, Elliott H. "Oil Demand: Emerging Markets Follow the American Roadmap." *Investing Daily,* August 2, 2010. Accessed November 7, 2015. https://www.investingdaily.com/13503/oil-demand-emerging-markets-follow-the-american-roadmap.

Johanningsmeier, Charles. "Unmasking Willa Cather's 'Mortal Enemy.'" *Cather Studies* 5. Accessed June 13, 2018. https://cather.unl.edu/cs005_johanningsmeier.html.

M., E. S. "Notes on the Periodicals." *Life* 63, no. 1645 (March 12, 1914): 444.

Macomber, Shawn. "Oil City Is Well Again." *The American Spectator,* January 26, 2009. Accessed June 25, 2018. https://spectator.org/42535_oil-city-well-again/.

Maranzani, Barbara. "Chicago Was Home to a Serial Killer During the 1893 World's Fair." History.com, May 1, 2013. Accessed October 5, 2017. http://www.history .com/news/7-things-you-may-not-know-about-the-1893-chicago-worlds-fair.

Munsey, Frank A. "The Making and Marketing of Munsey's Magazine." *Munsey's Magazine* 22, no. 3 (December 1899). Accessed June 1, 2018. https://books .google.com/books?id=irsmAQAAIAAJ&pg=PA323&lpg=PA323&dq=%22the +making+and+marketing+of+munsey%27s+magazine%22&source=bl&ots=d_ FkVGqW5B&sig=q4U8AIZu6F8se-SnVvh0UA5lfM0&hl=en&sa=X&ved=0ahU KEwjeq_Kz9LLbAhUSEqwKHflWCGYQ6AEILzAB#v=onepage&q=%22the%20 making%20and%20marketing%20of%20munsey's%20magazine%22&f=false.

Randle, Quint. "A Historical Overview of the Effects of New Mass Media Introductions on Magazine Publishing During the 20th Century." *First Monday* 6, no. 9 (September 3, 2001). Accessed November 16, 2018. http://firstmonday.org/article /view/885/794.

Romanes, George. "Mental Differences of Men and Women." *Popular Science* 31 (July 1887). Accessed October 6, 2017. https://en.wikisource.org/wiki/Popular _Science_Monthly/Volume_31/July_1887/Mental_Differences_of_Men_and_ Women.

Semonche, John. "Theodore Roosevelt's Muckrake Speech: A Reassessment." *Mid-America* 46 (1964): 114–25.

Shelley, Lorna. "Female Journalists and Journalism in Fin-de-siècle Magazine Stories." *Nineteenth-Century Gender Studies* 5, no. 2 (Summer 2009). Accessed November 16, 2018. https://www.ijpc.org/uploads/files/Female%20Journalists%20Lorna%20 Shelley.pdf.

Stephen, James Kenneth. "Lapsus Calami." Originally in Edmund Clarence Stedman, ed., *A Victorian Anthology, 1837–1895.* Cambridge, MA: Riverside Press, 1895. Accessed November 14, 2018. http://www.bartleby.com/246/1065.html.

Trambell, Caroline T. "Ida Tarbell and Her Farm." *Country Life in America* (November 1915): 19–22.

Whitman, Walt. "Tear Down and Build Over Again." *American Whig Review,* November 1845, 536.

Woolson, Constance Fenimore. "In Sloane Street." *Harper's Bazaar,* June 11, 1892. Accessed October 21, 2017. http://www.lehigh.edu/~dek7/SSAWW/writWoolson Sloane.htm.

Yergin, Dan. "The Pennsylvania Start-Up That Changed the World." *Forbes,* September 3, 2009. Accessed October 16, 2018. https://www.forbes.com/2009/09/03/oil -daniel-yergin-business-energy-oil.html.

## FILM

Burns, Ken. *The Roosevelts: An Intimate History.* Florentine Films: PBS documentary series, 2014.

Halligan, Liam. "The Unheard Story of Ida Tarbell." Video produced by UnHerd. Accessed April 23, 2018. https://unherd.com/2017/08/unheard-story-ida-tarbell -journalist-fought-big-businesses-time-won/.

# *Image Credits*

**1, 3, 4, 17, 21, 23, and 24:** Courtesy, The Lilly Library, Indiana University, Bloomington, Indiana

**2:** Courtesy, Special Collections and Archives, Knox College Library, Galesburg, Illinois

**5:** Lebrecht Music & Arts / Alamy Stock Photo

**6, 9, 10, 19, and 25:** Courtesy of the Ida M. Tarbell Collection, Special Collections, Pelletier Library, Allegheny College

**7 and 8:** Photographs by John Mather, Courtesy of the Drake Well Museum, Pennsylvania Historical and Museum Commission

**11:** Courtesy, The Jones Library, Inc., Amherst, Massachusetts

**12, 14, 15, and 18:** Courtesy, Library of Congress, Prints & Photographs Division

**20:** Photograph by Lawrence P. Ames, Courtesy, Library of Congress, Prints & Photographs Division

**22:** Courtesy, Frederick Dodds McClure Collection

# Index